stitch'n bitch
superstar
knitting

Coco Cardigan,
see page 332.

stitch 'n bitch
superstar
knitting

GO BEYOND THE BASICS

debbie stoller

with photography by Gabrielle Revere

WORKMAN PUBLISHING · NEW YORK

Button It! Kid's Sweater patches, see page 210.

Library of Congress Cataloging-in-Publication Data is available.

ISBN 978-0-7611-3597-5

Interior design by Sara Edward-Corbett
Page layout by Claudia Petrilli and Jen Browning
Cover design by Janet Vicario
Cover photo by Michael Lavine
Illustrations by Adrienne Yan

Workman books are available at special discounts when purchased in bulk for premiums
and sales promotions as well as for fund-raising or educational use. Special editions or
book excerpts also can be created to specification. For details, contact the Special Sales
Director at the address below or send an e-mail to specialmarkets@workman.com.

WORKMAN PUBLISHING COMPANY, INC.
225 Varick Street
New York, NY 10014-4381
www.workman.com

Printed in the United States of America
First printing October 2010
10 9 8 7 6 5 4 3 2 1

acknowledgments

This has been the longest, most postpone-iest book I've ever done. For their incredible patience and generosity in working with me and my busy schedule, and for allowing me the time I needed to recover from some health-related events, I am forever indebted to Peter Workman and especially Suzie Bolotin. I cannot express how thankful I am for their help, not just professionally, but also personally.

I am so very happy that my editor, Ruth Sullivan, was available to work on this book again. Not only did she manage to carefully edit a highly technical book even though she hasn't gone beyond the first Stitch 'n Bitch book's skills in her own knitting, but she also managed to do so while dealing with some health issues of her own. Even when it's wounded, her talented hand is able to make my writing so very much better, and I don't know what I'd do without her.

I'm equally glad that Janet Vicario was able to art direct the book and photo shoots once again; she always knows just what to do to make everything look great. On this book, she was assisted by Jen Browning and Claudia Petrilli, who brought a whole new level of cuteness to the page designs. And to Adrienne Yan, who had to draw my creaky hands over and over again, thank you so much. Also, a special shout-out to Julianna Cavano, Jodi Doff, and Peter Stoller for taking reference photos for all those illos.

Edie Eckman and Eve Ng brought their careful eagle eyes to their pattern tech-edits, and Irene Demchyshyn brought her No. 2 pencil to get all the copyediting done well and correctly. For their precision, patience, and good humor in the face of a lengthy and challenging project, I am ever thankful.

Photo editor Anne Kerman and her lovely team, including photo coordinator Danielle Hark and photo assistant Sophia Su, produced an exquisitely beautiful photo shoot for this book. I am most grateful to the talents of wonderful photographer Gabrielle Revere, amazing wardrobe stylist Ellen Silverstein and her assistant Lisa Metropolis, skilled hair and makeup gal Amy Schiappa, and photographer's assistant Hibbard Nash and digital tech, Jessie Adler. None of these projects would look nearly as adorable if they weren't being worn by such great models: Chyna, Ciara, Hannah, and Jeanette, as well as John, Shannon, and Dudly the dog of Ocean Grove, New Jersey, where these photos were shot. And, once again, I am grateful to Michael Lavine for taking such a nice cover photo despite the poor choice of model.

Of course, there wouldn't even be any projects to photograph if it weren't for the incredible talents of all of the designers who allowed me to include their patterns in this book. I am so amazed at their mad skillz, and insanely indebted to them for their contributions.

Every girl needs some backup, and I am so glad that Jennifer Wertkin and Sarah Graham were available to assist me with this book project, and thankful to Jill Astmann, Marney Andersen, and Jennifer Wendell for their helpful knitting hands.

My agent and fairy godmother, Flip Brophy, continues to make my life so much better, and I deeply appreciate the lovely ladies at BUST magazine, especially my biz partner Laurie Henzel, for giving me the space I needed to write.

Finally, for all the support they give me in everything I do, I want to thank my mom, Johanna Stoller, and my boo and best friend, Michael Uman.

contents

The Life Aquatic, see page 202.

Love Me or Leaf Me Bag, see page 250.

Tiger Lily Stuffed Animal, see page 345.

Sweetheart Sweater, see page 315.

PART II: HOW TO CREATE YOUR OWN PATTERNS

PART III: THE PATTERNS
COLOR BASICS AND STITCH WITCHERY

INTARSIA AND STRANDED KNITTING

CABLES, BOBBLES, AND TRAVELING STITCHES

LACE

BEADS AND EMBROIDERY

Little Red Riding Hoodie, see page 254.

iNtroductioN

In 1999, when I first got back into knitting, the world was a different place. In Manhattan, where I lived at the time, there were only two knitting stores that I knew of. When I took my knitting out in public, people would stare at me with the kind of curiosity usually reserved for side-show performers. And although all the older women on my mom's side of the family knit, I was aware of only two women in my age group who knew how to wield the needles. Desperate to learn as much about the craft as I could, I invited them, along with anyone else I could find who wanted to learn to knit, to come to a café in New York City's East Village every Wednesday evening to stitch and, you know, bitch.

That early Stitch 'n Bitch group was but one outlet for my knitting evangelism. As the editor in chief of *BUST*, the magazine for young women that I'd started in 1993 with a few friends, I had the opportunity to publish knitting patterns (including one for a knit bikini), recommend my favorite knitting magazines, and, of course, write about my Stitch 'n Bitch group and invite any of *BUST*'s readers to join us. And it wasn't just *BUST* that gave that early group coverage. The idea that young women were—of all things—getting into knitting was deemed newsworthy enough that we were visited by reporters from Fox News and *The Early Show*.

Nevertheless, it wasn't easy keeping that first Stitch 'n Bitch group from unraveling. At the beginning, eager learners would show up with their yarn and their needles, the enthusiasm in their eyes slowly draining away as they struggled to make clumsy rows of knit stitches. A few stuck it out through making a garter stitch scarf, never to knit again. Fewer still continued showing up regularly. That summer, especially, saw our numbers drop, from about 15 knitters down to only 3 and sometimes as few as 2 members gathering to knit together. Still, we kept meeting, and in Los Angeles and Chicago, women who learned about us

started up their own Stitch 'n Bitch gatherings. The next winter, our group picked up steam, and by 2001, we had to move to a larger café. The cat had been let out of the knitting bag, and there was no stuffing it back in.

All around us, a knitting trend was beginning to take shape, as people were drawn to the craft for a variety of reasons. Eager to opt out of what they perceived to be a global corporate culture that had little regard for the people making the products they produced and even less for the environmental impact those products had, more and more folks were getting interested in making things themselves. At the same time, a new generation of feminists were reclaiming women's traditional crafts. Rumors were even circulating that certain celebrities had taken up knitting. And it certainly didn't hurt that much of the fashion being paraded down the runways that season consisted of simple, hand-knit sweaters and scarves.

About that time, an editor at Workman Publishing who'd been following my knitting writing in *BUST* inquired whether I might be interested in writing a knitting book. My answer, of course, was yes—by that point I had taught so many people to knit, I felt that I had mastered what they felt were the biggest challenges. I also knew that there was a growing number of new knitters—both in my own Stitch 'n Bitch group and the ones I had become familiar with via a newfangled Internet phenomenon called "knitting blogs"—who were designing their own knitting patterns that were cuter and more youthful than anything commercially available at the time. I thought that if I wrote up the clearest instructions I could muster, explaining everything that I had struggled with when I was first starting, and asked my knitting friends and blogging contacts if they had any patterns they wanted to contribute, I could put together a book that would not only teach anyone to learn to knit, but also provide new knitters with the kinds of projects they were looking to make. I had originally called the book *Take Back the Knit,* in a nod to '70s feminists' "Take Back the Night" rallies and a reflection of my belief that feminists like me should embrace and respect handicrafts as an essential part of women's history. My publisher convinced me that *Stitch 'n Bitch* would make a better title, and, aside from a few issues we've had with the B word over the years, they couldn't have been more right.

As I spent weekend after summer weekend locked away writing, I noticed that other books were being published that were also aimed at the growing numbers of new, youthful knitters. Frustrated, at times I'd find myself wondering if I couldn't just insert my shopping lists into the middle of the text to fill up the pages. After all, would anyone actually read it? But once it was published and my publicist was able to book me on *The Today Show* (where I was luckily able to correct a misguided anchorwoman, who turned to me, just before we went on air, to confirm, "So, you're the 'Stitchin' Bitch,' right?"), I realized that there just might be some interest in what I had done. Partway through my book tour, I found out that the book had sold out and was going back to print, and in each city that I visited, with every TV, radio, and newspaper interview, word was spreading about just how fun knitting could be and how easy it was to set up a Stitch 'n Bitch group. I felt like the Johnny Appleseed of Knitting, making my way across the country, with newly formed Stitch 'n Bitch groups springing up in my wake.

In those days, the media dubbed knitting "the new yoga," comparing it to the Eastern exercise that had recently become a fad among young women nationwide. But soon they latched onto a new phrase: "Not your grandmother's knitting" is how every article about the knitting craze referred to it, and my book and I, along with the growing number of Stitch 'n Bitch groups, were frequently used as prime examples of the phenomenon. I have to say I found the media's phrase offensive. Not only did it seem to be an inherent dis to our grannies, but the fact was that what we were doing was, indeed, "your grandmother's knitting." It was all of our grandmothers' knitting, especially

mine, who'd knit for a full 90 years of her life, and whose knitting skills I could only hope to match someday. We weren't necessarily making our grandmothers' knitting patterns, but why would we? Having come of age in the '80s, I adored patterns (I still do) that incorporated punk rock themes—such as a skull and crossbones—which my Dutch Oma wouldn't have had any interest in (perhaps sweater patterns in the "flappers" style would have been on her must-make list, making them not *her* grandmother's knitting).

But it wasn't just the media that had it wrong. Some people who had been knitting for decades resented the attention being paid to these knitting upstarts, and saw the increasing numbers of new knitters traipsing through "their" yarn stores as some sort of invading army. Many of them mocked these young knitters for the miles of garter stitch scarves and acres of chunky sweaters they made, something I found equally infuriating. Who doesn't begin their knitting life with projects that can be completed in a reasonable amount of time? As far as I was concerned, when it came to knitting, the more, the merrier. And I was sure that as they became more comfortable with the craft, these new knitters would begin to take on more advanced projects.

Luckily, I was right. It's been 11 years since I picked up my needles, and I haven't put them down since. In the intervening time, so many more people have gotten addicted to the craft that I never have a hard time finding someone to knit with anymore. Yarn stores have cropped up all over the country, from the largest cities to the smallest towns; in my Brooklyn neighborhood, there are three yarn shops within walking distance from my house, and there are scores more in Manhattan. There are currently 694 Stitch 'n Bitch groups registered on my website, www.stitchnbitch.org, located in every one of our 50 states and across 29 countries. You can't swing a yarn ball on the subway without hitting a knitter fervently working away on her latest project, and there are extensive online communities where hundreds of thousands of Internet-savvy knitters can display their projects and share their knowledge. People no longer look at me sideways when they see me knitting in public; sometimes they can even identify the project I'm making ("Oh, I love that shawl pattern! I made the same one a few months ago!").

I was lucky enough to have the opportunity to write a few more knitting books, and even had the chance to start my own yarn line. And indeed, just as anyone would have predicted, those early enthusiasts, folks who had first learned to knit by making garter stitch scarves and chunky sweaters, became eager to take on projects involving lace, cables, complex colorwork, and more.

That's where this book comes in. As I watched these knitters boldly go where they had never gone before, I wanted to help them along. After all, even with all the available courses, online tutorials, and knowledgeable knitting-group attendees, many advanced knitting techniques can seem intimidating, overwhelming, or, at the very least, confusing. In fact, I've struggled to learn them myself. I got tangled in intarsia, was frustrated by Fair Isle, lost in lace, crippled by cables, and struck dumb by steeks. I collected bits and pieces from Web pages, magazine articles, online videos, knitting classes, and an abundant number of books, each focusing on only a single method. Designing my own sweaters proved particularly difficult, as it was almost impossible to find any references that explained it all. I paid dearly for rare, long-out-of-print books on the subject, scoured the Internet for information, and felt at times like I was trying to put together a variety of mismatched puzzle pieces, until I finally arrived at a sort of "best practices" method for pattern drafting.

In this book I've gathered together everything I've learned over the years in the hopes of encouraging you to become a knitting superstar—fearless when it comes to Fair Isle, unintimidated by intarsia, confident about cables, ready to lay down the law with lace, and able to stare down steeks. It is a manual of techniques that will help you take your work to the next level. In Part I, I'll teach you color knitting in all its forms—from stripes, slip stitching, and double knitting to intarsia and stranded

knitting. You'll learn textured stitches—including cables, traveling stitches, twisted stitches, bobbles, and lace—as well as embellishments, such as how to incorporate beads and embroidery into your work.

Even if you already know some—or all—of these stitches, I believe you'll still find this book helpful. That's because I've also included all the tricks and tips I've found to be central to each method. Cabling without a cable needle? As far as I'm concerned, it's the only way to fly if you're going to be serious about cabling. Weaving in your yarn while working stranded knitting? As essential to the technique as knowing how to knit and purl. Understanding how yarnovers and decreases work together to form lace patterns? Crucial if you want to save yourself hours of heartache. Knowing how to make one yarn stand out more than the other when working with two yarns at the same time? Don't leave home without it.

Just as in my other books, I've tried to make these instructions as clear as possible, paying special attention to anything that tripped me up when I was learning the techniques myself. That goes double for Part II of the book, where I explain how to design your own pattern. Now, I've taught a basic sweater-design class quite a few times, and I have to admit: People don't find it that much fun. That's because, at its heart, designing a knitting pattern is as much about figuring out a complicated math problem as it is about creative expression. In fact, drafting a knitting pattern is a bit like drawing up the plans for a house: It's all about blueprints, calculating precise measurements, and doing the math so that everything will fit together perfectly.

Now, there are software programs out there that can help you calculate all the measurements you need to knit a sweater, and I have nothing against them. But I think that the only way to really and truly understand what goes into designing a knitting pattern—to really become a master of it—is for you to create a pattern, like your knitting project, completely by hand. After all, there are knitting machines, too, but you'll never learn to knit by using one. The methods

I explain are simple and straightforward, but take those DIY chapters a little bit at a time so you don't get overwhelmed. Even if you never design your own pattern, understanding how they are created will blow your mind, and you'll never look at knitting patterns the same way again.

Part III is the icing on the cake; there you'll find 41 fantastic projects that will give you a chance to use your newfound skills (or inspire you to get on the stick and learn them!). For the patterns, I turned to the now vast community of knitters. Their projects reflect just how far our knitting culture has come over the years. Many of these designers—some with published patterns under their belt; some who are brand-new—only picked up knitting in the past decade but were able to take their recently acquired skills and turn them into amazingly fun and sophisticated original knitwear. But don't let their brilliance scare you away: Some of these projects are easy enough for you to make with only a bit of new knowledge. It will take more practice to master the skills for other patterns. The main thing is to know, with 100% certainty, that when it comes to knitting, there is nothing that is out of your reach.

So get ready to take your knitting in all sorts of directions you didn't believe were possible when you struggled your way through your very first row of stitches (remember that?). After all, with ten years and counting, knitting has made it past the "trend" stage and has graduated to becoming as much an important, and respected, part of our culture as any other skilled leisure activity, such as fishing, playing soccer, or cooking. New Stitch 'n Bitch groups seem to be popping up every week, and the community of knitters —both online and off—becomes stronger all the time. And it seems that the longer we stick with our knitting, the more we follow in the footsteps of those who came before us. After all, these knitting techniques were developed over a long period of time by women and men as a way to keep their knitting fun and lively. In other words, this is not just your grandmother's knitting, it's also your great- and great-great-grandmothers' knitting. And now it's yours, too.

PART I
the stitches

rows are red, rows are blue

COLOR KNITTING USING ONE COLOR AT A TIME

If knitting with one ball of yarn is still a bit of a struggle for you, then knitting with more than one color may seem intimidating. But in this chapter you'll learn the many ways that you can add color to your knitting and still work each row with only one ball of yarn. Adding stripes is one of the most basic methods of making knit fabric in more than one color, and slip-stitching, which creates the look of knitting with two colors but is worked with only one color of yarn per row, is a fun technique that yields impressive results. Tubular knitting takes slip-stitching to a whole 'nother level: It lets you create two-sided fabric with one color on one side and another color on the other side, while still working with only one color at a time. And double knitting is tubular knitting on steroids, allowing you to make color patterns on both sides of the fabric at the same time.

Even if the idea of working with two yarns at once doesn't faze you, this chapter still holds plenty of useful information. There are tips and tricks for making your striped knitting look better, and you may find the possibilities of the slip-stitching technique to be something of a revelation. Plus, having tubular and double knitting in your repertoire of techniques will truly broaden your knitting horizons.

stripes? cripes!

Stripes are the easiest way to add color to your knitting. In fact, you might think that stripes are so basic and straightforward that knitting them requires about as much thought as breathing. But there's more to stripes than you might think.

Stripes are the color equivalent in knitting of a drumbeat in music. They create a rhythm that can be as regular and booming as a John Philip Sousa piece, as surprising and unpredictable as an improvisational jazz jam session, or as energizing and sexy as a hip-hop hit. You create these rhythms with different colors, which are like the different types of drums in a drum kit, including the cymbals. And if you add just a little bit of trickery to your striping work, you've got a slip-stitch pattern, which looks about as much like stripes as a piano sounds like a bongo. Of course you know how to knit stripes back and forth, but if you want to become a master knitter, you need to know your stripes backward and forward.

The first thing you need to know is how to add a new color of yarn. My favorite way is less than straightforward, but it's worth learning. To do it, I borrow a trick from intarsia knitting (coming up later) to link my new yarn in with the old right from the start. Here's how:

To start new yarn knitwise:

1 With the old yarn in back, insert your needle into the first stitch knitwise.

2 Drape your new color yarn across this needle from back to front, leaving about a 6" tail hanging in back and to the left, and the ball end in front and to the right.

3 Twist the new yarn with the old yarn like so: Take the ball end of the new yarn and bring it in front of, then under, and up behind the old yarn. You are twisting it around the old yarn.

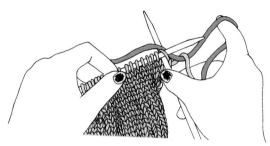

4 Hold the old yarn down with any old finger you can find, and wrap the new yarn around the needle as you would to make a knit stitch.

5 Carry the stitch on the left-hand needle *and the new yarn's tail* over the new stitch, and off the needle. (This maneuver is somewhat more challenging to execute if you are a Continental knitter than it is if you are an English knitter, but it can be done.)

Now you have a stitch that is wrapped around the old yarn, as well as its own tail, and it's pretty damn secure. You can go on knitting down the row, but hang on to the tail in your left hand for just a few stitches to make sure it doesn't go anywhere.

To start new yarn purlwise:

❶ With your old yarn in front, insert your needle into the first stitch purlwise.

❷ Drape your new color yarn across this needle from front to back, leaving about a 6" tail hanging in front and to the left, and the ball end in back and to the right.

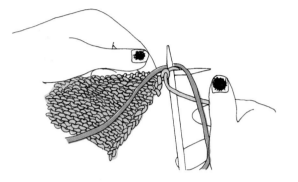

❸ Twist the new yarn with the old yarn like so: Take the ball end of the new yarn and bring it in front of, then under, and up behind the old yarn. You are twisting it around the old yarn.

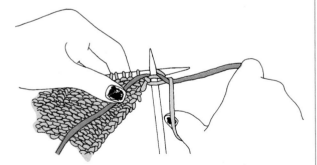

❹ Hold the old yarn down with any old finger you can find, and wrap the new yarn around the needle as you would to make a purl stitch.

❺ Carry the stitch on the left-hand needle *and the new yarn's tail* over the new stitch, and off the needle. (Again, this maneuver is somewhat more challenging to execute if you are a Continental knitter than it is if you are an English knitter, but it can be done. Sorry, haters.)

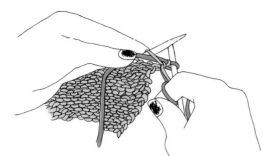

Go on purling down the line—just hang on to that tail for a few stitches to make sure it doesn't slip away.

If you cut your yarn every time you finish knitting a stripe and then start a new length of yarn for each new stripe, you will end up with a whole helluva lot of yarn ends to weave into your work when you are done, and as every knitter knows, that is one sucky job. To save you from this nightmare scenario, stripes are often knit in even numbers of rows (two rows of color A, four rows of color B, two rows of color A), which allows you to "carry" the yarn you aren't using up the side of your work until you are ready to use it again, instead of cutting it. Carrying your yarn will let you avoid leaving a big, ugly loop o' yarn along the side of your work when you need to start a new row with a color you haven't used for a while. All you do is wind the yarn you're knitting with once around the yarn you leave hanging at the end of your rows, thereby "carrying" it along with you up the side of the work (so that the yarn is never farther than two rows below where it needs to be when you want to use it again). This is usually called "twisting" the yarn together. You simply twist the yarn

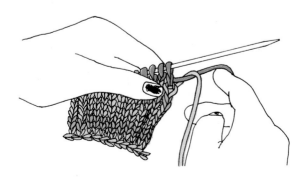

you're knitting with around the old yarn—catching it in a sort of yarn hammock—before you start knitting a row.

As I said, this technique works nicely if your stripes consist of even numbers of rows, because you'll always be starting and ending your colors on the same side of your work. But what happens if you are working an uneven number of rows? You'll be ready to stop knitting with red and start knitting with green and—uh-oh!—the green yarn won't be at the beginning of your work, where you need it to be, but at the end. Sure, you can use the old cut 'n start again method, but you have a better option. Just work back and forth on circular needles instead of straight needles; then, when you need to use a yarn that's on the far side of your work, just slide your stitches to the other end of your needles, where the yarn will be waiting for you, and start knitting from that side. Using this method, you can even knit single-row stripes without creating a giant hairball of hanging ends at the sides of your work. Just carry the yarn up the side as before, but work back and forth on circular needles and slide your work this way and that as you need to.

Presto Chango!
MAKING CLEAN COLOR CHANGES IN RIBBING

If you are knitting in stockinette stitch and change colors, the color change will be beautifully clean when seen from the knit side of your work. But on the purl side, things will look kind of ugly, with a jumble of new-color stitches visibly poking down into the old color, and old-color stitches poking up into the new-color stripe. Since the purl side will usually face where the sun don't shine, that's not much of a problem. But what do you do when you are knitting stripes in ribbing, and half of your stitches on the right side of the work are purls? Well, if your stripes are made of more than one or two rows, you can use my very favorite trick to keep the color change as clean as a kitten's paws: Just knit the entire first row of the new color, instead of alternating knits and purls as you normally would for ribbing. After that, go back to your regular ribbing pattern. How can this work, you ask? Won't it completely mess up your ribbing? Well, it will make your ribbing just a bit less stretchy. But that's a small price to pay for a color change so clean you could eat off of it.

Striped ribbing worked normally

Striped ribbing worked by knitting (no purling) on color-change rows

give Your knitting the slip

KNITTING COLORFUL PATTERNS USING SLIP STITCH

You know that slipping a stitch simply means transferring a stitch from one needle to another without doing anything to it. But what you might not know is that by not doing anything to some stitches in some rows, and then *doing* something to them in later rows, but with a different color, you can create some amazing effects. I don't see slip-stitch knitting used very often in patterns, and I think it's a shame. It's a way to make it look as if you used a much harder technique, but it's done using only one color in a row at a time. I'd really love to meet the person who invented slip-stitch knitting and shake her hand, because this method is so incredibly simple yet can yield such gorgeous results, it's truly nothing short of magic.

The basic idea is simple: You work a number of stitches in a row and slip some others. Then in a later row, you slip the stitches you worked previously, and work the stitches you slipped, but using a different color. To "slip" a stitch means to just pass it from one needle to the other without doing anything to it—like passing the Olympic torch. One thing to pay attention to in slip-stitch knitting is making sure you slip your stitch *purlwise*, so it doesn't change its orientation from one needle to the next. The "leg" on the right side of your stitch will be in front of the needle when the stitch is on the left-hand needle, and that leg will *still* be on the right and in front of the needle

Color by Numbers
DESIGNING STRIPES ACCORDING TO THE FIBONACCI SEQUENCE

There's a method of planning stripes in knit fabric that's been popular among knitters—and especially knitting math geeks—for quite a few years now. It's called the Fibonacci progression, and although it may sound like a delicious pasta dish, it's actually quite a nice way to get a stripe rhythm going in your work. To do it, you start your first stripe with a single row of color. The next stripe will be the number of rows in the previous two stripes added together. Your last stripe was only one row, and there was no stripe before that, so 1 and 0 makes 1. The next stripe will be, again, the number of rows in the previous two stripes added together. In this case, a 1 and a 1, that makes 2. And so on, so that each stripe is the number of rows in the previous two stripes added together.

(Or, 1 and 2 makes 3.) You won't want to do this for too long, however, or you'll end up with some mighty wide stripes, so at a certain point, you can either start working this sequence all over again, or start working it in reverse, so that your stripes get narrower and narrower again, all the way back to 1. But whichever way you do it, following the Fibonacci series can lead to some nice-looking stripes, just like the 13th-century mathematician Leonardo of Pisa intended it to when he introduced this numerical sequence, which mimics patterns found in nature. Talk about old school!

after the stitch is transferred. (This is what is meant by "stitch orientation"—it has nothing to do with whether your stitch prefers Adam or Eve.)

Another thing that really matters in slip-stitch patterns is where you hold the yarn while you are slipping the stitch. Slip-stitch patterns will usually say "sl 1 wyif" or "sl 1 wyib," which refers to where you hold your yarn when you slip—in front (as you would if you were going to make a purl stitch) when it says "wyif" (with yarn in front), and in back (as you would if you were going to make a knit stitch) when it says "wyib" (with yarn in back). In general, you will be holding your yarn on the wrong side of the work while slipping stitches.

This also means that after you've slipped your stitches and go back to knitting or purling again, you'll be leaving short lengths of yarn behind (or in front of) those stitches, also called "floats." (I really love calling them floats. It's such an airy, pretty way of referring to those ugly hanging strands!) Floats need to be loose enough not to pull your knitting together accordionlike, and just tight enough to float straight across behind your stitches instead of creating gross, dangling loops. (For more on this, see "Float Like a Butterfly," page 25.)

A very simple slip-stitch pattern that illustrates the method better than anything I can tell you is the 2-stitch check pattern, shown above, right. It looks like it was created by alternating stitches in two different colors across a row, but the truth is, each row was knit using only one color—the checked pattern is completely the result of slipping certain stitches.

If you've never tried slip-stitching before, whip out some needles and two colors of yarn and take it for a test drive.

Begin with a multiple of 4 stitches.

ROW 1: Knit with color A.

ROW 2: Purl with A.

ROW 3: With B, k3, *sl 2 wyib, k2, rep from *, end k1.

ROW 4: With B, p3, *sl 2 wyif, p2; rep from *, end p1.

ROWS 5 AND 6: Repeat rows 1 and 2 with A.

ROW 7: With B, k1, *sl 2 wyib, k2; rep from *, end sl 2 wyib, k1.

ROW 8: With B, p1, *sl 2 wyif, p2; rep from *, end sl 2 wyif, p1.

Once you've done this for a bit, you'll be scratching your head in bewilderment. How the hell does it work? Why do the color A stitches look like they are part of row B? The answer, my friends, is that knit stitches are stretchy and will adjust themselves as needed. The color A stitches are a bit stretched out, if you look at them carefully, but the stitches in the color B rows are more than happy to squash themselves down a bit, and that makes everything look a bit more even-steven. This bit of squashing does mean, however, that it will take more rows to knit, say, an inch of fabric using a slip-stitch pattern than it would using plain old stockinette stitch. And, even if you make the most perfect floats in town, your fabric will still be a bit less stretchy and more narrow than it would be if you weren't carrying yarn along behind your work. So deal with it.

As impressive as the 2-stitch check pattern is, it's just the tip of the slip-stitching iceberg. This little trickster can be used to create all sorts of complicated-looking color and texture patterns.

CIRCULAR LOGIC
SLIP-STITCHING IN THE ROUND

Slip-stitch patterns are almost always written in rows, not rounds, and they are so mysterious, you might be afraid to try using them on a project, like socks, that is knit in the round. But fear not! With a few adjustments to the stitch pattern, most slip-stitch patterns can work in the round as well as they do in back-and-forth knitting. The trick is to convert the wrong-side rows in the pattern to right-side rows. So, if the pattern says to knit on a wrong-side row, you purl; if the pattern says to hold your yarn in front, you hold it in back, and vice versa. Alternatively, you can simply knit from the chart, reading each row from right to left and skipping any edge stitches in the original chart so that your pattern will go round and round seamlessly. Also, leave out edge stitches in your count when you are casting on.

Slip 'N Slide
USING SLIP-STITCHING TO MAKE TWO-COLOR TUBULAR KNITTING

Earlier in this chapter, I talked about the fact that when you make color changes while knitting stripes in stockinette, one side of your fabric will look nice, and the other—not so much. And I'm sure that at some point in your life you've sought the beginning knitter's holy grail: a stockinette-stitch scarf that won't roll. While the latter is quite impossible, there is a stitch that creates fabric that lies completely flat, looks like stockinette on both sides, and will let you make stripes with beautifully clean color changes. What is this miracle stitch you ask? It's tubular knitting, done using slip-stitching, and it's just lovely. It creates fabric that's basically a sort of tube, with a layer of stockinette fabric on both sides (so it's twice as thick as regular stockinette-stitch fabric), and it's just perfect for scarf knitting. Best of all, when done with

two balls of yarn (in two different colors), you'll get a piece of fabric that is one color on one side, another color on the other. And you'll do it all using only one color per row.

To do it, cast on an even number of stitches that is twice the number you'd need if you were knitting the piece in plain stockinette stitch (so, if a 4" piece in stockinette stitch would require 16 stitches, cast on 32 stitches for a 4"-wide piece of tubular knitting).

ROW 1: *K1, sl 1 purlwise wyif; rep from * to end of row. Rep this row.

To add a stripe in a second color, you should begin on an odd-numbered row.

To create tubular knitting that is one color on one side and another color on the other side, the process is a bit different. You'll need to use two double-pointed needles or one circular needle. With color A, cast on an even number of stitches that is twice the number you'd need if you were knitting in plain stockinette stitch. Continue as follows:

ROW 1: With A, *k1, sl 1 next stitch purlwise wyif; rep from * to end of row.

ROW 2: Slide all stitches to other end of the needle. With B, *sl 1 purlwise wyib, p1; rep from * to end of row.

ROW 3: With B, *k1, sl 1 purlwise wyif; rep from * to end of row.

ROW 4: Slide all stitches to the other end of the needle. With A, *sl 1 purlwise wyib, p1; rep from * to end of row.

Repeat rows 1–4.

To make sure that your work is closed at each end, twist yarns A and B at the beginning of rows 1 and 3.

Tubular knitting is a bit slow since you are making two passes to complete each individual row. But you will end up with an awesome piece of double-thick, two-colored fabric that looks good on both sides. And how often can you say that in knitting?

doubLe knitting

ADVANCED TUBULAR KNITTING WITH TWO COLORS

Now, how about mixing things up and knitting with *both* colors on one side and *both* colors on the other side? You can do this, and it's called double knitting. It's almost the same as tubular knitting, only it isn't, because instead of slipping stitches you'll be knitting or purling them, and instead of working with only one color on each side, you'll be working with both colors at the same time. (I know I promised you'd only be using one color per row in this chapter, but at least double knitting doesn't involve any of the challenging stranding and catching that regular two-color knitting requires.) The coolest thing about double knitting is that each side will be the exact color inverse of the other. A purple field with a white diamond on one side will automatically become a white field with a purple diamond on the other.

Here's how: Cast on twice as many stitches as you need for the width of your piece. Holding both color yarns at the same time (see chapter 3, "Strand and Deliver," for methods of doing this), knit the first stitch with A. Then bring *both* colors to the front of your work (between the needle points) and purl the second stitch with color B. Now bring *both* colors to the back of your work and knit

the next stitch with color A. Continue alternating knit and purl stitches, always knitting with color A and always purling with color B and always bringing both yarns to the back before making a knit stitch, and both to the front before making a purl. As you continue to work, you will always alternate between knitting and purling, but you will not always alternate A and B in this same order. The color that you use to knit the first stitch of each knit/purl pair will be determined by your knitting color chart. The purl stitch, however, will always be made with the other color yarn.

Since double-knit fabric doesn't have a right side and a wrong side (both are "right sides"), you can start working the color pattern whenever you like. Let's say you are working with purple and white yarn; we'll call one side the "purple" side and the other the "white" side.

Double-knit swatch as seen from "purple" side

Double-knit swatch as seen from "white" side

The chart below shows a purple background and a white diamond. It shows how you will work when you are on the "purple" side. When you work your way back, the white side will be facing you, and you'll do exactly the opposite of what's in the chart.

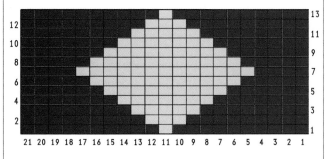

Reading the first row of the chart, from right to left, we see ten purple stitches, followed by one white stitch, followed by ten more purple stitches. The chart is showing us what we need to do with the *knit stitches only*. The purl stitches will simply always be made in the opposite color. So, to work row one, you would knit one purple stitch, then purl a white stitch, and repeat that nine more times. This gives you the first ten purple boxes of the chart. The next box in the chart is a white one, and remember, the chart only shows us the knit stitch, so that means you will knit the next stitch with the white yarn, and purl the stitch after that with the purple. Then, you've got to knit one stitch with purple and purl the next stitch with white ten times.

The truly tricky part comes in the next row. Now not only are you keeping track of your knits and purls and purple and white, but, since you're working on the other side of the fabric, you'll need to knit the opposite color of what you see on the chart. Our chart says we are to knit nine purple, three white, and nine more purple stitches. But on this row, we are going to do the exact opposite of that: We'll knit nine white, three purple, and nine more white. The purl stitches in between will all be done in the other yarn. So we knit white/purl purple nine times, then knit purple/purl white three times, and then knit white/purl purple nine times again.

Don't forget to twist your yarns at the end of the row by bringing the new yarn up from under the old yarn at the beginning of each color change.

knit,
if you
will, a
picture

CREATING
IMAGES WITH
INTARSIA

Say you want to knit a picture—like a bunny rabbit or some detailed flowers—on a project. You'll need to use a technique called intarsia. The word *intarsia* comes from a method of woodwork that uses different-colored pieces of wood glued together like a puzzle to create an image, and intarsia knitting works in somewhat the same way: Individual blocks of color are knit to form an image or pattern. And, just as a woodworker needs to use some sort of glue to keep different blocks of color from falling apart, one of the tricks of intarsia is to link your various pieces of color together. Unlike a woodworker, however, you won't do this after all the pieces are made, but instead, you'll connect the different color areas to each other as you are knitting them.

With intarsia, the idea is to make it look like your yarn magically changed color from one stitch to the next. The way you work with different colors in intarsia is easy, but getting it to look perfect can be a bit harder. I like that challenge, however, and that's why intarsia is one of my most favorite knitting methods.

the rules of the game

Intarsia is knit one row at a time, just like any other kind of knitting, but each area of color is knit with its own length of yarn—in intarsia, you do *not* carry your yarn across the back of your work. Instead, each time you change from one color to the next in a row of knitting, you drop the first color and continue working the row with the next color. This is sometimes hard for people to wrap their heads around, so let me clarify: If you are knitting a purple circle in the middle of a field of blue, you will need to use three separate lengths of yarn, two blue and one purple: one length of blue yarn to knit the stitches up to where the circle begins, then the purple yarn to knit the circle, and then the second piece of blue yarn to knit from the circle to the end of the row.

Intarsia knitting as seen from the front

Lemme give you another example, because I see people doing this incorrectly all the time: If you are knitting a cream-colored sweater that has red-and-black poppies scattered across it, you will use lots and lots of different pieces of yarn. Think about it—you'll need individual lengths of red and black for each individual poppy, *and* you'll need separate lengths of cream-colored yarn for knitting the spaces *in between* the poppies. And, depend-

ing on how the poppies are designed, you may even need more than one length of red and black to knit 'em.

In other words, the die-hard rule of intarsia is this: You should not, you may not, and you *will* not carry any length of yarn behind *any* stitches in order to continue knitting with it on the other side. This means that, on the back of your work, you will never see any strands of yarn that lead from one area of color to another. You know how Joan Crawford felt about wire hangers, don't you? Now picture her yelling this at you so you really get it through your wooly head: NO! MORE! YARN! STRANDS!

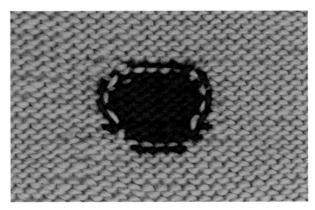

Intarsia knitting as seen from the back

The only real trick to intarsia is understanding how to connect color areas by linking yarns at each color change. I've told you that intarsia is worked using individual lengths of yarn for each color area, almost as if you are knitting a jigsaw puzzle where each puzzle piece is knit with its own length of yarn. But you need to link your stitches together every time you change colors (where the edges of the puzzle pieces meet), because if you don't, you will end up with something that is just like a real puzzle. With nothing holding them together, all the pieces fall apart. So, if you are knitting a purple circle in the middle of a blue field, without linking your stitches, the circle would be connected to the fabric at its top and bottom, but the sides would be flapping loose like a pair of fish gills. When I'm teaching intarsia, I usually ask three students to help me in a demonstration—two wearing similarly colored shirts, and the third wearing a different-colored shirt—and I line them up like this:

Let's call these volunteers Mary Ann, Gilligan, and Ginger. Now, pretend Mary Ann and Ginger are each an area of red stitches, and Gilligan is an area of white stitches. I then ask Gilligan to take a step forward while Mary Ann and Ginger stay in place. He does this, showing how these areas of stitches are not connected at all. Next I ask Gilligan to link arms with Mary Ann and Ginger, and ask him to take a step forward while Mary Ann and Ginger stay where they are. Obviously, he can't do it. Now that they've linked their arms, these areas of colors are connected together as one piece. That's just how it works in intarsia, where you

link the "arms" of your stitches when you change from one color to the next. The way you do that is really simple, so don't worry about the technique; I'll show it to you in a second. What's really important is that you remember that your stitches *have to be linked* at every color change, or you'll have a disaster on your hands—like Gilligan all alone, without his Ginger or Mary Ann.

THE RIGHT YARN FOR THE JOB

When you are working in color, whether you are working an intarsia design or stranded pattern, the yarn you choose for your project will make a big difference in how good it will look. Slippery, smooth yarns, such as 100% cotton—especially shiny, mercerized cotton—will never yield as nice a result as something that is even just a little bit fuzzy, such as a 100% wool or wool blend yarn. That's because the fuzziness will sort of fill in the empty spots between the stitches, and whether you're working in intarsia or stranding, changing from one color to another always makes the areas between your stitches a bit more janky than if you were just knitting with a single color. Cotton blended with wool—even a little bit—will give you a much better result than cotton alone. There are some wools that have been spun in such a way as to yield a yarn that has almost no fuzziness to speak of, and those should also be avoided for this type of colorwork.

great Lengths

YARN LENGTHS IN INTARSIA

So, how do you go about dealing with all these lengths of yarn? Many books will recommend that you wind the different lengths of yarn onto bobbins. Others will tell you to put your yarn into different bowls.

I've tried all of that, and my bobbins would wind around each other and my yarn would get tangled in no time flat. It was a huge pain trying to free all my yarn from this mess every time I needed to make a different colored stitch, and I didn't like knitting intarsia at all. But then I discovered a different, much simpler method. Instead of putting my yarn on bobbins, I just break off a nice, long piece of yarn—about a "wingspan" (the distance from hand to hand when your arms are spread out to your sides). I let that yarn dangle down behind my work, and no matter how much it twists around with the other yarns, it's easy to pull it out from those strands and knit with it again.

You might think that you'd continuously run out of yarn with this method and have to start new pieces, which would mean having to work in a horrible number of ends later. In some instances that's true. But here's a trick to lengthen any piece of yarn that's 100% wool. When you are getting to the end of your rope, so to speak, just spit-splice another wingspan's length of yarn to it and keep knitting. To spit-splice yarn, first fluff out the last ½" of each piece of yarn a bit by pulling it apart, then wet those ends in your mouth. Yes, you can dip them in a glass of water, but your mouth is so much more convenient. When the ends are nice and moist, place them in your palm, overlapping the wet parts, and rub your hands together so hard that you feel warmth. The warmth is important: What you're really doing is felting these two ends of yarn together, so you need all three ingredients—water, friction, and heat—to make the magic

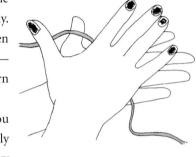

happen. Rub quickly while you count to ten slowly. When you are done, open your hands and voilà— your two pieces of yarn will have become one!

One caveat: If you are knitting with relatively thick yarn—say, heavy worsted or thicker—you will end up with a really thick knob where you spliced. To avoid that, after you've fluffed out the ends of your yarn, rip off about half of the thickness of each of your ends. Continue as usual.

There's one exception to the above technique, however: If you're working some sort of multicolored image in the middle of a large, solid-colored background—say, an adorable green, yellow, and black frog in a pale blue field—use these wingspan lengths for the frog colors, but use full balls for the background color. Plan ahead to have one ball of light blue for the knitting before you get to the motif, and another ball of light blue for the knitting that comes afterward. (If the pattern only calls for a single ball of light blue, wind off a nice-size second ball before you start.)

go figure

MAKING A FIGURE EIGHT YARN BOBBIN

If you are working intarsia with only a few different colors, you can make a center-pull figure eight, or "butterfly," bobbin out of the yarn like this: With your left hand in a "stick 'em up" position, hold the end of the yarn in your three closed fingers and start winding the yarn, in a figure eight, around your thumb and forefinger.

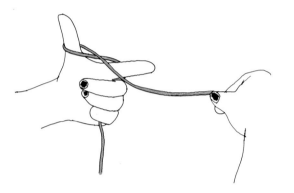

When you have a nice amount of yarn—about 15 or so figure eights—break the yarn off from the ball, wrap it a few times around the center of the eight, and pull it through the last wrap to secure.

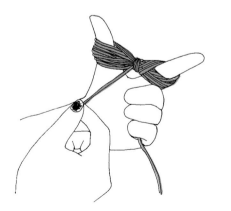

To use it, start with the tail, and pull out a bit of yarn from the butterfly as you need it. Yarn butterflies are light and will hang nicely at the back of your work. Yarn wound onto bobbins, on the other hand, are heavier and have a tendency to get really naughty and start twisting around each other. It's like knitting with yo-yos hanging at the back of your work. Hell to the no!

start me up

ADDING A NEW COLOR YARN

Up until now in your knitting life, you've been told to only start new yarn at the beginning of a row. But guess what? In Intarsialand, you'll be adding new yarn in the middle of a row, because that's where it will be needed.

You can always add new yarn in the middle of a row using the method described in chapter 1 (page 3), which incorporates the intarsia trick of twisting new yarn around the old yarn. But there's a second method that works especially well for intarsia, and it's sure to freak people out when they see it, which is a plus.

For this method, knit (or purl) up until you need to make a stitch in the new color. Then bring the new yarn between your needles, leaving about a 6" tail hanging *at the front* of your work, bring your old yarn up and to the left so that it crosses over the top of this new piece of yarn, then pick up the new yarn (it will now be coming from underneath the old yarn) and knit (or purl) the next stitch with this new color yarn.

Leave the tail that's weirdly hanging in front of your work so it doesn't get confused with the umpteen other lengths of yarn at the back, the ones you are actually working with. I've had it happen more than once while doing intarsia that I thought I was knitting with a new piece of yarn only to find that I was accidentally knitting with someone else's tail. Later on, you can put that tail behind you by simply pulling up the loop in the back of your work that he's attached to, *et voilà*—the most beautiful, undetectable new yarn addition ever.

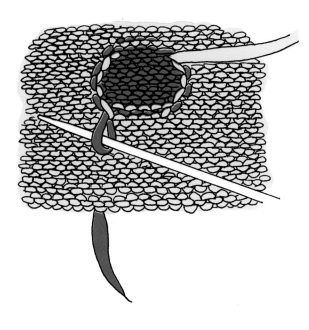

connecting the dots

LINKING YOUR YARNS TOGETHER

When you first add a new color of yarn using either of the ways I just described, it will already be linked with the old yarn. On the following rows, when you are changing colors in the middle of a row, it's quite simple to link the old and the new. For the last stitch of the old color, bring the old yarn up and to the left,

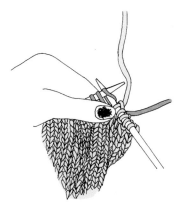

and bring the new yarn up from underneath it to make the stitch.

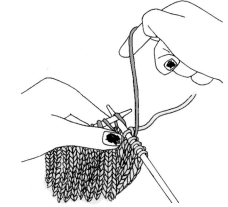

You are catching the old yarn in with the new yarn, making a little yarn "hammock," just like you do when carrying yarn up the sides of your work. While people make all kinds of fuss about how to link yarns in intarsia, that's really all there is to it. You use the same method whether you are making a color change on the knit or the purl side of your work.

Years ago, when I was first learning to knit intarsia, I would find that my yarn changes looked a bit crummy from the front. So, studious girl that I am, I began reading every book I could find on the subject of intarsia (um, there really aren't that many) to see how I could perfect my technique. I tried every method suggested and could still never get the front of my work to look right, until I finally realized that the front side of intarsia *never* looks very good while you are knitting it and won't reach true beauty until after it's been blocked and the edge stitches have been adjusted (see "Nip/Tuck," page 20). Sometimes, it won't look perfect even after you've fixed it up. In fact, I can show you more than one knitting book about intarsia on which the edges of the projects displayed on the *cover* look crappy!

In the end, it turns out that there really is only one way to link your yarns together at the color change—and it's the same whether the new yarn is coming from the stitch right below, or below and to the right or left—and that's the way I explain above: Take your old yarn up and to the left, bring the new yarn up from underneath that yarn and make your stitch.

A tigHt-kNit group

MAKING THE EDGES OF YOUR COLOR CHANGES AS NICE AS POSSIBLE

To keep the stitches at the edges of your color changes from being too loose, as they often are, tighten the last stitch before the color change by giving your yarn a good tug after completing the stitch. You also want to tighten the first stitch of your new color, but do it like so: Knit the first stitch in the normal way, linking it with the previous stitch of the old color. Then, on the next stitch in that color, insert your needle as if to knit (or purl) but don't wrap the yarn yet. Instead, tug on the yarn to tighten up the previous stitch. Then wrap the yarn and complete this stitch. You'll still need to touch up your edge stitches later on, but this trick will definitely help.

Why do the stitches at intarsia color changes often look so distorted? Because what makes a knit stitch a perfectly shaped knit stitch is the direction that the yarn on either side "travels" into that stitch. Think of a knit stitch as the legs of a prima ballerina doing a plié in first position—which, if you've never taken ballet, means that the heels of her feet are together, her feet are pointing straight to each side, and her legs are slightly bent. Her weight is distributed nicely over her feet, and they are bent in exactly the same, graceful way. Now imagine that you take one of her feet and change its orientation—for example, you cut a hole in the ground under her foot and pull down on her toes, or you tie a rope to the toes of one foot and tie the other end to the ceiling, making her toes point up in the air, or you twist her foot so that it is pointing down and behind her. Can you see that this would make it very difficult for her to keep her legs in the same perfect plié shape as when her feet were both evenly sticking out to each side? When working intarsia, your knit stitches are like the legs of this poor tortured ballerina. Linking the stitches

together is an attempt to get the yarn to seem like it's coming into the stitch from the sides—like the feet of the ballerina before we started messing with her, and like normal knit stitches when you aren't changing colors in the middle of a row. But in intarsia, the yarn leading up to a stitch at the edge of a colored area is coming from the row below, not the stitch next door—sometimes directly below, which isn't so bad (the foot through the floor thing above), but often from below and a few stitches before or after the stitch you are making, which is like taking that foot and pointing it in every other crazy direction you can think of. The yarn "exiting" your edge stitches isn't necessarily going on to create the next stitch, either—it

may be going to make a stitch in the row above, possibly right overhead, or above and a few, or even quite a few, stitches to the right or left. That means our ballerina's feet are going to get quite twisted and turned, and it also means that when you are knitting intarsia, the stitches on the edges of your color areas are naturally going to be somewhat wonky. All you can do is try your best not to pull your yarn too tight or leave it too loose while making your stitches, and concentrate on linking your colors together as you go. Later, when your work is done, you can fix up those gross edges with a bit of a knitting facelift. (See "Nip/Tuck," page 20.)

COMbiNAtion pLAtter

USING INTARSIA AND STRANDED KNITTING TOGETHER

Remember Joan Crawford earlier? And how she told you never to carry your yarn behind your stitches? Well, don't tell her I said so, but sometimes you can do just that. If you're working an intarsia pattern that has just a few stitches outside the main color area, or a few details inside of a larger design, you can go ahead and carry your yarn over there to knit those few stitches, as long as they aren't too far away. Your intarsia may not be completely street-legal if you do this, but you will keep your head from exploding as a result of dealing with too many lengths of yarn, and that's an important consideration. A long time ago, I was making a baby sweater that had many small flower sprigs sprinkled across it, with leaves and stems and flower buds. I was so committed to practicing perfect intarsia, I didn't let a single length of yarn ever cross another length of yarn, so each flower sprig required many strands, plus I needed tons of pieces of yarn to create all the bits of background color between each flower sprig. As I worked, I found myself cursing the designer, and cursed her even more when I walked into my LYS to find a sample of this very sweater in which the background color yarn was carried behind each of the flower sprigs, as were some of the colors in the flower sprig itself. The sweater looked perfect, and whoever knit the sample went through a lot less hell than I did, with fewer ends to work away.

There are two instances in which you might want to combine some stranding with your intarsia. If you have a number of small color designs scattered over a single-color background (as in my torture sweater above), you should use separate lengths of yarn to make your small designs, but strand the background yarn behind them. Here you'd be working intarsia within a stranded piece. Alternatively, you might work some stranded knitting *within* an intarsia piece. For instance, in an American flag design worked in intarsia using separate lengths of red, white, and blue, you might work the stars by stranding the white yarn behind the blue.

Be careful, though, of other times when you might be tempted to strand—such as stranding your background color behind a narrow vertical stripe, or a larger, solid stripe. If you do that, not only will your fabric pucker and distort like nobody's business, but your color changes will also be a mess.

If, however, your design includes vertical or diagonal lines that are only a single stitch wide, you're best off not knitting them into your design at all, but instead adding them at the end of the work using duplicate stitch (see "All Stitched Up," page 81) or crocheting them into your design, as explained next. Linking a single column of stitches using the intarsia technique is impossible. Duplicate stitch is your best bet for small details on your pieces as well, especially when they consist of only a few stitches in a different color.

one-stitch pony

MAKING SINGLE-STITCH VERTICAL COLOR COLUMNS WITH CROCHET

I encountered this method in a Dutch knitting pattern for a sweater that had vertical and horizontal stripes running across the sleeves in contrasting colors. The horizontal stripes were knit right in, but for the single-stitch-wide vertical stripes, the pattern directed me to knit purl stitches in the regular background color, then crochet the vertical stripes over these columns of purl stitches afterward. I've never seen this method show up in any American pattern (except for a pattern in one of my own books, where I put it in myself), but it's quite brilliant. While you're knitting, work the single-stitch vertical column in reverse stockinette stitch instead of stockinette stitch. That will leave a column of purl stitches running up your fabric. Then, holding your new color yarn at the back of your work, insert a crochet hook (one that's the appropriate size for your yarn) from the front of your work through to the back, underneath the lowest purl rung. Pull a loop of the new color yarn through to the front of the work.

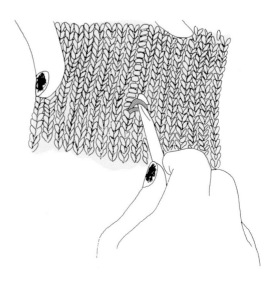

Insert the hook under the next rung up, wrap your yarn around the hook, and pull it through to the front and through the loop on the hook, so you are left with a single loop on the hook. You're really making a crocheted slip stitch. Work your way all the way up the column of purl stitches, securing your yarn and stitch at the end by whatever means necessary, and you'll see that you've created a

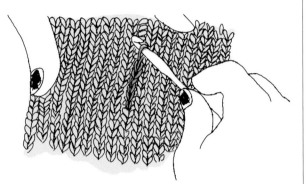

new column of stitches that, for all intents and purposes, look just like knit stitches. (In Nelson voice) HA-ha!

Nip/tuck

FINISHING YOUR INTARSIA WORK, FIXING IT UP, AND WORKING AWAY THE ENDS

Once you've completed knitting your intarsia piece, you still have a bit of work to do before it is truly finished. Start by stretching your work, top to bottom, side to side, and corner to corner, to sort of "settle" the stitches. Next, get out a knitting needle and prepare to fix up those ratty edges of your color changes. I've found the best way is to tighten each loose stitch by pulling up each arm of the V with a knitting needle and adjusting the stitch so that it's neither too loose nor too tight, then distributing the resulting slack across a few stitches. Thus, I pull up the arms of the next V, but not completely, so that some of the slack stays in that stitch, then on to the next stitch and leave a bit of the slack there, and on for a few more stitches until the looseness that was in the first stitch has been spread out among four or five stitches and is thereby imperceptible. Do this to all of the stitches at the edges of your colors that look ratty.

Next, it's time to work away your yarn ends. First, bring all the yarn ends that you've left hanging on the front of your work to the back by pulling up the loop on the back of your work where the yarn was started. (See "Start Me Up," page 15.)

The trick to weaving away the ends of intarsia work neatly is twofold: (1) Work the ends into stitches of the same color, and (2) make sure the stitches where the ends are coming from are not distorted in the process. One easy way to accomplish this is to simply weave the ends into the loops where the two different color sections were joined. Another undetectable way to secure your yarn is to stab your needle through the back loops of similar color stitches, thereby splitting them, as you are weaving away your ends. This keeps any yarn from showing through on the front side of your work.

circLe game

INTARSIA IN THE ROUND

'm a die-hard flat knitter, but I know there are some of you out there who are equally committed to knitting in the round. Intarsia, however, is really not intended for circular knitting. Think about it for a sec: You're knitting with color A, then you drop it when you get to color B, then you drop it when you get to color C. In flat knitting, you would go back the other way around, knit with color C till you get to B, and right there, color B is waiting for you. But in the round, after you've finished with color C and you want to start knitting with color A, you can't! Color A is hanging on the left side of that color block, and here you are at the beginning of the block—the right side—with no yarn to be had.

Knitting intarsia in the round can be done, but it's actually kind of a cheat. What you really do is knit back and forth on circular needles, and join the ends of each row so it sort of looks like a round. Nevertheless, it's a good technique if, for instance, you're knitting a sock with an intarsia motif on it— like a ball and pins for a committed bowler—you can knit the cuff in the round up until the intarsia motif, knit using the technique described at right on the bowling stuff, then continue in the round down to the heel and onward.

Here's how it's done:

❶ Knit in the round until you get to the intarsia section.

❷ Place a marker between the first and last stitches of your round. Begin the next row with a yarn over, then knit the rest of the row of your intarsia section the normal way. Knit up to one stitch before the yarn over. Make an ssk decrease with the last stitch and the yarn over together.

❸ Turn your work so the purl side is facing you. You may want to push your entire work through the needles, inside out, or turn your work so that the needle points are at the far end of your round. Yarn over and purl your way back, as you would for intarsia worked flat. Work your intarsia sections in the normal way. Stop before you get to the last purl stitch before the yarn over. P2tog with the last stitch and the yarn over.

❹ Turn your work so the knit side is facing you, and continue this method for the entire intarsia section. If your last row of intarsia is a knit row, just ssk at the end of the row, then continue knitting in the round. If that last row is a purl row, you'll need to p2tog at the end and turn and work a yarn over again at the beginning of the next knit row. Ssk at the end of that knit row, and then continue knitting in the round normally.

3

Strand and deliver

TWO-COLOR KNITTING USING THE STRANDED TECHNIQUE

 tranded knitting—also called "Fair Isle" or "jacquard" knitting—is the technique of knitting with two or more colors of yarn in a single row. Unlike in intarsia, in stranded knitting you hold both yarns throughout the entire row, using only the color you need for each stitch, and carrying the unused color behind those stitches until you need to use it again. This results in strands of yarn across the back of your work, hence the name. Some folks, myself included, usually refer to this kind of knitting as "Fair Isle," because it creates the kind of work you associate with Fair Isle sweaters: intricately patterned colorwork across an entire sweater, or just around the yoke. While you may feel free to call it that in the privacy of your own home, just don't get caught in public referring to any old kind of stranded knitting as Fair Isle because the Knitting Police will be sure to slap you with a summons and a fine, and point out that true Fair Isle knitting is not a technique but a particular type of design.

Learning to do stranded knitting can be quite challenging, because unlike any of the other skills you might associate with advanced knitting—such as intarsia, cable, or lace knitting—stranded knitting requires you to actually change the way you hold your yarn so that you can knit with two yarns at the same time. Remember how, when you were first learning to knit, trying to hold your yarn correctly would make your hand get all cramped, as you struggled your way through stitch after stitch? And remember how it wasn't until you finally got the feel of tensioning your yarn correctly—perhaps by winding it around your pinky and then over your index finger, or twice around your index finger, or whatever worked—that your knitting started to speed up? Well, learning to do stranded knitting will make you feel like you've been sent right back to square one, because it will feel just as awkward to hold two yarns at the same time and keep them each at the correct tension. But just like when you first learned to knit, if you just hang in there, eventually you'll find the way that works best for you, and it will all be worth it.

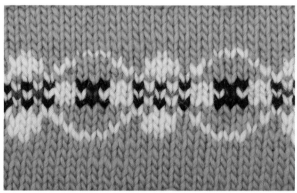
Stranded knitting as seen from the front

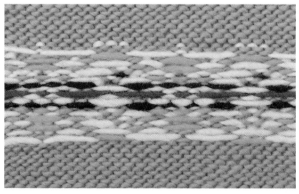
Stranded knitting as seen from the back, showing strands

PICKUP AND DROP-OFF
TWO-COLOR KNITTING WITH ONE HAND

If you're really opposed to holding two yarns at the same time, you can always use the "pickup and drop-off" method for stranded knitting, by simply dropping one yarn and picking up the other as you need it. This method is probably just fine if you are knitting a sweater in really bulky yarn, like a traditional Lopi sweater, similar to those overgrown ski sweaters of the 1960s. But when you are working at a gauge of 8 stitches to the inch, you'll be picking up and dropping off so often that it might take you an hour to knit a single row. At that point you just need to bite the bullet and learn to knit with both yarns at once. Besides, stranded knitting will open up all kinds of possibilities for you. You might even become obsessed with it.

the Hold Steady

FINDING THE RIGHT YARN HOLD FOR WORKING WITH TWO COLORS

There are quite a few different ways to hold your yarn for stranded knitting. If you can knit in both the English and the Continental methods, you can simply hold one yarn in each hand. This method makes it easier to keep both yarns tensioned equally, since they will be feeding off your hands completely independently of each other.

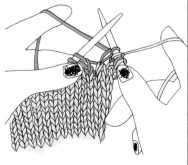

If, however, you are like me and really despise one of the two ways (I personally feel that Continental takes all the fun out of knitting; you might feel exactly the same way about English-style knitting—I know Elizabeth Zimmermann did), you can hold both yarns with the *same* hand. And just so you know, there is no *right* way to hold two colors of yarn. Holding both yarns in the right hand is the official way the folks in the Shetland Islands do it to make their famous Fair Isle knits, whereas holding both yarns in the left hand is the traditional way knitters in Finland, Denmark, Norway, and Sweden make those gorgeous Scandinavian yoked sweaters and colorful mittens.

The tricky part about knitting with two colors in the same hand is keeping the tension equal on both yarns, especially if you are using one color more frequently than the other in a row. If you have both yarns tensioned around your pinky, for instance, the one that is being used more often will also pull out the other yarn, which will quickly become too loose in your hand. This drove me crazy until I realized that I needed to wrap each yarn separately around my pinky, so that each could feed off my finger at its own rate. So I wrap one yarn around my pinky and lead it over my index finger, then I wrap the other yarn around my pinky and lead it over my middle finger. It's kind of a pain to set up, but it works.

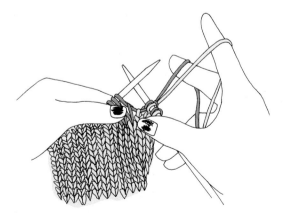

Alternatively, you can hold both yarns over your index finger, spread out a bit (one color between your nail and your knuckle, and the second color between your knuckle and your hand) and maintain the tension by holding the yarn against your palm with your lower three fingers. Though this method works, it can lead to a bit of cramping in those lower fingers.

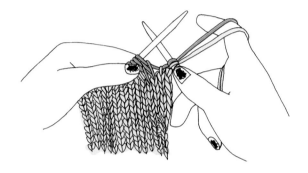

If you prefer to hold *both yarns in your left hand*, the most common method is to hold both yarns over your index finger, with one strand closer to your nail and the other closer to, or to the left of, your knuckle.

Another method would be to hold one yarn over your index finger and the other over your middle finger.

The middle finger can kind of stay out of the way and spring up only when needed, intermittently giving the bird to your knitting.

If holding two yarns in your left hand over one finger, you will need to adjust your knitting method slightly. When knitting (or purling) the yarn that is on the left-hand side of the two yarns, everything is as normal, but when you go to "pick" a stitch from the yarn that is on the right side, you will need to be sure that you bring the point of your right-hand needle *over* the yarn held on the left.

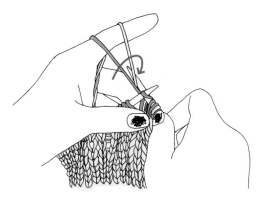

Alternatively, if one yarn is over your index finger and the other is over your middle finger, make the stitch with the strand on your index finger as usual, but make the stitch with the strand on your middle finger by first bringing your needle point *over* the strand on your index finger. In purling, this is reversed. The stitches you make with the yarn over your middle finger will be made as usual, but when using yarn that is on your index finger, be sure to pass your needle *under* the yarn that is on your middle finger.

You can also try placing something called a knitting thimble, or yarn guide, on your index finger and slip both yarns through. (I haven't tried this myself, but I know that the trick to making it work will still be to maintain equal tension on both yarns.)

float Like A butterfly

LEAVING LOOSE-ENOUGH STRANDS

Once you've got a yarn hold down, you pretty much knit as usual. Stranded knitting is most often done on stockinette fabric (no need to muck up any intricate color patterns by throwing in textured stitches), so once you're comfortable with your hold, knit holding both yarns all the way across your row, using the correct color yarn to make each stitch according to your color chart. Then turn around and purl all the way back, continuing to follow the chart. Or, if you are knitting in the round, you just continue knitting the next round.

The other beast to deal with in stranded knitting is the strands themselves. You already learned about these "floats" in chapter 1, and here, as in slip-stitching, it's crucial that they be not too tight, not too loose, and, very important, not too long. Most knitters who are first learning this technique tend to make their floats too short, which means the fabric will pull together and they end up with an accordion instead of a sweater. But even with perfect floats, a sweater knit using stranding will never be as stretchy as one without. Because knit stitches are shaped like Vs, they can spread out and compress like little tweezers, whereas yarn strands will always be straight lines that can only expand and contract so much. Stretchier yarn will result in stretchier floats, but no matter what kind of yarn you're using, you want to try to leave floats whose tension is *juuuuust* right.

Here are some tips: If you are knitting in the round, one way to force yourself to leave loose strands is to turn your work inside out, so that the purl side is on the outside, and the knit side is on the inside. You then knit with the needles on the far side of the circle, making regular old knit stitches that you can see on the inside of this tube. This leaves the strands around the outside of your knitting as you're working, and because of geometry (the circumference of the outer perimeter of your work is larger than the circumference of the inner perimeter), they will be a bit longer and therefore looser.

Eventually, however, you'll want to be able to knit circularly the way you're used to, with the good side of your work on the outside. And if you knit flat, you'll need a way to leave floats with the right amount of tension as well. There's got to be another way—and there is. I spread out the stitches on my right-hand needle before I create a stitch in the new color by pulling them away from the point of the needle, about as far apart as they'd actually be if the fabric was being stretched a bit. This way I leave a float that is close to the width of the fabric or just a bit wider, which leaves room for a bit of stretchiness in the completed fabric.

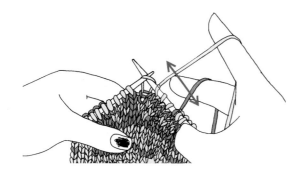

Of course, be careful not to pull this stitch tight when you're knitting it, or you'll undo the good of spreading out the stitches leading up to it. To make sure you're doing this correctly, stop and check that your knitting is stretchy enough and that the strands hang flat, neither pulling the fabric taut nor hanging down in unsightly loops. Eventually, you'll know instinctively to spread your stitches out and away from the needle before making a stitch in a new color, and your strands will always be at the correct tension.

who's on first?
YARN DOMINANCE IN STRANDED KNITTING

On the back of stranded knitting, if done correctly, the floats of the two colors should run parallel to each other, like train tracks, never switching sides. As a result, the floats of one color will always lie above the floats of the other. This will happen if you consistently carry the same yarn in the same hand, or in the same position if you're carrying your yarns with one hand. Let's say you are knitting with blue and yellow yarn: You might always hold your yellow yarn in your right hand and your blue yarn in your left hand. Or you might always hold your yellow yarn over your index finger and your blue yarn over your middle finger. If you do this while knitting, you will see that your floats never switch positions; in this example, the yellow floats would always be above the blue floats, and the blue floats would always be below the yellow floats.

What's really surprising, however, is the fact that which color yarn you carry above or below will affect the look of your design. In fact, *the color that is carried underneath will always show up better in the image.* Say that the pattern in the example described above had little blue flowers on a yellow background. You'd want the blue stitches to stand out and not get sucked up into the yellow background, so you'd be sure to always carry your blue yarn below the yellow yarn. But if your knitting design was yellow stars against a blue sky, you'd want to change the arrangement, and carry the yellow yarn below the blue yarn, so that the stars stand out in the sky.

I had a really hard time remembering which was which, until I came up with a catchphrase I could remember: *Dominant Goes Down.* That is, whichever color you want to be dominant—or stand out—in your knitting is the one you should hold below the other. Which hand or which position is the "lower" yarn is different for each yarn hold and sometimes even different on the knit and purl sides. If you're holding your yarn in two hands, the yarn you are holding in the right hand will lie above the yarn you hold in your left hand, and that's true whether you are knitting or purling. If you're knitting holding both yarns in your right hand over the same finger, the leftmost yarn will be underneath and dominant. If you're holding one yarn over each of two fingers, the yarn that is held over the finger farther away from your body will come to lie underneath and be dominant. On the purl side, this will be reversed. If you're knitting holding both yarns in your left hand, the leftmost yarn or the strand held over the finger closer to you will lie underneath and be dominant in your design; the same holds for the purl side.

In the top half of this swatch, the purple yarn was held in the lower position and the white yarn was held in the upper position. In the bottom half of the swatch, the white yarn was held below the purple yarn. As you can see, the white yarn is more dominant in the lower half of the swatch.

don't Leave Me Hangin'

HOW TO "CATCH" LONG FLOATS IN YOUR KNITTING

No matter how good you are at leaving floats with the correct tension, sometimes there are so many stitches before you need the same color again that you are left with lengthy floats that can get caught on fingers, toes, earrings, necklaces, and anything else that happens to cross their path. A float is considered "too long" if it is more than an inch in length. So if you are knitting with yarn that has a gauge of four stitches to the inch, you can leave your yarn hanging if you plan to use it again after four stitches. If not, you must "catch" it at the back of your work to keep it from getting too long. This means twisting the float with

In the lower half of the above swatch, shown from the front and from the back, long floats were left hanging. In the upper half, the long strands were caught every four stitches or so.

the yarn you're using, catching it behind your work. It's a way of invisibly "tacking" these long floats so all your bits aren't hanging loose. This "catching," also called "weaving" or "trapping," is the last of the stranded knitting bugaboos that you need to learn.

Consider that you are knitting with two yarns. Let's call them Abe and Bee. Catching Bee while knitting with Abe is done in one way while knitting and a different way while purling, and catching Abe while knitting with Bee is also done differently while knitting than while purling. This means you need to learn all four different ways of catching your yarn. Plus, it is done differently, depending on what yarn hold you use.

C'mon out from under that chair! It's not going to be all that bad. And I'll tell you something: Once you learn this fancy trickery, you can easily impress all your friends, both knitting and non-, by whipping out your stranded knitting anywhere and strutting your yarn-weaving techniques. It's like a complicated square dance done with yarn, and it's pretty magical-looking stuff.

For one thing, most of them aren't even so much "catching" methods as they are, to extend the fishing metaphor, "catch-and-release" methods. You'll often be wrapping the yarn you want to "catch" around the needle, and then you'll be unwrapping it before you make the actual stitch. That's important to remember. The second thing is that the yarn won't really be "caught" until you create the next stitch. So you always need to do your yarn "catching" at least one stitch in from the last stitch in your working color.

You don't have to worry about any of this catching business unless you've got *more* than an inch of knitting in a single color, and you'll want to catch the yarn in the middle of your float. If, for example, you're going to be leaving a 1½"-long strand of yarn at the back of your work, weave it at around the ¾" mark, so you are left with two ¾"-long strands at the back of your work. If you've got many rows of this same pattern, don't do your stranding on the same stitch every time. So, if the 1½" of a single color is, say, ten stitches, then on one row or round catch it on the fifth stitch,

and on the next row make it the sixth stitch, and on the next row, the fourth stitch, and so on. That's because there will be the tiniest bit of a pucker on the front of your work where the nonworking yarn was caught, and if you make it at the same point on every round, that pucker will become a quite noticeable line.

In the following directions, I've identified, for each method, which yarn will create the "upper" or "lower" strand at the back of your work. Whether you're catching or not, hold the yarn that you'd like to appear dominant in the design in the lower position (remember, dominant goes down), and the background yarn in the upper position.

Pick the yarn hold that's most comfortable for you, and skip to the directions that pertain to that hold.

CATCHING TECHNIQUES WHEN HOLDING YARNS IN BOTH HANDS
ON THE KNIT SIDE

When knitting, the yarn being held in the right hand will be the upper yarn, and the yarn being held in the left hand will be the lower yarn.

To catch the yarn in the right hand (upper) on a knit stitch:

1 Insert the needle into the next stitch as if to knit.

2 Wrap the yarn being held in the right hand around the needle as if to knit.

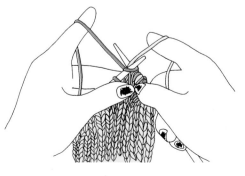

③ Wrap the left-hand yarn around the needle as if to knit.

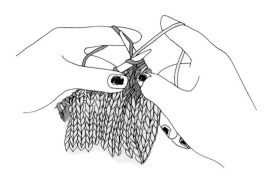

④ *Unwrap* the yarn that's being held by the right hand.

⑤ Complete the knit stitch.

To catch the yarn in the left hand (lower) on a knit stitch:

① Insert the needle into the next stitch, and at the same time go *under* the strand coming from the left hand.

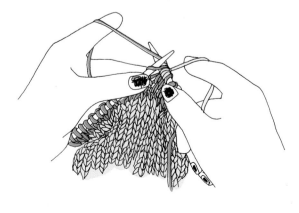

② Wrap the yarn being held by the right hand around the needle as if to knit, and complete the stitch.

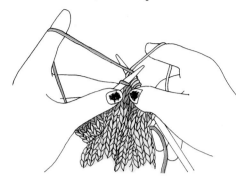

ON THE PURL SIDE

When purling, the yarn being held in the right hand will be the upper yarn, and the yarn being held in the left hand will be the lower yarn.

To catch the yarn in the right hand (upper) on a purl stitch:

① Insert the needle into the next stitch as if to purl.

② Wrap the yarn in the right hand around the needle *in the opposite direction* you would to make a purl stitch (clockwise under the needle).

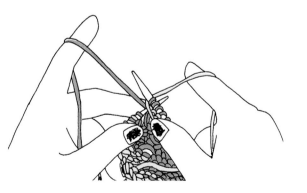

③ Wrap the yarn in your left hand around the needle as if to purl.

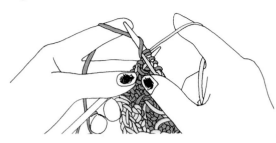

④ *Unwrap* the yarn being held by your right hand.

⑤ Complete the stitch.

To catch the yarn in the left hand (lower) on a purl stitch:

① Insert the needle into the next stitch as if to purl.

② Wrap the yarn being held in the left hand around the needle as if to purl.

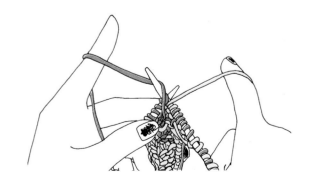

③ Wrap the yarn being held in the right hand around the needle as if to purl.

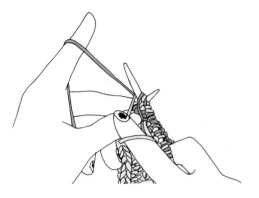

④ Unwrap the yarn being held in the left hand.

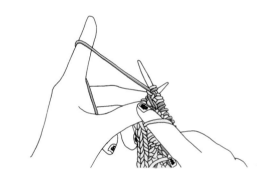

⑤ Complete the purl stitch.

CATCHING TECHNIQUES WITH BOTH YARNS IN THE RIGHT HAND

While knitting, if you are holding the yarns over two different fingers, then the yarn on the finger closest to you (usually your index finger) will be the upper yarn, and the one on the finger farthest from you will be the lower yarn. If you are holding both yarns on the same finger, then the one on the right will be the upper yarn, and the one on the left will be the lower yarn.

ON THE KNIT SIDE

To catch the upper yarn on a knit stitch:

1 Insert the needle into the next stitch as if to knit.

2 Wrap both yarns around the needle as if to knit.

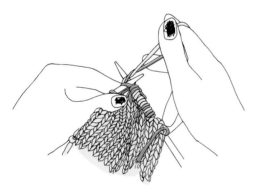

3 *Unwrap* the upper yarn and complete the stitch.

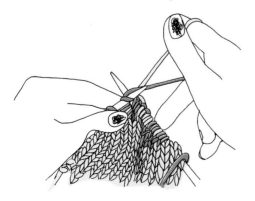

CATCH O' THE DAY:

CATCHING LONG FLOATS ON THE FOLLOWING ROW

If you are just starting out with stranding—struggling to learn how to knit with two yarns at the same time—and the idea of learning to weave in your yarn at the same time seems too daunting, don't fret. There is a sort of "training wheels" method of float-catching in which your lengthy floats are caught on the following row. To do this, simply knit according to your design, leaving floats even if they are more than an inch long. Then, on the next row, when you get to the stitch that's roughly at the center of the long float, simply insert your needle into that stitch and also underneath the float. Make your knit stitch and bring the new

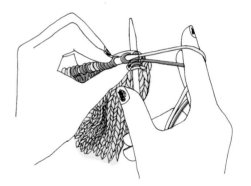

stitch underneath the float as well as through the loop to complete the stitch. Float caught! (On a purl side, it's only slightly different: Insert your needle underneath the float first and then into the stitch.) It's a good trick, but it does require you to keep track of when your long floats are coming around to where you're knitting. On the purl side, they're facing you, but on the knit side you need to peek over the top of your needles every so often so you know when another long float is coming. You'll spot the ones that are too long right away.

To catch the lower yarn on a knit stitch:

① Insert the needle into the next stitch as if to knit.

② Wrap the lower yarn around the needle *in the opposite direction* you would to make a knit stitch.

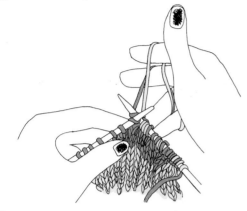

③ Wrap the upper yarn around the needle as if to knit.

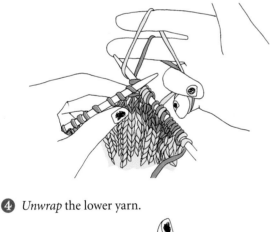

④ *Unwrap* the lower yarn.

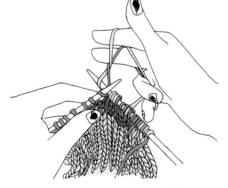

⑤ Complete the stitch.

ON THE PURL SIDE

While purling, the positions of upper and lower yarns are reversed: If you are holding the yarns over two different fingers, then the yarn on the finger farther from you will be the upper yarn, and the one on the finger closer to you will be the lower yarn. If you are holding both yarns on the same finger, then the one on the left will be the upper yarn, the one on the right will be the lower yarn.

To catch the upper yarn on a purl stitch:

① Insert the needle into the next stitch as if to purl.

② Wrap the upper yarn around the needle *in the opposite direction* you would to make a purl stitch.

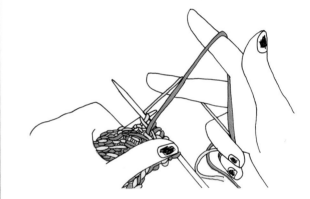

③ Wrap the lower yarn around the needle as if to purl.

④ Unwrap the upper yarn.

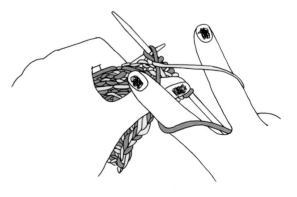

⑤ Complete the stitch.

To catch the lower yarn on a purl stitch:

❶ Insert the needle into the next stitch as if to purl.

❷ Wrap both yarns around the needle as if to purl.

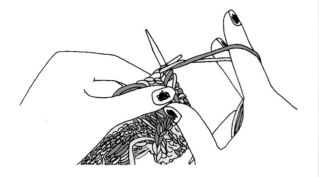

❸ *Unwrap* the lower yarn.

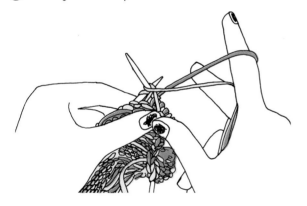

❹ Complete the stitch.

CATCHING TECHNIQUES WITH BOTH YARNS IN THE LEFT HAND

Weaving yarns when both are held in the left hand is ridiculously simple on the knit side. However, it is such a miserable experience when done from the purl side that I would quickly give up high-level national secrets (if I had any) if I were forced to purl even a single row on a stranded sweater this way—it's sheer torture. This may be the reason I was not able to find references to weaving on the purl side when holding two yarns in the left hand in any knitting book ever written. Avoid it like the plague; either work your projects in the round by knitting circular yoked sweaters or using steeks (see "Steek 'Em," page 35), or learn to purl with your right hand and work your purl rows holding one yarn in each hand, as above. Nevertheless, for those of you who want to give it a try, the directions are below.

ON THE KNIT SIDE

If you are knitting and holding the yarns over two different fingers, the yarn on the finger farther from you will be the upper yarn, and the one on the finger closer to you will be the lower yarn. If you are knitting and holding both yarns on the same finger, the one on the right will be the upper yarn, and the one on the left will be the lower yarn.

To catch the upper yarn on a knit stitch:

❶ Insert the needle into the next stitch as if to knit.

❷ Swing your needle to the right *over* both strands of yarn, then to the left *under* both strands, and catch the lower yarn on the back of your needle.

③ Push the new stitch back underneath the upper yarn and complete the stitch.

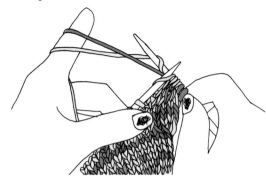

To catch the lower yarn on a knit stitch:

① Insert the needle into the next stitch as if to knit.

② "Pick" the yarn from the rightmost (upper) strand by going *under* the leftmost (lower) strand and complete the stitch.

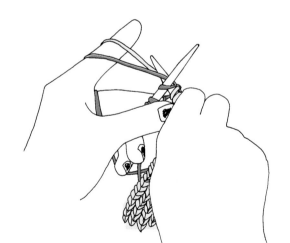

ON THE PURL SIDE

If you are purling and holding the yarns over two different fingers, then the yarn on the finger farther from you will be the upper yarn, and the one on the finger closer to you will be the lower yarn. If you are purling and holding both yarns on the same finger, then the one on the right will be the upper yarn, the one on the left will be the lower yarn.

To catch the upper yarn on a purl stitch:

① Insert the needle into the next stitch, and go *over* the rightmost (upper) yarn to grab the stitch from the leftmost (lower) yarn.

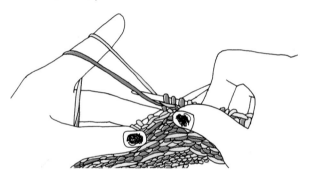

② Complete the stitch.

To catch the lower yarn on a purl stitch:

① Insert the needle into the next stitch, bring the needle around and over both upper and lower strands of yarn, then under the leftmost (lower) yarn to grab the stitch from the rightmost (upper) strand.

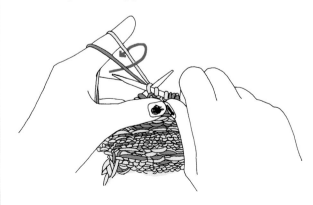

❷ Bring this new stitch back around and underneath the leftmost (lower) strand.

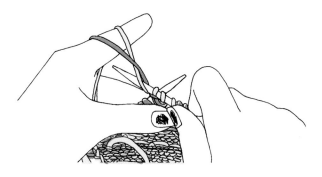

❸ Complete the stitch.

ʃteek 'em

WORKING IN THE ROUND AND CUTTING YOUR WORK USING STEEKS

I've already told you that working the purl side of stranded knitting is no walk in the park. And that's why in countries where this type of two-color work is most popular, garments are made in the round, so that the knit side always faces the knitter. It's a lot easier to avoid errors in your pattern knitting this way as well. But how can you knit a sweater completely in the round? Turns out there are two different ways to do it. The classic ski-style sweater, which features a ring of color design around the neck and across the shoulders only, is accomplished by knitting the body completely in the round from the bottom up to the armholes, and knitting the sleeves in the round from the cuff up to where the armholes would begin. At this point, both sleeves and the body are placed on one giant circular needle (leaving a few armpit stitches on holders) and the yoke—where the color-work will appear—is entirely knit in the round. You totally avoid any of those awful purl stitches.

But what about different styles of sweaters—drop-shoulder sweaters, for instance, or cardigans? How can

these be done completely in the round? There is a way, and it's accomplished by using a method known as steeking. *Steek* (rhymes with "eek!") is a Scots word that means to "shut" or "close," and that's exactly what it does. A steek is made up of anywhere from 3 to 12 stitches, and closes, or bridges, an area (such as where an armhole would be) so that knitting can continue in the round. Later on, when the knitting is done, these steeks are cut open, and voilà— an armhole is born! Steeking can also be used if you'd like to knit a cardigan in the round. You'd just make a steek up the front of your sweater, and when your knitting is done, you cut the steek open, knit on a front band, and there you go—a pullover is now a button-down cardigan.

LET'S TALK ABOUT STEEKS, BABY
HOW TO MAKE A STEEK IN YOUR KNITTING

If a pattern uses steeks, it will usually tell you exactly how and where to make them. But the beauty part is, once you learn this technique, you can use it on just about any sweater. You need to be knitting in the round to use steeks, so if your pattern has separate directions for front and back, convert it to a sweater knit in the round like so: Cast on all stitches for front and back, subtract 4 (these would be the seam stitches), and get knitting.

For anything but a cardigan, the first time you'll encounter steeks in a bottom-up sweater is when you reach the armholes. Here's the most common scenario: Knit until you get to the point when you would normally bind off stitches, and instead, put them on a stitch holder or a piece of waste yarn. Now look at what you have. If you want to keep knitting, you have to get to the stitches on the other side of this area of stitches. So how do you bridge the gap? With a steek! Just place a marker at this point on your needles and cast on anywhere from 3 to 12 stitches (how many stitches and whether you cast on an even or odd number depends on how you plan to finish your steek; see "Different Steeks for Different Freaks," facing page), place another marker, and continue knitting on the other side of the gap. This "bridge" of stitches will be cut open down the middle after all your knitting is done. And while the idea of cutting your knitting might terrify you, there are a number of things about the way a steek is knit, as well as the way it is finished, that will keep it from unraveling, so don't be scared. Folks have been doing this for a couple of centuries now, and what you're learning here is a method that has truly passed the test of time.

When you cast on those stitches that will bridge the gap, you'll want to use both colors of the yarn you're working with. The easiest way to do this is to use the long-tail cast-on (page 90), pretending that one color of yarn is the tail end, the other color the ball end. On the next round, you'll set up the pattern for these stitches.

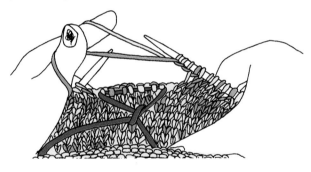

Here are a few things to keep in mind: The first and the last stitches of the steek are traditionally done in the background (nondominant) color of your pattern. Some folks like to knit their steeks in long vertical stripes, but I suggest that you alternate color stitches and make a sort of checkerboard; then, when you go to reinforce a column of stitches, which you will do before cutting, that column will include stitches in both colors. Having the outer steek stitch in a single color helps by providing a guideline for where to pick up stitches later for knitting on button bands, sleeves, or a collar. So, for instance, if you are knitting a six-stitch steek in yarn colors A and B, with A being the background color, you might alternate your stitches

like so: A B A B A A, and, on the next round, you'd knit A A B A B A. The stitch on each side of the outer edge of this steek will be a column in color A, while the inner four stitches will alternate on each round, forming a checkerboard pattern. The basic idea here is that you are seriously weaving your yarns together throughout the steek, which will also help the stitches hold together after you cut the steek open. Don't worry about how your steek looks—this part of your sweater will be folded to the inside where no one but you will ever see it.

Once you've set up your steek stitches you can continue working your sweater in the round, shaping your armholes with decreases—although you might want to reverse the slant of the decreases you are instructed to make. So if the pattern calls for a right-slanting decrease, make a left-slanting one instead, and vice versa. That will work better later when you need to turn the steek to the inside. Either way, it's gonna be a bit strange-looking, 'cause your steek stitches are a straight band while the sleeve hole is shaped, and so the sweater may pucker here and there, but don't sweat it. When the steek is cut, everything will be as it should.

Once all the knitting is done, with bridges in place, it's time to get ready to cut those steeks open. What? you're probably thinking, You can't cut knitting! All the stitches are going to unravel! You must be mad! Well, believe it or not, you *can* cut the steek open, and your stitches won't unravel, for a few reasons. First, stitches don't unravel side to side, they unravel downward—the proverbial dropped stitch runs down, not sideways. We're not cutting the knitting horizontally across a row, but rather vertically, down a column of stitches, so there will be no downward running of stitches. Second, knitting that is going to be steeked is often done in 100% animal fiber yarns that will felt together with a bit of wash and wear. Third, most folks choose to reinforce the area around the cutting line with sewing or crocheting before even picking up a pair of scissors. Finally, steeks are most often at least six stitches wide, so even if some stitches do come undone a bit, you'll still have quite a few stitches of "padding" between the cut edge and where you'll be picking up stitches or adding edgings—a true margin of error.

DIFFERENT STEEKS FOR DIFFERENT FREAKS

Although knitting a steek is basically the same for all the steeking methods I'm going to be explaining here—cast on stitches to make the steek, then knit these steek stitches for every round that you need 'em—once your steek is complete, it will be time to do the dirty deed: cutting it. Since that seems pretty frightening, there are some folks who prefer to reinforce their stitches before cutting anything at all, thereby giving them a bit of reassurance that their fabric won't unravel all over the place. These reinforcements are made on either side of the cutting line and are created with a sewing machine, a needle and thread, or a crochet hook and some yarn. Other folks, however, don't make any reinforcements at all, and rely on the stickiness of their yarn and the width of their steeks to keep things from going all to hell after the cut. There are different methods of finishing the cut ends, as well: They can be folded to the inside to form a small facing and stitched down, or they can be left as is. Which method of reinforcing and finishing you choose is up to you, but the type of yarn you are using may mean that one method is preferable over another. Here are the three main ways that you can choose to cut and finish your steeks.

THE TRADITIONALIST: CUT AND FINISH

Number of steek stitches: An even number of stitches, usually between 10 and 12.

Reinforcement method: None!

Prerequisites: This method of steeking works only if you are using 100% natural animal fiber yarn that is sticky, like traditional Shetland wool is, and are working it at a relatively tight gauge.

Finishing method: Steeks are trimmed and stitched down inside the garment using a whipstitch.

Upside: No chance of distorting knitting with sewn reinforcements; no need to take extra reinforcing step.

Downside: Wider steeks necessary for insurance; requires plenty of trimming and stitching to complete.

This is the method of steeking that is most often used by traditional Fair Isle knitters. You'll need some balls to take it on, however, as the steeks aren't reinforced by anything at all: You just cut right into them, then neaten them up and stitch them down later. But if you're working with the traditional, sticky DK weight Shetland wool yarn, it's a good one to try because that type of yarn sticks to itself as if it were made of Velcro and is not very prone to unraveling. If you are working with heavier or nonsticky yarn, however, stay away.

To execute it, work your steeks the usual way, with the two outermost stitches in the background color, and the inner stitches worked in a checkerboard pattern. When all your knitting is done, using a sharp pair of scissors, carefully cut through the rungs between the two center steek stitches. Next, pick up stitches for the sleeves or bands and knit these. When the sleeves or front bands are complete, return to your steek and trim it to only two or three stitches wide. Fold it to the inside of your work, tuck in the outermost stitch, and, using a thinner yarn or your knitting yarn split into fewer plies to keep it from becoming too bulky, tack it as follows: Make a line of whipstitches along the edge, piercing through the yarn on the back of your work with each stitch to hold the facing in place and keep these stitches from showing on the front. If you'd like, you can

make a second line of whipstitches going back down that will cross with the first line of stitches and form nice little X's. This second row of stitches would just be to keep the cut stitch nicely tucked in; you don't need to tack it down with this set of stitches.

THE CONSERVATIVE: SEW, CUT, AND FINISH

Number of steek stitches: Even number of stitches, usually around six.

Reinforcement method: Machine or hand-stitched.

Prerequisites: You must know (or be willing to learn) how to work a sewing machine or know how to make a back-stitch by hand with needle and thread.

Finishing method: Steeks are stitched down inside the garment using a whipstitch.

Upside: The most secure method, suitable for all yarn types; narrower steeks and less cleanup of raw edges.

Downside: Sewing your knitting may not leave your fabric as stretchy; need to get out yucky heavy sewing machine; sewing by hand takes a long time.

Sewing through your knitting, whether with a machine or by hand, is certainly one way to be certain your steek stitches aren't going to unravel anywhere. This method comes to us from the Norwegian tradition, where sweaters are knit with no steek stitches at all—as a simple tube—then rows of stitches are made with a sewing machine on either side of where an armhole needs to be cut, and then the knitting is simply sliced up between the machine stitches.

However, the machine- or hand-sewing method is also quite frequently used by knitters who are using the steeking method. For these, the steeks need not be quite so wide, because you don't need the security cushion of additional stitches. A steek of six stitches is enough. There are a few different ways to secure the steek with sewing

before it is cut down the center. The basic idea is that you are sewing stitches on either side of where the steek will be cut to secure it. Here are a few of the most common methods. You can:

Ⓐ Use your sewing machine to make a line of zigzag stitches that are about as wide as a column of knit stitches over the columns of stitches one stitch in from the right and left edges of your steek.

Ⓑ Use your sewing machine to make two lines of small straight stitches, right next to each other, down the centers of the columns of stitches one stitch in from the right and left edges of your steek.

C Using a sewing needle and thread, hand-sew a line of small backstitches down the center of the columns of stitches one stitch in from the left and right edges of your steek.

After you've reinforced your steek in this way, take out sharp scissors and slowly and carefully snip the steek open by cutting between the center two columns of steek stitches.

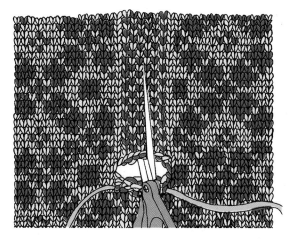

Next, pick up stitches for sleeves or front bands as usual. After you're done, turn the tiny facing to the inside of your work, and whipstitch it down, as in the traditionalist method (page 37).

THE UPSTART: CROCHET AND CUT

Number of steek stitches: An odd number of stitches, usually three or five.

Reinforcement method: Crochet stitches along edges to be cut.

Prerequisites: You must know (or be willing to learn) how to crochet slip stitches.

Finishing method: None.

Upside: Quick to execute; leaves a very pretty edging that can be done in contrasting yarn for additional adorableness points; no need to finish edges after cutting.

Downside: The least secure method; can be pulled loose, especially if worked on slippery yarn.

While the first two methods described here both have their beginnings rooted in regional knitting traditions, the crocheted method of steek finishing is a much more recent development. Nevertheless, because it is so simple to execute and leaves such a nice edge, it is gaining in popularity and has been appearing on knitting blogs all up and down the Internet. Meg Swanson, daughter of knitting guru Elizabeth Zimmermann, is a big proponent of this method. Unfortunately, I've seen her method mistaught and mangled many a time, especially by folks for whom crocheting is a bit of a foreign language, so listen up and learn it right.

While this method is quick and cute, it's also a bit dangerous because it is the least secure of the three methods. Don't you dare use it on anything knit with slippery or smooth yarns. You'll end up with a gorgeous crocheted edging encasing your cut edges, but it will pop off like an ugly scab if it is pulled on too much, which can easily happen if you are knitting on edgings just a few stitches away.

This method requires fewer stitches than the others because there is no trimming to be done once the steek is cut. To do it, knit your steek of three to five stitches in the usual way. Then, when your steek is done, use a length of contrasting slippery yarn to baste down the center stitch. (This is just a marker to help you see the center more clearly.)

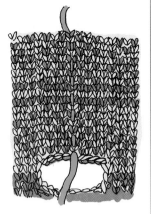

Next, get out a crochet hook that's a bit smaller than the gauge of your knitting needle, and some yarn that can also be a bit finer than the yarn you used for your garment (or use your project yarn if it's not too bulky). For added fun, use some nice contrasting yarn, because the crocheting will show on the inside of your project and it can look cool in a different color. Put a slip knot on your crochet hook. Fold your work along that basted line and turn it 90 degrees to look at the edge horizontally. You'll see a column of V's running across the top of your fold line that actually consist of the left arm of the center stitch, and the right arm of the stitch just to the left of it.

If you love to crochet, you might begin to drool at this point, because what you're seeing looks almost exactly like the top of a row of crochet stitches. In fact, we're going to treat them as if they were crochet stitches, and we're going to crochet a chain right on top of them. To do that, insert your hook from front to back underneath both legs of the very first V, wrap your yarn around your hook, pull that loop out to the front from under the legs of the V, then pull it through the slip knot on the hook. This stitch is called slip stitch, and you'll be making a chain of them all the way across this column of stitches.

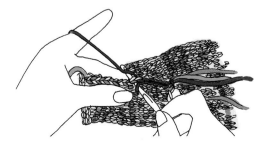

PICKUP ARTIST
PICKING UP STITCHES ON STEEKED PROJECTS

You've probably picked up stitches before, from around a neckline to knit a crewneck, or from the sides of a sock after turning the heel. In most instances, when you are picking up stitches in knitting, you are picking them up right from the edge. But here in Steekland, you will be picking up stitches from the middle of your fabric—in between the body of your garment and the edge stitches of your steek. How can you best pick up stitches in this situation? It's easy. Start by holding your yarn behind your work and insert your needle into the "ditch" between the column of stitches that is the edge of your work and the column of stitches that is the edge of your steek. Wrap your yarn around the needle and pull that loop up. Continue working this way, inserting your needle between the "rungs" of these stitch columns. You'll probably want to pick up two stitches for every three rows (each row will have its own "rung") because knit stitches are about two thirds as tall as they are wide. Thus,

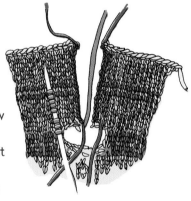

the fabric you'll knit from these picked-up stitches will be the same width as the rows from which you picked them up.

At the end of the column, break your yarn, pull it through the loop on the hook, and pull to finish off this chain. Then turn your work around and do the exact same thing on the other side, using the right leg of the center column of knit stitches together with the left leg of the stitch just to the right of it as your new set of V's to crochet into.

When both crochet chains are done, it's time to cut. Pull out the basting thread and cut up through the rungs of the center stitch of the steek.

Have a look at the edges of your work. They will look just gorgeous, like you wrapped them up in a beautiful snuggly little crocheted cover.

Nevertheless, even though the crochet edging is cute, you might still want to tack your facing down after knitting on your sleeves or front bands. If so, just keep it simple with an easy whipstitch.

ALL'S WELL THAT ENDS WELL

STARTING AND ENDING YOUR YARN IN THE MIDDLE OF STEEKS

Stranded knitting, since it uses lots of different colors, is notorious for leaving you with tons of yarn ends to work away. Happily, you can use a little trick with your steeking method to ensure that you don't have to work away any of them at all! Simply begin your knit rounds in the center of your steek; in this way, the ends from newly started yarn will be left hanging there, as will those of yarn that you need to leave hanging at the end of a round. Then, once you've reinforced your edges with whatever method you prefer and have snipped up your steeks, just trim those yarn ends when you trim up your steeks. Hooray! Yarn ends be gone!

cables and bits

**ADDING TEXTURE
IN YOUR
KNITTING WITH
CABLES, TWISTED
STITCHES,
BOBBLES, AND
MORE**

W henever I knit cables, I find myself wondering how they were invented. It's true that adding cables to your work both breaks up the monotony of knitting a sweater in stockinette stitch, and also results in thicker—and thereby warmer—fabric, but who is it that hit upon the idea of knitting stitches in a different order than they appear on the needle in the first place? Because, in the end, that's all that cable knitting really is. Perhaps it was, like so many great inventions, simply a happy accident.

However it came about, there's *less* to knitting cables than meets the eye. The stitches involved in a cable are knit in stodgy ol' stockinette most of the time and are only made to cross each other every once in a while. In cable-knitting, a stitch or a number of stitches are usually slipped onto a cable needle, the following stitches are knit as usual, and then the stitches on the cable needle are knit. This creates an actual crossing of the first and second columns of stitches, and yields a gently twisting cable. If the cable needle is left to hang to the front of the work, the stitches on it will cross in front of the stitches that follow. Since they're in front, these are the stitches you see "moving" in the cable, and because they start out on the right of the second set of stitches and end up to the left of them, this kind of cable is called a "cable to the front (or left)." If you take the first few stitches and hang them to the back of your work, they will end up behind the next group of stitches. Now it is that second group of stitches that lies on top and appears to travel from left to right, so this is called a "cable to the back (or right)." I don't like either of these names, really, because in both cases half the stitches that twist are in the front, and the other half are in the back, and also, in both cases, half of the stitches are moving to the right while the other half are moving to the left. But I don't suppose it matters how I feel about the nomenclature of cables, for I am but a lowly scribe.

To the left and right of the column of stitches that create the cable there are usually purl stitches, or some other low-lying stitch such as seed or moss stitch, to create even greater contrast between the cable and its surrounding fabric. The cable itself can range anywhere from two to eight stitches wide, with half of the stitches crossing over the other half to make the cable and with the crosses usually occurring over the same number of rows as the cable is wide—so, if the cable consists of six stitches, it will cross every six rows; if the cable is made of eight stitches, it will cross every eight rows. However, that's not a hard-and-fast rule. Another non-hard-and-fast rule is that the columns of stitches that are doing the crossing most often consist of stitches worked in stockinette stitch (I mean, like, 99.9% of the time), but there are some more intricate cable patterns where this section is knit in ribbing, or even garter stitch.

On the left, two back-crossing cables; on the right, two front-crossing cables

Because cables are usually made with simple knit and purl stitch areas, and the action happens only every six rows or so, it's a deceptively simple technique that yields impressive results. But from small acorns grow mighty oaks, and over the past century, clever and inspired knitters have created elaborate cable stitch patterns, with columns of stitches slithering this way and that, twisting around other columns of stitches before returning to their original locations; cables that perform double, triple, and quadruple lutzes across their smooth-as-ice purl backgrounds before landing and weaving themselves over and under other stitches; and cables that appear to never cross at all, instead splitting over and over again into antler- or horseshoe-like shapes.

Let's try one of the simplest cables, the C4F, or "cable four to the front," which means it is a cable over four stitches, and we'll hold the stitches on the cable needle to the front.

On the row where your pattern directions instruct you to cross your cable, work until you reach the first stitch of the cable panel. Slip this stitch and the next one onto a cable needle as if to purl.

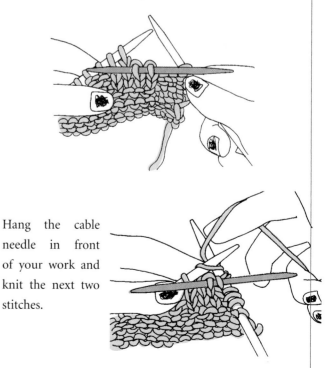

Hang the cable needle in front of your work and knit the next two stitches.

Now knit the two stitches on the cable needle. You may

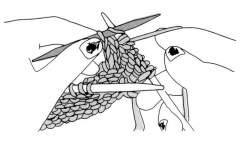

have to pull and tug on the cable needle a bit to get to those stitches—things are gonna be a little tight up in there. Then continue working stitches according to your pattern.

A C4B, or "cable four to the back," is worked in much the same way, but you will hang the stitches you've slipped onto the cable needle to the back of your work.

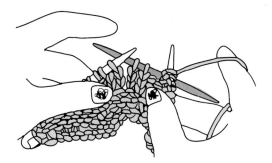

Knit the next two stitches on your needle, then pull the cable needle with the stitches on it around to the front, and knit those two stitches. That's it!

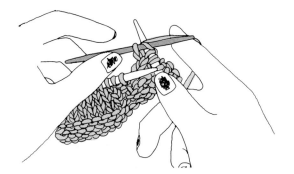

Lefty Loosey

Some knitters find that the last knit stitch of their cable tends to be a real horror show—much larger and looser than the rest of the stitches. One way to avoid this is to purl the stitch that follows the last knit stitch a bit differently. Insert the needle into that purl stitch and wrap the yarn in the *opposite* way you normally would for a purl stitch—from left to right, clockwise around the back of the needle, and complete the stitch. You'll end up with something that looks just like a purl stitch, but it will be oriented the wrong way on the needle. When you get back to that stitch on the wrong side of your work, you'll knit it through the back loop, so you don't twist it. Creating a purl stitch by wrapping your yarn the opposite way uses just a bit less yarn than a normal purl stitch and thus can help keep that last knit stitch of your cable just a bit tighter.

Look ma! No NeedLe!

CABLING WITHOUT A CABLE NEEDLE

Okay—now that the kids are out of the room, I'll let you in on a little secret. Unless I'm dealing with a truly complex triple-strand cable, I never use a cable needle. A cable needle is fine and all, but it's a pain to have to pull it out of (a) your knitting bag, (b) your knitting itself, or (c) your mouth every time you need to use it. But don't worry: There is a better way. With just a slight bit of jostling, you can knit your cables without a cable needle.

CABLE 6 TO THE FRONT WITHOUT A CABLE NEEDLE

On the row when you need to cross your stitches, knit up to the cable panel. Then slip the next six stitches purlwise onto the right-hand needle. Insert the left-hand needle into the front loops of the first three stitches you slipped,

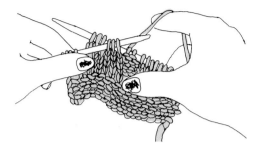

and drop the other three stitches off the right-hand needle—for a second!

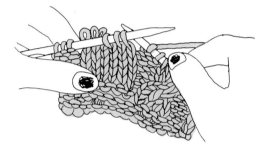

Keeping your left needle in front, quickly snatch those three kamikaze stitches back up onto the right-hand needle,

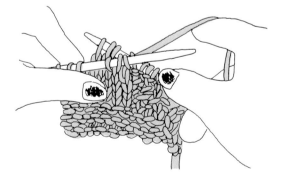

transfer them back to the left needle, then knit all six stitches in the order they appear on your needle. You've made a cable without a needle! Good times.

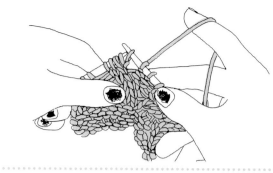

CABLE GUIDE

When you're working a cable, you'll often use something called a "cable needle." If you've never seen one of these doohickeys, they're basically a stumpy knitting needle that can hold your stitches until you're ready to knit them. Cable needles come in a number of different shapes and sizes. One popular type is shaped like a U, with one side longer than the other. The way to use this type is to slip the stitches onto the short end of the U, then pull it through so it can hang from your work for a few seconds. When you're ready to knit the stitches on this holder, pull them through and knit off of the long end. Another type looks a bit like a Q-tip: It's basically a stubby knitting needle, with each side of the needle being a bit thicker than the center. For this one, slip your stitches onto the cable needle, hang them to the front or back of your work, then work the stitches off the cable needle. Because it's a bit thicker at each end, your stitches shouldn't go flying off until you are ready for them.

If you find yourself up a cabling creek without a cable needle, no worries. You can always use a double-pointed needle (just keep an eye on it to make sure it doesn't slip out of the stitches while it's holding them), or use a short circular needle to do the job.

You can use whichever needle you like best. The only thing to keep in mind is that you'll want to use one that's approximately the same diameter as the needles you're knitting with. If you don't, the stitches on the needle will tighten up while they're on the holder, and they'll be difficult to knit off of it later on.

Of course, you can use this exact same technique with a 4-stitch cable, by slipping the four stitches onto your right-hand needle and inserting your left-hand needle into the front loops of the first two stitches, and you can probably use it with wider cables as well, although the wider the cable, the more difficult it becomes to slip the last stitches from the right-hand needle back onto the left-hand needle.

CABLE 6 TO THE BACK WITHOUT A CABLE NEEDLE

Proceed as for the front left-twist cable by first slipping all six stitches to the right-hand needle purlwise. Now insert your left-hand needle into the *back* loops of the first three stitches you slipped (your left needle will be behind your right needle).

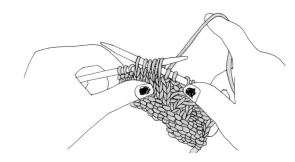

Carefully pull the right needle out of the six stitches,

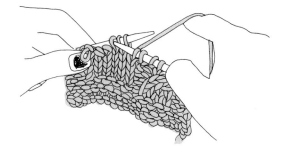

bring it in front of the stitches that are being held by the left needle, and rescue the three loose stitches.

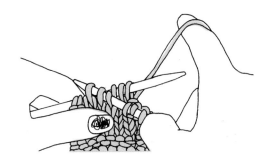

Slip those stitches onto the left needle, one by one, then knit the stitches in the order that they appear on the left needle.

Again, this same method can be used with 4-stitch cables.

RAMBLIN' MAN
TRAVELING STITCHES

Cable panels don't always have to cross each other; sometimes you can cross a cable panel with its background, which doesn't look like a twist at all, but instead just looks like a column of stitches is slithering across the fabric. That's called traveling cables or traveling stitches. Many of these traveling stitches moving left and right and weaving over and under each other on a background of purl or knit stitches is called a braid. When a cable panel of knit stitches is shifted over a set of purl stitches, it is often crossed over a single purl stitch at a time. So, you might be slipping two knit stitches to a cable needle, purling the next stitch, then knitting the two stitches from the cable needle. With traveling stitches, you always cross the knit stitches in front of the background purl stitches and never behind them, but whether that means you are holding your stitches in front or behind your work depends on whether the knit section is crossing to the left or to the right. So if you've got knit stitches on your cable needle, you'll be hanging them to the front. And if you've got purl stitches on the cable needle, you'll be hanging them to the back.

When single knit stitches are traveling over single purl stitches, you won't want to get your cable needle involved at all. See below for a variety of ways to accomplish this. One more thing about traveling stitches: While they are mostly done with knit stitches traveling over purl stitches, sometimes they are knit stitches traveling over other knit stitches. Is that so wrong? And finally, in some knitting traditions, when you have a single knit stitch traveling over a background of purl stitches, the knit stitches are twisted (knit through the back loop on the right side; purled through the back loop on the wrong side) to make them stand out even more from their background. More on that later.

Traveling stitch braid

tHe LittLest caBLe

2-STITCH CROSSES AND TWISTS

The 2-stitch cable is made by simply crossing one stitch over, or behind, another stitch, and it can be used in many different ways. And yet, this little stitch has some sort of Napoleonic complex, because there are not just 2 variations on this stitch, as there are with larger cables, but more like 12. Unlike wider cables, it is frequently worked from the wrong side as well as the right side of your work (although you'll

only see it from the right side). Its stitches can be worked the standard way, or so that they are twisted, with their legs crossed. To complicate matters further, it also has many different names, sometimes being called a right or left cross, or a right or left twist, or a right or left traveling stitch. And even when it is referred to as a "twist," that alone doesn't mean that the stitches themselves will be knit twisted (so twisted stitches can be knit twisted or untwisted).

LEFT, RIGHT, FRONT, BACK, WHAT?

The naming conventions of cables can be really confusing. A cable to the front at least means you're hanging your cable needle to the front, and a cable to the back means you're hanging your cable needle to the back, but what about when you're not using your cable needle? What's up with that "left cross" and "right cross" business? The first group of stitches *always* travels to the left, and the second group of stitches *always* moves to the right—after all, they're switching sides. The thing to remember is that when knitters say "left cross" or "right cross," they are really referring to the direction that the stitches *in the front* of the cable appear to be moving. So, *left cross* means that the first group of stitches crosses *in front of* the second set of stitches (they move to the left on your needle). And *right cross* means that the second set of stitches crosses *in front of* the first set of stitches (they move to the right on your needle), which is the same as saying the first set of stitches crosses in back of the second set of stitches. As for *front cross* and *back cross,* that refers to the first set of stitches only. Use whatever nomenclature works for you, but if you can really picture where those stitches are going and whether they are moving in front and to the left, or in front and to the right, you will always get it right (or left).

Why bother with all these variations? A 1 x 1 cross can enable you to create columns of single stitches that travel across a field of purl or other knit stitches, forming graceful lines that, like synchronized swimmers, gently curve together and cross over and under each other. These patterns of traveling stitches can also be arranged to resemble wide, elaborate cables, but since they are flatter than wider cables, your fabric won't become quite so bulky. And when those traveling knit stitches are worked through their back loops so that they become twisted, it makes these meandering curves even crisper. And if these little crossed-stitch pairings are simply worked in a column, they yield an adorable panel of mini-cables.

KNIT CROSSING OVER KNIT

Let's start with the simplest variation of a 2-stitch cross: a simple knit stitch crossed over (or under) a second knit stitch. You can knit this as a true cable, by slipping the first stitch to a cable needle, holding it in front of (or behind) your work, knitting the next stitch, then knitting the stitch from the cable needle. Better still is to work it as a 2-stitch cable without a cable needle. But there is also a much easier (and funner) way. This method is often called a "right or left twist," and even though it isn't exactly the same as the 2-stitch cable, or cross, described above, in most cases you can make a right or left twist whenever a 2-stitch right or left cable (or cross) is called for. Here's how:

Right twist:

Knit two stitches together but leave them both on the left-hand needle,

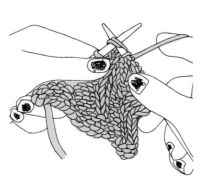

knit the first stitch, then drop the stitches off the needle. Easy peasy!

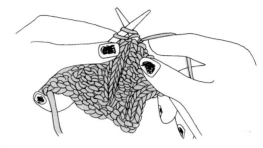

Left twist:

This one's just a tad more difficult. With the right needle behind the work, skip the first knit stitch and knit the second stitch through the back loop.

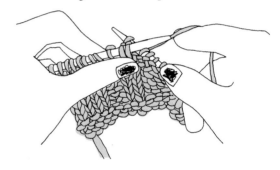

Leave both stitches on the needle and knit through the first stitch.

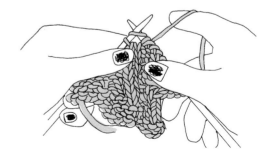

Then slide both stitches off the needle.

It won't happen very often, but on occasion you may need to execute this maneuver from the purl side of your work. Here's how:

Right twist (purl side):

Purl the second stitch, then purl the first and second stitches together. Drop both stitches off the needle.

Left twist (purl side):

Slip two stitches knitwise to the right-hand needle, then return them to the left-hand needle. Purl both together through the back loop, then purl the first stitch through the back loop. Drop both stitches off the needle.

KNIT CROSSING OVER PURL

When single knit stitches are traveling over a purl background, the knit stitch will always cross in front of the purl stitch, whether it's a right or left cross. And because that means the purl stitch will always be in back where it won't be seen, you can cheat and use the same, simple knit-crossing-over-knit methods you learned in the previous section. Of course, you can also get out the old cable needle, but if you're not crazy enough to use a cable needle just to make a 2-stitch twist, you can use the following cabling-without-a-cable-needle method.

Right twist, knit over purl, method #1:

Slip the next two stitches (a purl and a knit) onto the right-hand needle. Insert the left-hand needle, from behind, into the back of the purl stitch. Pull the right needle out, bring it in front of the purl stitch, and catch the knit stitch. Slip the knit stitch back onto the left-hand needle. Knit the first stitch, purl the next stitch.

Left twist, knit over purl, method #1:

Slip the next two stitches (a knit and a purl) onto the right-hand needle. Insert the left-hand needle, from the front, into the front of the knit stitch. Pull the right needle out, bring it in back of the knit stitch, and catch the purl stitch. Slip the purl stitch back onto the left-hand needle. Purl the first stitch, knit the next stitch.

There's also another way to do this, which is to knit and purl the stitches out of order while they are still on the needle, dropping them only when you are done with both. The right knit-over-purl twist is a breeze, but the left knit-over-purl twist is hellish. Nevertheless, here they are should you want to try this method.

Right twist, knit over purl, method #2:

With the yarn in back of your work, knit the second stitch on your left-hand needle but do not drop it off the needle. Bring your yarn to the front and purl the first stitch on the left-hand needle, then drop both stitches off the needle. And . . . scene!

Left twist, knit over purl, method #2:

A bit trickier, but doable. With the yarn in front of your needle, purl the second stitch on the left-hand needle through the back of the stitch, and leave it on the needle. Then knit the first stitch on the left-hand needle and drop both stitches off the needle. (I'll admit purling that second stitch through the back loop can be a doozy, so you may want to execute this twist as you would any other.)

tHAt ʃounds deLicious

BAVARIAN TWISTED STITCH

In what's known as "Bavarian twisted stitch," patterns are made up of knit stitches crossing over a background of purl stitches, but with a twist—literally. In this type of knitting, which has its roots in the Alpine region of Germany (and is sometimes called Alpine knitting), all knit stitches, as seen from the front of the work, are twisted. This means that all knit stitches are knit through the back leg on the right side, and purled through the back leg on the wrong side. This twisting raises the knit stitches a bit from their purl background, which makes them more prominent.

In Bavarian knitting, knit stitches are always traveling in front of purl stitches, so you can create them in the same way as described above, crossing knits over purls without a cable needle. The only difference is that, when working the right side of your fabric, you'll knit the knit stitches through their back loops in order to twist them, and when you're working the wrong side, you'll purl the purl stitches through their back loops in order to twist them.

RIGHT OR LEFT TWIST, KNIT OVER KNIT (BAVARIAN)

Although it's rare, sometimes Bavarian knitting is done by making twisted stitches over a stockinette stitch background. If you're making a twist this way, cross one knit stitch over the other knit stitch with or without a cable needle, and knit the stitch that's crossing in front through the back loop to twist it. Alternatively, you can use the instructions below to work your stitches while leaving them both on the left-hand needle, then dropping them off when you're done with 'em.

Right twist, knit over knit (Bavarian)

With the yarn in back, insert the right-hand needle between the first and second knit stitches, and knit the second stitch through the back loop. Knit the first stitch in the normal way, then drop both stitches off the needle.

Left twist, knit over knit (Bavarian)

With the yarn in back, bring the right-hand needle behind the first stitch and knit the second stitch through the back loop. Then knit the first stitch through the back loop, and drop both stitches off the needle. (This also twists the stitch in back, but it won't be seen anyway.)

RIGHT OR LEFT TWIST, KNIT OVER PURL (BAVARIAN)

Just as for the non-Bavarian version of a knit crossing over a purl stitch, whether to the left or right, the knit stitch will always cross in front of the purl stitch. Since that purl stitch won't show much, you can be sneaky and use the above knit-over-knit method to cross these stitches. That's appealing, because those stitches are easy to do.

And, as with the non-Bavarian methods, you can be a technical perfectionist and cross these stitches using a cable needle, or just forgo the cable needle and do it without one, as follows:

Right twist, knit over purl (Bavarian):

Slip the next two stitches (a purl and a knit), onto the right-hand needle. Insert the left-hand needle, from behind, into the back of the purl stitch. Pull the right needle out, bring it in front of the purl stitch, and catch the knit stitch. Slip the knit stitch back onto the left-hand needle. Knit the first stitch through the back loop, purl the next stitch.

Left twist, knit over purl (Bavarian):

Slip the next two stitches (a knit and a purl), onto the right-hand needle. Insert the left-hand needle, from front, into the front of the knit stitch. Pull the right needle out, bring it in back of the knit stitch, and catch the purl stitch. Slip the purl stitch back onto the left-hand needle. Purl the first stitch, knit the next stitch through the back loop.

When Bavarian twisted knitting is worked in the round, with the twists occurring on each row, use the directions for left and right purl twists, above. But if you are knitting flat, you'll need to know how to do this from the purl side as well. Of course, on the purl side, your knit stitches will look like purls and your purls will look like knits. You can use the same directions as above to cross a knit stitch over a purl stitch in whatever direction your pattern calls for. Just remember that from the back of your work, it will still always be knit stitches crossing in front of purl stitches, but you'll work those *purl* stitches through the back loop, in order to twist them, and the knit stitches normally (since they are the purl stitches on the front of the work—and those don't get twisted).

fake it tiLL You make it

MOCK CABLES

Twist stitch mock cables on left, 3-stitch mock cables on right

Since cables are so friendly, you might wonder why anyone would want to mock them. But even without a cable needle, cabling can slow down your work a bit, and mock cables are a quicker way to put some twisty-looking stitches into your project. The tiniest little mock cable is simply the right or left twist (knit over knit) described above. When worked every four rows, surrounded by purl stitches, they will give the effect of a tiny cable winding up your fabric.

Another popular mock cable is worked over three knit stitches, and surrounded by purl stitches on either side. The twist is worked as follows:

3-STITCH MOCK CABLE

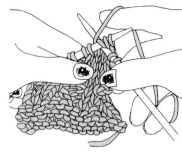

With the yarn behind your work, skip the first two stitches and insert the needle, from front to back, into the third stitch as if to knit, and knit it. Don't drop any stitches off the needle yet. Then knit the second stitch on the needle in the same manner, and then the first. Drop all three stitches off the needle. Work this twist every four or every six rows.

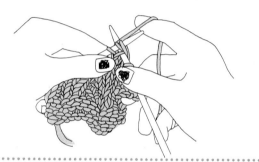

crossed signals

HOW TO FIX MISCROSSED CABLES

When you are working a cable pattern, even if it is very complex, eventually you will be able to see whether you are crossing a cable to the left or to the right. And with the clarification given here (see "Left, Right, Front, Back, What?" page 47), you should be able to cross your cables correctly. However, mistakes happen to the best of us (I won't give away the name of a major knitting magazine that once had a model on the cover wearing a sweater with a cable crossing in the wrong direction) and sometimes aren't noticed until you are rows beyond where the error is made (or, in the case of said magazine, don't notice at all until the sweater is finished, the photograph taken, and the magazine printed!). But have no fear. First of all, as my example shows, miscrossed cables aren't really that big of a deal and are usually barely noticeable, if they're noticed at all. But second, if you haven't gone too far past it, you can easily recross a miscrossed cable, with the help of a trusty crochet hook.

I've seen instructions for fixing miscrossed cables tell you to unravel all the stitches down to the beginning of the cable and knit the stitches all back up, crossed correctly, but I don't understand that at all. If you look at a miscrossed cable, all you really want to do is take that one column of stitches and bring it in front of the other column. And in fact, that's all you have to do.

Begin by identifying the stitches that make up the column that is mistakenly crossing *behind* the other column of stitches (this might be the stitches to the left or

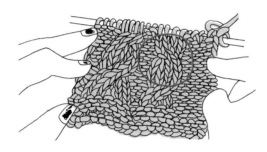

the right). Knit your way to just before those stitches, then place your work on a flat table in front of you and drop the miscrossed stitches off the left-hand needle. Using your fingers and keeping the work lying flat, unravel these stitches, releasing each individual rung of yarn, one row at a time.

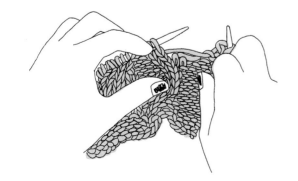

Working slowly and carefully, keep going until eventually the loops will "pop" to the front—you are looking for them to get back to their original position before they were crossed with the other stitches. You may have to help the stitches along a bit with your fingers and they may not quite "pop," but if you keep your eyes on the prize, you will see when they are back to starting position.

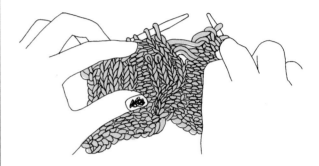

Now, bring those loops to the front and run a cable needle through them to keep them from unraveling any farther. Keeping the work flat so the rungs stay spread out, cross the stitches on the cable needle in front of the other panel

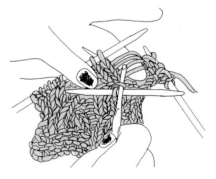

of stitches, and transfer the innermost loop to a crochet hook (this will be the leftmost stitch on your cable needle if you are re-creating a right-crossing cable, or the rightmost stitch if you are re-creating a left-crossing cable).

Next, pick up the new column of stitches, rung by rung, grabbing the part of the rung that is closest to the remaining column of cable stitches. You are picking up your rungs from the inside of the cable, leaving as much yarn rung on the outside as possible. Bring the stitch all the way up to the top and pop it onto the left- or right-hand needle, whichever one is holding the remaining cable stitches. Repeat with the second stitch on the cable needle,

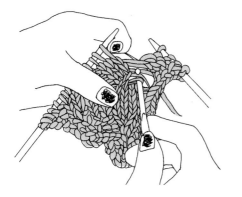

and continue until all stitches have been brought back up. If the recrossed stitches are now on the right-hand needle, slip these stitches back to the left-hand needle and work them. Pull your cable widthwise to settle everybody into place. And there you have it. This one makes for a great party trick!

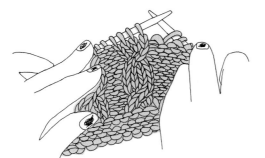

the color cable

CABLES IN TWO COLORS (OR MORE)

If you were a kid and you looked at a knit cable, you would probably think, hey, that looks like snakes! And then you might want to see blue and yellow snakes wrapping around each other, and maybe a red snake getting involved

at some point as well. As a knitter new to cables, you might think that would be impossible, since the snakes aren't really all separate entities. But in fact, it can be done.

To make a multicolor cable, you can knit different sections of stitches in different colors, stranding the unused color along the back of your work. Or, depending on the design you are working, you might be better off using the intarsia method (page 16) to create your different colored sections and linking your yarn at each color change.

cable distortion

ADJUSTING YOUR FABRIC FOR CABLES

Cables pull your fabric in widthwise quite a bit, so a sweater knit with cables will take many more stitches around, and a lot more yarn, than a sweater knit in plain stockinette stitch. As a result, the sweater will be a lot thicker, and thus warmer. But you need to be prepared for the fact that cables pull your fabric in like an accordion when they cross, because if you don't, the fabric before the first cable crossing or after the last cable crossing can flare out, and you want to avoid that.

Most sweater patterns will have you increase stitches after ribbing to make sure you have enough stitches so that the cable won't distort, or pull in, the ribbed section. If you decide to add a cable to a sweater pattern where there is none, be sure to add stitches in order to make up for the fact that the cable will make a much narrower piece of fabric over the same number of stitches than a section of stockinette stitch would.

To keep a cabled area from flaring out as you cast off, it helps to perform some preemptive decreases. To do that, decrease about one stitch out of every four by binding off two stitches in the usual way, then knitting two stitches together and binding off, and repeating this two-normal,

Stitch 'n Bitch Superstar Knitting

two-together bind-off pattern. You need to do this only over the stitches that are involved in the cable; the other stitches, such as the background, can be bound off in their usual way.

bobble Heads

MAKING BOBBLE STITCHES

While cables are one great way to add some real three-dimensional textures to your knitting, they are often combined with another technique, that of making knit bobbles. A bobble is sort of like a tumor on your knitting, and it's kind of created that way as well. Just as a real tumor is created when some cells go mad and start increasing, a bobble is made by increasing a whole bunch of stitches into a single stitch, usually with a series of knit stitches and yarn overs, and then decreasing them all back again. Sometimes the stitches are all decreased on the same row where you create the bobble, and sometimes they are decreased on the following row. This leaves a big old lump in your knitting, and although it may sound somewhat horrifying, it can be quite cute. One thing to remember: If you're going to need to knit or purl all the stitches together to make the bobble, be sure to make your knits and yarn

overs *loosely* (see "Know Your Nupps," page 73). Here is an example of a simple bobble:

K1, yo, k1, yo, k1 into a stitch.

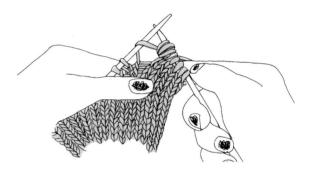

Turn your work and knit into these five stitches.

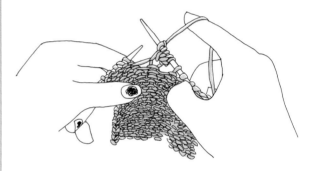

Turn again, knit all five stitches, then pass four of the stitches over the last stitch, one at a time.

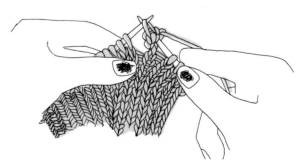

5

Lace

THE FINAL FRONTIER

**A**s far as I'm concerned, knitting lace is about the most impressive thing you can do with two sticks and some yarn. The intricate interplay between open spaces and solid areas, separated by gently bending lines of stitches, is the closest thing I can think of to making your yarn dance. And best of all, it's really fun and satisfying to do.

Lace in knitting can cover a lot of ground—from shawls so delicate and spiderweb-like that they can fit through a wedding ring to chunky dresses with openwork panels down the front; from bags that look like they are made of netting to sweaters with carefully placed holes that form a pattern of cat's paw prints. There is really only one thing that any knitting that can be called "lace" must include: holes in the fabric, more politely known as "eyelets." These holes may be separated by nothing more than strands of yarn, or they may be placed on a background of stockinette stitch or garter stitch. They can be small or quite large, surrounded by visible lines of stitches or seemingly poked right through the fabric.

The holes in lace knitting are almost always created using a maneuver called a "yarn over." Yarn overs not only create holes, but they also create new stitches—every yarn over is an increase. In some cases, increasing the number of stitches on your needle is exactly what you want in lace knitting. For instance, circular lace shawls are started in the very center with just a few stitches; as yarn overs are made, they extend the fabric into larger and larger rounds of stitches, so that a shawl of the correct circumference is eventually created. Many triangle shawls are also created this way, starting with a few stitches and becoming wider and wider at the top as more and more yarn overs are made in each row, extending the fabric widthwise.

But if you're working on a sweater or socks or a scarf in a lace pattern, you usually don't want your fabric to keep growing wider, which is why most lace patterns include a decrease to counteract each yarn over. Those decreases are sometimes made on the same row as the yarn over, or sometimes on a later row. They may be made right next to the yarn over, or a few stitches over; they may be made singly, knocking out one stitch at a time, or doubly, taking out two stitches at once; they may be made to be decorative, forming beautiful lines of winding stitches on your fabric, or invisibly, and they may lean left, right, or line up in the center. But if your fabric is to keep from growing wider and wider, there will be a *decrease for every yarn over in your knitting pattern,* and they are as central to lace knitting as the holes that make lace lacy.

Once you master the yarn over (easy) and the various decreases (also easy), you're all set to knit lace. And even more good news: In most lace-knitting patterns, you only make these yarn overs and decreases on the right-side rows; the wrong-side rows will be plain, usually a purl row. (By the way, this kind of lace-making is sometimes distinguished from the other, less common type where yarn overs and decreases are made on every row, by calling the former "lace knitting" and the latter "knitted lace." I think that's pretty silly, and use them interchangeably, but I'm just letting you in on this bit of lingo in case the Knitting Police are about.)

What makes lace knitting challenging, however, is the fact that you must follow a stitch chart with an eagle eye, placing your yarn overs and decreases exactly where they need to be, because even a single stitch made incorrectly

will throw everything off. Moreover, lace patterns can be quite complex and can be difficult to follow just by looking at your stitches, unlike color knitting, where you might see immediately where you made a mistake. And what's worse, all but the simplest errors in lace knitting are notoriously challenging to correct.

But as you will learn in this chapter, there are ways to avoid these types of lace-knitting disasters. For one, you will come to understand how yarn overs and decreases work together to create various types of fabric, which will help you to "read" your stitches better and avoid working away blindly from a chart. You'll also see how some common errors can be fixed. And finally, you'll learn some tricks that lace knitters have come up with over the years to help you keep from making errors in your work, and even how to buy yourself some knitting insurance so that you're covered in case you do.

Lace exploration

SELECTING YOUR MATERIALS

Like any other type of knitting, to make lace you need yarn and some needles. The very thinnest yarn is called "lace weight," but lace can be made with any weight of yarn; remember, what makes lace lace is the holes, not the thinness of the yarn. The lightest lace weight yarn is used for gossamer-like shawls, but airy shawls can also be made out of fingering, sport weight, or even worsted weight yarn, depending on the stitch pattern used. However, since lace fabric depends on creating a contrast between the holey and solid areas of stitches, yarn that is smooth or only slightly hairy (such as mohair) is much more appropriate than eyelash yarns, yarns with bobbles and bits, or yarn that changes from thin to thick. Solid-color yarns often show off lace to its best advantage, whereas variegated yarn, especially if the color changes from quite light to quite dark, tends to detract from the pattern created by the combination of solid and open areas.

There are also a few things to consider when selecting needles for lacework. For one, just as the size of your knit stitches is determined by the diameter of your needles, the holes in lace will come out bigger when made on larger needles, and smaller when made on smaller needles. Since the holes are what make lace, it is important that they be large enough to be seen, and so lace is usually worked on knitting needles that are larger than what's recommended for a given weight of yarn. Sport weight yarns, for instance, usually knit on needles sized 4–6 (3.5–4.0mm), might be worked over size 8 (5.0mm) needles in a lace pattern. The needle size can't go up too far, however, because the solid areas of knitting, which are essential to any lace pattern, need to be solid enough to contrast with the open holes. In general, however, the larger the needles, the lacier and airier the fabric.

Since lace knitting requires so much care to avoid making errors, you also want to select needles that aren't too slippery. I like to use bamboo or wooden needles for knitting lace, but flexible plastic needles also work well; just leave those supersleek needles in your knitting basket when making lace. Needles that are pointier will make manipulating the stitches in lace easier—lifting single stitches up and over others, inserting your needle into multiple stitches, and picking up strands between stitches. Finally, if you are knitting lace on circular needles, make sure that the join (the place where the needle meets the plastic "thread" that leads to the second needle) is very, very smooth. More so than regular knit or purl stitches, stitches that are made of nothing but yarn overs will get caught on there like nobody's business, and your lace knitting will not be fun.

the Lace knitter's tooL kit

THE MOST COMMON STITCHES USED IN LACE KNITTING

Aside from the old knit and purl, there are a few basic stitches you need to be familiar with in order to create lace. The first, of course, is that all-important yarn over. In most cases, you'll be making it between two knit stitches, which is quite simple. But sometimes you'll need to make one between a knit and a purl or between two purls, so you should know those, too. And although no one really ever mentions it, they are accomplished slightly differently if you're knitting English style versus Continental, so I've given you both versions.

YARN OVER

YARN OVER BEFORE A KNIT STITCH, ENGLISH STYLE

Make the first knit stitch, bring the yarn (in your right hand) to the front of the work between the points of the needles (or leave it there if you've just made a purl stitch). With the yarn in front (sometimes abbreviated as "wyif"), make your knit stitch.

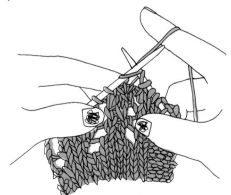

YARN OVER BEFORE A KNIT STITCH, CONTINENTAL STYLE

Bring the yarn, which is in your left hand, in front of the right-hand needle and wrap the yarn over the right-hand needle from front to back; put your right index finger on that strand of yarn to hold it in place and make a knit stitch.

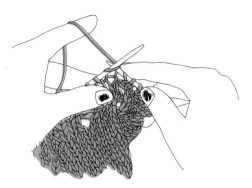

YARN OVER BEFORE A PURL STITCH, ENGLISH STYLE

Bring the yarn to the front of the work (or leave it there if you've just made a purl stitch), then bring the yarn over the top of the right-hand needle from front to back and wind it 360 degrees around back to the front, then make the next purl stitch.

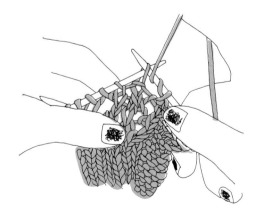

YARN OVER BEFORE A PURL STITCH, CONTINENTAL STYLE

Bring the yarn in front of the right-hand needle, then over the top of the right-hand needle from front to back and wind it 360 degrees around back to the front; place your right index finger on that strand of yarn to hold it in place and make a purl stitch.

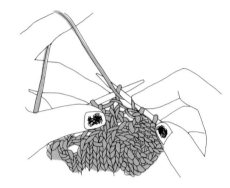

MULTIPLE YARN OVERS

Some lace patterns will require that you make extra big yarn over loops, and these can be created with ease. Once you've created the required yarn over as above, bring the yarn a full 'nother 360 degrees around your needle, keep calm, and carry on.

DECREASES

As I explained above, to counteract all the yarn overs you'll be making and keep your work from becoming ever wider, decreases are strategically placed in every lace-stitch pattern to keep things at the same stitch count. But decreases in lace are not only functional; they are usually also decorative, and can add almost as much to the lace design as the holes do. There are only six decreases you need to know, and two of those are just different ways of making the same decrease, so no worries there. Plus, you've probably already made most of these decreases plenty of times in your knitting career. However, this time I want you to really understand these decreases, because understanding what your stitches are doing in lace will help you "read" your work (one of the goals here) and thereby make fewer mistakes.

In a lace-knitting workshop I took given by the awesome lace knitter (and opera singer) Lisa Daehlin, she talked about decreases leaning left and right, and how they made her think of synchronized swimmers. I loved the image; for me they conjure up ballet dancers. When you make a k2tog, the second stitch will lie on top of the first stitch in the finished product, and that's why your stitch will slant to the right. Here, let my ballet dancers show you:

But even with visions of pretty ballet dancers in my head, I'll admit to having had the hardest time trying to remember whether a particular decrease slanted to the right or the left—until Lisa also noted in her class that *whichever stitch your needle goes into first* when making a decrease is the stitch that will *wind up on top* when done. Thus, you can predict that the stitch on the left will end up on top of the stitch on the right when making a k2tog, because, when you make it, your needle *first* enters the stitch on the left, then the stitch on the right. Think about it: How could things have ended up any other way?

There are two different ways to do the left-slanting decrease, and I'll show you both. But whichever way you

execute it, the stitch on the right will end up on top of the stitch on the left, and hence your decrease will slant to the left. Again, bring on the ballet:

SINGLE DECREASES
RIGHT-SLANTING: KNIT TWO TOGETHER (K2TOG)

To make a k2tog, just insert your needle into the next two knit stitches at once, knitwise, and knit through them both.

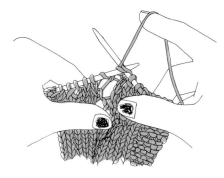

You've now made one stitch out of two, so you've decreased a stitch. But in lace knitting, it's also very important to know that this decrease—the k2tog—is a right-slanting decrease.

LEFT-SLANTING: SLIP, KNIT, PASS SLIPPED STITCH OVER (SKP)

Slip the first stitch from the left needle to the right as if to knit, knit the next stitch, lift the stitch you slipped over the knit stitch and off the needle (just like you would when binding off). Decrease made. And here, of course,

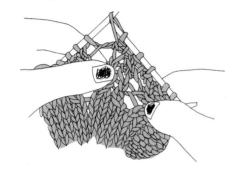

the stitch your needle went into first? The stitch on the right. That's the guy who ends up on top of the stitch on the left, although I will admit that the skp does not lay your stitches on top of each other as neatly oriented as the k2tog does in the other direction. That's just the nature of the beast.

LEFT-SLANTING: SLIP, SLIP, KNIT (SSK)

Slip, slip, knit is another way to accomplish the same thing, and it is preferred by many knitters. To do it, slip the first stitch from the left needle to the right needle as if to knit, then slip the second stitch from the left needle to the right needle as if to knit, then insert your left needle into these two stitches from the front and knit them together. Again, the first stitch, the one on the right, ends up on top.

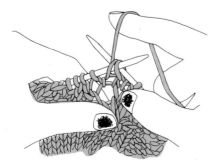

Below is an image of what you end up with using each of these ways of making a left-slanting decrease.

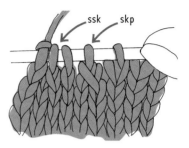

Notice anything? The structure of the finished stitch is exactly the same! So why do some knitters prefer the second method? Because when you are doing the "pass slipped stitch over" part of a "slip, knit, pass slipped stitch over," you have to pull on that stitch a bit, and that may result in its being just a bit bigger and floppier. When you do slip, slip, knit, you're not pulling on one stitch more than the others, and some folks feel that gives you more even results. Go ahead and try them both out yourself to see which one you prefer. Me, I likey the ssk, always have.

DOUBLE DECREASES

RIGHT-SLANTING: KNIT THREE TOGETHER (K3TOG)

If you can knit two stitches together, surely you can knit three together too, right?

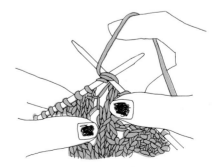

And of course, since your needle enters the leftmost stitch

first, that's the stitch that ends up on top with this decrease, meaning that this one slants to the right. Lemme bring the dancers to the stage to prove it.

Just as the left-slanting single decrease had two variations, so does the left-slanting double decrease.

LEFT-SLANTING: SLIP, SLIP, SLIP, KNIT (SSSK)

Slip the first stitch from the left needle to the right needle knitwise; slip the second stitch from the left needle to the right needle knitwise; slip the third stitch from the

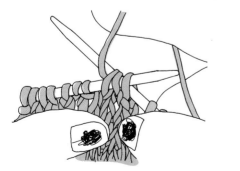

left needle to the right needle knitwise. Then insert the left needle into all three stitches on the right needle from the front and knit all three together. Who's on first? The

rightmost stitch, of course. She will end up in front of her sisters and lean to the left, just like the dancers do above.

LEFT-SLANTING: SLIP ONE, KNIT TWO TOGETHER, PASS SLIPPED STITCH OVER (SK2P)

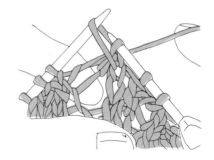

Slip the first stitch from the left needle to the right needle knitwise, knit the next two stitches together, lift the first stitch over the second stitch, and drop it off the needle. You put your needle into the rightmost stitch first, so that one lands on top.

CENTERED: SLIP TWO TOGETHER, KNIT ONE, PASS TWO SLIPPED STITCHES OVER

This decrease is not quite a toughie, but it is a bit less elegant than any of the others. To make it, first slip two stitches *together* knit-wise from the left needle to the right needle. Knit the next stitch, then pass

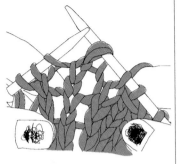

both of these slipped stitches over that knit stitch and off the needle.

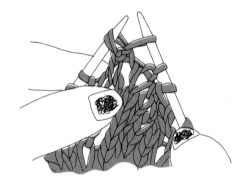

Did you catch that? The first stitch you put your needle into was the one in the middle of these three stitches. Thus, this middle sister will end up on top of the other two, and your decrease is nicely centered. I'll bring out the dancers one last time to show you.

PURL DECREASES

Okay, I admit it, I lied. There are a few other decreases you may encounter in your lace-knitting explorations, especially if you're doing one of those "knitted lace" thingies where yarn overs and decreases are happening on every row, rather than on every other row. Your pattern will explain these decreases to you, but basically, these purl decreases will be exactly the reverse of your knit decreases, and are accomplished in the same way, only with purl stitches. So if your chart shows you a left-leaning decrease (remember, a knitting chart only shows you the front of the work), then you'd need to execute a right-leaning decrease from the purl side. And vice versa.

To make a purl decrease that leans to the left (giving you a right-leaning decrease when seen from the front side of the work, are you following me?) you just purl two stitches together (p2tog).

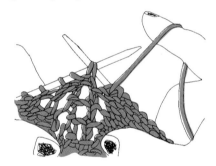

To make a purl decrease that leans to the right (which results in a left-leaning decrease when seen from the front) you need to work an unpleasant stitch called a slip, slip, purl2togtbl.

To do it, you slip one stitch knitwise, then slip the next stitch knitwise,

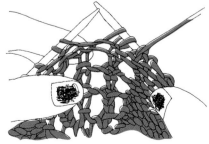

slip them both back to the left-hand needle,

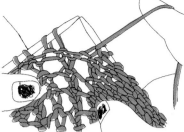

and purl them together through their back loops.

To make a double purl decrease that leans to the left (for a right-leaning decrease in the front) just purl three together.

To make a double purl decrease that leans to the right (yielding a left-leaning double decrease when seen from the front) you will be doomed to creating a slip, slip, slip, purl3togtbl (slip one stitch knitwise, slip the next stitch knitwise, slip the third stitch knitwise, slip them all back to the left-hand needle and *purl three stitches together through the back loop*).

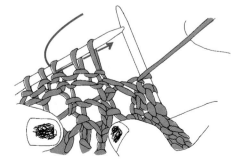

Oh, I know, you still need a centered double decrease from the purl side, don't you? Sure thing: Slip one stitch knitwise, slip the next two stitches *together* knitwise, slip them all back to the left-hand needle, and purl all three stitches through the back loop. It works, but I ain't gonna lie: It's unpleasant.

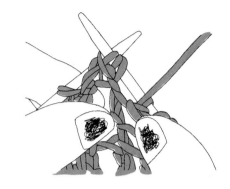

thinking outside the box

READING LACE CHARTS

You've probably already gotten a pretty good sense of how to read lace charts by following the examples in the previous section, but let me lay it out for you just in case. As you do with all knitting charts, when reading a lace chart you start with the bottom row and work your way up. These charts usually show you which stitch to work when you are looking at your work from the front, so, for instance, an empty box will mean you'd make a knit stitch if the front of your work is facing you, but it would mean a purl stitch if you are working the back side of your work. Conversely, a box with a dash means a purl stitch should be created there when working the front of your piece, but a knit stitch should be made if you are working on the back. The first row of a knitting chart is usually a right-side row and is read from right to left—which only makes sense, since you work stitches off the needle from right to left. (The number 1 will often be printed to the right of that first row to show that that's where you start. If the number 1 is on the left-hand side of your chart, however, it means you will be starting with a wrong-side row.) If you are working back and forth, the next row of your chart will be a wrong-side row, and it will be read from left to right. If, however, you are working in the round, then the next row is also a right-side row and will also be read from right to left. Don't let this get you in a tizzy; it all makes sense if you think about how you are really working the stitches off your needles.

When working lace charts, pay attention to the numbers next to the rows. That's because some charts won't even include the wrong-side rows—the row numbers will jump from 1 to 3 to 5. In lace patterns where every other row is worked plain (purled if working back and forth, or knit if working in the round), this is done to save space. So be sure you check for that before you get yourself in a jam.

To keep your place in a knitting chart, you might place a large Post-it note just *above* the row you are working. Placing your Post-it there rather than over the rows you've completed, as some folks do, means you can use the stitches in the previous row as landmarks, and that can keep you on track when you're knitting a complex pattern.

There's one other thing to be aware of in lace charts: the big black box. In some lace patterns, where the stitches increase over a number of rows in order to change the shape of the piece—a shawl widening, for instance—the later rows will show all of the stitches, but the earlier rows, which have smaller stitch counts, will have shaded or black boxes. You'll also find black boxes in lace patterns where increases are made on one row, but aren't decreased until a later row. That does not mean that you have to create a big black hole when you get to those boxes; instead, you are supposed to skip over those boxes and continue on the other side of them. So, when you come across them, just think: "Nothing to see here, just move along."

Nevertheless, even if the chart sort of gives you an idea

of what your lace pattern will look like once it's knit, it can be difficult to understand how your knitting compares to the chart when working lace. That's why beginning a new lace project, and following your first few rows of a chart, is kind of like going on a blind date. In the beginning, you sort of follow along, but you really don't know much about the pattern. You are just discovering it, learning new things about it with each stitch, and each row. And that time can be awkward—terribly, terribly awkward. But eventually, after enough rows (and enough dates), you come to really understand how the stitch pattern works. This is when lace knitting (and dating) finally becomes enjoyable. You can see how the decreases are working together to create the lines in your pattern and when they need to lean left or right; you understand where the yarn overs need to be placed in order to create the lines of eyelets. You become far less fearful of making mistakes, and if you do make errors, you recognize them much sooner. I still wouldn't advise taking a complex lace project with you on the subway or to your local bar—lace knitting requires fewer distractions—but when you get to this point with your work, you can relax into the rhythm of your lace pattern because you understand what you're doing.

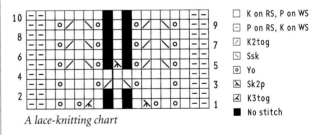

A lace-knitting chart

the Hole story

HOW YARN OVERS AND DECREASES WORK TOGETHER TO CREATE LACE

Now that you know the stitches and how simple they are to make, you may be wondering just how such innocent-looking yarn overs and decreases can come together to result in incredibly intricate lace patterns. So with these building blocks, I'm gonna show you just how these stitches interact to create various textures and patterns that all add up to lace.

At right you'll see a chart with a number of arrangements of yarn overs and decreases. The yarn overs form a line that leans to the right, creating eyelets on a diagonal; this is something that you'll encounter very frequently in lace patterns. On the bottom right of the chart, each yarn over is preceded by a left-leaning decrease. On the bottom left of the chart, each yarn over is preceded by a right-leaning decrease. On the top right, each yarn over is followed by a left-leaning decrease, and on the top left each yarn over is followed by a right-leaning decrease. Now that we've got all our bases covered, let's see how this knits up.

Look at the bottom right of the swatch below it and you'll see what we get by preceding yarn overs that travel to the right with decreases that lean to the left. We've got a nice line of eyelets all right, but those decreases aren't doing anything for them. But on the lower left of the swatch, we see that by preceding yarn overs that travel to the right with decreases that also lean to the right, we get a nicely defined line of stitches, and our eyelets are open— I like it. This is how you will often see yarn overs and decreases paired in lace patterns.

Now, let's look at the top half of the swatch. Here you might have predicted that the top right wouldn't look so nice, since again we've combined yarn overs that travel to the right with decreases that lean to the left, and indeed, this combination looks like crap. You might, however, have expected the top left to look better, since there we've got yarn overs traveling to the right paired with decreases that lean to the right. But that side doesn't look so good, either. What happened to the eyelets? On both the top right and the top left of the swatch, the eyelets are tiny and squished, and the decreases don't form a nice line in either pattern. The problem here is that the decreases are landing above

the yarn overs in the previous rows, and so the yarn over itself is getting pulled into the decrease and thus is closing up. So neither of these arrangements is any good. Of the four, clearly, the lower-left one wins.

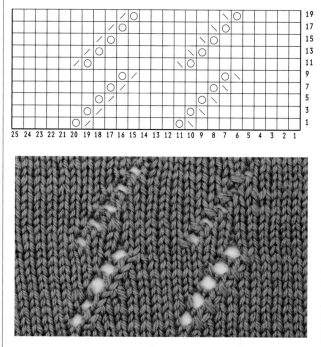

So, here's a puzzle. Say you want to knit up a diamond shape out of eyelets, and you want the decreases to form nice, prominent lines next to each line of eyelets. Where do you put your decreases?

The answer can be seen in the swatch and chart on page 66: We put right-leaning decreases to the right of yarn overs that travel to the right, and we put left-leaning decreases to the left of yarn overs that travel to the left. If you think of the yarn overs as a sort of a ladder, this arrangement keeps the decreases always *underneath* the ladder and never above it. That's a good thing, because that way they don't pull the eyelets closed. And by making them lean in the same direction that the yarn overs are traveling, they form nice, prominent lines of stitches. It all adds up to a pretty decent diamond, don't you think? Diamonds like this, and chevron shapes of V's and upside-down V's, are a favorite lace motif, and now you know why.

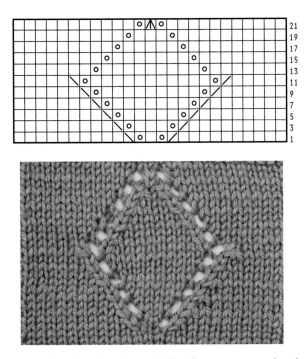

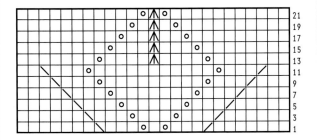

In the examples above, all the decreases were placed right next to the yarn overs. Something quite magical happens, however, when you place the decreases a few stitches away from the yarn overs, as you can see in the swatch (and the corresponding chart) below.

In the lower half of the diamond, the decreases were placed three stitches *before* the right-slanting line of eyelets, and three stitches *after* the left-slanting line of eyelets. And just look at what happens to those three stitches on either side of the eyelets—they slant right along with the decrease lines. In the top half of the diamond you see the same effect, but this time I placed a centered double decrease in *between* the eyelets, and as you can once again see, the stitches between the decreases and the eyelets are leaning toward the decrease. This effect is really quite cool, and is the basis of many leaf patterns in lace.

Of course, holes do not need to be placed at an angle in lace patterns. In the chart and swatches on the facing page, the holes are arranged in vertical columns. The rightmost pattern is sometimes referred to as a "faggot stitch" panel (see "Who You Calling a Faggot?" page 68), and it is a very common motif in lace knitting. It also officially qualifies as "lace knitting" since the yarn overs and decreases are made on every row, but it is a very simple stitch to execute. The pattern in the center is similar to the previous one but here the yarn overs and decreases are made on every other row. The leftmost pattern is a bit of a trick. This stitch contains no yarn overs at all. Instead, the holes here were made by dropping a column of stitches. To control how far the stitches drop, however, a make 1 increase was created between two stitches at the bottom of the "rung." This newly created stitch was knit on every row until it came time to drop it down. Then, of course, it only dropped to the point where it was born—where the make 1 had been placed—and stopped there. Sometimes referred to as a "snowshoe" stitch because the rungs tend to be narrower at the top and bottom of the drop than in the center, this easy stitch can be used in a variety of ways to liven up your knit fabric.

The order in which yarn overs and decreases are arranged can lead to an unexpected result: If every decrease is placed before a yarn over, and never after, the knit fabric will bias—that is, the bottom edge will be straight, but the side edges will lean off to the left or the

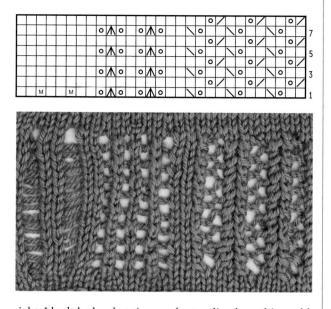

right. I had the hardest time understanding how this could be happening, until I realized that if you are always taking stitches away from the right side and always adding them to the left, which is what happens if you are always making your decreases before your yarn overs, then naturally, the right edge is going to pull in, while the left edge will push out, and vice versa. Some lace designs take advantage of this fact to make their side edges go zigzaggy. Other lace designs correct for this by alternating the decreases in the pattern, with some coming before and some coming after the yarn overs, which keeps the fabric from skewing left or right.

The bottom part of the swatch at right was created by repeating a yarn over followed by a k2tog, all the way across the work as in the chart below. Since the yarn overs always appear on the right of the decrease, the swatch leans to the right.

Following that, this order was reversed; a decrease (ssk in this case, to make things prettier) was always followed by a yarn over, all the way across the row. Here, the swatch leans to the left.

Finally, in the top third of the swatch, these two patterns alternate: a yo/k2tog row, then a purl row, followed by a ssk/yo row, and a purl row, as per the chart below.

As you can see, this keeps things straight. This swatch is also a nice demonstration of the fact that when you make nothing but yarn overs and decreases, you get yourself a truly open mesh pattern.

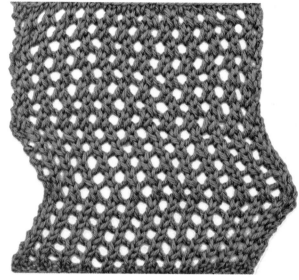

There are other ways, too, that lace patterns create jaggedy, zigzaggedy, or curvy edges. One common method, especially for lace that is intended as an edging, is to increase stitches over a number of rows on one side of the work, then decrease those stitches on a later row by simply binding off a number of stitches on that same side. You'll come across others in your lace knitting career as well. But now that you understand how the building blocks of lace—those simple yarn overs and decreases—come together to create a variety of effects, you'll never look at another lace pattern with your mouth hanging open. Instead, you'll have an understanding of how the stitches were put together to achieve those results, and that will help you a lot when you start knitting it up yourself.

Lace bandages

PREVENTING AND DEALING WITH MISTAKES IN LACE KNITTING

If you knit, you're going to make mistakes, and that goes for lace knitting as much as anything else. But while undoing an error in most knitting is no big whoop, unraveling a row or two or three of intricate lace knitting and trying to catch the original stitches back on the needle is a task I wouldn't wish on my worst enemy: Yarn overs that were made a few rows back will evaporate, decreases will slip away, and you will begin to lose your mind. And while you

WHO YOU CALLING A FAGGOT?

As offensive as it may sound, there is such a thing known as "faggot stitch" and "faggot lace stitch," although you may get a different definition of what they are, depending on whom you ask. "Faggoting" is an old term that predates knitted lace and comes from old-fashioned lace-making techniques and patterns. In knitted lace, *faggot stitch* is sometimes used to refer to the type of pattern you get when you have eyelets stacked vertically one above another, or beside each other on a diagonal line, so that they are separated by only two twisted strands of yarn (as in the swatch examples in this chapter), and *faggot lace* is achieved when yarn overs are made on every row rather than every other row. If there's a definitive definition of *faggot stitch* I have yet to come across it, but I'll be willing to bet that anything called "faggoting" is going to have eyelets placed right beside each other, separated by those twisty strands. Not that there's anything wrong with that.

may be able to unknit a row or two stitch by stitch, that's a slow and time-consuming process. So here are some ways to prevent making mistakes, take out insurance in case you do have to rip back, and repair some simple errors.

MARK THAT STITCH

Lace patterns usually repeat over a number of stitches—6, 8, 12, whatever. It can therefore be really helpful to put stitch markers in between each of these sets of repeats. That way, if you suddenly have too few stitches to complete the repeat, you'll know exactly in which section something's gone wrong, and you'll be able to fix it there, instead of carrying that error all the way across the entire row. Eventually, when you come to know your lace pattern backward and forward, you can ditch the markers. But especially if you are a beginning lace knitter (or you are just starting to get used to your stitch pattern), putting those markers there can really help you stay on track.

STITCH OVERBOARD
HOW TO ADD A LIFELINE

Inserting a "lifeline" into your lace knitting is like taking out an insurance policy on your project. A lifeline is simply a long piece of yarn threaded through your project at a particular row and left there while you continue knitting, so that when you get to a point where you realize you've made a mistake, you can rip back to where you've placed the lifeline, just like going in a time machine back to the point before you made your error. Of course, this works well only if you place a lifeline pretty often; ripping back 20 or 30 rows to your last lifeline is not much of a help. Many lace knitters put their lifelines in after they complete a pattern repeat—if your stitch pattern is six rows of knitting, you'd place a lifeline every six rows. But don't hesitate to place a lifeline more frequently than that. It's easy to do and will save you lots of time and trouble in the long run.

To add a lifeline, use a long piece of smooth yarn, like cotton, in a contrasting color to the yarn you are knitting with. Thread it through a tapestry needle, then draw the

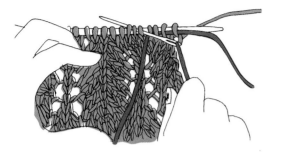

yarn through the bottom of every stitch on your knitting needle, making sure you don't thread it through any stitch markers (just go underneath them). Leave long tails hanging out on each side of your work (really long tails—you don't want the lifeline itself to go running away). Then carry on

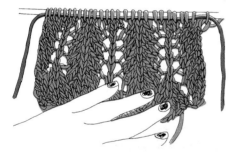

with your lace knitting, being supercareful not to include your lifeline in any of your stitches. Now, when you realize you've made a mistake, carefully rip back to the stitches just above your lifeline, then start transferring the stitches on the lifeline, one by one, back onto a knitting needle and gently pull out that last row (you can use a smaller-size needle than the one you've been knitting with to make this a bit easier). You don't need to remove the lifeline, because you just might need to make use of it again (although I hope you won't). When you go back to knitting again, make sure your stitches are seated correctly on your needle, and flip any that are facing the wrong way before you work them.

YARN OVER BOARD
RE-CREATING A MISSED YARN OVER

One of the easiest and most common mistakes in lace knitting is forgetting a yarn over somewhere along the way. A yarn over is easy to re-create, even if you are one or two rows past where it was supposed to be. That's because in between every two knit stitches lies a yarn over just waiting to happen. If you discover that you've left out a yarn over, knit (or purl) to the spot where the yarn over was supposed to be. If this is just one row down, simply pick up the horizontal strand of yarn that lies between the stitch you just worked and the following stitch, and place it over your left-hand needle so that it is oriented correctly, with the "leg" on the right in front of the needle, and the "leg" on the left in back. Now just knit (or purl) it like you were supposed to. If the yarn over was two rows down, you can still re-create a yarn over, and the purl stitch that was made into it. Again, just knit (or purl) your way to the point where the yarn over was supposed to appear.

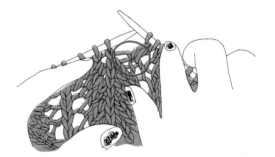

Now, take the horizontal strand that lies between the stitch you just worked and the following stitch, and, using your fingers, the points of your knitting needles, or a crochet hook, bring it around and up from underneath the horizontal strand in the same location one row down. That

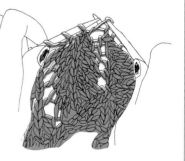

strand has now become the yarn over, and the horizontal strand you just pulled through it is the purl stitch that would have been made into it on the wrong side. Place this loop onto your needle in the correct orientation and work it as usual. Fiddle with the eyelet you just created a bit so it is close to being the same size as the others. And carry on!

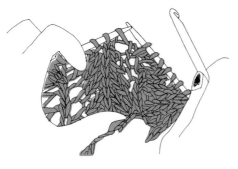

ADVANCED TOPICS IN CALAMITY KNITTING
RE-CREATING A MISSED DECREASE

This is the toughest repair of the bunch, but since by now you understand so well the principles of left- and right-leaning decreases and how they are made, you should be able to pull it off. You may notice that you have too many stitches at some point because you forgot to make a decrease, and instead of knitting two stitches together (or slip, slip, knitting them), you just knit them instead. On the next right-side row, work to the point where the stitches that would have been made into the decrease are. Drop them both down to the row where the decrease should have been made (okay, it's best to attempt this maneuver if the decrease should have happened only two rows down), and pull out the horizontal rungs that are left in their wake.

Now, using your fingers, a crochet hook, or another needle, cross the right stitch over the left stitch if the decrease was to lean left, or the left stitch over the right stitch if the stitch was to lean right.

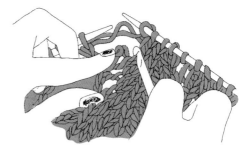

Pull the bottom-most yarn rung through both loops,

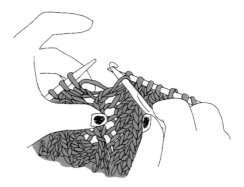

then pull the next rung through this single loop and place the stitch back on the needle.

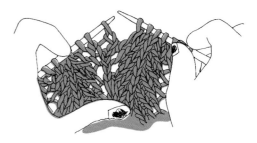

Work it as normal. The stitches around it may be a bit more loosey-goosey than they should be, but that will all even out once you block your project. If you're up to a challenge, you can even try this with a double decrease—just be sure that the decrease leans left, right, or is centered.

getting in Shape

SHAPING IN LACE KNITTING

You already know that lace is created by pairing increases (yarn overs) with decreases. But what about when you are making decreases or increases to shape your fabric, as you do in sweaters—decreasing along armholes, increasing to shape sleeves, etc. How do you keep that from messing up your entire lace pattern?

Turns out there are a couple of different ways to handle this. When decreasing, the simplest but least attractive solution is to discontinue knitting your lace pattern as soon as you no longer have enough stitches for a full repeat. Instead, knit the stitches between your decrease and the next lace pattern repeat in stockinette stitch. Of course, this is going to make an area of solid stitches along the edges of your work. If your stitch repeat is only a few stitches that won't be so noticeable, but if your stitch pattern is say, 12 stitches, you'll have a big ole' solid area of fabric, and you probably don't want that.

You can use this same simple-but-ugly method when increasing your stitches: Just keep knitting the new stitches in stockinette stitch until you've created enough new stitches for a full repeat of your lace pattern, then begin knitting those stitches according to your lace pattern. But here, again, you'll end up with bands of stockinette stitch along the edge of your work, and if those bands are wide, they may look awful.

The better solution, however, is quite a bit more complex. For this method, you continue to create every yarn over in your lace pattern as long as you still have enough stitches to complete its corresponding decrease, and you continue to create every decrease in your lace pattern as long as you have enough stitches to complete its corresponding yarn over. In order to execute this method, you should first take a good, close look at your lace pattern itself and try to identify which yarn overs go with which decreases. Starting from the right, look for the first decrease (or yarn over). The next yarn over (or decrease) to the left of this is the one it is paired with. If there is a double decrease, then you need to find the two yarn overs that it belongs to (they will most likely be the closest yarn overs to the left and right sides of the decrease).

Next, you'll need to keep very careful track of the number of stitches at the edges of your work, and the best way to do that is to place a marker after your first full lace pattern repeat and just before your last full lace pattern repeat. Let's say your lace pattern is eight stitches wide; you'd put a stitch marker after the first eight stitches, and before the last eight stitches. (If your lace pattern has an edge stitch, as many of them do, place your first marker after the first nine stitches and before the last nine stitches.)

Now let's say your pattern instructs you to "k1, ssk, knit in lace pattern to last 3 sts, k2tog, k1." Once you've done your edge stitch and your first decrease, you'll have used up the first two stitches of your pattern repeat (in the ssk), and you'll only have six stitches left. What were those first two stitches supposed to be? If neither of them was a yarn over or a decrease, you don't need to worry about a thing. But if one of them was a yarn over, then you should know that you'll need to eliminate the first decrease you come to (just work it like two regular stitches). However, if it was a single decrease, you need to eliminate its corresponding yarn over—just don't make it. If you can make a single decrease for every yarn over in the remaining stitches, go ahead and do so. But if you have only enough stitches left to make one yarn over, and two single decreases, then don't make the first of those single decreases. Make the yarn over, and one of the single decreases, and those two will cancel each other out. Don't make the other decrease, because without its friend, the yarn over, it will actually change your stitch count, and you want it to remain at six until you need to do more shaping.

You can also fudge this a bit: Say your remaining stitches required you to make a yarn over and a double decrease; you could simply change that double decrease to a single decrease to keep your stitch count from changing.

You need to calculate things in the same way at the end of your row by knocking off the last yarn overs or decreases according to whether you are able to complete their corresponding decrease or yarn over. Can't do the yarn over? Don't make the decrease. Not enough stitches to make the decrease? Don't make the yarn over. Don't do the crime if you can't do the time.

The same principle applies when you are increasing your fabric. Place markers to indicate where the new stitches are being added, and as soon as you have enough new stitches to create both a yarn over and its corresponding decrease, go ahead and do that. This way you are increasing in pattern, and that's a nice thing to do.

I'm the first to admit this is complicated. So to make things easier on themselves, some folks take the time to chart out all their increases and decreases, actually drawing out all of those rows on graph paper, filling in their lace pattern, adding in the decreases or increases for shaping, and then eliminating the yarn overs and decreases as is necessary. Once that's done, they can just knit according to their own chart and they don't have to think at all.

ʃtarting And ʃtopping

CAST-ONS AND BIND-OFFS FOR LACE

Some lace is so delicate and dainty that a regular old cast-on and bind-off doesn't do it justice; it needs a cast-on and bind-off that can stretch and block along with the lace. After all, a good part of lace is made of air, and when it's done, it will open up and stretch out quite a bit as a result. Your cast-on and bind-off need to be able to stretch right along with it.

My favorite cast-on method is the long-tail (sometimes called "slingshot") cast-on. And if you're making a project that just has a bit of lace in it—say a lace panel down the center—that cast-on will probably do you just fine. But if you are making something in an all-over lace stitch, you'll want to avoid the long-tail cast-on because it just isn't stretchy enough. A better one to use is the knit cast-on (page 88).

There is also another type of cast-on you should know if you are going to really become a lace-knitting pro. Lace shawls are oftentimes made so that it looks as if there was no cast-on at all. How do they do it? With something called a provisional or invisible cast-on. Both of these cast-on methods create a needleful of stitches, as any cast-on would. But they also do something else: They leave a series of loops below the stitches you've created, which are kept from unraveling with a piece of waste yarn or a crocheted chain until you're ready for them. When you are, you pull out the waste yarn or crocheted chain, transfer these "live" stitches to a knitting needle, and start knitting in the opposite direction. The result is fabric made of uninterrupted knitting, hence, the cast-on is "invisible."

Finally, when you're all done with your lace project, you'll want to be able to bind it off in a way that is as loose and airy as your knitting itself. You have a variety of options for this, including the sewn bind-off (page 101), the Russian lace bind-off (page 102), and the knit together bind-off (page 101).

the AMaZing Lace

BLOCKING YOUR PROJECT

Blocking lace can be truly transformational. That's because as you knit with stretchy yarn, your yarn overs may tend to collapse in on themselves. In fact, many all-over lace projects can look a bit of a mess when they first come off your needles. Only when you block them is their true nature revealed. The yarn overs all become perfectly open eyelets, any angled or pointed edgings make their crisp appearance, and the lace emerges in its best light.

To block lace, dunk your project in lukewarm water, then roll it in towels to squeeze out water. When your lace is "damp" rather than "wet," lay it out on a few thick towels. Gently pull it this way and that and, using straight pins placed every few inches or so, pin the lace to the towel, making sure your eyelets are held nice and open. Then, as with any other blocking project, you need to just walk away from it. The next day, carefully remove the pins. Your lace will look lovely!

Know Your Nupps

You may never encounter a stitch known as a "nupp" (rhymes with "loop") in your life, but if you do, you'll be thankful you read what I'm about to tell you.

Nupps are a type of bobble stitch common in Estonian lace knitting. I came across them in a supercute lace shawl I was working on. A nupp is made in two steps. The first step is easy. You knit into a stitch without dropping it off the needle, then yarn over, then knit into that same stitch again, and yarn over again, and then knit into the stitch again before dropping it off the needle. In this way, you've made five stitches out of one. Some nupps have you make more stitches, some have you make less. On the next row, the wrong-side row, you purl into all of these stitches at once.

Doesn't sound that bad, does it? That's what I thought, so while working on my shawl, I obediently made my knits and yarn overs when called for. But when I tried purling them together on the next row, I found myself in a major pickle. How could my needle fit into all those stitches? The loops were wrapped snugly, so that each time I tried to insert my needle

into one or two loops, it made the remaining loops tighten around the needle in a stranglehold. This was torture. How could I ever finish the shawl, which called for row upon row of these monsters? I tried using a thinner needle. I tried a crochet hook. Nothing worked, and I started breaking into a sweat. While I was struggling, I was watching a documentary about people whose plane had crashed in the Andes and who had to live off nothing but snow and other people's remains. Listening to them discuss their horrible suffering seemed to only amplify my own nupp-related distress.

I eventually made it across the row—I think it took me more than an hour. Sweaty and frustrated, I looked up nupps on the Internet, and found a video in which Nancy Bush, Estonian lace-knitting expert, demonstrated her nupp-making trick: *She makes each knit stitch and each yarn over very loose!* That's right: Instead of making a knit stitch the usual way, she pulls up her knit loop a bit after creating it and keeps her yarn overs loose as well. That was the key! It left the stitches loose enough to be purled together easily. I tried it. I was a nupp-hater no more. And now you won't have to be, either.

6

knit bLing bLing

ADDING A LITTLE SUMPIN' SUMPIN' TO YOUR KNITTING WITH BEADS AND EMBROIDERY

ou've learned so far that you can add an endless variety of textures and patterns to your knit fabric by using more than a single color of yarn, or by incorporating cable patterns or lace stitches. Each of these is done by manipulating the yarn itself while knitting, but there are other ways to add decorative elements to your knitting, and in this chapter we'll deal with two of those: knitting with beads and embroidering onto knit fabric.

Knitting with beads has got to be one of the most delicious crafts going: Not only do you get to work with sumptuous, beautiful yarn, but you're also playing with glittering, sparkling beads. And I don't know about you, but when it comes to glittery, sparkly things, I'm all for 'em. While knitting with beads doesn't require a lot of technical skill, there are a variety of methods for incorporating beads into your knitting, and almost all of them involve first stringing a whole bunch of beads onto your yarn. You then knit from this beaded-yarn source and slide up a bead to include in your knitting as you need it. So the first thing to know is how to get those beads on that yarn. Next, there are a number of ways that the bead can be positioned on your fabric, and for each, a slightly different method of creating the stitch is used. Knitting with beads can be a bit more slow-going than other knitting, but the results are well worth it.

But before you can knit with beads, you need to have some yarn . . . and some beads. Just as yarn comes in various thicknesses (or weights), beads come in a variety of diameters. Seed beads, the ones most commonly used in beaded knitting, go from being teeny-tiny to being, well, just small, and they are given numbers according to their size, with 1 being the largest size, and 15 being the smallest. That's right: Unlike US knitting needle sizes or, in fact, just about anything else in this world, with seed beads, the larger the number, the smaller the bead, and vice versa. This wackadoo naming convention comes from the approximate number of beads per inch—so, for instance, about 15 size 15 beads lined up in a row makes up about an inch, whereas about 6 size 6 beads make an inch. It's not an exact formula, though, and size 1 beads are definitely not an inch wide.

However, you won't often encounter size 1 beads. Sizes 6, 8, and 11 are the ones most frequently used in knitting, and a good rule of thumb is that any light worsted or DK yarn, for which the yarn label will usually recommend using a size 6 (4.0mm) needle, will work well with a size 6 bead. Go down in yarn weight, and you can go up in bead number (which actually means going down in bead size). Yarn that is heavier than a DK or light worsted is most likely not going to work well in bead knitting because the yarn has to be able to fit through the hole in the bead.

Getting the beads onto the yarn can be done one of three ways. If you can find a needle that is both thin enough to pass through the bead completely and has an eye that is large enough for you to thread your yarn through, you can simply slide the beads onto the needle and then onto the yarn. Chances are, however, that any needle big enough to thread your yarn through will be too much of a fatty to fit through your beads. There is such a thing as a "large-eye" needle, however, and it can be picked up at beading and craft supply stores. Less a sewing needle than it is a wire that is twisted on one side, leaving an open "eye" on the other, a big-eye needle allows you to thread your yarn through one side, then slide beads onto the other. Since it is really just a twisted wire, the large eye can compress as the bead is passed over it and onto the yarn. And since it is usually rather long, you can pick up quite a few beads at once, then push them all onto your yarn.

Unfortunately, my life is a big black hole for those big-eyed needles, and whenever I buy one, I seem to lose it within the first 24 hours of owning it. But do I let that keep me from bead knitting? I do not. That's because my favorite way of stringing beads onto yarn involves the creation of my very own DIY big-eye needle. To make it, all I do is thread a very thin sewing needle (thin enough to fit through my beads) with about a 6" length of thread. I tie a knot in the thread, then insert the end of my yarn into this loop of thread, leaving about a 6" tail hanging out. Now, I pick up beads on the needle, then slide them down over the doubled thread and then over the doubled yarn.

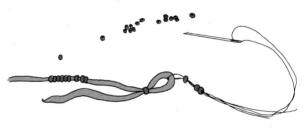

Works like a charm, and I never have to worry about losing or misplacing it, because I can easily create a new one. There is one thing to be careful about with this method, however, and that is that the thread, given enough pressure from the bead passing over the doubled yarn, could quite possibly cut into the yarn. So I just move the yarn every so often so that it isn't folded over the thread at the exact same spot while I am stringing beads.

Although many a beaded knitting pattern will tell you to string all of your required beads onto your yarn before you start knitting, this can cause quite a bit of wear and tear, both on your yarn—by fraying it and making it weaker—as well as your beads, which run the risk of having their linings rubbed off. So you might just want to string as many beads as you can deal with—say, 40 or 50 beads—and plan on breaking your yarn, restringing beads, and restarting your yarn at a later point in your knitting. I also find that, possibly because of the way I knit, the yarn that is strung with beads tends to get very, very wound up, the way an overused telephone cord can. To untwist it, I stick a stitch holder through my yarn ball and close it off to keep the ball from unwinding, then let the ball dangle, beads and all, and spin itself out. To check whether it's back to normal, I just fold the yarn in half and see whether it winds around itself or hangs loose. If it winds around itself, then it's still too twisted, and the ball needs some more unspinning. If it hangs loose, then I remove the stitch holder and continue my knitting.

beads on a wire

VARIOUS POSITIONS FOR BEADS ON YARN

Just as there are a number of different ways to sit on a horse for riding (sidesaddle, bareback, etc.), there are a number of different ways that a bead can "sit" on a knit stitch. As shown in the diagram below, a bead can (1) sit on the right arm of a knit stitch; (2) sit on the strand between two knit or purl stitches; (3) sit on a strand in front of a slipped stitch; or (4) wrap around both legs of a knit stitch.

The first three methods require that you prestring your beads; the last one is done with a crochet hook or a needle with a length of thread, and involves sliding a bead over the

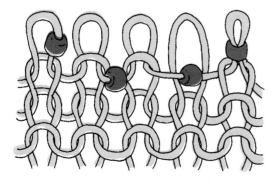

top of a loop of yarn just before you knit into it. Why so many methods? Well, for one thing, each technique has an effect on how your bead will be oriented on your knitted fabric: A bead that sits on the "leg" of a knit stitch will lie on a diagonal seen from the front of your work; a bead sitting on the strand between two stitches or on a strand in front of a slipped stitch will lie horizontally, and a bead that's placed around both legs of a stitch will lie vertically. Depending on the type of bead you are using, one of these methods might be preferable over the others. For instance, if a sequin is placed on the horizontal strand between two stitches, it will stick straight out from your work like a circular saw, and all that will show is the sharp edge. Place it on one leg or over both legs of a stitch, however, and it will lie flatter, like the scales of a fish, which is what you want.

BEADING BETWEEN THE LINES
PLACING A BEAD ON THE STRAND BETWEEN TWO STITCHES

It's very easy to place a bead between two stitches, but in order to have it show on the front of the work, you need to place it between two purl stitches. So this method works best with reverse stockinette stitch, garter stitch, or on stockinette stitch fabric, where each bead is surrounded by two purl stitches. The fun part about this technique, aside from its ease, is that you can place more than a single bead between stitches, thereby spreading them apart and shaping your work. It's frequently found in those little clutch bags where growing numbers of beads are used to widen the bottom of knit fabric into a purse.

To place a bead between two knit stitches:

Knit the stitch that comes before the bead, slide the bead up the yarn until it is lying right next to the knitting needle,

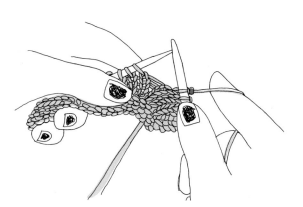

and knit the following stitch. The bead will show on the other side of the fabric.

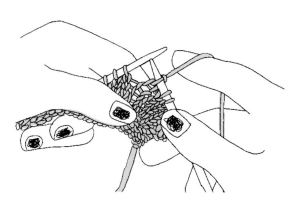

To place a bead between two purl stitches:

Purl the stitch that comes before the bead, slide the bead up the yarn until it is lying right next to the knitting needle,

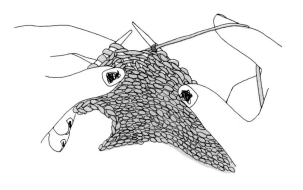

and purl the following stitch. The bead will show on the side of the fabric that is facing you.

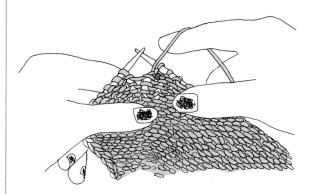

THE BEAD GOES ON
PLACING BEADS ON THE LEGS OF STITCHES

This method of placing beads is probably the oldest, and one could even argue the most authentic, way of placing beads in your knitting. Placing beads on the legs of stitches can be done from the knit side or the purl side, and the beads themselves will show up on the knit side of your work (yay!). Here's how.

To place a bead on the leg of a stitch while knitting:

Insert your needle into the stitch where you will place the bead, wrap the yarn around the needle as if to knit, then slide the bead up to the needle, make the knit stitch and pull the bead, along with the new stitch, to the front. The bead will be sitting on the right (front) leg of the newly created knit stitch.

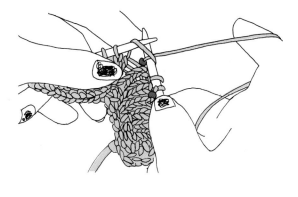

To place a bead on the leg of a stitch while purling:

Insert your needle into the stitch where you will place the bead, wrap the yarn around the needle as if to purl, then slide the bead up to the needle, make the purl stitch and

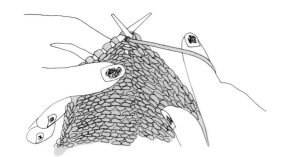

push the bead, along with the new stitch, to the back. The bead will be sitting on the right (front) leg of the stitch when viewed from the front.

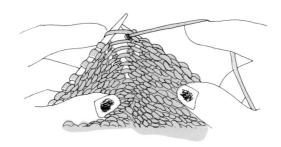

Beads sitting on stitches this way have a tendency to squirm around and may try to hide on the back leg of the stitch as you go along. One way to keep them in place is to knit or purl into the back leg of the stitch that has a bead on it in the next row. This twists the stitch above the bead and leaves a smaller, tighter hole so that it is less likely to be naughty and slip through. Alternatively, you can knit or purl through the back leg while placing the bead, which pretty much accomplishes the same thing, although this also gives you a smaller hole to bring the bead through in the first place. That's not so bad with a knit stitch, but it can be a monster when trying it from the purl side.

If you are looking to knit with sequins, this method is one to try. Since the sequin will sit on a diagonal rather than a horizontal strand, as it would in the between-the-stitches method, it will be oriented so that it can lie flat on your fabric and you will see the shiny part of the sequin, and not just the side of it. To make sure it stays in place, it's a good idea to knit into the back of the stitches when you place sequins. One more thing: If you're using faceted sequins, ones that have a bit of a cuplike shape, you'll want to thread them so that the open part of the cup is facing the ball of yarn. When you knit them into your work this way, the cup will face outward, and that's a good thing, because it's the facets in the cup that reflect the most light.

BEAD ALL THAT YOU CAN BEAD

ALL-OVER "BEAD KNITTING"

What we've learned so far—sprinkling beads over knit fabric for decorative purposes—is known as "*beaded* knitting." That's so that it can be distinguished from "*bead* knitting," which, believe it or not, refers to something quite different. With bead knitting, the entire surface of your work is covered with beads, with very little yarn showing through—it's as if the fabric itself is made of beads. A pattern is often created by the varying colors of beads, for example a heart made of red beads on a white bead background. In order for the design to come out correctly in your knitting, the exact order that the beads are strung on your yarn is very important. One bead in the wrong place and your heart will look like it had a heart attack, so you need to pay very close attention while stringing.

In bead knitting, beads are placed on each stitch and each row. You place the beads in the same way as described above for placing a bead on a leg of a stitch—that is, you pull a bead through to the front while making a knit stitch, or push it through to the back when making a purl stitch—which isn't so hard. However, since you are placing a bead on each stitch, in every row, you need to make sure that the bead that is already on the stitch that you are knitting or purling into stays on the right side of your work—and trust me, it will try to escape. To make sure it doesn't, see to it that the bead on that stitch is kept *underneath* your right-hand needle when you insert it to make the new stitch. The same goes for when you're creating a purl stitch.

In bead knitting, beads are placed on every stitch and every row.

Now, you know how the "leg" of the knit stitch is one-half of a V and, as such, is a diagonal line, right? Well, if you place a bead on every stitch and every row in the same way, all those beads sitting on all those diagonals will end up skewing your fabric—the entire piece of knitting will sort of lean to the right, just like the front leg of your knit stitch does. This is just the nature of bead knitting. In order to correct for that skew, however, you can knit through the back legs of your stitches in one row, and purl through the front legs of your stitches, as usual, on the following row. Not only does this twist the stitches in the row below your knit row, thereby keeping the beads in place, but it also reverses the angle of the front leg of that row of stitches, which will correct for the skew.

BEADING AROUND THE BUSH
PLACING A BEAD IN FRONT OF A SLIPPED STITCH

Your bead will lie nice and horizontal when you place it between stitches, but in order for it to show, it needs to be placed between two purl stitches. On the other hand, it can easily appear on a field of stockinette stitches if you place it on the right leg of the stitch, as earlier, but then the bead will be sitting at an angle. But what if you want your bead to both lie horizontal *and* sit on a field of stockinette? This too can be accomplished, using the following slip-stitch method of bead placement. This method requires that your beads be prestrung on your yarn.

To slip a bead on a knit (right-side) row in stockinette stitch:

Simply knit to the location where you want to place your bead, bring your yarn to the front of your work and slide a bead into place, slip the next stitch purlwise,

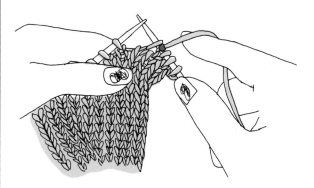

then bring the yarn to the back of your work again, leaving the bead (or beads) in the front of your work. Carry on knitting.

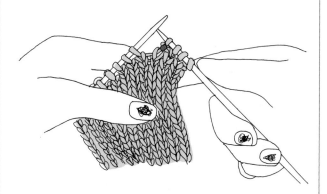

***To slip a bead on a purl (wrong-side) row in
stockinette stitch:***

Purl to the location where you want to place your bead,
bring your yarn to the back of your work and slide a bead
into place, slip the next stitch purlwise, then bring the yarn
to the front of your work again, leaving the bead (or beads)
in the back (right side) of your work. Carry on purling.

One cool thing about this method is that you can
leave more than one bead in front of your work, say, two
or three, and simply slip the corresponding number of
stitches. Another good thing is that you can do this on
every row. But there is a downside to this method as well:
Your slip stitches will need to be worked on the following
row or they risk getting too stretched out, and that means
that you can't work a vertical line of beads placed this way
over every row. You can, however, work a vertical line over
every other row, and that will most likely suffice.

BY HOOK OR BY CROOK
PLACING BEADS ON INDIVIDUAL
STITCHES USING A CROCHET HOOK

Let's say you want your bead to hang with its hole oriented
vertically—up and down. By hanging beads individually
on stitches as you need them, and basically pulling the
entire stitch through the bead so that the stitch is wearing the bead around its neck like a necklace, you can do
that. And placing beads this way also doesn't require that
you string 'em all up in advance. But since a loop of yarn
is obviously too thick to push through a hole in a bead,
you'll need a little helper to get this job done, and you can
get it in the form of a teensy crochet hook. The crochet
hook you use for this will be one of those steel jobbers
made for very fine crochet work, because it needs to be
small enough to fit through the hole in the bead. At the
same time, it needs to be large enough to grab onto your
stitch and pull it through without making the yarn get all
splitty. You'll just have to experiment with your yarn and

beads till you find a hook that can do both of those things
without too much difficulty.

To do it, work up to the stitch onto which you want to
place a bead. Pick up the bead with a crochet hook. Then
use your crochet hook to remove the next stitch from the
left-hand needle,

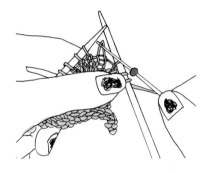

and pull it through the bead already on the hook (yes,
you'll need to have Mr. Thumb and Ms. Forefinger help
out here by pushing the bead down over the stitch).

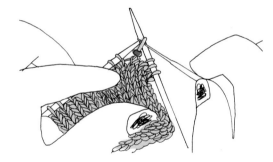

Then place the stitch back onto the left-hand needle.
You can knit (or purl) this stitch, but since it is now being
held in a stranglehold by your bead, the loop through
which you can make
a stitch is much,
much smaller. Better
to just slip it purl-
wise onto the next
needle and work it
normally on the fol-
lowing row.

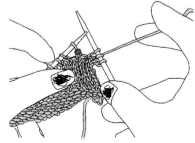

If you can't find the right-size crochet hook to pull off this maneuver, there's also a poor man's method with a needle and thread, although it is much slower. Knit up to the stitch where you want the bead, then take a sewing needle with a short length of thread and pick up the bead. Remove the stitch from the left-hand needle and pass the needle and thread through it. Then pass your sewing needle back through the bead in the oppo-  site direction. You have now created a loop of thread through the center of the stitch, and the loop has a bead on it. Push the bead down so it leaves the thread and goes onto the stitch, then pull the needle and thread through so it exits the stitch. Replace the stitch onto the left-hand needle and carry on as above.

ALL Stitched Up

EMBROIDERY ON KNITTING

Whether you're using it to add an intricate design onto otherwise plain knitting or just to add detail to an intarsia pattern, embroidering on knit fabric can kick your work up a notch. By using a few basic embroidery stitches, you can take a sweater from drab to fab, a hat from shitty to pretty.

Embroidery is most often done on a stockinette stitch background because that is nice and smooth, and the little V's of your knit stitches form a sort of grid that can help with the placement of your embroidery stitches. For stitches that are worked around your knit stitches, such as the dupli-cate stitch, cross-stitch, and chain stitch, you'll want to use a blunt tapestry needle with a hole large enough for your yarn to pass through. For other embroidery stitches, you can still use a blunt needle, but for more precise stitch placement,

In this swatch, a floral motif was created using duplicate stitch, cross-stitch, and a variety of other embroidery stitches.

you may prefer to use a pointed embroidery needle with a large hole, so that you can pierce your fabric at the exact point where you want your yarn to enter or exit the fabric. Of course, if you are embroidering on felted knitting, you'll definitely need to use a pointy needle.

DUPLICATE STITCH

One of the most basic forms of embroidery on knitting is the duplicate stitch, in which you simply follow the path of the stitch with another length of yarn (in a different color, of course, otherwise what would be the point?). You can use this to make a correction in a stranded or intarsia pattern, or to add details to your fabric, or to create an entire design. Duplicate stitch can also be considered the lazy man's intar-sia or even Fair Isle: Some folks prefer to add simple color designs to their work after it's been knitted, rather than as they go. And indeed, you can create some really nice-looking designs with carefully placed duplicate stitches. Duplicate stitch is also a good method to use

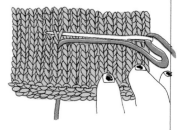

when adding single-stitch diagonal lines to an argyle pattern. Because it exactly duplicates a stitch (duh!), duplicate stitch is worked only over knit stitches, and most often on stockinette stitch fabric.

To make a duplicate stitch, simply bring a needle up at the base of the knit stitch, slip it under the legs of the stitch right above it, bring

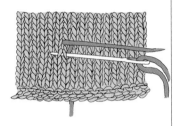

it back down where you came out, and come back up at the bottom of the next stitch you want to duplicate. Try to keep your duplicate stitches nice and loose, so they are just sitting on top of the underlying stitches like mustard on a pretzel and aren't squishing them out of shape.

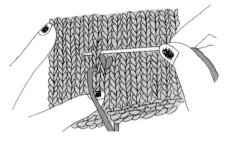

STITCHING LIKE A BIG GIRL

How do you embroider? Do you stick your needle up through your fabric, pull the entire length of your yarn through, then insert your needle into the fabric and pull the entire length of yarn all the way through again? Well, listen, son, you need to get schooled! You may have seen this kind of time-consuming business in the movies or in a cartoon, but in the real world, almost every embroidery stitch is meant to be completed using a gesture in which you insert your needle into the fabric at one point, and then bring it back out again at another point a small bit away—it's like weaving your needle in and out. Your needle goes in one place and out another, and *then* you pull the needle and the yarn all the way through—so your yarn and your needle are always above your fabric, where you can see 'em. Keep the fingers of one hand behind your work, however, and press a finger underneath the fabric so that it can help guide the needle to come up at the right spot. If you're embroidering with a blunt tapestry needle, that finger is out of harm's way. If you are using a pointy needle, as you would if you were embroidering through felted fabric, then that finger may get pricked. Now you know why thimbles were invented—consider it a helmet for your finger. Pop one on that bad boy and he can still do his job of helping your needle know where to go without getting hurt.

CROSS-STITCH

Cross-stitch is another nice stitch to use on knit fabric, especially since the knit V's form a clear grid on which to work it, and each cross-stitched X will sit neatly over each knit V. Before you try this, take a look at your stockinette stitch fabric. You'll see that each knit V is surrounded by four little holes, one in the upper right, one in the upper left, one in

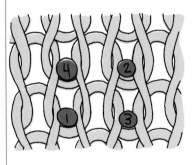

the lower right, and one in the lower left. To make a cross-stitch, start by bringing the yarn up through the hole in the lower left. Insert a needle into the hole at the upper right of the V, then bring

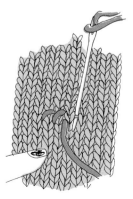

it out again at the lower right, and pull the yarn through. You have one half of the X—a small, diagonal stitch. Now, if you've got more of these cross-stitches to make to the right of this one, repeat that last gesture—in at upper right, out at lower right— as many times as necessary.

To finish the X, insert the needle into the upper left hole, and out again at the lower left hole if you've got more stitches to complete, otherwise leave the yarn at the back.

Cross-stitch is, in my mind, an often underutilized and misunderstood stitch. It doesn't look like much by itself, but it can be used to make all kinds of intricate figures on your knitting. And when done correctly—with all of the diagonal stitches that are on the top of the X leaning in the same direction—it can be quite pretty, and fast.

CHAIN STITCH

The chain stitch can be accomplished by a single in-and-out movement of your needle, although it's pretty much up to you where your needle should enter and exit the fabric. For chain stitch, you'll want to concentrate more on making your stitches a similar length than on exactly where in your fabric your needle is going in and coming back out. To make it, bring the yarn up at the point where you'd like the chain stitch to begin. Insert the needle back into the same point where the thread just came out, and then back out again about ¼" away, making sure that the yarn loops *under* the needle. Pull the yarn through.

Insert the needle back where you came out, and bring it up again about a quarter-inch away.

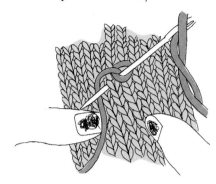

Create a single chain stitch, and tack down the loop by reinserting the needle over the loop and drawing it to the back of your work, and you've made what's called a lazy daisy stitch, often used for making flowers or small leaves.

A line of chain stitches can also be worked with a crochet hook, especially if you want to make vertical lines across your work. (I mentioned in the Intarsia chapter that if you need to make a vertical column of a single stitch, you are better off adding it with a crochet hook using this method.) But you can also make chain stitches with a crochet hook that travel any old way across your work. To do it, hold the yarn at the back of your work, and insert a crochet hook.

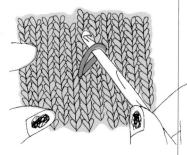

Pull a loop through to the front, reinsert the hook one or two stitches away, then pull up another loop through the fabric and through the loop that is on the hook as well.

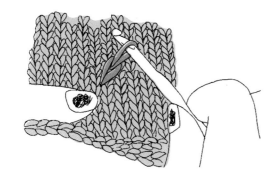

If you want perfect diagonal or vertical lines, insert the hook in the center of the V each time, moving up one stitch, or up one stitch and over one stitch, as necessary. Otherwise, just insert the hook wherever seems best to create the line. When you're done, pull the strand of yarn all the way through to the front of your work, thread a needle with it, make a small, straight stitch to fix the last loop onto your fabric, and work the yarn end away on the wrong side.

Duplicate stitch, cross-stitch, and chain stitch can all be made quite nicely using the knit stitches in stockinette stitch fabric as a sort of grid and creating your embroidery stitches around the knit V's. You can work the following embroidery stitches around your knit stitches, or use a pointed needle and work them *through* your knit stitches, piercing them whenever you need to in order to create the embroidery stitch the way you want it to be. There is no way to maintain the natural stretch of your fabric when making embroidery stitches, but at least be careful that you don't bunch up your fabric while doing them. (By the way, if you were thinking about using an embroidery hoop with your knit fabric, *stop right now.* You will stretch it out, and when your embroidery is done the fabric will contract again and the results will be complete crap.) Just hold your knit work in your hand, unstretched and relaxed, and try to create embroidery stitches that lie flat on the fabric

without pulling it together. Of course, if you're working embroidery stitches on felted fabric, no worries.

STRAIGHT STITCH

The straight stitch is the one to use when making a series of short lines in any direction. It's also the easiest: Just bring the yarn up from behind where you want the base of the stitch to be, then bring the embroidery needle back down into the fabric where you want it to end, and up where you want the next stitch to begin.

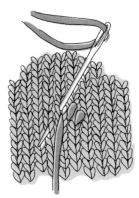

STEM STITCH

Stem stitch is a nice way to make a straight line as an outline for a design, or, obviously, for a stem. Working from left to right, bring the yarn up from behind your work at the point where you want your line to begin. Then insert the embroidery needle back into the fabric about ¼" to the right of this point, and bring it back up again about halfway between where the yarn started (about ⅛" to the left, in this example), holding the yarn below this point and pulling through.

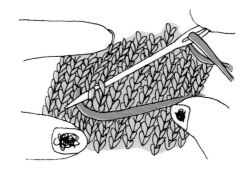

Keep inserting the needle into the fabric where you want the line to continue, bringing the needle back up again a bit to the left, holding the length of yarn below the needle, and then pulling the yarn all the way through. This stitch is perfect for making slightly curved lines; you'll end up with a line that is a bit thicker than the yarn you are using to embroider with.

BACKSTITCH

The backstitch is familiar to anyone who's ever done any hand-sewing. It creates a nice, solid line that is exactly as thick as the yarn you are using. This stitch is worked from right to left. Bring the yarn up where you want to begin, and pull it through. Next, insert the needle about ⅛" to ¼" to the left of this point and then bring it up again ⅛" to ¼" farther to the left. Pull the yarn through. Insert the needle back into the same point where the first stitch ended, and bring it up again about ⅛" to ¼" to the left of where the second stitch is ending. Continue this way, being very careful not to make your stitches too wide (because on the wrong side of the work, your strands of yarn will be twice this length), and being careful to neither stretch out nor bunch up your fabric while creating this stitch. The backstitch is very sturdy and does not stretch.

SATIN STITCH

When you want to create a solid, filled-in shape with your embroidery, look to the satin stitch. It's nothing more than a number of straight stitches lying next to each other like so many matches in a matchbox. It is created in the same way as a straight stitch, too. While it looks simple, executing an exact shape with satin stitch can be quite challenging, especially if you want to make something like a perfect circle. In this case, it's easier to start by making an outline of the shape in small backstitches, using a strand or two of embroidery floss, and then covering the outline completely with your satin stitches.

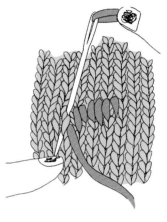

FRENCH KNOT

A French knot is the go-to stitch for making animal eyes or anything else that looks like a little bump; it's pretty fun to make, too. Begin by bringing a needle up where you want the knot to appear, and pull the yarn all the way through. Then hold the needle flat along the surface of your knitting, right above where the yarn exited the fabric, and wrap the yarn around the point twice.

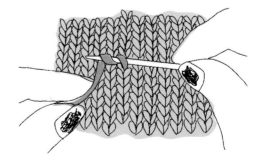

Hold that wrapped yarn in place with your pointer finger, reinsert the needle close to where it came out, and pull

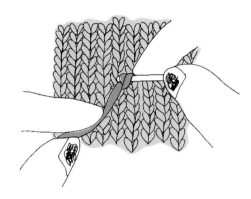

through carefully so that the wrapped yarn stays in place (you may hold it there with your finger). French knot made! Ooh-la-la!

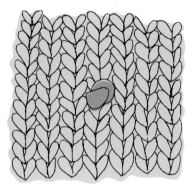

FLY STITCH

Another stitch that can be quite decorative on knit fabric is known as the fly stitch. This is a V-shaped stitch in which the bottom of the V is held down with a straight stitch. When these V's are spaced apart, the stitch creates some-

thing that looks a bit like the leaf of a fern; when the V's are spaced closer together and altered in their width and depth, they can make a very nicely formed leaf shape. Start by bringing the needle up at the point where you'd like the top of the left side of the V to begin and pull the yarn

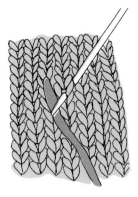

through. Bring the needle back down to the right of this point, where you want the top of the right-hand leg of the V to be. Hold the yarn down with your thumb at the point where you'd like the bottom of the V, and bring the needle back up just *above* this point.

Pull the yarn through. Reinsert the needle below this point, underneath the V, to make either a short or a longer straight stitch to hold down the bottom of the V, then bring the needle back up again where you'd like the top of the next V to appear, and repeat the process. The V's will be stacked on top of each other, for a pretty, feathery look.

7

I f you're reading this book, you already know how to cast on, bind off, knit, and purl. You also know how to increase and decrease when you want to shape your fabric. But just as an artist has different brushes for different types of strokes and effects, a well-rounded knitter should have at her disposal an arsenal of stitches to deploy when needed. For instance, all cast-ons are not created equal: Some are firmer, some are stretchier. You want to be able to pick the best cast-on for a given project. How about putting an edging on a neckline? You have a wide variety of options for that as well. In this chapter, you'll learn more cast-ons and bind-offs than you can shake a stick at, a couple of increases and decreases, variations on Kitchener stitch, cords, and buttonholes, and finally, how to make short rows, and why. Once you've got all these options in your back pocket, you'll be prepared to handle any kind of stitchy situation.

stitch witchery

A USEFUL ASSORTMENT OF CAST-ONS, BIND-OFFS, INCREASES, DECREASES, CORDS, AND BUTTONHOLES, AND AN INTRODUCTION TO SHORT ROWS

Start Me Up

CAST-ONS

BASIC CAST-ONS

BACKWARD LOOP CAST-ON

This cast-on gives a soft edge and is especially useful when you need to cast on stitches at the end of a row. It can also work well as the beginning of a lace project. It's ridiculously easy to do, but the first row can be hell to knit because there is nothing to fix the size of these loops and they can get really tight. Also, the strand between the stitch you just knit and the next one on the needle will seem to get longer and longer with each new stitch, which tends to make this cast-on look sloppy.

1 Make a slip knot and place it on a knitting needle.

2 Holding the yarn in the palm of your left hand, make a "stick 'em up" gun with your thumb and forefinger.

3 Bring your thumb under the strand from back to front.

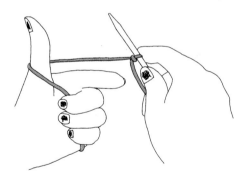

4 With your right index finger on the slip knot to keep it in place, bring your right needle down and scoop up the strand that is on your thumb from front to back.

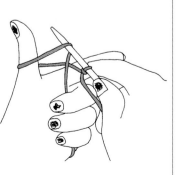

5 Drop the strand off your thumb and tighten the loop.

Repeat steps 2–5 until all stitches have been cast on.

KNIT CAST-ON

Another soft cast-on that is good for lace. This is many folks' go-to cast-on, although I find it much slower going than the long-tail cast-on (page 90). But if you have to knit down at some later point, this stitch is very easy to unpick.

1 Make a slip knot and place it on a knitting needle.

2 Take the needle with the slip knot in your left hand.

3 Knit into the knot

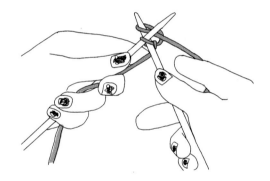

and place the resulting loop back onto the left-hand needle. Make sure to place it onto the left-hand needle correctly: The left-hand needle should go completely in front of the new loop, then enter it from right to left. Snug up the new loop but don't make it tight.

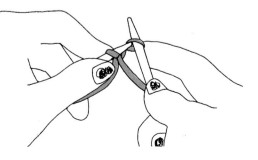

4 Knit into the new loop.

5 Place this loop on the left-hand needle as in step 3.

Repeat steps 4–5 until all stitches have been cast on.

CABLE CAST-ON

Similar to the knit cast-on, above, but makes a firmer edge. It's good for when you want some structure at the beginning of your project, but not good if you want any stretch.

1 Make a slip knot and place it on a knitting needle.

2 Take the needle with the slip knot in your left hand.

3 Knit into the knot and place the resulting loop back onto the left-hand needle. Make sure to place it onto the left-hand needle correctly: The left-hand needle should go completely in front of the new loop, then enter it from right to left. Snug up the new loop but don't make it tight.

4 Insert the right-hand needle in between the two stitches on the left-hand needle,

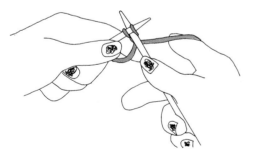

wrap the yarn as if to knit, and pull up the loop.

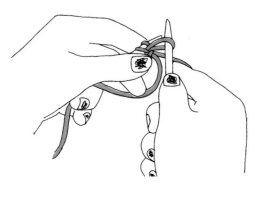

5 Place this loop onto the left-hand needle as in step 3.

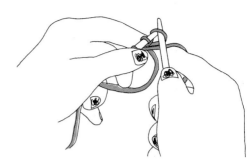

Repeat steps 4–5 until all stitches have been cast on.

ALTERNATE CABLE CAST-ON

Similar to cable cast-on, of course, but is somewhat stretchy and works well for 1 × 1 ribbing ("1 × 1 ribbing" just means a knit one, purl one ribbing). It's not as nice for ribbing as a tubular cast-on (page 95), but it's much simpler to execute.

1 Make a slip knot and place it on a knitting needle.

2 Take the needle with the slip knot in your left hand.

3 Knit into the slip knot and place the resulting loop back onto the left-hand needle. Make sure to place it onto the left-hand needle correctly: The left-hand needle should go completely in front of the new loop, then enter it from right to left. Snug up the new loop but don't make it tight.

4 Insert the right-hand needle in between the two stitches on the left-hand needle from back to front as if to purl. Wrap the yarn as if to purl and pull up the loop.

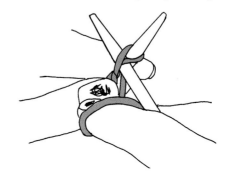

⑤ Place this loop onto the left-hand needle as in step 3.

⑥ Insert the right-hand needle in between the two stitches on the left-hand needle, from front to back, wrap the yarn as if to knit, and pull up the loop.

⑦ Place the new loop onto the left-hand needle as in step 3.

Repeat steps 4–7 until all stitches have been cast on.

To work the first row of ribbing, knit through the back loop of the first stitch if the last cast-on stitch was a knit; purl the first stitch if the last cast-on stitch was a purl. Alternate knit and purl for 1 × 1 ribbing, but continue to knit all stitches on this first row through the back loop.

LONG-TAIL CAST-ON

My beloved and most favoritest cast-on in the universe. Once you get used to this maneuver, you can whip out new stitches a mile a minute. It's stretchy enough to use for ribbing, but may be a bit too sturdy to use for lace. The long-tail cast-on actually produces something like a row of single cast-on loops plus the first knit row of stitches (if you look at it closely, you'll see what I mean). One thing that sucks about this cast-on is that if you ever have to knit down from your cast-on stitches (to lengthen a sweater or fix some kind of error), it is very difficult to unpick. If you want to make sure this cast-on is stretchy enough for, say, the top of a sock, cast on over two needles held together, then pull one of them out before you start knitting.

❶ As its name suggests, you need to begin this cast-on with a long tail of yarn—about three times the width that your first row needs to be. Make a slip knot at this point and place it on your right-hand needle (or try it without a knot; see "Look, Ma! No Knots!", facing page).

❷ Hold the ball and tail ends in the palm of your left hand, with the tail end to the left and the ball end to the right, and close your lower three fingers over them. Insert your thumb and index finger through the two strands from behind and

spread out the strands. Make sure that the tail end is the one over your thumb. Place your right-hand index finger on top of the slip knot to keep it from slipping off the needle, and bring your right-hand needle down so it is below the thumb and forefinger of your left hand.

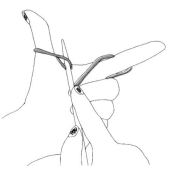

❸ With the right-hand needle, scoop up the strand of yarn that is over your thumb from underneath.

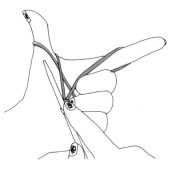

❹ Swing the right-hand needle, clockwise, over the top and then underneath the strand of yarn that is coming from your index finger and leading to the needle.

5 Bring the right-hand needle through the loop on your thumb, then drop the loop off your thumb.

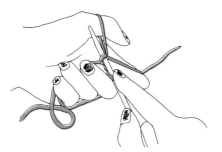

Snug up the stitch, but don't make it tight, by gently pulling on the tail end of the yarn.

Repeat steps 3–5 until all stitches have been cast on.

VARIATION #1: LOOK, MA! NO KNOTS: STARTING A LONG-TAIL CAST-ON WITHOUT A SLIP KNOT

You can easily begin your long-tail cast-on with no slip knot at all, which will leave a first cast-on stitch that has more give than one created with a slip knot. To do it, hold the yarn as you normally would for a long-tail cast-on, with the long tail end over the thumb of your left hand, the ball end over the index finger of your left hand, and the ends of the yarn in the lower three fingers of your left hand. Since the yarn is not attached to the right-hand needle by a slip knot, there will be a strand of yarn running straight across from your thumb to your index finger. With the other knitting needle in your right hand, bring the needle behind this strand and then pull it toward you. Place your index finger on top of the strand to hold it in place on the needle and proceed with the long-tail cast-on step 3. Cool, right?

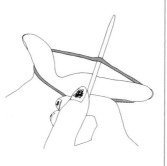

VARIATION #2: THE INFINITE TAIL: STARTING A LONG-TAIL CAST-ON WITH TWO BALLS OF YARN

This ingenious trick is particularly useful if you are casting on a large number of stitches, like a hundred or more, and you're terrified of getting to stitch number 90 only to find out that you've run out of tail. To do it, you use two balls of yarn (or the end and beginning of the same ball). This method also doesn't use a slip knot, so pay attention:

1 Hold the ends of both balls of yarn in the bottom fingers of your right hand—and hold a knitting needle in that hand as well.

2 Hold on to the yarn with your left hand in the usual way for the long-tail cast-on, but now both the index finger and the thumb will have ball-ends of yarn over them.

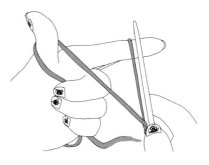

3 Begin casting on with step 3 of the long-tail cast-on, and don't let go of the yarn ends in your right hand until after you've cast on a few stitches. When you've cast on as many stitches as you need, cut one of the balls of yarn off, leaving a long strand, and carry on knitting with the other ball.

OLD NORWEGIAN CAST-ON (AKA GERMAN TWISTED CAST-ON)

This cast-on is very similar to the long-tail cast-on, but it is quite a bit stretchier, which has made it the "It" cast-on among sock knitters, who like to use it for the tops of socks. This cast-on can also become very tight, so if you want to be sure that it stays loose enough, cast on over two needles, then pull one out before you begin knitting.

❶ Begin this cast-on with a long tail of yarn—about three times as wide as your first row needs to be. Make a slip knot at this point and place it on the right-hand needle.

❷ Hold the ball and tail ends in the palm of your left hand, with the tail end to the left and the ball end to the right, and close your lower three fingers over them. Insert your thumb and index finger through the two strands from behind and spread out the strands. Make sure that the tail end is the one over your thumb. Place your right-hand index finger on top of the slip knot to keep it from slipping off the needle, and bring the right-hand needle down so it is below the thumb and forefinger of your left hand.

❸ Swing the right-hand needle underneath both strands on your thumb, from front to back,

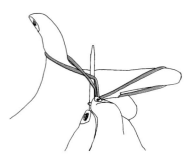

then weave it over the strand that's farthest from you and under the thumb-strand that's closer to you.

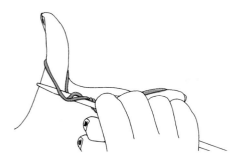

❹ Swing the right-hand needle clockwise, over then under the strand on your index finger that leads to the right-hand needle.

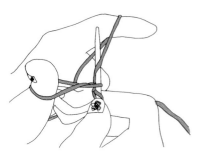

❺ Rotate your thumb clockwise until it points down so that the loop on your thumb is no longer crossed,

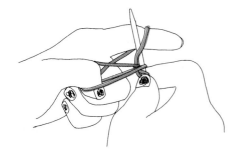

then bring the right needle through this loop and drop the loop off your thumb.

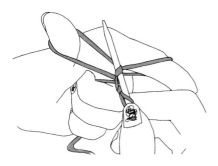

❻ Snug up the stitch.

Repeat steps 2–6 until all stitches have been cast on.

provisional cast-ons

If you ever need to knit downward from your cast-on edge—in order to add an edging or to continue your work in the opposite direction—you can unpick any of the cast-ons above to reveal "live" stitches to put on your needle. Some of those cast-ons are easy to unpick, while others are more difficult. But if you already know that you're going to need to do this, you should cast on using one of the provisional cast-on methods below, because with them you don't have to unpick anything: The live stitches will be there, waiting for you when you need 'em. You should be aware that these live stitches at the bottom of your work are actually situated *in between* the stitches that you'll be working from the bottom up, and as such they will be one half-stitch off from them. If you're going to be knitting stockinette or adding ribbing, that doesn't matter at all. But if you have been working some sort of knit-and-purl or stranded colorwork pattern in the upward direction and plan to continue the same pattern going downward, the stitches won't line up. You can fudge this a bit by creating some sort of separation—a few rows of reverse stockinette stitch or a stripe in a contrasting color, for instance—before you start knitting your pattern stitch going downward.

CROCHET METHOD

This method is easy to remember and is great fun when you need your live stitches: You just pull on the tail of the base row of crochet stitches and they'll easily come loose, one at a time, revealing loops that you can quickly snatch up with your knitting needle. The method is a bit like picking up stitches, only instead of picking them up from the center of other knit stitches, you are picking them up through the bottom loops of crochet chains. It does require a crochet hook and that you know how to crochet a chain, though, so crochet haters should choose another technique.

❶ With a length of smooth, slippery yarn (cotton is nice for this) in a contrasting color and using a crochet hook that's about the same thickness as the needle you plan to knit with, make a length of crochet chains that is a few chains longer than the number of stitches you need to cast on. Insert the end of the yarn through the last chain, and pull to close.

❷ Flip the chain over so that all of the V's are facing down and the back of the chain—which will look like a dashed line of little purl-like bumps—is facing you.

❸ Hold the crochet chain in your left hand, and insert your needle through the rightmost "bump," wrap your yarn as if to knit,

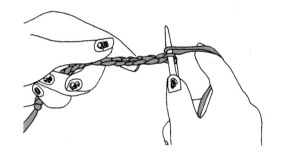

and pull up a stitch (this is similar to picking up stitches). Continue pulling up stitches through each crochet bump until all stitches have been cast on.

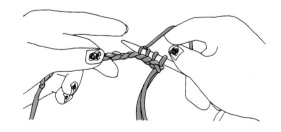

When you need to free the stitches at the bottom of the cast-on edge, just undo the last chain and then gently pull on the end of this yarn. The crochet chain will come loose one chain at a time, revealing a live stitch that you can quickly pop onto a needle. You may want to use a thinner needle just to catch the stitches, then transfer them all to the needle you intend to knit with afterward.

LOOPING METHOD

This method is mad cool, but requires all kinds of wackadoo twisting and turning to get the stitches on the needle. It will most likely take you a few attempts before you get it right. It's worth the effort, however, because at the end you'll have all your live stitches waiting for you on a strand of waste yarn, making them supereasy to transfer to a needle when you need them.

❶ Make a slip knot in a long length of smooth, slippery waste yarn and place it on two knitting needles held together. Make a slip knot with your working yarn and also place it on the needles. Place your right index finger over both slip knots to keep them in place when you begin this cast-on. Hold the two yarns in your left hand as for the long-tail cast-on (page 90), with the waste yarn over your thumb, the working yarn over your index finger, and the ends held in your palm with your lower three fingers.

❷ Bring the right-hand needle down between the yarn strands and swing it counterclockwise under and then over the working yarn.

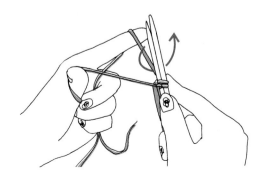

❸ Now swing the needle counterclockwise over and then under the waste yarn, bringing the needle up in the middle of the two strands.

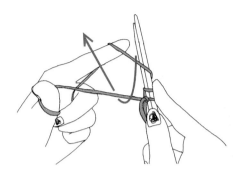

❹ Swing the needle clockwise over and then under the working yarn, and then under the waste yarn, bringing the new loop to the front.

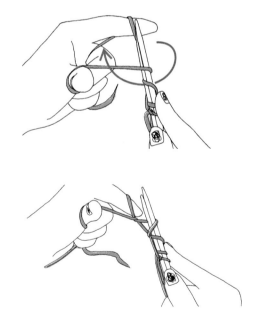

Continue in this way, repeating steps 2–4, until all stitches have been cast on, being careful to keep the waste yarn at the bottom of all the stitches (this may take some finagling). Then remove the bottom needle and work your way across the row, knitting the backward-facing stitches through their back loops (every other stitch will be situated this way). At the end of the row, drop the waste yarn's slip knot off your needle. You now have a long length of waste yarn at the bottom of your knitting, which is holding all the live stitches. When you need them, insert the needle into the live stitches (you might want to use a smaller-size needle than you plan to knit with for this). You can pull out the waste yarn one stitch at a time, or wait until you've inserted your needle through all the stitches and then pull out the waste yarn all at once.

This cast-on method produces two stitches at a time. If you need to cast on an odd number of stitches, just cast on one extra and work the first two stitches together on the next row. Also, since the "live" stitches on the waste yarn are coming from in between the knit stitches, you will have one less stitch on the waste yarn than you have on the needles. If you need to have the same number of stitches when you knit in the other direction, just increase a stitch at the end of the row.

LONG-TAIL PROVISIONAL CAST-ON

This method is perhaps the easiest, and it's pretty much just like the long-tail cast-on. The downside is that, while the live stitches are easy to slip onto your needle, it is much more difficult to unpick the length of waste yarn that's holding them.

Work this cast-on exactly as you would the long-tail cast-on variation #2—the one with an infinitely long tail (page 91). However, instead of using a second ball of yarn, you'll use a long length of smooth, slippery waste yarn.

❶ Making sure that the waste yarn is the one over your thumb, cast on as many stitches as necessary with the working yarn, then knit as usual.

❷ When you need to grab the live stitches at the bottom, you can unpick the waste yarn and, as each stitch is freed, place it on a knitting needle (use a smaller-size needle for this part).

Alternatively, holding the work so that the side where the waste yarn cast-on looks like a series of dashes fac-

ing you, take a smaller needle and insert it, from front to back, into the loop of the working yarn that is below and between these dashes. Then you can unpick the waste yarn.

Either way, unpicking this waste yarn is not going to be fun (you have to pull it out through each loop not once but twice), and it's simplest to just snip right through those "dashes" with a pair of scissors and pull out the waste yarn a small little piece at a time. Just be careful not to accidentally cut through your working yarn.

TUBULAR CAST-ONS

Don't bother with tubular cast-on for anything other than ribbing. It creates a little tube of ribbing at the base of your knitting, and it is superstretchy—like the ribbing itself. This is sometimes called an invisible cast-on; it's a wonder of knitting technology and worth attempting at least once in your life. Be aware, though, that this cast-on cannot be worked in the round, so if you want to use it for the tops of socks, for instance, you'll need to cast on and work your first four rows back and forth before continuing in the round. Later, you can stitch the two sides of the tube together.

TWO-STRAND TUBULAR CAST-ON

This cast-on might seem like the looping provisional cast-on (facing page), but it isn't, so be careful not to do it incorrectly.

❶ Use a needle two to three sizes smaller than the needles you plan to knit your piece with. Leave a long tail, at least four times as long as the width of the piece you'll be casting on. Make a slip knot and place it on your needle. Take this needle in your right hand and hold the yarn in your left hand the same way as for the long-tail cast-on (page 90).

❷ Swing the needle clockwise over and then under the strand of yarn that's over your index finger, and bring the point of your needle up in between the strands.

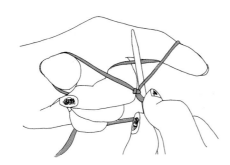

3 Now swing your needle counterclockwise over the strand of yarn that's over your thumb. Do not come up between the strands—instead, continue swinging the needle in a counterclockwise motion, bringing it all the way under and up behind the strand of yarn over your index finger. See how the yarn on your index finger is in front, at the base of this stitch you just made? That means you've just cast on a purl stitch.

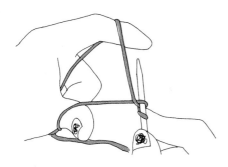

4 Now we'll do the same thing, but in reverse: Swing the needle counterclockwise over and then under the strand of yarn on your thumb, and bring the point up in between the strands.

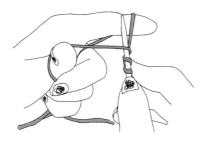

5 Next, swing the needle clockwise over and then under the strand on your index finger, but don't come up in between the strands. Instead, swing the needle underneath the strand that is over your thumb and come up for air in front of that strand. See how the strand on your thumb is behind the base of this stitch? That means you've just cast on a knit stitch.

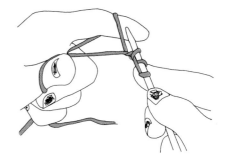

Repeat steps 2–5 until all stitches have been cast on. Tie the tail end to the working end under your needle.

Although I've referred to these cast-on stitches as knits and purls, what you've really done is create a bunch of stitches that are doing a back bend around your needle, with their heads and tails meeting underneath it.

In order to make this tubular cast-on into a tube, you first need to knit four rows of what's known as *tubular ribbing stitch*. To do this, continue with the smaller needles and work the first stitch as an edging stitch. Now, if the next stitch is a purl stitch (it will have a little strand of yarn across the bottom of its "feet," and it will be situated on the needle correctly), slip the stitch with the yarn in front. If the next stitch is a knit stitch (it will be situated on the needle backward), knit into the back of it. Then just continue slipping the purl stitches purlwise with the yarn in front, then knitting the next stitch through the back loop, all the way across.

On the next row, knit the knit stitches and slip the purl stitches with the yarn in front, always working the first and last stitches of the row as edge stitches. You do not need to knit into the backs of the knit stitches on this or any following row, because after the first row they will be situated on the needle correctly.

Repeat this last row two more times. Then switch to the larger needles that you intend to work your project with, and knit the knit stitches and purl the purl stitches for a 1 × 1 ribbing. After you've gone for a while, you can take a look at what you've just created: a small tube of ribbing at the bottom of your work that leads right into your ribbing. Miraculous!

If you are going to work a 2 × 2 rib (k2, p2), you need to add one more step when you are beginning to knit with your regular-size needles. Work the edging stitch as normal. Then work the next stitch (knit or purl, whichever it is). The stitch that follows this one will not be the right stitch for a 2 × 2 pattern. What you need to do here is swap the order of this next stitch and the stitch after it on the needle. To do that, slip the next two stitches to the right-hand needle purlwise. Then insert the left-hand needle into the back loop of the first stitch you slipped. Slide the right needle out of both stitches, then bring it in front of the stitch that is now on the left-hand needle and catch the free-hanging stitch. Slip that stitch back to the left-hand needle. *Now* the next stitch on the needle is the stitch you need for your 2 × 2 rib, so knit it if it's a knit, or purl it if it's a purl. Repeat the next time you encounter a stitch that is not the one you are looking for, which will be three stitches later. Continue to repeat this maneuver every four stitches until you are done.

YARN OVER TUBULAR CAST-ON

This one is easier than two-strand tubular cast-on, although not quite as miraculous, and it requires the use of waste yarn and a provisional cast-on. If you're up for that, give it a go.

❶ Using knitting needles two or three sizes smaller than what you are going to knit your project with and a contrasting, slippery yarn, cast on half the number of stitches you need using the two-strand provisional cast-on

method. (If you need an odd number of stitches, round up to the next even number.) Alternatively, you can just loosely crochet a chain that is at least half the number of stitches you need.

❷ With the working yarn, knit a stitch, then yarn over and repeat that all the way across the row. (If you've started with a crochet chain in step 1, make your knit stitches into the "bump" on the back of each chain stitch, as you would when making a crocheted provisional cast-on.) Knit the last stitch. You'll end up with an odd number of stitches. If you need an even number of stitches, just increase a stitch at the end of the first row of tubular ribbing stitch (facing page).

❸ Using needles two to three sizes smaller than what you'll be knitting with, work the tubular ribbing stitch as for the two-strand tubular cast-on as follows: Slip the purl stitches with the yarn in front (the first and last stitches of the first row will both be purls), then bring the yarn back to knit the yarn overs on the first row (you don't need to knit the yarn overs through the back loops because they will already be oriented on the needle correctly). Work three more rows of tubular ribbing stitch, knitting the knits with the yarn in back, and slipping the purl stitches with the yarn in front.

❹ Now switch up to your normal-size needle and continue knitting in knit 1, purl 1 ribbing. If you need to work 2 × 2 ribbing, switch the order of the stitches as necessary (see directions under two-strand tubular cast-on, page 95).

❺ Unpick your waste yarn.

TURKISH CAST-ON

This cast-on is frequently used when starting socks from the toe up, although it has other applications as well. Basically, what you are doing here is casting on for circular knitting, but instead of knitting something like a doughnut, with a hole in the center, you're knitting more of a danish, with a closed center. You do this by putting stitches on a needle in such a way that you can knit from both the top and the bottom of the first row of stitches. If you do that row after row—knitting from the top and the bottom of the work, and pulling the yarn tight between each of these rows—you'll end up with a little pocket, perfect for sticking your toes in. It is often done using circular needles, but I'll give the directions for using double-pointed needles first, which is a bit tight going, then explain how to do it on circs, which is actually easier.

1 Place a slip knot on one of your double-pointed needles, then hold both needles together in your left hand, one above the other, with the needle with the slip knot on it at the bottom. With your right hand, wind the yarn once around both needles counterclockwise for half the number of stitches that you need. Bring the yarn to the back between the two needles after the last round.

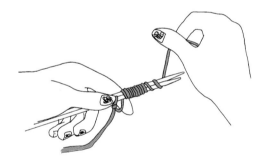

2 Get out a third double-pointed needle. Working between the two needles, knit through each loop on the top needle, being careful not to let any loops drop off the bottom needle. Things will get a bit tight here. Just work through it.

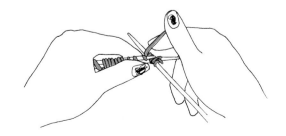

3 Turn the work 180 degrees. Drop the slip knot off the needle that is now on top. Then, working between the needles again, knit through each loop on the top needle, being careful not to let any stitches fall off the bottom needle.

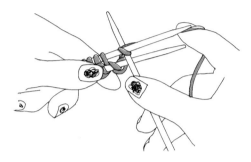

4 Turn the work 180 degrees. Knit the stitches on the top needle, making sure to pull the yarn tight after the first stitch.

Repeat step 4 for as many rows as your instructions tell you.

Doing this over two circular needles is less difficult because you can pull one of your needles through while knitting the loops, and since the cable that connects two circular needles is thinner than the actual needle, this will make things a bit less tight. Step 1 is the same as above, only you wrap your yarn over the points of two circular needles held together. After all the stitches are wound on, pull the bottom needle through the loops so that the loops come to rest on the cable. Then knit through the loops on the top needle with the other side of the same circular needle that they are sitting on. Rotate the work 180 degrees, and pull the left side of the top cable needle so that the stitches come to rest on the needle part rather than the cable part of this needle. Now you need to pull the bottom needle through the stitches so that they are resting on the connecting cable. Continue as above, using the other side of this same needle to knit the loops on the top needle.

Happy endings

BIND-OFFS

Just as there's more than one way to cast on stitches, there are also many ways to bind off. And just as with cast-on methods, these bind-offs vary in their firmness, stretchiness, appropriateness for ribbing, and more. Here are just a few of the many variations that you may find useful.

CHAIN BIND-OFF

This bind-off is the most basic—no frills—and works well for most situations. It leaves a nice row of V's that look like a chain across the top of your work, which is how this bind-off got its name. It's somewhat firm and not very stretchy, so if you are binding off something like a neckline or the top of a sock where it's important that things stay stretchy, bind off super loosely (or use the suspended bind-off, below).

1 Knit (or purl) the first stitch.

2 Knit (or purl) the next stitch.

3 Lift the prior stitch over this stitch and off the needle.

Repeat steps 2 and 3 till the end. When you have only one loop left on the right-hand needle, cut the yarn and pull it through this loop.

You'll get the best results with the chain bind-off if you bind off in pattern, which just means that you'll knit the knits and purl the purls on the bind-off row.

SUSPENDED BIND-OFF

I find this method pretty yucky, but if it's looseness and stretchiness you're after, this bind-off will give it to you and then some.

1 Start like the chain bind-off (above), but after you

insert your left-hand needle into the first stitch to lift it up and over the second stitch, don't drop it off the left-hand needle.

2 Work the next stitch on the left-hand needle (you'll need to work behind the stitch still hanging out on the needle for a knit, or in front of that stitch to make a purl).

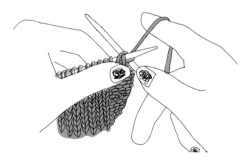

3 Drop both stitches off the left-hand needle. Continue across the row. This method also yields a chainlike edging, but each chain is elongated.

Personally, if I want stretch, I just bind off using a much larger needle, or very, very loosely, as if I were a bit drunk.

TUBULAR BIND-OFF FOR 1 X 1 RIBBING

You didn't think I'd leave you high and dry at bind-off time after we went through all that trouble to make a tubular cast-on (page 95), did you? Here's the corresponding bind-off. As with the tubular cast-on, this is meant to be used with 1 × 1 or 2 × 2 ribbing only (see directions for binding off 2 × 2 ribbing, facing page). But of course, it doesn't have to be paired with the tubular cast-on. For instance, if you've knit a crew neck on a sweater in ribbing, it would be just lovely to end it with this tubular bind-off: It will give the crew neck a much more finished look, and it will also be nice and stretchy so you don't have to worry about your head not fitting through.

Like the tubular cast-on, this bind-off actually creates a small tube of ribbing at the end of your knitting, and the tube is connected on both sides to the ribbing below it. It's as if your stitches are doing a back bend over the edge of your work, and it is magnificently cool. However, unlike the tubular cast-on, this bind-off is done with a tapestry needle instead of a knitting needle; you aren't so much knitting stitches off the needles as you are sewing them off.

Okay, enough jibberjabber, let's get to the bind-off. First of all, it's best if you knit four rows of tubular ribbing before you bind off, so you should end your 1 × 1 ribbing about two rows early (two rows of tubular ribbing are the same height as one row of regular ribbing). To do this, knit the knit stitches and slip the purl stitches with the yarn in front for four rows, if you are working flat. Unlike the tubular cast-on, the tubular bind-off can be worked in the round. To work tubular ribbing in the round, knit the knit stitches and slip the purl stitches with the yarn in front for the first round, then purl the purl stitches and slip the knit stitches with yarn in back for the second round. Repeat these two rounds. But whether you are knitting back and forth or in the round, what you are really doing is creating two layers of knitting here, a front and a back layer. When you connect these layers at the tippy top, voilà, you've created a tube!

After these four rows, you are going to graft the front and back layers of stitches together. The easiest way to do this is to slip all the purl stitches to one double-pointed or circular needle, and slip all the knit stitches to another double-pointed or circular needle, then just Kitchener stitch them together (see page 107).

If you want to go for the gold, you can graft the stitches together while they are still all on one needle. But let me warn you: Getting this right takes concentration and a bit of practice. Don't attempt it in the middle of your next Stitch 'n Bitch meeting; instead, save it for when you are in a quiet, well-lit spot. And before you work it on your actual knitting, I suggest working it on a test swatch. Once you get the rhythm of the stitching down, it's not that hard, but you don't want to mess it up on the real thing, because it's not easy to undo.

❶ Begin by breaking off the yarn and leaving a long tail—about three times the width of your piece. Thread this tail through a tapestry needle.

❷ Insert the needle into the first stitch on the knitting needle knitwise (if the first two stitches are both knit, insert the tapestry needle through both knit stitches together, knitwise), and drop that stitch off the knitting needle.

❸ Insert the tapestry needle into the second stitch on the left-hand needle—which will be a knit stitch—purlwise, pull the yarn through, and leave this stitch on the knitting needle.

❹ Insert the tapestry needle into the purl stitch you just skipped over, purlwise, and drop this stitch off the needle.

5 Now here's the toughie: Bring the tapestry needle behind the work, and insert it knitwise through the second stitch on the needle, which will be a purl stitch. Pull the yarn through.

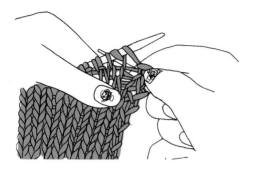

Repeat steps 2–5 until all stitches have been worked off the needles. While it may be difficult to discern a rhythm here, what you're actually doing is pulling your yarn through each stitch twice: The first time, the tapestry needle is inserted in the opposite direction of the type of stitch it is (purlwise on knit stitches, knitwise on purl stitches), and the second time, the tapestry needle is inserted in the same direction as the type of stitch (knitwise for knit stitches, purlwise for purl stitches), and this is when they are dropped from the needle.

TUBULAR BIND-OFF FOR 2 X 2 RIBBING

To bind off 2 × 2 ribbing, we first reverse what is done when a tubular cast-on is turned into 2 × 2 ribbing:

1 Knit and purl across the row as for 1 × 1 ribbing, swapping the order of knit and purl stitches as necessary (crossing the knit stitch over the purl stitch). Thus, you'll knit the first edging stitch, then knit the next stitch, purl the next stitch, and then you'll encounter a second purl stitch (this is 2 × 2 ribbing after all), when what you want is another knit stitch.

2 Slip this purl stitch and the following knit stitch onto the right-hand needle, insert the left-hand needle into the back of the purl stitch from behind, slip both of these

stitches off the right-hand needle, and catch the free-range knit stitch back onto the right-hand needle and slip it onto the left-hand needle. You've just reversed the order of your knit and purl stitches. Knit the knit stitch, purl the purl stitch. Next you'll get a knit and purl, just as you want 'em. After that, you'll need to swap your stitches again.

Once that's done, work two rows of tubular ribbing as for 1 × 1 tubular bind-off, then bind off as for 1 × 1 ribbing with a tapestry needle.

KNIT-TOGETHER BIND-OFF (AKA LACE BIND-OFF, KNIT BIND-OFF, OR DECREASE BIND-OFF)

The following bind-off works well for ribbing but is even better for cable patterns because it can keep them from flaring out like 1970s bell-bottoms when you bind them off. In fact, you can use the chain bind-off over any stockinette sections and switch to this bind-off over only the cable stitches to get a really nice effect. It is also quite useable for lacework, where you want some—but not too much—stretch, and it leaves a nice edging.

1 Knit two stitches together through their back loops.

2 Put the resulting loop back onto the left-hand needle.

Continue steps 1 and 2 until all stitches have been bound off.

SEWN BIND-OFF

Here's a favorite for all-over lace projects, such as shawls and the like. After knitting your last row, cut your yarn to a length of three times the width of the area you need to bind off. Thread the yarn through a tapestry needle and follow these directions:

1 Insert the tapestry needle purlwise through the first two stitches on the needle. Pull the yarn through.

2 Reinsert the needle into the first stitch knitwise and drop that stitch off the needle. Repeat steps 1 and 2 until all stitches have been bound off.

RUSSIAN LACE BIND-OFF (AKA PURL BIND-OFF)

This one is very similar to the knit-together bind-off (page 101), but it's worked a bit more loosely, and by purling instead of knitting, it gives you a very lovely, stretchy, non-distorting bind-off for your lace projects.

1 Purl two stitches together.

2 Loosen up the resulting loop and place it back on the left-hand needle.

Continue steps 1 and 2 until all stitches have been bound off.

EDGING BIND-OFF

Let's say you want to add an edging to your work, the kind of edging that is knit in a narrow band (as so many lace edgings are worked), or just a band of garter stitch, or moss stitch. You could bind off all your stitches, knit up the edging until it's long enough, then sew the edging onto the bound-off edge. Or you could knit the edging right onto the knitting, without binding anything off. Sounds more appealing, doesn't it? Better yet, it's exceptionally simple.

1 Cast on as many stitches at the end of your row as you need for your edging (or you could cast on stitches at the beginning of your row if required).

2 Knit your edging with these edging stitches, and when you get to the last stitch (the first one you cast on), just knit (or purl) it together with the following live stitch. If necessary to keep things flat and even, you can knit it together with two live stitches. Eventually, you'll run out of live stitches, and your edging will be done.

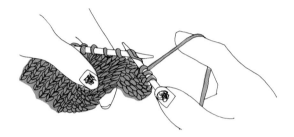

A similar technique can be used to knit an edging onto stitches that have already been bound off (see instructions for attached I-cord edging, page 110). In that instance, instead of knitting the last stitch together with the first live stitch, pick up a stitch from the unbound edge, and decrease a corresponding stitch from the edging.

PICOT BIND-OFF

Is this a practical bind-off that you will find yourself using all the time? No. Is it a lovely bind-off that you will find reasons to use just because it is so purty? Yes, that it is.

A picot bind-off is gorgeous at the end of sleeves or sweaters knit from the top down, especially children's sweaters, or as an edging around a neckline. Best of all, it gives a dainty, fancy look but is dead simple to execute.

1 Beginning with the first stitch of the row, cast on two stitches using the knit cast-on.

❷ Bind off these two stitches using the chain bind-off, and bind off one more stitch, leaving one loop on the right-hand needle.

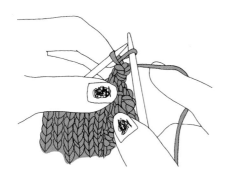

❸ Transfer the loop on the right-hand needle to the left-hand needle.

❹ Cast on two stitches using the knit cast-on.

Repeat steps 2–4.

This method will produce picot stitches that are all right next to each other and, depending on what kind of stitch you used for your knitted fabric, this may be too many picots in too small of a space—they will make the edge of your work flare out. To correct this, place more stitches in between the picots by binding off a few additional stitches, using the chain bind-off method, before making the next picot.

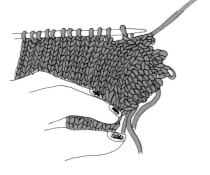

3-NEEDLE BIND-OFF

Like the edging bind-offs above, this one manages to kill two birds with one stone. And the first bird in this case is

binding off; the second bird is connecting two pieces of knitting to each other.

To work it, you'll need two sets of "live" stitches on two different needles, and, of course, you'll also need a third needle. (Duh!) Each needle should have the same number of stitches. This is great for binding off the shoulders of a sweater—instead of binding off the back, just put the last row of stitches on stitch holders and do the same with the front. Then you can work your three-needle bind-off on each shoulder.

You can make this bind-off so that it doesn't show by holding your needles with the right sides of the two pieces of knit fabric facing each other. Or, if you prefer, make it visible by holding your needles so that the wrong sides of the knit fabric face each other.

❶ Insert a third needle into the first stitch from each needle at the same time, and knit them together. Or, if you are working purl stitches, insert the needle purlwise into both of these stitches and purl them together.

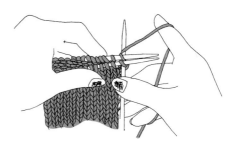

❷ Continue as for the chain bind-off, knitting (or purling) the next two stitches together, then lifting the first loop on the needle up and over this new loop, and off of the needle.

❸ This bind-off creates a chain of stitches at the top of your work, with the knit side facing one way and the purl side facing the other way. If you want it to look similar on both the front and back of your work, alternate knitting together, then purling together your stitches, and binding off in knit and purl (you're really binding off in 1 × 1 ribbing).

More or Less

A SMORGASBORD OF INCREASES AND DECREASES

Of course you already know ssk, and k2tog. You probably also know the make 1 increase, and the bar increase (knit into front and back of the same stitch). In the lace chapter, you were introduced to a whole bunch of other decreases, including left, right, and center double decreases, and the increase you can make with a yarn over (which leaves a hole).

But there are still a few more ways to increase and decrease, and they are worth adding to your repertoire, Some are decorative, and some blend invisibly in with your fabric. Some lean left and some lean right. Some are easier to make, some are more complex. Which increase or decrease you use is largely up to you, so if any of these are new to you, try them out. You may discover a new way of doing something that you like much more than what you've been using all along.

INCREASES

MAKE 1

You already know the make 1, but you may not realize that there is a right-leaning and a left-leaning way to make it.

Right-leaning:

With the right-hand needle, lift up the horizontal strand between the last stitch and the next stitch from the front and transfer it to the left-hand needle by inserting the left-hand needle into the loop from back to front.

Knit through the front loop to twist it.

Left-leaning:

With the right-hand needle, lift up the horizontal strand between the last stitch and the next stitch from the front and transfer it to the left-hand needle by inserting the left-hand needle into the loop from front to back. Knit through the back loop to twist it.

BAR INCREASE

You probably know this one, but what you might not know is that it is technically a right-leaning increase. To make it, knit into the front loop of the stitch but don't drop it off the needle; then knit into the back loop.

This is called the "bar increase" because it leaves a little bar—a horizontal strand of yarn across the front of the stitch, which results when you knit into the back loop.

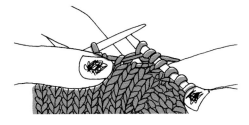

The benefit here is that you can clearly see where you made your increases and thereby easily count how many you've done.

You can also make this increase on the purl side: Just purl into the front and back of the stitch (purling into the back of a purl stitch can be quite a hassle, but if you ask a few of your fingers to lend a helping hand, you can make it happen).

KNIT AND PURL INCREASE

Like the bar increase above, this one also leaves a little bar. But unlike the bar increase, it has left- and right-leaning versions.

Right-leaning:

Purl, leaving the stitch on the left needle, then knit into the front loop of the same stitch.

Left-leaning:

Knit, leaving the stitch on the left needle, then purl into the front loop of the same stitch.

LIFTED INCREASE

This increase has both a left- and a right-leaning version, and can be pretty invisible.

Right-leaning:

Turn down your left-hand needle so you can see the purl bumps at the back of your work. Insert your right-hand needle, from the top down, into the purl bump at the base of the first stitch on your left-hand needle. Knit the stitch, then knit the stitch on the left-hand needle.

Left-leaning:

Knit one stitch. Insert the left-hand needle into the left leg of the stitch *below* the stitch you just dropped off the needle (not the stitch you just made), from the back. Knit through the back of this stitch.

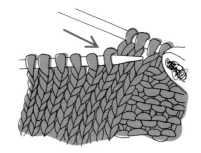

ROW-BELOW INCREASE

This increase may leave a bit of a hole.

Right-leaning:

Knit into the stitch below the next stitch on the needle, then knit into the next stitch.

Left-leaning:

Knit into the next stitch on the needle but don't drop it off the needle. Knit into the stitch below, then drop both stitches off the needle.

DECREASES

For all intents and purposes, the k2tog for the right-leaning decrease and the skp or ssk for the left-leaning decrease are all you'll ever need. (If you're making lace, you'll also need the double decreases covered in the lace chapter.) Most folks use the two left-leaning decreases interchangeably, and it's true: If you look at the results of these decreases carefully, you'll see that they have the same exact structure. However, the slip-knit-pass-slipped-stitch-over version is always a bit more visible than the other one, because you are stretching that loop out a bit when you pass the slipped stitch over. The slip, slip knit is really the more exact match for the k2tog, because it doesn't pull on any of the loops. What you may not have realized is that there is a right-leaning decrease that is a better match for the slip, knit, pass-slipped-stitch-over as well. Each of these methods is shown below.

KNIT TWO TOGETHER DECREASE (AKA KNIT DECREASE)

Right-leaning:

Knit two stitches together.

Left-leaning (ssk):

Slip the first stitch as if to knit; slip the next stitch as if to knit. Insert the left needle into the front legs of these two stitches, and knit them together.

DECREASE INVOLVING SLIPPING, KNITTING, AND PASSING STITCHES OVER EACH OTHER (AKA SLIP DECREASE)

Left-leaning:

Slip the first stitch knitwise, knit the next stitch, pass the slipped stitch over the next stitch, and drop it off the needle.

Right-leaning:

This is the surprise decrease you've probably never heard of: Knit one stitch, then transfer this stitch back to the left needle without twisting it. Pass the next stitch on the *left-hand* needle over this stitch and off the needle. Slip the stitch back to the right-hand needle purlwise.

TWISTED DECREASE

The left-leaning version of this one looks more like k2tog than either of the options above and is sometimes preferred by lace knitters. However, it's called "twisted decrease" for a reason: It twists the legs of the stitches, and this may or may not be desirable in your work. Again, it may come as a surprise to know that there is also a right-leaning version of this decrease.

Left-leaning:

Knit two stitches together through their back loops.

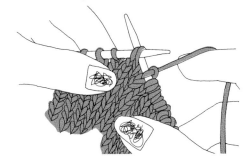

Right-leaning:

Slip the next two stitches, one at a time, as if to knit. Transfer these stitches back to the left-hand needle without untwisting them. Knit them together through their front loops.

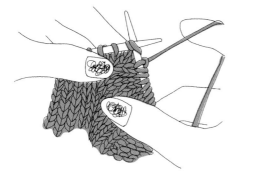

if YOU CAN stand the Heat

KITCHENER STITCH EVERY WHICH WAY

You've most likely encountered, and probably already used, the Kitchener stitch to graft two sets of live stitches together; it's very often used to close off the toes of socks that are knit top-down. When you've used it, you've probably used the stitch to graft knit stitches together. The Kitchener stitch basically connects the two pieces of knitting by creating a new row of knitting in between them. Only thing is, you create this row of knitting with a tapestry needle and some yarn. When done correctly, the connection looks seamless.

But what if you have to connect two sets of ribbing stitches? Or pieces of fabric knit in garter stitch? Yes, Virginia, there really is a way to use Kitchener stitch in these instances.

We'll begin with a refresher course in Kitchener stitch for two pieces of knitting done in stockinette stitch, then move on to other variations.

KITCHENER STITCH FOR STOCKINETTE

Hold two knitting needles together with their points facing to the right, and the wrong sides of the fabric together. Break off a long length of yarn from either the front or the back, and thread a tapestry needle.

❶ Insert the tapestry needle into the first stitch on the front needle as if to knit, and slip this stitch off the needle.

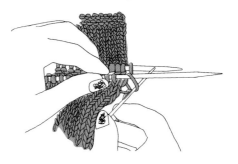

❷ Insert the tapestry needle into the next stitch on the front needle as if to purl, but leave the stitch on the needle.

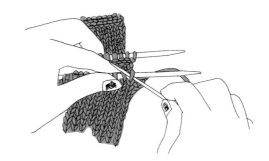

❸ Insert the tapestry needle into the first stitch on the back needle as if to purl, and drop the stitch off the needle.

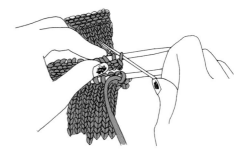

④ Insert the tapestry needle into the next stitch on the back needle as if to knit, and leave the stitch on the needle.

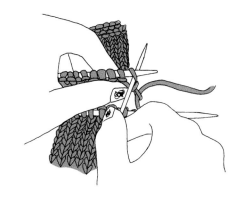

Repeat steps 1–4 until the end.

KITCHENER STITCH FOR REVERSE STOCKINETTE

Okay, remember how I explained that Kitchener stitch basically creates a new knit row in between two knit rows? So here, instead of trying to create a new purl row in between two purl rows, just flip the dang thing the other way and work your Kitchener stitch as above. Easy peasy.

KITCHENER STITCH FOR GARTER STITCH

Although you create garter stitch by knitting every row, when you look at it from the front, what you are seeing is one knit row followed by one purl row. As a result, to graft two pieces of garter stitch fabric together using Kitchener stitch, you'll need one piece that has a knit row on top (if you pull down on your work a bit, you'll see the V's of the previous row below the stitches on the needle), and one piece that has a purl row on top (if you pull down on your work a bit, you'll see only purl bumps right underneath the stitches on the needle).

Make sure that the purl side is showing on the front needle and the knit side is showing on the back needle.

Break off a long length of yarn from either the front or the back, and thread a tapestry needle.

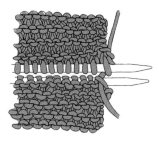

① Insert the tapestry needle into the first stitch on the front needle as if to knit, and drop that stitch off the needle.

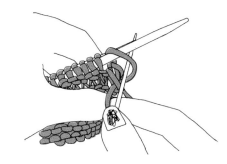

② Insert the tapestry needle into the next stitch on the front needle as if to purl, and leave that stitch on the needle.

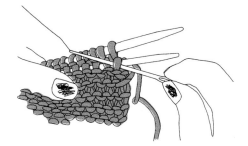

③ Insert the tapestry needle into the first stitch on the back needle as if to knit, dropping it off the needle.

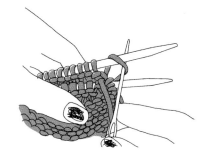

④ Insert the tapestry needle into the next stitch on the back needle as if to purl, and leave that stitch on the needle.

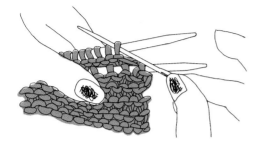

Repeat steps 1–4 until the end.

KITCHENER STITCH FOR RIBBING

Okay, listen to me carefully: When you are grafting two pieces of knit fabric together using Kitchener stitch, you are not really connecting the heads of the stitches on each side together—that's not really possible because they would sort of crash into each other. Instead, what you are really doing is connecting the heads of the stitches on one piece of fabric with the stitches that are formed *in between* the stitches on the other piece of fabric. The stitches in between knit stitches can easily form either knit or purl stitches; that's why you can graft in stockinette or garter stitch. It works like a charm. But when you have two pieces of ribbing, you really want the heads of each piece to connect to each other: You want the knits to continue as knits; you want the purls to continue as purls. Unfortunately, it can't be done. I didn't know this wasn't possible, and at one point spent hour upon hour trying to figure out how to graft ribbed fabric together. Even Mary Thomas, in her knitting classic, seems to think it's possible; it's obvious she never tried it herself. It simply isn't.

There is a passable alternative, though. To do it, you'll need two double-pointed needles and two stitch holders. Slip all the knit stitches to one double-pointed needle, and the purl stitches to a stitch holder.

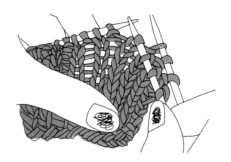

Do the same on the other piece of ribbing. Now, you can Kitchener stitch the two sets of knit stitches together. Afterward, turn your work around, slip the stitches that are on holders to two double-pointed needles, and Kitchener them together.

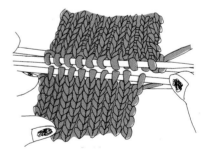

cords

There comes a time in every knitter's life when a cord of some sort is called for. They can be used to tie the earflaps of a hat around your head, or tie together the opening of a sweater or hoodie, or even as the handles of a bag. You have a number of options when making cords; here are some of the simplest:

CAST-ON, BIND-OFF CORD

This sneaky little cord is a nice one. Just cast on as many stitches as you think will make up the length of the cord, then bind off all these stitches on the very first row. There ya go: A cord is born.

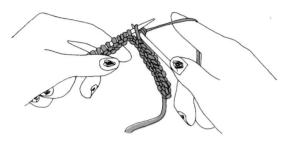

TWISTED CORD

This one's not even knit, but is nice. Cut a number of lengths of yarn three times as long as you'd like your cord to be. Tie these lengths of yarn together at each end with an overhand knot. Hang one end over a doorknob, stick a pencil through the other end, and turn, turn, turn, turn until that cord is as twisted as it can get, keeping tension on both ends as you twist. Then bring the two tied ends together and the cord will twist around itself, and stay that way. Secure both ends with a knot when you're done.

I-CORD

In this, the I is short for Idiot. Why? Cause it's so easy, even an idiot could do it. Or, because you are knitting without turning your needle, like an idiot might do.

To make it you need a pair of double-pointed needles. Cast on the number of stitches for your I-cord (usually a very small number, like three or five). Knit one row.

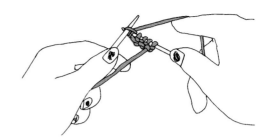

Now, don't turn your work, but instead just push all the stitches to the other end of the double-pointed needle and knit the row again.

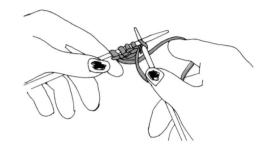

Be sure to pull your first knit stitch tight; it is really the stitch that is pulling this cord together into a tube.

ATTACHED I-CORD EDGING

An I-cord can also be knit right onto a piece of knit fabric to form a nice, rolled edging. There are a couple of ways to attach the I-cord as you are knitting it.

Method 1:

Knit to one stitch before the end of the I-cord, slip the last stitch. Pick up a stitch from the fabric, knit that stitch, and pass the slipped stitch over it and off the needle.

Method 2:

Knit to one stitch before the end of the I-cord. Slip the last stitch knit-wise, pick up a loop from the fabric, and slip that stitch knitwise onto the right-hand needle,

then insert the left-hand needle under the front legs of these two stitches and knit them together.

buttonHoLe Surfers

When it comes to making buttonholes, you have a lot of options. Unfortunately, not all of them are good ones. Many patterns will instruct you to make the classic two-row buttonhole, which is done as follows: On the first row, you work up to where the buttonhole should start, knit the next two stitches, then lift the first stitch over the second, dropping it off the needle. Bind off the number of stitches you need for the buttonhole this way, and continue working to the end of the row. On the second row, you work to the gap made by the bound-off stitches, then cast on, using the backward loop method, the same number of stitches that you bound off, and work your way to the end of the row. Buttonhole made: The bottom of the buttonhole is the bound-off stitches, the top is the cast-on stitches.

Although this method of buttonhole making is easy to remember, the results are a hot mess. There is a visible bump at the beginning of the bound-off stitches and an ugly loose strand at the start of the cast-on stitches. For this kind of buttonhole to be workable, it needs to be firmed up by sewing all the way around it, using something called a buttonhole stitch (page 113). Not fun.

Luckily, knitters dissatisfied with this subpar buttonhole have come up with alternatives. Each improves on the original buttonhole by making the bind-off and cast-on prettier and more sturdy, and also by keeping any random strands from forming. The best also see to it that the bind-off and cast-on edges are mirror images of each other, and that they don't flip to the outside like a pair of flapping lips, but instead form neat and tidy edges that roll inward.

I've tried out just about all of these, and I have to say that the undisputed champion is a method I first came across in Maggie Righetti's brilliant book *Knitting in Plain English*. This is the one I'm going to share with you now. It's done in one row instead of two and it's easy to execute, but not so easy to remember. So write down these directions on a slip of paper and just keep it in your knitting supply bag for when you need them.

THE BESTEST BUTTONHOLE

1 Work to the point where the buttonhole should start.

2 Slip the next stitch knitwise.

3 Bring the yarn to the front of the work.

4 Slip the next stitch knitwise.

5 Pass the first slipped stitch over this stitch and drop it off the needle. First stitch "bound off" for the buttonhole.

Repeat steps 4 and 5 until the correct number of stitches have been bound off.

6 Slip the last stitch from the right-hand needle back to the left-hand needle. Turn your work around.

7 Cast on one more stitch than you bound off, using a variation of the knit cast-on method in which you purl, rather than knit, the stitches that you are casting on. Turn the work around.

8 Slip the first stitch on the left-hand needle to the right-hand needle,

and being careful not to pull it out too much, lift the extra cast-on stitch up and over this slipped stitch and drop it off the needle. Slip the stitch back onto the left-hand needle. Continue working to the end of the row.

VERTICAL BUTTONHOLES

The above buttonhole is a horizontal one. That is, it creates a horizontal slit, one that's parallel to the rows of knitting in your knit fabric. However, sometimes you may need to make a buttonhole oriented the other way in your fabric—vertically, or perpendicular to your rows. Of course, the buttonhole will run horizontally when worn, but if you are knitting a front band onto a sweater from stitches you picked up from the side edge of a cardigan, in order for the buttonhole to lie horizontally, you need to knit it vertically.

Making a vertical buttonhole is very easy, although a bit annoying, especially because you need to be working on all these buttonholes at the same time, at different points along your row. And every time you want a buttonhole to start, you have to stop knitting at that point, pick up a new ball (or long length) of yarn, and go on knitting. You may end up with quite a few lengths of yarn at the same time if you are knitting a buttonhole band that has more than one buttonhole in it (as most do). Just keep knitting back and forth this way, dropping the yarn on the last stitch before

the buttonhole, picking up the yarn on the other side, and continuing to work the row. When the buttonhole is as long as you want it to be, you can go back to working all the way across the row with a single ball of yarn.

There are some steps you can take to make this type of buttonhole look its best. The first is to make sure you are creating neat selvedges at either edge of the buttonhole. My preferred method of selvedge making is to be sure to pull my yarn tight when my needle is inserted into the stitch that follows the edge stitch, before I actually make that second stitch. The other trick is to add a new stitch on the second side of the buttonhole with a lifted right increase (see page 105). That stitch becomes the edge stitch on the left side of the buttonhole, and when you are done, you knit the edge stitch on the right side together with this extra stitch on the left side, which both gets rid of the extra stitch and also makes a nice, tight closure at the top of the buttonhole.

The easiest buttonhole of all is quite small, but might be all you need for a small button, or a ball-shaped one. To make an eyelet buttonhole, make a yarn over followed by k2tog. That's it!

As I mentioned above, the two-row buttonhole, if you are determined to make it, requires some cleanup work at the end, and you might want to do the same for an eyelet buttonhole. To firm it up, just work a buttonhole stitch all the way around the opening, making your stitches as even and neat as possible.

Buttonhole Stitch

The buttonhole stitch is basically the same as the blanket stitch, only you're making it much smaller. Start by making a few small straight stitches with a tapestry needle at the right corner of the buttonhole, at the back of the work, to tack your yarn in place. Bring the tapestry needle through the buttonhole to the front. Working from right to left, insert your needle into the fabric just below the lower edge of the buttonhole, then bring it up again through the buttonhole, holding the yarn behind the needle point. Make the next stitch just slightly to the left of this first stitch in the same way—inserting your needle down just below the edge of the buttonhole, and bringing it up through the buttonhole, holding the yarn behind the needle.

When you get to the edge, make one or two stitches in the side of the buttonhole, and then along the top of the buttonhole, turning your work as you go.

If your buttonhole is nothing more than an eyelet, you can try just whipstitching around the edges to reinforce it.

Short rows

What do you do when you want to add a bit of fullness to a piece of knit fabric? Say, for instance, that you are particularly well endowed up top, but if you make a sweater to fit your chest it becomes too wide altogether. What you really want is just to add a bit more fabric around the boob area without having to add more knit fabric to the entire body of the sweater. What if you could knit a few more rows just around the bust without adding more rows to the overall length of the sweater? Something a bit pouchlike that would give the boobs some more room to spread out without pulling the whole sweater up?

Yes, you can do that. It's called short-rowing, and it's used to do exactly this—add fullness at the bust of a sweater, and for other pouchlike extrusions in a tube of fabric, such as the heel of a sock, or even shoulders, when something like a set-in sleeve cap is being created on a sleeve that is knit from the top down. This technique can also be used to add a bit of fullness at the back neck of a sweater that is being knit in the round, or in the front of a sweater to make room for a beer belly.

The idea behind short rows is simple: You add some fullness to knit fabric by slipping in a few extra rows in the center of your fabric. These rows don't extend all the way to the edges of your fabric, and that's why they're called short rows. And, just like they sound, they are worked by knitting or purling to a certain point in a row, then turning around and working back in the opposite direction, and turning around again before the end of that row is reached. If you picture in your mind what would happen if you did this a number of times, you can see that it would create some pouching.

But also, picture what happens if you knit and then turn around in the middle of a row and start knitting in the other direction. You're going to get a hole—and we need to do something to keep our short row connected to the rest of the fabric. What if there was a way to hitch our turning row to the rest of the fabric somehow? In short rowing, that's exactly what you do: You work your way across a certain number of stitches, then wrap your yarn around the next stitch, sort of like hitching a horse to a post, before turning and heading back the other way. This connects your short-row fabric to the rest of the fabric without creating a hole. When you are ready to work across all of the stitches again, you knit this wrap (the "hitch") together with the stitch its wrapped around in such a way that the wrap falls to the back of the work, where it won't be seen.

WRAPPING & TURNING

This method works for either knitting or purling.

1 Work to the point where you want to turn around, but before turning, slip the next stitch to the right-hand needle purlwise.

2 Transfer the yarn, between the needle points, to the opposite side of the work,

slip the stitch on the right-hand needle back to the left-hand needle,

and transfer the yarn to the opposite side of the work again.

3 Turn your work and knit or purl in the opposite direction.

Do you see what you did with that yarn swapping and stitch slipping? All you did was just wrap the yarn around a stitch in the fabric that you aren't going to work right now in order to connect it with the part of the fabric that will have some short rows.

HIDING THE WRAP

When you have finished short-rowing, you will go back to working full rows of knitting or purling. When you do this, however, you need to work the wrap that's wound around a stitch together with its stitch, and you need to do this in such a way that the wrap falls to the back of the fabric, where it won't be seen. This is done a bit differently for purling than for knitting.

When purling:

Work up to the wrapped stitch. With the right-hand needle, insert the needle under the back strand of the wrap and place it onto the left-hand needle.

Now purl the wrap and its stitch together. This keeps the wrap at the back of the work.

When knitting:

Work up to the wrapped stitch. Insert the needle up into the wrap from underneath, and then into the knit stitch it is wrapped around. Knit these stitches together. This pops the wrap behind the knit stitch, to the back of the work.

PART II

How to create
your own patterns

diY: design it Yourself

**SKETCHING,
SWATCHING,
MEASURING,
AND DRAFTING**

Say you have an idea for something you want to make and just can't find a pattern that matches what's in your head. Or maybe you bought some yarn that is simply itching to be made into something very specific. How do you translate your idea into something made of yarn? Although it may seem overwhelming, the basic challenge in creating a knitting pattern is figuring out how to knit a specific kind of fabric into a very specific shape (or shapes), and this process can be divided into two main steps. The first is the "designing" part of the process—when you find your inspiration, sketch ideas, and play with yarn. The second is the "drafting" part of the process, when you turn those sketches and swatches into an actual pattern that can be knit. This is when you figure out your stitch and row gauge, multiply them by particular measurements, and write it all up in a set of knitting instructions that, when followed, will result in the exact thing you had sketched out.

Step 1:
dream a
Little dream

DESIGNING YOUR PROJECT

In the design phase of a knitting project, you work out the shape of the garment you want to make, as well as the kind of fabric out of which you'd like to make it. This is what some folks would consider the creative part of developing a knitting pattern. It's when you sketch and swatch—and swatch and swatch and swatch. Once you have the idea in mind, sketching your project-to-be might not take that much time, but swatching to arrive at the right combination of needle size, yarn, and stitch pattern to create the fabric you want *does* take time, and plenty of it. So go slow with this part—it's the key to everything else. And enjoy it, too. Because once you've determined your shape and your fabric, you're pretty much done with the designing part.

SKETCH AND KVETCH

SKETCHING YOUR DESIGN

Most designers begin with inspiration. Yours can be as straightforward as a sweater you saw in a catalog and want to re-create, or as spirited as a pastry that gave you an idea for a hat. However you arrived at your idea, you'll want to sketch it out. The quality of your sketch doesn't matter one bit; what matters is that it contain key information about the pieces of fabric that need to be made—and in what shapes and sizes—in order to bring your project to life. When sketching a scarf, for instance, you might want to sketch it being worn by a person (it can be nothing more than a stick figure). That way you can begin to work out how long you'd like it to be. Once it's wrapped around the person's neck, how far should each end reach? Above the

boobs? Below the boobs? To the hips? You can sketch in a simplistic version of your stitch pattern as well. If you're thinking of a double-knit scarf with a repeating insect motif, how large are the insects? Sketch them in roughly. And the width of the scarf—is it as wide as the neck is long, from the shoulder to the chin? Or is it narrower? Each of these design details holds important information you'll need when you start working out your schematic— the illustration that shows the exact dimensions of your scarf—as well as how large your insect chart should be.

When you're sketching a sweater, you'll need to make quite a few more decisions that will impact your final pattern. What do you want for a neckline? A simple crew neck, a deep scoop neck, a wide boatneck, a V-neck, a turtleneck? And how will the neck be finished? With simple ribbing or a picot stitch? Will your sweater have a collar? A hood? Then you'll want to think about the edging at the bottom of your sweater and sleeves. Many sweaters are knit in stockinette stitch or a variation thereof, and stockinette has a tendency to roll. Unless you want your sweater to look (and act) like a window shade, rolling up when you don't want it to, you'll need some sort of edging at the bottom to keep it hanging straight. Many sweaters start with a ribbed edging, which not only straightens out the bottom but also ensures that the bottom of the sweater and sleeves cling snugly to the body and wrists. You can also work a simple moss stitch, which won't pull in at all, at the bottom of both body and sleeves. There are tons of other edgings to consider that you can find in books on the subject.

But of all the decisions you make during your sketching phase, the biggie is how the sleeves will attach to the body. Although it may surprise you, this is one of the main architectural challenges of sweater construction, and in the past 300 years or so, knitters have come up with four basic solutions to this problem, each defined by how the sleeves are attached to the body: drop-shoulder, raglan, yoked, and set-in sleeve. Each method has its strengths and weaknesses, as described below, and has particular implications for your design. Which one you choose will depend on a variety of factors, including how you'd like the sweater to fit, what kind of stitch design you're featuring, and what kind of knitting you prefer (in the round or flat), so deciding on a sweater type is something you'll want to do now, while you're sketching. It's a bit like building a house. There are really only a few basic house types—ranch, colonial, Victorian, for example—and each type requires a different set of blueprints. But it is the details—the siding, the paint color, the number of turrets, the roofing material, the windows—that make each one different. In the later chapters in this part, I'll give you the directions—the blueprints, so to speak—for how to make each of these basic types of sweaters. It will be the details you choose—the stitch pattern, the yarn, the colors, the fiber, the neckline, the edgings—that will make your design unique.

DROP-SHOULDER SWEATER

The drop-shoulder is one of the oldest styles of sweaters. With this one, the body is a simple tube with a hole for the neck, and the sleeves are two tapered tubes that get connected directly to the body. The body tube remains the same width from the bottom of the sweater to the top and is based on the chest size. But because shoulders are narrower than chests (and when knitters talk about the width of your shoulders, they mean only how far apart your shoulder *sockets* are), the upper part of this type of sweater

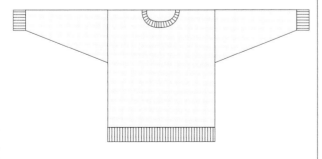

hangs down over the tops of the arms a bit (hence the name "drop-shoulder"), and the sleeves hang down off that.

Because the drop-shoulder is made of the simplest shapes—rectangles and trapezoids—it's the easiest to design. The fact that the sweater body is a big rectangle makes it a wonderful canvas for complex colorwork or for featuring a stitch pattern, such as involved cablework.

However, because it's not fitted at the shoulders, a drop-shoulder sweater has a pretty baggy shape—comfy and cozy rather than sleek and sexy. Think about it: The sweater is wider than your shoulder sockets, which means it extends past your armpits, and that extra fabric has to go somewhere. With your arm down, that fabric just kind of folds over itself—hence, bunching at the underarm. For this reason, the drop-shoulder style is often made as an oversize sweater. With roomy sleeves, there is plenty of space between your armpit and the fabric, so the bunching is less problematic. There is a modification of this style of sweater—often called, appropriately, a modified drop-shoulder—in which this underarm bunching is reduced a bit by creating a very rudimentary armhole in the body of the sweater. With either a drop-shoulder or a modified drop-shoulder, you're pretty much limited in your sleeve length. You can make long sleeves, obviously, or possibly even three-quarter sleeves, but a cap sleeve would be impossible (since the sweater body kind of already forms a cap at the top).

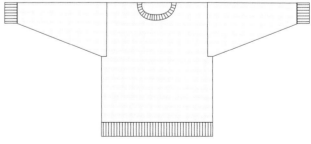

RAGLAN SWEATER

The raglan is also one of the older styles of sweaters and was probably originally only knit in the round, although these days many patterns will present it as something you knit flat. The raglan style takes care of the issues of the unsightly underarm bunching that is the curse of the drop-shoulder style by decreasing stitches on both the body and the sleeve from the armpit to the neck, resulting in a closer fit. Imagine a navel orange cut into quarters. If you think of the peel as the sweater and the navel as the neckhole, then the way the four pieces come together at the top is pretty much the way a raglan sweater is constructed.

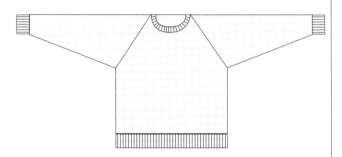

With a raglan, the angles that form the top of the sleeves and the top of the body are exactly the same—that's the only way to fit them together perfectly (remember the orange peel). This means that the number of stitches decreased after the armpit, and the number of rows to decrease them over, is exactly the same on all four pieces. And because each piece has exactly the same number of rows, it is easy to match any horizontal stitch patterns—such as stripes, knit and purl patterns, or beading—across all four pieces. However, the raglan shaping forms diagonal lines that cut across the sweater from the armpit to the neckline, and they will interrupt any vertical stitch patterns, such as cables, that you might have in your design. On the other hand, the decreases at these points can be made quite prominent to become a design element. For example, the sleeves can be one color and the body another, or the body knit in one stitch pattern and the sleeves plain (or vice versa). And with a raglan sweater, you can make your sleeves any length you want to. (Of course, since the top of the sleeve forms part of the body, a sleeveless raglan is out of the question.)

CIRCULAR YOKE SWEATER

In many ways, the shape of a yoked sweater is similar to that of a raglan sweater, except that rather than having the decreases on the sleeves and body made in a diagonal line, the sweater is knit all in one piece from armpit to neck—the yoke—and the decreases are spaced evenly and distributed over fewer rounds (think of that orange peel again, only without its being sliced up at all). As a result, the decreases blend in and don't form any lines between the armpit and neck. None of this much changes the fit of a yoke sweater versus a raglan sweater, but it does mean that you can have a design that travels around the neckline and across the shoulders—like a stranded colorwork design of kitties and skulls—without its being interrupted. A sweater with a circular yoke is almost always knit in the round, so if you don't like circular knitting, avoid this design.

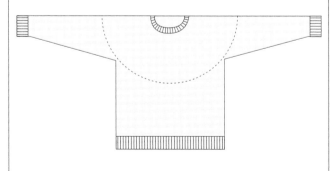

SET-IN SLEEVE SWEATER

Many designers fear the sweater with set-in sleeves. That's because the geometry needed to chart the cap of the sleeve so that it fits perfectly into the armhole gives some knitters major math anxiety. But it really isn't that difficult, and it's worth taking on, because set-in sleeves allow for many more variations in fit and sleeve length—long, short, three-quarter, cap, or none at all. And because the sleeve fits as comfortably into the sweater as your arm fits into its socket, these sweaters can be made very, very fitted.

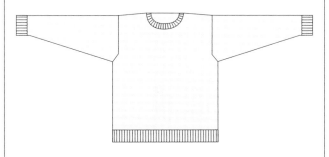

The set-in sleeve does not have a very long history in knitting and in fact borrows the idea for armhole and sleeve-cap shaping from the world of—gasp!—sewing. In these sweaters, decreases are made at the top of the sleeves to form a nicely rounded cap, and the body of the sweater is created with an armhole into which this sleeve cap will fit perfectly. Because of this armhole, vertical designs on the body will be interrupted, although not nearly as much as they are in raglan sweaters. And because there are never as many rows in the sleeve cap as there are in the armhole (more on this later), it is impossible to have any horizontal patterns (stripes, etc.) run uninterrupted across both the body and the sleeves.

Aside from the fact that it may require a bit more time at the charting stage, sweaters with set-in sleeves are a great solution for most designs; they offer a nice, wide canvas for any kind of stitch pattern you might like on the front and back of your sweater, and the sleeves fit comfortably, without any excess underarm fabric.

SWATCH WATCH
DECIDING ON YOUR KNIT FABRIC

Once upon a time, you may have hated knitting gauge swatches. But that was before you decided to try your hand at design. Because as a designer, you are going to learn to *love* to swatch—or you'd better hang up your designer's hat right now.

Swatching as a designer is much more fun than just checking your gauge before knitting a project. The latter can sometimes feel like homework that some invisible teacher is demanding you complete before you go out and play. But when you're trying to come up with the perfect fabric for a knit design, swatching is a process of discovery. In fact, it's an adventure. Here's where you'll decide on your color scheme, your texture, and the drape and feel of your fabric. And for design swatches, you don't have to follow any rules. Later on, once you've determined your ideal stitch pattern, yarn choice, and needle size, you can make the master swatch from which you'll get those all-important stitch and row gauge counts. But for now, you're just exploring.

But where to start? If you're looking to do simple stockinette, you might want to begin with the needle size suggested on the yarn ball band. Cast on enough stitches to make a good-size swatch—at least 5" wide—and knit for several inches (5" is a good amount). To keep things from getting too curly-whirly (stockinette likes to roll up on itself), knit the first four rows after casting on in garter stitch, and knit the first four and last four stitches of each row in garter stitch as well. Knit the last four rows in garter stitch, and bind off.

When you're done, feel up your swatch. Is it loose? Is it stiff? If it were made into a sweater, how would it hang off your body? Would it stick out from your boobs like a barrel, or would it gently cling to your curvy bits? When you place it over a finger pointed in the air, does it hang down like a tent (meaning it has quite a bit of "drape") or stick straight out like a Frisbee (no drape at all)? If you're swatching for a knit jacket or a bag, you might want your fabric to be rather solid and a bit stiff. If you're swatching for an elegant sweater, you'd want it more drapey. Now, make another swatch in the same way, but this time using a needle one size smaller, for tighter fabric, or larger, for looser fabric. Is that more to your liking? Are you having fun yet? Don't forget to label your swatches (I use the kinds of tags that folks use for tag sales), noting the needle size you used to knit each.

The process is similar if you are testing out stitch patterns. Work it for a few inches, break it up with a few rows of garter stitch, and continue with a different size needle. If you think your fabric will change quite a bit after blocking (lace definitely does), block it and see how you like it then.

Swatching also gives you the opportunity to alter stitch patterns as you see fit. The bobbles in that bobble stitch you like may need to be spaced farther apart in order to keep your fabric from looking like a knit version of gooseflesh. The cable pattern may benefit from throwing in another couple of rows between stitch crossings. Maybe the lace panel could use some faggoting (see "Who You Calling a Faggot?", page 68) to better separate it from the stockinette stitch that surrounds it.

Swatching to a knitwear designer is like sketching to a painter. You may want to add something here and subtract something there (unlike a painter, however, you can't erase your sketch; instead, you have to reknit a new swatch for each change). Because no matter what your stitch book shows you or your yarn ball band tells you, you can never be sure what you'll end up with when you combine needles, yarn, and stitch. In that way, swatching is like a box of chocolates: You never know what you're gonna get.

Step 2: talk Nerdy to Me

PATTERN DRAFTING

Once you've finalized the shape you want your project to be, along with the stitch pattern, needle size, and yarn you want to use to create the fabric, it's time to start figuring out how to knit your desired fabric into your desired shape. This is the math-y part of the pattern design process and will require truckloads of patience and precision. So tread slowly and carefully, and be sure to check your numbers before you start knitting. After all, there's nothing worse than making a mathematical error in your pattern and winding up with a sweater sporting armholes so tight they could double as tourniquets.

MEASURE TWICE, KNIT ONCE

CALCULATING YOUR GAUGE

When drafting a knitting pattern, the first things you'll need are the stitch and row gauges from your swatch. This process is a bit different for a stitch pattern where the stitches are easy to see (such as stockinette) than for stitch patterns where counting stitches and rows is more difficult (such as lace or cable stitches). For stockinette or other easy-to-count stitches, start with a nice, blocked, 5" × 5" swatch. Lay it down, relaxed and flat, and place a ruler on top of it. You want to take your measurements from the 2" at the center of the swatch, at least ½" in from the edge. Place pins at 0 and 2", and count the stitches in between the pins. Don't forget to count half-stitches as well, but that's as far as you need to take it; don't try to estimate what a third or a quarter of a stitch would look like. Take a measurement from a different area of your swatch as well, as a double check. Divide the number by 2 to get your stitches-per-inch gauge, and round it up or down to two decimal points. Do the same for your rows by laying your ruler vertically on your swatch.

For a lace, cable, or other stitch pattern where it's difficult to clearly see the stitches and rows, you want to start with a different type of swatch. In this case, make your swatch by casting on enough stitches to knit at least two full pattern repeats, and add eight stitches so you can still make your garter stitch edgings. Knit at least two pattern repeats vertically as well, or however many it takes to get at least 5" worth of fabric (but be sure to knit full repeats, so if the pattern is 14 rows, knit all 14 rows). The reason for two pattern repeats is that it gives a better average gauge than a single repeat would.

Block the swatch before measuring. Then measure the swatch width just inside your garter stitch edges, and divide that by the number of stitches you cast on minus 8 (the edge stitches) to get the number of stitches per inch. Measure the swatch length as well, leaving out your beginning and ending garter stitch rows, and divide by the number of rows you knit. This gives you the number of rows per inch.

MEASURING UP
TAKING BODY MEASUREMENTS FOR PATTERN DRAFTING

Once you've got your measurements from your swatch, you need another set of measurements as well—your own.

Not all sweater styles require all of the following measurements, but why not write everything down while you've got the measuring tape out? The numbers are sure to come in handy at some point. It's no sweat to take someone else's measurements, but if you need your own, ask a friend to help you out.

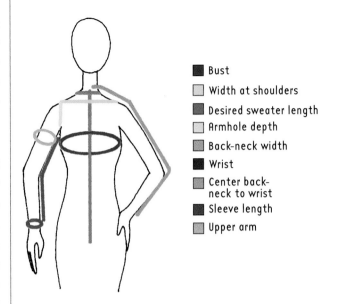

- ■ Bust
- □ Width at shoulders
- ■ Desired sweater length
- □ Armhole depth
- ■ Back-neck width
- ■ Wrist
- ■ Center back-neck to wrist
- ■ Sleeve length
- □ Upper arm

BUST: This is the chest at its widest point. If you're measuring a woman, be sure she's wearing a bra (if she plans to wear one with the sweater, that is), and measure around the widest point of the boobage. That pretty much means around the nipple area (same holds for dudes, too, but no bra is required).

WIDTH AT SHOULDERS (also called "cross-back width"): Feel around at the top of the shoulders till you feel a bump. Measure the distance, across the back, from this bump on the left to the bump on the right.

DESIRED SWEATER LENGTH: For this, it helps if the person holds a piece of string or a tape measure around the body at the point where he or she wants the sweater to end. Then feel around in the back of the neck till you find a little bump poking out—that's the top of the spine. Measure from that bump down to the bottom of the string/tape measure to determine how long the sweater should be.

ARMHOLE DEPTH: This is one of the most difficult, as well as most crucial, body measurements to take. The one thing nobody wants is to have an armhole that's too tight. But there are a number of factors that go into getting the correct measurement here. Before you start measuring, place one finger on that bump at the back of the neck that you used to measure sweater length, above, and another finger on the bump at the top of one of the shoulders, which you used to measure shoulder width, above. Notice something? The neck bone is higher than the shoulder bone—usually about an inch higher. Now, in some styles of sweaters—for instance, drop-shoulder and raglan—the armhole starts somewhere below the armpit and continues to the height of that neck bone. But others—such as fitted-sleeve-cap sweaters—have an armhole that begins somewhere below the armpit and then ends right there at the top of the shoulder, where the shoulder bump is. The sweater body continues, however, and doesn't end until the neck bump. The fabric on either side of the neck runs at an angle from the length at shoulder point to the length at the neckline, and this is called "shoulder shaping"—it offers a better fit. So, for sweaters with shoulder shaping, the armhole depth would be the measurement from the shoulder bump to the armpit, with about an inch added in so that the armhole doesn't jam right into the armpit. For raglan and drop-shoulder sweaters, however, the armhole is yet another inch deeper than this, because the armhole ends at the height of the neck instead of at the top of the shoulder.

I wish I could give you one simple way for measuring the armhole, but unfortunately, I can't. And because this is such a critical measurement, I'm going to give you a few options and a way to double-check your figures.

For the first method, have the person stick a knitting needle under his or her armpit, and measure from the bump on the shoulder down to the needle. Add at least an inch to this measurement to give the armpit some breathing room, and also so that the wearer will be able to raise his or her arms.

The second method tries to get an exact measurement of the armhole for those sweaters without shoulder shaping. Have the person hold a knitting needle in the armpit as above, then try to visualize an imaginary line running from the person's armpit straight across the back, parallel to the floor. Measure down from that bump on the back of the neck to this imaginary line. Add at least an inch to this measurement to keep the armhole from landing right in the wearer's armpit.

The third method is also for a sweater without shoulder shaping, and you can use it alone or as a double check to the above method. To take it, just jam the tape measure into the person's armpit and measure down to where he or she wants the sweater to end. Subtract this measurement from the "desired sweater length" you took above for the armhole depth. But again, add at least an inch to the armhole depth here to keep the armhole from cutting off the wearer's blood supply.

BACK-NECK WIDTH: Hold a tape measure straight across the back of the person's neck where it attaches to the body.

WRIST: For this, you might think you should measure a person's wrist. But since the entire hand needs to fit through the entire length of the sleeve when he or she is putting the sweater on, without getting stuck anywhere along the way, it's safest to measure around the knuckles with the hand closed in a fist, which is the widest the hand would ever be.

Alternatively, you can measure around the wrist about 2½" above the wrist bones and add an inch to that (to give room for the hand to fit through). The bottom of most sleeves will have ribbing, so the sweater will lie closer to the wrist when worn, but we're actually measuring how wide the sleeve needs to be *above* the ribbing (ribbing itself is very stretchy and can expand to at least this width).

CENTER BACK-NECK TO WRIST: This is an odd measurement, but you'll need it to calculate sleeve length on a drop-shoulder sweater. You want the person to stand with his or her arm bent a bit, and measure from that bump in the back of the neck, all the way down and around the slightly bent arm to the wrist.

SLEEVE LENGTH: To measure the sleeve length from underarm to wrist, stick your measuring tape into the person's underarm and measure from the slightly bent arm to the wrist bone. Now, because you don't want the sleeve to start right in the armpit, you'll subtract an inch from this number. That's the sleeve length from underarm to wrist.

UPPER ARM: Measure around the widest part of the upper arm, about halfway between shoulder and elbow. And no, they don't need to be flexing their muscles when you do this. You can check out the gun show later.

KNITTING BY THE NUMBERS
THE PATTERN-DRAFTING PROCESS

Now that you've got your stitches- and rows-per-inch gauge, and whatever body measurements you need, it's time to start drafting your pattern. I like to do this in four steps:

❶ Translate a sketch into a schematic.

❷ Fill in the schematic with measurements.

❸ Translate those measurements into stitch counts.

❹ Transform those measurements and stitch counts into written directions.

To demonstrate this process, let's start with something supersimple: a scarf. We'll begin by looking at a sample sketch of a regular old scarf.

To start the schematic, or blueprint, for this scarf, I'll just draw a long rectangle.

Now I need to figure out the actual dimensions of this rectangle, of which there are only two: length and width. I'll take my cues from the sketch to determine what those measurements are. I see that the scarf wraps once around the neck, then hangs down to just below the boobs. I also see that the scarf is about as wide as the neck. So, I take a piece of yarn and wrap it once around my neck, then cut it so that both ends hang just below my boobs. Next I measure this piece of yarn: Turns out, it's 52" long. That's the length of my rectangle. Then I take a tape measure and measure the length of my neck. From shoulder to chin, my neck measures 4" long. I fill both of these measurements in on the schematic.

4"

52"

Instead of yarn, you could use a tape measure to get the length. Alternatively, you could measure a scarf you already own if its length and width are just right for this project.

Now comes the time to pull out your calculator, 'cause we're going to turn these lengths and widths into stitches. Say I want to knit this scarf in a 2 × 2 rib. I've already knit up a gauge swatch in the ribbing stitch I intend to use, and it turns out that my gauge is 4.5 stitches per inch, and 5 rows per inch. Now I just multiply the number of inches wide I want my scarf to be by the number of stitches to one inch, to get the number of stitches wide the scarf will be: 4.5 stitches per inch × 4 inches = 18 stitches.

Let's look at that number for a moment. I know I'm knitting this scarf in a repeat of 4 stitches (k2, p2). But the number 18 doesn't come out to be a repeat of 4—the closest repeats would be 16 or 20. Here I have a couple of options: I can add or subtract a few stitches so that it's a multiple of 4 and every row of my pattern will start with a k2 and end with a p2, or I can just leave it as is and not worry about whether it ends with 2 knits or 2 purls. In this case, I'll leave it as is and put that number, 18, into my schematic. I'll put it in parenthesis so I can keep track of which figures represent the number of inches and which represent the number of stitches.

I'll also multiply the number of inches long I want my scarf to be by the number of rows I need to knit to get one inch of fabric: 5 rows per inch × 52 inches = 260 rows. I'll put this number into my schematic as well. However, I'll also let you in on a little secret: When you are knitting something that involves no shaping (meaning no increases or decreases), row gauge is not nearly as important as stitch gauge. The goal here is to wind up with a scarf that is 52" long, not just to be able to say, "Hooray! I knit 260 rows! I'm done!"

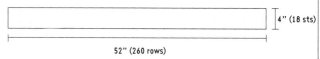

52" (260 rows)

4" (18 sts)

Finally, I'm ready to write my pattern, which becomes: CO 18 sts. Knit in 2 × 2 rib for 260 rows or until the scarf measures 52". BO all stitches.

Got it? Good. Now you're ready to begin drafting your very first sweater pattern.

drop it Like it's Hot

DRAFTING A DROP-SHOULDER OR MODIFIED DROP-SHOULDER SWEATER

As we saw earlier, a drop-shoulder sweater is basically two rectangles, the only difference between the front and the back being that the front will have a bite taken out for the neck. For the schematic, we can draw just one rectangle with the neckline marked and know that when we knit the back, we won't worry about the neckline. The sleeves are trapezoids, but we only need one schematic because both sleeves will be made the same. The sweater we'll be drafting has standard details: ribbing at the bottom of the sweater and the sleeves, and a regular old crew neck.

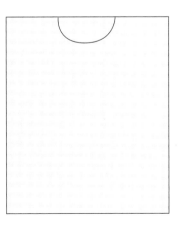

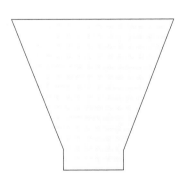

filling in the Measurements

BACK AND FRONT

Let's start with the standards. The standard length of ribbing on sweaters is 2½"; the standard width of a crew neck edging is 1". I'll add the measurements for the ribbing to my schematic, but I'll leave out the crew neck because that will be knit on after the front and back are done; I'll just make a note of that measurement so I don't forget about it. And I have one more standard as well: the depth of this neckline. The bottom of an adult human neck averages about 1½" lower than the shoulders, and I don't want this sweater to come right up to the base of the neck in front. In fact, I want it to be about ½" below the neck. That means I know that the neckline is at least 2" deep (1½" + ½"). And since I'm going to be adding that 1" of crew neck ribbing after my sweater is done, I can also calculate that the depth of my neckline will be 3". Let's put that measurement into the schematic, too.

The remaining measurements need to be taken from an actual body. For the front and back of the sweater, I need to know the width of the sweater, the length of the sweater,

and the width of the neck. For the sleeve of the sweater, I need to know the width of the sleeve at the top, the width of the sleeve at the bottom, and the length of the sleeve.

Let's take these one at a time. To calculate the width of the front and back, we first need to figure out the full circumference of the sweater. We'll start with the bust measurement and then add some ease to this number to decide the actual circumference of the sweater (see "All About Ease," page 129). Two inches is the amount of ease for a standard sweater, and since this example is all about standards, we'll add 2" to this measurement. Because the front and back of the sweater each account for half of this entire circumference, we'll divide this number by 2 to get the width of the front and back pieces. For our example, let's say the person's bust is 38". We add 2" to that and get 40". Divide 40" by 2 and you get 20", so the sweater body will be 20" wide.

Next, I'll need the full length of the sweater. So, if the desired sweater length was 23¼", we'll put 23¼" in the schematic. We'll also mark off where the sleeve will start on the schematic. We can take the measurement for the armhole using any of the methods described on pages 122–123; just be sure to add an inch to keep the sweater from being jammed into the armpit (and, if measuring the armhole from the top of the shoulder, add another inch because this sweater will not have any shoulder shaping). For our example, let's say that we measured from the armpit down to the desired length of the sweater and got a measurement of 14¼". Subtract 1" to give the armpit breathing room and get 13¼", which is how far we have to knit before we put a marker for where the sleeve needs to be attached, leaving an armhole depth of 10". We'll add both these numbers to the schematic.

To calculate the width of the neckline, start with the measurement of the person's neck at the back, and leave room for the crew neck, which is 1" wide on each side of the neck. If the width at the back of the neck is 5", then 5" + 2" = 7". So we'll put 7" in the schematic.

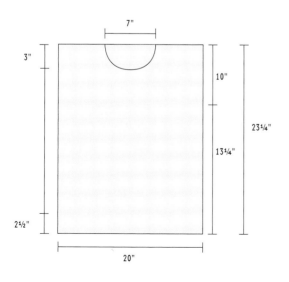

SLEEVES

The top of the sleeve on a drop-shoulder sweater is exactly two times the armhole depth. That's not so surprising, since the sleeve will get folded in half and sewn to the body from the marker we placed, identifying where the sleeve will start, to the top of the sweater, so it needs to measure twice that length, or $2 \times 10" = 20"$. We'll write that in.

For the bottom of the sleeve, we'll just take the wrist measurement we calculated on page 123. For our example, let's say the circumference around the person's arm 2½" above the wrist is 6½"; we'll add 1" to that and get 7½".

Our last measurement, sleeve length, is a bit weird to calculate on drop-shoulder sweaters. We take the "center back-neck to wrist" measurement and subtract half of the width of the back of the sweater to get the sleeve length. Why don't we just measure the arm? you might ask. Recall that a drop-shoulder sweater really does drop down over the shoulder, so part of the body becomes the top part of the sleeve. If you wanted to measure sleeve length by measuring the arm, you'd have to subtract the amount the sweater drops over the shoulder. But you don't know how much that's going to be, exactly. What you do know, however, is how wide the back (and front) of the sweater will be. So to calculate the sleeve length of a drop-shoulder sweater, you take the center back-neck to wrist measurement and subtract half of

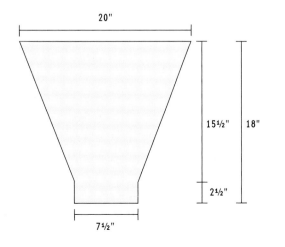

the width of the sweater back. If this measurement is 28, you'll subtract one-half of the back width, or 10 inches ($20" \div 2 = 10"$) and get 18".

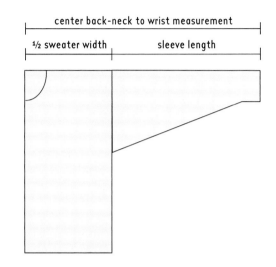

We'll put ribbing at the bottom of the sleeve, and the standard for that is 2½". That means we'll be knitting for 15½" after the ribbing to complete the sleeve ($18" - 2½" = 15½"$). We'll write this in, too. That's it! We've got all of our measurements. On to the next step!

filling in the stitches

BACK

Now we need to translate our measurements into stitch counts. Let's say our gauge is 5 stitches per inch wide and 7.5 rows per inch long, in stockinette stitch with size 8 needles. And let's say we're gonna make this sweater in stockinette stitch. The bottom of both the front and the back of the sweater is 20" wide. If it takes 5 stitches to make 1" and we need 20", then 5 stitches per inch × 20 inches = 100 stitches.

ALL ABOUT EASE

ou might think that if you wanted to make a nice-fitting sweater, you'd just measure around your body and then make some fabric that size. But think about it: If you make a sweater that has the same exact circumference as your body, you'll be making something that is the same circumference as your skin! And unless you're planning on performing some kind of knit version of *The Silence of the Lambs*, you usually don't want your sweater to fit like skin. That's why designers usually add a few more inches to the actual body measurement to determine the final sweater measurement. This little bit of extra is known as *ease*, and the amount you add depends on the result you'd like to achieve.

- For a normal sweater, one that you plan to wear with just a bra or undershirt underneath, add from 2" to 3" to the bust/chest measurement.

- For a cardigan or other type sweater that you plan to wear over something else, like a T-shirt or a blouse, add from 4" to 6".

- For something like a knit jacket or coat, which you plan to wear over something heavier—maybe even another sweater!—you'll want to add from 6" to 8".

Because knit fabric is stretchy, you can knit something without adding any ease at all, but it will cling to your every curve (and bulge) and will be slightly stretched when worn. And if you want something to really be stretched over your body, you can even add what's called "negative ease"—which means you would *subtract* about 2" from the bust/chest measurement.

Ease is not only added to the chest measurement, however. On sweaters with raglan or fitted sleeves, you'll also add ease to the upper arm measurement—about 50% of the amount of ease you added to the body.

For most sweaters, you won't need to add ease anywhere else, but if you're making a sweater to be worn over light clothing, you can add ½" to the shoulder width measurement and ¾" to the armhole depth; and if it's to be a coat or something worn over heavier clothing, add ¾" to the shoulder width and as much as 1½" to 2" to the armhole depth.

Add a stitch on each side for the seam (if you're knitting in the round, you wouldn't add these stitches). So, the bottom of the sweater is 102 stitches wide.

We'll work our ribbing over this number of stitches, as well as the remaining front or back of the sweater, which we'll be working in stockinette stitch. But just to make sure the ribbing is nice and snug, we'll work the ribbing on a needle that's two sizes smaller than the needle we are using for the rest of the sweater body. Also, I'm planning to work the lower ribbing of this sweater in 2 × 2 rib—a stitch pattern with a repeat of 4. The number 102 is not divisible by 4, so I'll start and end my work with a knit stitch, because I like having a column of knit stitches to work my mattress stitch when I seam these pieces together. This also means that the ribbing pattern will continue uninterrupted when I sew the front and back together.

We won't worry about rows on the back of the sweater because, as with the scarf example in the previous chapter, there's no shaping going on here. All we need to do is keep knitting until the piece is 23¼" long, then bind off.

FRONT AND NECK

Let's consider the front of the sweater. Here, we also want to knit until the piece is 23¼" long, like the back, but we have that neck shaping to deal with. What we know from the schematic is that the neck shaping begins 3" before the top of the sweater—in other words, the neck shaping begins when the sweater is 20¼" long—however many rows it takes us to get there.

Now let's take a look at the neckline. Since we know that the neck is 7" wide, we multiply that by our gauge of

5 stitches per inch and get 35 stitches. Write that in. Now let's work out how many stitches are in each shoulder: If the sweater is 102 stitches wide in total, and 35 stitches make up the neck, then 67 stitches make up the rest of the width of sweater—and each shoulder would be half that number. But—yuck!—that's an odd number of stitches, and we can't divide it in half equally. We want our shoulders to be even-steven, so let's add another stitch to the neck stitches—making it 36 stitches—so we now have an even number of stitches left: 102 body stitches − 36 neck stitches = 66 stitches. Dividing these stitches in half gives us 33 stitches for each shoulder. Let's write these numbers into the schematic.

Note: Here's a handy rule: To have the same number of stitches for each shoulder, the neck stitches should be even if the number of stitches in the front and back are even, or odd if the number of stitches in the back or front are odd.

Now for the creation of that neckline and how to take that 3"-deep "bite" out of the front of the sweater. There are a number of ways this can be done, but here's mine: We start by binding off half of the neck stitches at the beginning—in this case, that's 18 stitches. Write that in. Next, we'll bind off 1 stitch at each neck edge every other row until we've gotten rid of all 36 stitches. Then we need to knit straight until the sweater measures 23¼" in total. Since we started this neck shaping when the sweater was only 20¼" in total, that means our neckline will be exactly 3" deep.

Before we move on, we need to check something. We'll be getting rid of 9 stitches on each side of the neck, and doing that with every-other-row decreases will use up 18 rows. And it took us 2 rows to bind off the first 18 stitches, for a total of 20 rows. The thing is, we want our neck to be only 3" deep. Can we fit those 20 rows into 3"? Here's the one time we need to check our row gauge, which is 7.5 rows per inch: 3" of length × 7.5 rows per inch will require 22½ rows. Yay, we can definitely fit in our 20 rows of bind-off and decreases before reaching 3". So we have nothing to alter here. If we were going to run out

of rows before we used up our every-other-row decreases (which could happen with a wider neckline and a shallower depth), we would just add a few more stitches to the center neckline bind-off.

There's one more thing: How many stitches do we knit before we get to the spot for the initial bind-off? This is easy: The body has 102 stitches, and we're going to be binding off the center 18 of them. Subtract those 18 stitches from the 102 and we get 84. Divide 84 in half and we get 42—which is how many stitches we'll be knitting before that 18-stitch bind-off, and also how many stitches after. Might as well write those numbers into the schematic, too.

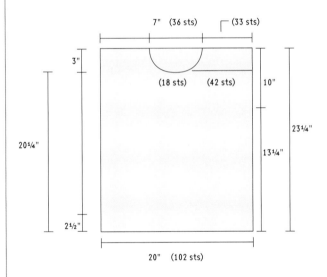

SLEEVES

These sleeves will be worked from the bottom up, so let's start with the wrist. We arrived at a measurement of 7½", so we multiply 7.5 by our stitch gauge of 5 stitches per inch, and we get 37.5 stitches. Boo! We can't cast on 37½ stitches, so we round up to 38. However, 38 isn't divisible by 4 (our 2 × 2 ribbing stitch pattern); I need to either add or subtract 2 stitches from that number if I want my ribbing to continue uninterrupted. I'll add 2, giving me 40. Then I'll add 2 stitches for the seams, resulting in 42 stitches. I'll put that number on the schematic.

So now let's go to the top of the sleeve. This measurement was 20" wide, and multiplied by our 5 stitches/inch gauge, we get 100 stitches for the top of the sleeve. Adding in the seam stitches gives us 102 stitches.

The sleeves need to increase from 42 stitches at the bottom, after the ribbing, to 102 stitches at the top. Since there is shaping in these sleeves, we need to know our row gauge. So let's figure out how many rows we have available over which to make these increases. Our total sleeve length is 18": 2½" of that will be the bottom ribbing, and I'd like to end my increases at least 1" before the top, so that gives $18" - 2\frac{1}{2}" - 1" = 14\frac{1}{2}"$ over which to increase stitches.

That 14½" times our row gauge of 7.5 rows per inch will give us the number of rows over which we can make those increases. So, $14.5" \times 7.5$ rows per inch $= 108.75$ rows. We'll round that down to the next lowest number, in this case, 108 rows.

If we subtract the number of stitches at the wrist from the number of stitches at the top, the result is the number of stitches we need to increase (which here is $102 - 42$, or 60 stitches) over 108 rows. When knitting sleeves, we like to keep things balanced, and that means increasing 2 stitches at a time—one on each side of the sleeve. Divide the total number of stitches we need to increase in half, and we'll get the number of increase rows we need to have: Here, that's $60 \div 2$, or 30 increase rows. We want to space those 30 increase rows evenly over the 108 rows we have available. If we just divide 108 by 30, we get 3.6.

Obviously, we can't place our increases every 3.6 rows. We also can't just round that down, willy-nilly, and increase every 3 rows, either, because we need to increase 30 times, and $30 \times 3 = 90$, which is less than the 108 rows we have available. We might want to do a bunch of increases every 3 rows and then a bunch more every 4 rows, to even things out. Not only would it take a bunch of trial and error to figure out how many increases to put every 3 rows and every 4 rows, but placing increases every 3 rows means we'd be making our increases on wrong-side rows, and it's really much nicer always to put the increases on right-side rows. But don't worry: There is a pretty nice formula to help you figure out exactly how to do that. I call it "the Magic Formula" (see page 133) because it really is.

The way it works is like this: Instead of rounding 3.6 down to 3, we round it down to the nearest even number: in this case, 2. And we also figure the next-higher-up even number, which in this case is 4.

Then we figure out how many rows we would use up if we made all of our increases using the lower of these two numbers. In this case, that would be 2×30, or 60 rows. Next, we figure out how many rows that would leave over: $108 - 60 = 48$ rows. Divide this number by 2—because we're making increases only on even rows—and that gives us 24. And this number—24—is the number of times we are going to make increases using the *larger* even number, 4. The remaining increases will be made using the smaller even number. Here, we have 6, because 30 (total number of increase rows) $- 24 = 6$.

So, we'll increase each side every 4 rows 24 times, and every 2 rows 6 times. Let's see if that works: Every 4 rows $\times 24 = 96$ rows; every 2 rows $\times 6 = 12$ rows; and 96 rows $+ 12$ rows $= 108$ rows. We've used up our 108 rows, and also our 30 increase rows. Abracadabra! It's magic!

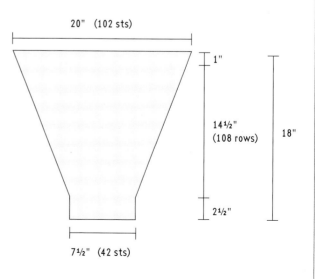

write on

WRITING OUT THE DROP-SLEEVE SWEATER PATTERN

Finally, we're ready to write up the pattern in words. It looks like this:

SIZE

Finished bust: 40"

Finished length: 23¼"

NEEDLES

US 8 (5mm) needles

US 6 (4mm) needles

US 6 (4 mm) 16" circular needle

GAUGE

20 sts and 30 rows = 4" in St st using size 8 (5mm) needles

BACK

With smaller needles, CO 102 sts.

ROW 1 (RS): K1, *k2, p2; rep from * to last st, k1.

ROW 2: P1, *k2, p2; rep from * to last st, p1.

Rep rows 1 and 2 until piece meas 2½" from beg, end with a WS row.

Change to larger needles. Work in St st until piece meas 13¼" from beg. Place marker in fabric at this point to mark armhole.

Work even until piece meas 23¼" from beg. BO all sts.

FRONT

With smaller needles, CO 102 sts.

ROW 1 (RS): K1, *k2, p2; rep from * to last st, k1.

ROW 2: P1, *k2, p2; rep from * to last st, p1.

Rep rows 1 and 2 until piece meas 2½" from beg, end with a WS row.

Change to larger needles. Work in St st until piece meas 13¼" from beg. Place marker in fabric at this point to mark armhole.

Work even until piece meas 20¼" from beg, end with a WS row.

NECK SHAPING

NEXT ROW (RS): K42, join a 2nd ball of yarn and BO next 18 sts, k to end.

Working both sides at the same time, BO 1 st at each neck edge every other row 9 times—33 sts each side.

Work even in St st until piece meas 23¼" from beg. BO all sts.

SLEEVES

With smaller needles, CO 42 sts.

ROW 1 (RS): K1, *k2, p2; rep from * to last st, k1.

ROW 2: P1, *k2, p2; rep from * to last st, p1.

Rep rows 1 and 2 until piece meas 2½" from beg, end with a WS row.

Change to larger needles. Work in St st, inc 1 st each side every 4th row 24 times, then every other row 6 times—102 sts.

Work even in St st until piece meas 18" from beg. BO all sts.

FINISHING

Sew shoulder seams.

With circular needle, pick up sts along neckline (see "One, Two, Pick up Stitch," page 162), and work in 2 × 2 rib for 1". BO loosely.

Sew in sleeves.

Sew side and sleeve seams.

the magic formula

EVENLY SPACING INCREASES (OR DECREASES) OVER A GIVEN NUMBER OF ROWS

1 Take the number of stitches that need to be increased (or decreased) and divide by 2. This is the total number of increase (or decrease) rows that need to be made.

2 Divide the number of rows over which the increases (or decreases) can be made by the total number of increase (or decrease) rows. (If the result is less than 2, stop here and read the Note at right). If your result is an even number with no decimals, this is your answer! Increase (or decrease) every time you reach this number of rows and skip the next steps. Otherwise, carry on.

3 If this number is odd, round down to the nearest even number. If it's even with a decimal, drop the numbers after the decimal. This will be your smaller number. Add 2 to this number to get your larger number.

4 Multiply the smaller number by the total number of increase rows that need to be made.

5 Subtract the total number of rows available by the result you got in step 4.

6 Divide this number by 2. This gives you the number of times you need to space your increase rows by the *larger* of your two even numbers.

7 Subtract the result in step 6 from the total number of increase rows to get the remaining number of increase rows. This is the number of times you need to space your increase rows by the *smaller* of your two even numbers.

Note: The magic formula won't work if the result you get in step 2 is less than 2, which indicates there are too many increases (or decreases) to be made over too short a length for them to be made every other row—some decreases will need to be made *every row*. How many can you make of each? This puzzled me for a while until I figured out the following formula. First, take the result you got in step 2 and subtract 1. Multiply by the total number of decrease rows you need to make, and round to the nearest whole number. This is the number of times you can make decreases on every other row. The remainder of your decreases will need to be done every row. For example, say you need to space 23 decrease rows evenly over only 40 rows; 40 divided by 23 is 1.739. Subtract 1 from that and we get .739. Multiply that by the number of decrease rows—23—and we get 16.997, which, rounded to the nearest whole number, is 17. Thus, we can make 17 decreases every other row, which will use up 34 rows, and we'll need to make the remaining 6 decreases every row over the remaining 6 rows, giving us 40 rows in total.

Tricks Are for Knits
THE MODIFIED DROP-SHOULDER SWEATER

As you know, in a drop-shoulder sweater, there is always some fabric bunching up under the arms. One easy way to get rid of a bit of that extra fabric is as follows: On the body of the sweater, when knitting the front and back, instead of simply placing a pin to mark the beginning of the armhole, bind off about 1" of stitches on each side. Then, when the sleeve reaches the desired length, instead of binding off, knit straight for an additional inch of length. This extra inch will fit perfectly into the shallow, rectangular armhole you created in the sweater when you bound off that inch of stitches.

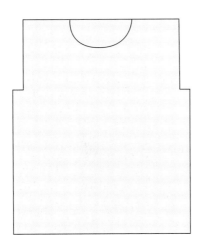

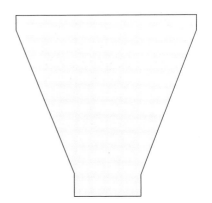

10

**DRAFTING
RAGLAN-SLEEVE
AND CIRCULAR
YOKE SWEATERS**

et's take a look at a raglan sweater schematic. The front and back start just like the drop-shoulder sweater in the previous chapter. At the armhole, however, things change. First, about an inch of stitches are bound off on each side. Then, stitches are decreased until only the neck stitches are left on the back, and until no stitches are left on the front and only a few stitches are left on the sleeves. Basically, after the bind-off at the base of the armholes, the front and back stitches are decreased to the width of the neckline.

The sleeve is quite a bit different from the drop-shoulder sweater sleeve. First, stitches are increased after the wrist edging, along the length of the sleeve from wrist to underarm, until

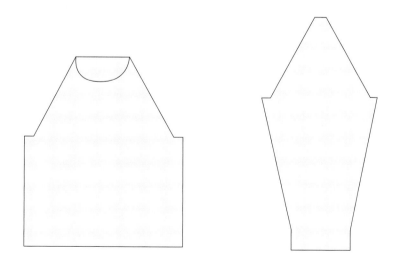

they reach the width of the upper arm plus ease. There, an inch of stitches are bound off on each side, just as they are on the front and back pieces. On the part of the sleeve from the armpit to the top (known as the "sleeve cap"), stitches are decreased *in the exact same way as the stitches on the body,* leaving only 1–1½" of stitches to be bound off at the end.

You'll notice I emphasize that the decreases on the sleeve cap *exactly match* the decreases at the upper part of the body. Getting that to work out takes a bit of fussing, but it's worth the trouble. Some folks might tell you to work out those decreases separately, just so long as they are the same length, but the number of stitches being decreased on the body and the sleeve can be different (which means they won't match up). I don't like that method, because it's nice to make the decreases decorative on a raglan sweater, and it will look best if those pieces line up perfectly. Also, if you'd prefer to knit your raglan sweater in the round, you'll need these decreases to match up, so why not do so when knitting flat as well?

Now let's take a look at what happens when a raglan sweater is put together.

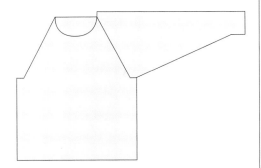

As you can see, half of that 1–1½" of fabric at the very top of the sleeve cap becomes part of the neckline. Also, it contributes to the overall length of the sweater. In fact, you can see that the front and back of the sweater are just a bit shorter than the total length of the sweater. If the top of the raglan sleeve cap is 1" wide, then the sweater front length will measure ½" less than the total desired sweater length. Also, the neckline will be ½" shallower on the front piece of the sweater than the total depth of the neckline, because the other ½" of depth will be coming from the top of the raglan sleeve. Do you get that? If you don't, don't move on to the next step yet; keep looking at that illustration (below, left) until you understand. It's important.

filling in the measurements

BACK AND FRONT

Let's begin by filling in the measurements, but *use a pencil,* because we may need to adjust some to get everything to work out. Start with the measurement at the bottom of the front and back. (This is done in the same way as for the drop-shoulder sweater, page 127.) The actual bust measurement for this example will be 38", to which we added 2" of ease, resulting in a 40" finished circumference. Half of this is 20", so we'll write that in.

Next, the length on the front and back from armpit to bottom of sweater is the measurement we took from armpit to where we want the sweater to end, *minus* 1" to give that armpit some breathing room. We don't need to worry about how many rows it will take to get there, because there is no shaping in this lower part of the sweater. We measure this length to be 14¼", so taking away an inch makes this measurement 13¼". We'll write that in.

On raglan sweaters, we always begin the armhole shaping by binding off 1" of stitches at each armhole, so write this onto the schematic. Also write in the width of the sweater after the underarm stitches are bound off—in our case, that's 20" − 2" = 18".

Let's jump to the neckline and ignore the middle part for now. The bottom of an adult human neck averages about 1½" lower than the shoulders in the front, and I want this sweater to come ½" below my neck. And since

I'm going to be adding 1" of crew neck ribbing after my sweater is done, I can calculate that the depth of my neckline will be 3". I also know that the desired full length of the sweater is 23¼". Subtracting 3" from 23¼" means that the neck shaping will begin when the sweater body is 20¼" long from the cast-on edge. I can figure out the width of the neckline by taking the back-neck width measurement, which for this example will be 5", and adding 1" in width on each side to allow for that crew neck (which will be knit on later), which results in 7". Write in these measurements—width at neckline, length from bottom of sweater to beginning of neckline. Looking at my schematic, I can see that for this type of sweater, I'm going to need to decrease the yoke from 18" above the armhole bind-offs to 7" at the neck. This means I'll be decreasing this area by 11" in overall width. This number—11"—is important. Keep it in mind.

SLEEVES AND ARMHOLE DEPTH

We take the wrist measurement from a person's body (see page 123). For this example, we'll use 7.5" and write that in. Now we need to take two additional body measurements for the raglan sweater, which we didn't need for the drop-shoulder sweater: the sleeve length from underarm to wrist and the upper-arm circumference.

The length of the lower section of the sleeve—from wrist to underarm—should be equal to the sleeve length measured from the underarm to the wrist, minus an inch to give the armpit room to breathe. Let's say we measured the arm from armpit to wrist to be 19"; subtracting an inch from that, we get 18". Write that in. Now for the width at the upper arm. For our example, we measured this to be 13". To add ease to the upper arm circumference, the standard is to add 50–100% of the body ease. Let's start by adding just 50% (we may end up adjusting this later).

Our body ease is 2", and 50% of that is 1". So our total sleeve width at the upper arm is 13" + 1" ease = 14". Let's write that in. After binding off 1" at each side, we end up with 12" just above the upper arm. Let's write this in, too.

Okay, now for the somewhat tougher part, where we may need to jiggle up our numbers a bit.

First of all, I want the sleeve at the very top to be only 1–1½" wide—that's a standard for this type of sweater. I know that I need to decrease the front and back of the sweater from 18" wide at the armhole to 7" wide at the back of the neck. And I know that this means I have to decrease 11" worth of stitches. I'm going to pull out some stitch counts here for just a minute to prove a point.

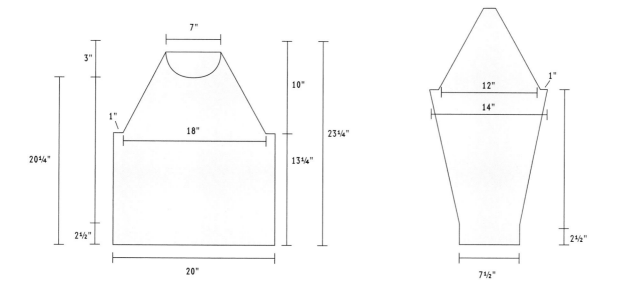

Multiplying 11" by my stitch gauge of 5 gives me 55 stitches that I'll need to decrease, which I'll round up to 56 so I can decrease them 2 stitches at a time. And dividing this number in half means that I'll have to evenly space 28 decrease rows over some, as yet unknown, total number of rows.

I promised you that the decreases for the sleeve cap and the front/back decreases were *exactly the same*, right? That means if I'm making 28 decrease rows on the front, then I also need to make 28 decrease rows on the sleeve cap, and they need to be spaced apart in the same way. And if I'm making 28 decrease rows for the sleeve cap, that means I'm decreasing 56 stitches on the sleeve cap (remember, we always decrease two stitches on a decrease row—one on each side). And if I'm decreasing 56 stitches on the sleeve, that means I'm decreasing 11" (56 divided by 5) from the sleeve after the armhole bind-off. Do you recognize that 11"? It's the same width we decreased on the body to get to the neck width. Remember? When making a raglan sleeve sweater, the decreases on the body from the armhole bind-off to the neck are the *same* as the decreases on the sleeves from the bind-off to the top—that is, if you want them to match up and be all purty.

This means that since we removed 11" of stitches from the body, we have to decrease 11" worth of stitches from the sleeve as well. We have 12" at the upper arm after the bind-off, minus 11, giving us 1". And that's exactly what we want to end up with at the very top of our sleeve. Everything is going to work out, we don't need to juggle any numbers, and we can start calculating our stitches, rows, and everything else. But there's one measurement we still need in order to be able to finish drafting up this pattern, and that's the length of the sweater from the armhole bind-offs to the top. Refer back to the diagram on page 136, which showed how raglan sweaters are put together, and you'll understand that this length is the total armhole depth minus half of the width at the top of the sleeve. We measured the underarm depth to be 10", so that means that our front and back from armpit bind-off will measure 9½". And finally, what is the length of the sleeve cap itself? That's easy: In a raglan sweater, the sleeve cap depth is the same as the length we calculated for the sweater front and back after the armhole bind-offs. It may seem weird that the length of the sleeve cap is determined by the length of the sweater after the armholes, but how could it be any-

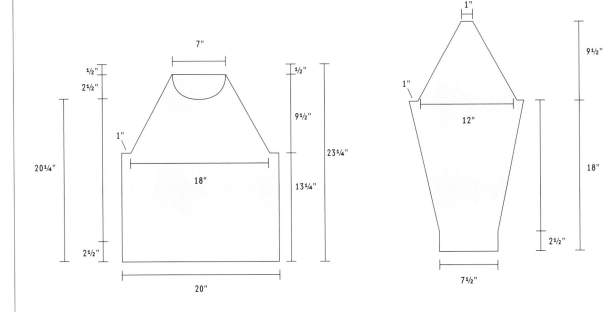

thing else? If the decreases on the front, back, and sleeves are all going to be created in exactly the same way, we need to make the same number of decreases over *the same number of rows.* Finally, we have all of our measurements. Now we can start putting in all the stitch counts, and working out our decreases.

filling in the stitches

BACK AND FRONT

First, just as we did with the drop-shoulder sweater, we'll begin with 102 stitches (20" × 5 stitches/inch + 2 seam stitches). Moving up the sweater, our 1" of bind-offs means we'll be binding off 5 stitches on each side.

I know that the total length of this section—from underarm bind-off to back neck—is 9½". Multiplying by my row gauge of 7.5 rows per inch by 9.5", I get 71.25, which I'll round up to 72 rows. At the bottom of this

sweater I have 102 stitches; then I bind off 5 stitches at each side, leaving me with 92 stitches. Now if I need to decrease from 92 to 36 neck stitches, how many stitches do I need to decrease? 92 − 36 = 56. I divide 56 stitches by 2 (because I'll be decreasing two at a time) to get to the number of decrease rows, and the result is 28. So I need to space 28 decrease rows evenly among 72 rows total. Running this through the Magic Formula (see page 133), I discover that I have to decrease every 4 rows 8 times, and every 2 rows 20 times. Now, what's the beauty of the raglan pattern when done this way? These are exactly the same directions I need to follow for the sleeve cap—decrease 2 stitches every 4 rows 8 times, and every 2 rows 20 times.

On to the front neck. The total number of stitches in the neck is 7" × 5, or 35, which we'll round up to 36 because the number of stitches in the width of the sweater is an even number—102. This way we know we'll be able to divide the stitches to the left and right of the neck in half evenly. And also, I know that I'll be binding off half of those 36 stitches—or 18 stitches—in the first row. After that, I'll bind off 1 stitch each edge every other row until all 36 stitches have been bound off.

SLEEVES

Here, all we need to do is calculate the increases on the lower half of the raglan sleeve. The cuff is calculated the same way as the drop-shoulder sleeve, so write in 42 stitches for the wrist. The widest part of this sleeve, the upper arm width, is 14", and at 5 stitches per inch, that's 70 stitches, plus 2 stitches for the seams, or 72 stitches. So we need to go from 42 stitches at the wrist to 72 stitches at the upper arm, meaning we have to increase 30 stitches, or 15 increase rows. The total length of the lower part of this sleeve is 18", and the first 2½" of that is ribbing, so that leaves us 15½". Again, I'd rather get all my increases done well before I start binding off, so I'll take an inch off that and give myself 14½" over which to space my increases. Multiplying 14.5 by the row gauge of 7.5 gives us 108.75 rows, which I'll round down to 108. Now I need to evenly

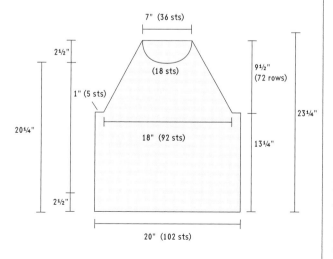

give you every inch of my Love

ADJUSTING MEASUREMENTS ON RAGLANS TO ARRIVE AT THE PERFECT SLEEVE CAP WIDTH

The example here just happened to work out perfectly, but many times your projects will not work out so neatly. To illustrate this, let's say I added 2" of ease to my upper arm measurement instead of 1" to give me a measurement of 15". After I'd bound off an inch at each side I'd have 13" left. And let's keep our 20" front/back width, and our 7" neckline. After I remove 2" at the armholes, that leaves me with 18" for the front, and to arrive at the 7" neckline means I have to decrease 11" worth of stitches (18 - 7 = 11). Subtracting this 11" from my upper arm width (13) now gives me 2"—more than I want for the top of my sleeve cap. This means that to get to that magical 1½", I need to get rid of a ½" of stitches from somewhere. One place could be to subtract a bit from my upper arm measurement, but I could also remove a bit from my neckline width, say ½". I would be decreasing my sweater from 18" after the bind-off to a neckline of 6½", increasing my total decreases on the body from 11" to 11½". And voilà! Subtracting 11½" from 13" gives me the 1½" that I want at the top of my sleeve cap. I could have added ½" to the front and back widths of the sweater and gotten to the same result. My sweater width would have been 18½" after

the sleeve bind-offs, and to decrease the neck to 7" I'd be losing 11½" in width.

If you need to get rid of even more stitches—say your sleeve cap calculates out to 3" somehow, you can split up the difference, taking 1" from one area, adding 1" to another area, until you get to your 1–1½". Now you see why I said to write the numbers into your schematic in pencil, because you may need to adjust some measurements before you make other calculations.

So, if you have *more* than 1–1½" of stitches at your sleeve top, you can:

1 Subtract a little from the neck width.

2 Subtract width from the upper arm measurement. Make sure you still have some ease left there, though.

3 Add a little to the body width.

If you end up with *less* than 1–1½" of stitches at the sleeve top, you can:

1 Add a little to the neck width.

2 Add width to the sleeve at the upper arm.

3 Subtract a little from the front/back width.

space 15 increase rows over 108 rows total. The magic formula then swoops down and informs me that this means I need to increase 1 stitch on each side every 8 rows 9 times, then every 6 rows 6 times.

And how to complete the second part of the sleeve, from the 1" bind-off at the armpit to the top? That's easy, because the beauty of this method is that I will use the exact same decreases that I already calculated for the body of the sweater: Decrease 1 stitch each side every 4 rows 8 times, and every 2 rows 20 times.

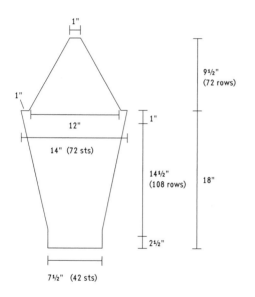

writing out the pattern

We're done! Here's how we'd write out this raglan sweater pattern:

SIZE

Finished bust: 40"

Finished length: 23¼"

NEEDLES

US 8 (5mm) needles

US 6 (4mm) needles

US 6 (4 mm) 16" circular needle

GAUGE

20 sts and 30 rows = 4" in St st using size 8 (5mm) needles

BACK

With smaller needles, CO 102 sts.

ROW 1 (RS): K1, *k2, p2; rep from * to last st, k1.

ROW 2: P1, *k2, p2; rep from * to last st, p1.

Rep rows 1 and 2 until piece meas 2½" from beg, end with a WS row.

Change to larger needles. Work in St st until piece meas 13¼" from beg. BO 5 sts at beg of the next 2 rows —92 sts.

Dec 1 st at each side every 4th row 8 times, then every other row 20 times—36 sts. BO all sts.

FRONT

With smaller needles, CO 102 sts.

ROW 1 (RS): K1, *k2, p2; rep from * to last st, k1.

ROW 2: P1, *k2, p2; rep from * to last st, p1.

Rep rows 1 and 2 until piece meas 2½" from beg, end with a WS row.

Change to larger needles. Work in St st until piece meas 13¼" from beg. BO 5 sts at beg of the next 2 rows —92 sts.

Dec 1 st at each side every 4th row 8 times, then every other row 20 times.

AT THE SAME TIME, when sweater measures 20¼" from beg, continue raglan decreases, work to center 18 sts, join a 2nd ball of yarn, BO center 18 sts, work to end. Working both sides at the same time, BO 1 st at each neck edge every other row 9 times. Work even at neck edge and cont raglan decs until no sts remain.

SLEEVES

With smaller needles, CO 42 sts.

ROW 1 (RS): K1, *k2, p2; rep from * to last st, k1.

ROW 2: P1, *k2, p2; rep from * to last st, p1.

Rep rows 1 and 2 until piece meas 2½" from beg, end with a WS row.

Change to larger needles. Work in St st, inc 1 st each side every 8th row 9 times, then every 6th row 6 times —72 sts.

Work even in St st until piece meas 18" from beg, end with a WS row.

BO 5 sts at beg of the next 2 rows.

Dec 1 st each side every 4th row 8 times, then every other row 20 times—6 sts.

BO remaining sts.

FINISHING

Matching bind-off areas at armhole on sweater front and back to bind-offs at sleeves, sew sleeves to front and back of sweater body.

With circular needle, pick up sts along neckline (see "One, Two, Pick up Stitch," page 162), and work in 2 × 2 rib for 1". BO loosely.

Sew side and sleeve seams.

round and round

HOW TO DRAFT A PATTERN FOR A RAGLAN SLEEVE SWEATER IN THE ROUND

A raglan sleeve sweater is supereasy to knit in the round; in fact, this is most likely how they were originally made. Work out your schematic, stitch counts, increases, and decreases the same as above, *except* leave off the seam stitches, because you won't need 'em. Raglan sweaters can be knit from the top down or the bottom up. Knitting from the top is nice because you can try on the sweater as you go. The instructions that follow are for knitting from the bottom up, which are more like the directions for knitting flat, but feel free to reverse all of this and knit from the top down. Just remember that all your increases become decreases, and all your decreases become increases (because you are knitting in the other direction).

To knit this sweater in the round, cast on all the body stitches—both front and back—on a circular needle. Place a marker to identify the beginning of the round (and the left underarm) and another halfway around to indicate the right underarm. Begin knitting in rounds until you get to the desired sweater length to armhole. On the last round end 1" before the end of the round. Remove the markers and put 1" worth of stitches from either side of the markers onto stitch holders (you have already calculated how many stitches this should be on the schematic). That makes a total of 2" of stitches for each underarm now on holders. Then put the body aside and begin knitting the sleeves on double-pointed needles, which you do by casting on the full number of stitches at the bottom of the sleeve, without seam stitches. Place a marker to mark the beginning and start knitting in rounds. Refer to your pattern for the length of ribbing and placement of increase rounds. When you reach an increase round, make an increase between the first two stitches after the marker, and another increase between the last two stitches before the marker. Continue knitting in this way until you reach the full sleeve length, transferring your stitches from double-pointed needles to a circular needle when necessary. Place the first and last inch's worth of stitches on a waste yarn and the remaining stitches on a separate waste yarn, so you now have 2" worth of underarm stitches on one waste yarn and the remaining sleeve stitches on a separate waste yarn.

Set this sleeve aside and knit another sleeve to the full sleeve length. Place the first and last inch's worth of stitches onto a waste yarn, and leave the remaining sleeve stitches on the needle for the left sleeve.

Now that you have both the body and the sleeves knit, you can put all the parts together and begin knitting the upper part of the sweater—the yoke. Since you'll be working on the body and sleeves together at this point, you'll need a longer circular needle. With the longer circular needle, knit all the left-sleeve stitches from the sleeve needle. Place a marker on the needle. Next, knit across the front of the sweater, then place a stitch marker here. Next, leaving the underarm stitches on waste yarn, place the right-sleeve stitches back onto the needle and knit across the right-sleeve stitches, place a marker, then knit across the back stitches until you get to the last stitch. Place a marker to indicate the end of your round, which is now between the back and the left sleeve.

At this point, you have all your stitches on one needle and four sets of underarm stitches (two from the sleeves and two from the body of the sweater) on their own stitch holders or lengths of waste yarn. And you have four stitch markers, indicating the beginning and end of each sleeve, and thus also the beginning and end of the sweater front and back. Now you begin knitting in the round. Refer to your schematic for the placement of decreases. When you reach a decrease round, decrease at the beginning and end of each sleeve and at the beginning and end of both front and back. Since the markers indicate where each part starts and ends, you will make your decreases just before, and just after, each marker, resulting in eight decreases on each decrease round. Continue in this way until you reach the round where the neck stitches need to be bound off. On that round, you will work to the neck stitches, bind them off, and complete this round. From that point on, you will work the sweater back and forth in rows, instead of in the round, decreasing stitches as per your schematic at each neck edge until all neckline stitches have been bound off and decreased. Continue until you are left with an inch's worth of stitches for each sleeve plus the number of stitches you need for the back neck (get this number from your schematic). Bind off all stitches.

You are almost done. I promised you there would be no seams on this sweater, but I didn't promise you no sewing! You still need to connect the underarm stitches to each other, and the most invisible way to do this is to graft them together using the Kitchener stitch (see page 107). Now your raglan-in-the-round is done.

circuLAr Yoke Jweater

If you want to make a sweater that has a circular design around the neck and shoulders—like those Icelandic ski sweaters from the 1960s—then you need to design a circular yoke sweater. The style is a lot like the raglan sweater knit in the round, above. However, instead of making your decreases from armpit to neckline in only four locations and spacing those evenly across your rounds, you'll spread your decreases evenly across only three or four decrease rounds. By not lining up your decreases in the same spot on each round, you avoid creating seamlike lines of decreases. This way you can create a circular design that is uninterrupted all the way around the yoke.

Circular yoke sweaters are different from raglan sweaters in another way as well: Whereas the neckline on a raglan sweater is usually deeper in the front and straight across in the back, the neck of a circular yoke sweater can be either equally deep in the front and the back, or only slightly raised in the back and slightly deeper in the front. Circular yoke sweaters are created by a series of circles, becoming ever smaller toward the neck. That lends itself to awesome circular decorations around the entire top of the shoulders all the way to the neck. But having a neckline that is not any lower in the front and not any higher in the back can lead to one uncomfortable sweater. We can easily correct this by extending the back slightly, which tips the neckline a bit forward, thereby making the sweater fit better. It's done by knitting short rows—rows that don't go all the way around the entire circle—to create a small wedge of fabric in the back of the sweater, below the neck.

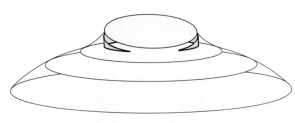

Yoke shaping with short rows

Finally, sweaters with circular yokes are most often worked out by using a percentage system. With this system, many of the numbers are not taken from body measurements, but are a percentage of some key number that is *based* on a body measurement—usually, the sweater circumference (body + ease). Elizabeth Zimmermann first worked this system out, and it was later refined by her daughter, Meg Swanson. There are many variations, but we're going to use the most common formula here. And although the percentage system can give you numbers for just about every measurement on a sweater apart from the body circumference, we're going to use as many actual body measurements as we can, and rely on the percentage system only for working out the yoke.

Start designing your circular yoke sweater the same way you would a raglan sweater knit in the round: Work out the number of stitches for the full body circumference,

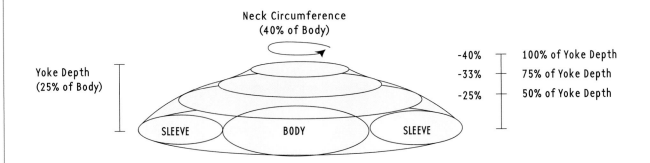

and how long you need to knit until you reach the armpit. Same thing for the sleeves: You'll knit them from the bottom up until you reach the armpit.

Now comes the land of percentages. The circumference of the neckline, before the edging, is going to end up being about 40% of the circumference of the body. Strangely enough, we don't even need to calculate what that number is, because the decreasing system you'll learn below will get us to exactly that number. What we do need to calculate, however, is the depth of the yoke over which we'll be making our decreases, and that number turns out to be a nice percentage as well: It is equal to 25% of the body circumference. We're going to make only three rounds with decreases in them, and we'll make them in three locations: The first is about halfway up the yoke depth. The second is about three-quarters up the yoke depth. Then, just about ½" before we get to the full yoke depth, we'll knit some short rows to raise up the back of the neck (more on that later), and then at the full yoke depth, we'll make our last round of decreases. At that point we'll be left with all the neckline stitches we need, and it will turn out that they add up to about 40% of the body stitches.

And how are we going to make those decreases? We're going to do those with percentages as well. On the first round of decreases, the one that we do halfway up the yoke, we'll decrease by 25%. The next round, three-quarters of the way up, we'll decrease by 33%. The last round, ½" before full yoke depth, we'll decrease by 40%. Decreasing by these particular percentages is quite wonderful: To decrease by 25%, or one-quarter, we want to ditch one out of every four stitches, and we do that by [k2, k2tog], all the way around. To decrease by 33%, or one-third, we want to decrease one out of every three stitches, and we do that by [k1, k2tog] all the way around. And to decrease by 40%, or four-tenths (which is the same as two-fifths), we want to get rid of two out of every five stitches, which you can accomplish by working [k1, k2tog, k2tog] all the way around. No magic formulas, no calculators, no nuthin'. Just superduper nice percentages that are easy to work.

BODY AND SLEEVES

For our circular yoke sweater, we'll start the same way we did for the raglan sweater in the round: We'll knit the body and the sleeves in the round up to the armpits, with the necessary increases along the sleeve to arrive at the desired upper-arm width at the underarm (see illustration below). Then we'll put 2" worth of stitches for the underarms from each sleeve and 2" from each side of the body on separate

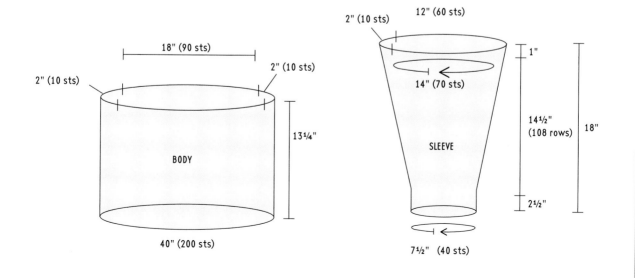

stitch holders. We'll put all of our stitches from body and sleeves onto a giant circular needle, first the left sleeve, then the stitches for the front of the sweater, then the right sleeve, then the stitches for the back of the sweater. With a stitch gauge of 5 stitches to the inch, 2" = 10 stitches on each holder, so 200 body stitches + (70 sleeve stitches × 2) − (10 stitches × 4 holders) = 300 stitches on our giant circular needle.

YOKE

Now let's calculate the yoke. Our original body circumference was 40", and 25% of that is 10, meaning that our yoke is going to be 10" deep. So, when we have reached 5", or half of that depth, we'll do a round of [k2, k2tog], decreasing our round by 25%. We start with 300 stitches on the needle, and we'll end up with 225 stitches. Next, we'll continue to knit until our yoke measures 7½". Here we'll do our 33% decrease round: [k1, k2tog] around. We are left with 150 stitches.

When we get to 9½" of yoke, it's time for our short rows, to lift up the back neck for a nicer fit. This is not hard at all. The trick is to work about an inch of short rows, which will usually be from 4 to 10 rows. Since our gauge is 7.5, let's round it up to 8. We'll create these rows across the right sleeve, back, and left sleeve, leaving the front as it is. To make the first short row, knit the round across the back till you get to the end of the left sleeve, then wrap and turn (see "Wrapping & Turning," page 114) and purl your way back to the end of the right sleeve, then wrap and turn. You've completed one set of short rows. Knit to about an inch before the end of the left sleeve, wrap and turn again, and purl your way back to about an inch before the end of the right sleeve, then wrap and turn. Continue this way, with every two short rows completing one "set," and each set ending about an inch before the previous set. For our 8 rows, we'll be doing 4 sets of short rows. Once I'm done, I need to work my way all the way around the circle, picking up the "wraps" together with the stitches (see "Hiding the Wrap," page 114).

Finally, I'm ready for the last decrease round: I decrease 40% of my remaining stitches by doing [k1, k2tog, k2tog] around, and I end up with 90 stitches. Now I'm done knitting the yoke. All I need to do is knit on my neckline edging (probably about an inch of ribbing for a nice crew neck), graft my body and sleeve stitches together at the underarm using the Kitchener stitch, and I'm finished.

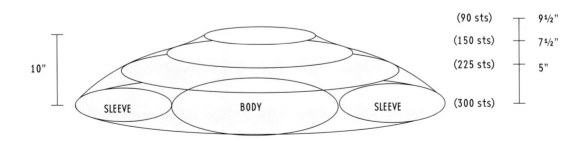

PLACING DESIGNS AND FUTZING WITH THE FORMULAS

When you're designing a sweater with a circular yoke, the most fun part is that you can make cute designs that travel all the way around in a circle. Usually, these sweaters have a series of little designs, one after another. The trick is to place your decrease rounds in between the design rounds, usually in a plain round so that they can't be seen. In order to make that work out, you might need to make your decrease a few rows later or earlier than the above method prescribes; you have my full permission to do so.

You can also tweak the formula to make a sweater that is more closely based on actual measurements rather than percentages. Place a piece of yarn around your neck and expand and contract it until it is sitting on your neck exactly the way you'd like your neckline to sit (before the edging), and place another string around your body just an inch below your armpits. Measure down from the neck string to the armpit string to get the yoke depth; then take the yarn off your neck, measure it, and multiply by your stitch gauge to get the number of stitches you want to decrease to for your neck. (And hey—don't forget to take that string out from under your armpits before you leave the house.)

bringing out the big guns

THE SET-IN SLEEVE SWEATER

he sweater with a set-in sleeve is the type that strikes fear into the heart of many a would-be knitwear designer. But while it's true that working out the sleeve cap of this type of sweater can be a bit more complex than what we saw in the drop-shoulder or raglan sleeve, it really isn't all that bad. Let's take a look at the schematic first.

As you can see, the front and back of the sweater look pretty familiar: It's just a rectangle with the same neck-bite. But a fitted-sleeve sweater reduces the upper part of the sweater to the width of the person's shoulders, and it does that by creating two armholes on the sides, which are very easy to calculate. It also gives a more fitted look by adding shoulder shaping.

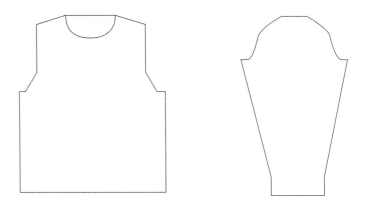

The lower part of the sleeve is exactly the same as the lower part of the raglan sleeve, but that upper part, the sleeve cap, is what freaks people out. That's because the geometry required to get that sleeve cap to fit the armhole perfectly is a bit complicated. For one thing, the measurement around the outside of the sleeve cap needs to be the exact same as the measurement around the inside of the armhole. It can be a bit longer, and can be eased into the armhole, but it can't be shorter, or your sleeve will look crazy.

The question is, How can we make sure that these two measurements are the same? Some people actually knit the front or back of the sweater, measure the armhole and double that number to get the full armhole measurement, and calculate the sleeve cap based on that. Others draw the front or back on knitter's graph paper, then measure that with a tape measure and do some calculations of what that would be in inches.

I don't know about you, but I'd rather have my whole pattern written out before I start knitting. And really, measuring a curve on graph paper with a tape measure doesn't seem like it would be very accurate. I don't understand why anyone would do either of these when you can figure out everything you need to for a sleeve cap just by using a little bit of mathematical perfection called the Pythagorean theorem.

Do you remember this formula? The Scarecrow in *The Wizard of Oz* recites it after being told he already has a brain, only he says it incorrectly. But I'm telling you that you don't need to go see any wizard in order to get the brains to understand this formula. You already have plenty of brains. So let me show it to you.

The Pythagorean theorem states that in a "right triangle"—a triangle that has a 90-degree angle—there is a very specific relationship between the lengths of the three sides. Let's call the side opposite the right angle the "hypotenuse," because that's what it *is* called. It turns out that the square of the length of the hypotenuse is equal to the sum of the squares of the sides (or the other two legs of the triangle). And remember that a square of a number is just the number multiplied by itself. Here's the formula:

side 1 squared + side 2 squared = hypotenuse squared

or $a^2 + b^2 = c^2$. Here it is in a picture:

In knitters' terms:

length squared + width squared = diagonal squared

Why is the Pythagorean theorem our new best friend? Because these kinds of right triangles happen all the time in knitting—decreases or increases often create a diagonal line, and they are spread out over a certain width of fabric (a specific number of stitches) and a certain length (a specific number of rows). With this theorem, we can figure out the measurement of any of the three sides as long as we have the measurement of any two sides, and when we're working out a sleeve cap, that's exactly what we'll need to do.

Let me give you a demonstration of the power of this theorem in knitting. Let's say you were knitting up a piece of fabric at a gauge of 4 stitches per inch and 6 rows per inch, and you need to decrease 8 stitches over 18 rows. That makes a right triangle, as shown on page 150. Now, let's say I asked you for the measurement of the diagonal side of that triangle, because I want to knit a lace edging for that side, and I don't want to have to do any more knitting than I need to. Would you be able to tell me what that length is? Oh sure, you could take out your knitting and knit it up and then measure it. But why bother? Just whip out the Pythagorean theorem instead, because you know two sides of this triangle, and you can figure out the third. You know that the bottom of the triangle is exactly 2" wide, because 8 stitches divided by 4 stitches per inch equals 2". And you know that the vertical side of this triangle is 3" long, because 18 rows divided by our row gauge of 6 rows per inch equals 3.

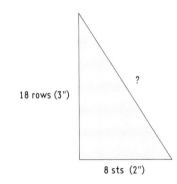

So the theorem tells us that 2 squared + 3 squared = the diagonal squared. Use your calculator to figure out 2 squared or just multiply 2 × 2, and you'll get 4. Same for the other side: 3 squared = 3 × 3 = 9. Since 4 + 9 = 13, that means that 13 equals the diagonal side squared. But does that mean that the third side of this triangle is 13"? No, 13 is the diagonal side *squared*. We need to take the square root of the diagonal to figure out what its actual length is. Grab your calculator (or use the calculator on your computer) to get the square root of 13 (the square root thingy looks like this: $\sqrt{}$). My calculator tells me that the square root of 13 = 3.61 (rounded up). I'm sure your calculator tells you the same. So you'd say, "The length of the diagonal side is 3.61 inches. Suck it, Stoller!"

This works another way, too. If I know the length of the diagonal and either one of the sides, I can figure out the length of the third side. Say I want that diagonal side to be exactly 5", and I've got 16 stitches to decrease. Over how many rows do I need to make those decreases in order for the hypotenuse to measure exactly 5"? Well, using my stitch gauge above, I know that those 16 stitches = 4", which is the width of the bottom side of my triangle.

So I'll whip out my formula: length squared + width squared = diagonal squared. Plugging in the numbers I

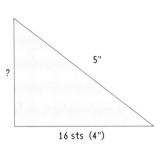

know, it gives me: length squared + 4 squared = 5 squared. Now, 4 squared equals 16 and 5 squared equals 25. So that means that: length squared + 16 = 25. Hey, you're a smarty pants by now. You can see that if you subtract 16 from 25, you'll end up with the value of that "length squared," or 9. Now if we take the square root of that, we get 3. So we have 3" over which to decrease those stitches. And 3 times the row gauge of 6 rows per inch equals 18 rows. I need to decrease 16 stitches over 18 rows to end up with a diagonal measurement of exactly 5". Yay.

filling in the Measurements

BACK AND FRONT

The bottom part of the back and front will be the same as the other two sweaters you've learned about. When we get to the armhole, we'll bind off 1" of stitches on each side, just like for the raglan sweater. But after that, we'll decrease one stitch each side every other row until the upper body equals the width of the person's actual body from shoulder to shoulder. Narrowing the body fabric to this width means we'll have no more issues with bunching fabric under the arms. Then we'll keep knitting straight until the armhole reaches our desired armhole length, which will now be 1" less than on the other two sweaters. Why? Because we're going to end the armhole right at the top of the shoulder. But we aren't going to end the sweater there. The front and back will continue on for 1", over which we are going to shape the shoulders of the sweater, for an even nicer fit. Why exactly 1"? Because that's the standard shoulder slope, and I like standards when I can get 'em.

For the sleeves, we'll start by increasing stitches until we get to the desired upper arm width. Then we're going to bind off 1" of stitches on each side. Next comes the tricky part that requires calculations: We're going to bind off one stitch each side over a particular number of rows in a way that will give us a nice curve. In the last ½" of the sleeve cap, we're going to bind off an inch of stitches on each side. And then we're going to bind off all the remaining stitches, giving us a flat part at the top of the sleeve cap. This flat part will be 25% of the sleeve width at the upper arm (usually from 3" to 5").

On the front and back, we know from our previous examples that the bottom of the sweater measures 20" wide. We also know that the desired total sweater length is 23¼". The armhole measurement (from the top of the shoulder bone point to the armpit itself) is 8", but, as always, we need to add an inch for breathing room, which gives us 9". That number—9"—is our armhole depth. We'll add that to the schematic. We're going to bind off 1" of stitches on each side as soon as we reach the desired body length to armpit, and we'll write that in as well. We know we want the neck to be 7" wide and 3" deep (see

previous examples), so we'll write those numbers in, too.

There is only one more measurement for the front and back that we need to enter—the width from shoulder to shoulder. This is a measurement you get from the body (see page 122). For this example, let's say we measured this and it came out to be 14½". We'll write this in, too. Now we have all the measurements we need for the body schematic.

SLEEVES

Taking numbers from our previous examples, we know that the width at the wrist is 7½", and that the width at the upper arm is 14" (the actual measurement was 13", plus 50% of the 2" of body ease—1"—equals 14"). We also know that the desired sleeve length is 18" (this is measured from the armpit to the wrist, minus 1" to give some room in the armpit), and we're going to knit the first 2½" in ribbing. We're going to bind off 1" of stitches on each side, just as we did on the body, before we begin the cap shaping, so we'll write that in, too.

SLEEVE CAP

Let's start by filling in the width of the top of the sleeve cap, which we will calculate as 25% of the upper arm width. I've seen this calculated as 20% of the body circumference, but just because I've got big boobs doesn't

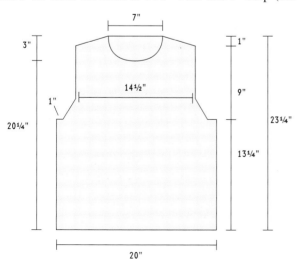

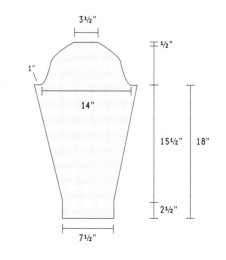

mean I've got large arms, and vice versa. I prefer it to be a percentage of the upper arm, and 25% does the trick. This means multiplying our upper arm width by .25, and 14 × .25 = 3.5. This is the width at the top of our sleeve cap, so we'll write that in.

It's another rule of thumb that we will bind off 1" of stitches on each side of the sleeve in the last ½" of rows before the final bind-off, so we'll put that into the schematic as well.

Now, the last part of the cap is the length from under-arm bind-off to the final bind-off. How long is that? Well, it's a toughie, and I'll show you why. Let's take a close-up look at the armhole on the sweater and the sleeve cap itself. We need that sleeve cap to fit into that armhole perfectly. Since we'll be sewing together the front and the back of the sweater to make the armhole, half the sleeve cap needs to fit perfectly into the front of the sweater, and the other half needs to fit perfectly into the back.

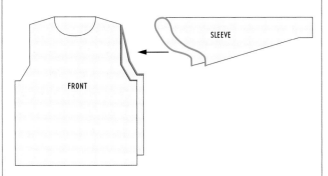

That means that *half* of the sleeve cap needs to fit perfectly into *half* of the armhole made by the front and back of the sweater together. Let's take a close-up look at those two parts alone. You can see that the inside edge of the armhole and outside edge of half the sleeve cap—indicated by the blue line in the diagram—need to measure *exactly* the same if the full sleeve cap is going to fit into the completed armhole. (We don't need to worry about the 1" worth of bound-off stitches on either the armhole or the beginning of the sleeve cap since we

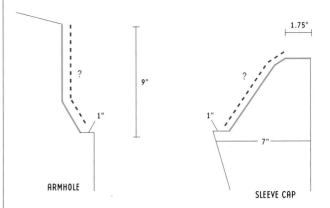

already know they'll match up.) If we put in the measurements that we know so far, we can see what parts of those edges we still need to work out, indicated by the red dashed line in the diagram.

In order to complete the sleeve cap, we first need to figure out the total measurement of the armhole. And what is that measurement? You might raise your hand and say, "I know! It's 9 inches!" To which I'd have to say, No, that's the armhole *depth*, not its measurement. If the armhole were completely straight without that angled line of decreases at the bottom, then yes, it would measure exactly 9". But we need to figure out what the measurement of that angled part is and add it to the remaining straight part if we want to know the *exact* measurement.

We can figure out what the straight part measures by taking the full armhole depth and subtracting the amount of depth that is taken up by that angled part. How do we get to that? We need to figure out how many rows we will have to work to get the right number of decreases, then convert that to inches, and finally, subtract it from the armhole depth. Have no fear: We can do this.

We start out with 102 stitches at the bottom of this sweater (see previous examples). After we've bound off an inch on each side—5 stitches on each side, so 10 stitches in total—we're left with 92 stitches. Now, we want to decrease 1 stitch each side every other row until we reach the width of the sweater at the shoulders. Our shoulder width is 14.5", multiplied by our stitch gauge of 5 stitches per inch = 72.5, which I'll round down to 72 stitches. We have 92 stitches and we need to decrease to 72 stitches, so we need to get rid of 20 stitches. That's only 10 stitches on each side, but since we're only working 1 decrease each side *every other row,* it will take us 20 rows to do this. Dividing that by the row gauge of 7.5 inches gives us 2.67.

So, if I'm spending 2.67" worth of rows decreasing stitches, and then knit the rest straight until I reach the armhole depth, it means that the straight bit is going to be the armhole depth minus the height of these decrease rows. We take our armhole depth of 9" and subtract 2.67", and we get 6.33". And *that's* the length of the straight part of the armhole.

But we still don't know the measurement of the angled part. Yet are we frightened? No, we are not. That's because we have our friend the Pythagorean theorem in our back pocket. That angled part is really the hypotenuse of a triangle made up of the length of the area in which we made our decreases, as well as the width. We just calculated the length, above (it was 2.67"). The width we already figured out, too, when we worked out that we needed 10 stitches to decrease on each side after the bind-offs, so one side of our triangle is 2". Now we just need to figure out the hypotenuse. Length squared + width squared = diagonal squared. So $(2 \times 2) + (2.67 \times 2.67)$ = diagonal squared.

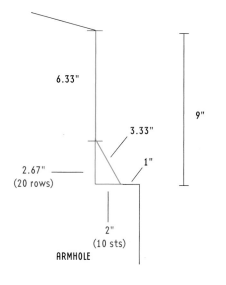

That comes out to be 11.13, and the square root of that is 3.33. The length of that diagonal part is 3.33". So the total measurement of the armhole is 3.33", plus the straight part, 6.33", for a total of 9.66".

Now back to the sleeve cap. We'll just look at half of it, since this is what is going to have to fit into that 9.66". We'll work our way down from the top. First, we know the width of the flat top of the sleeve is 3.5". (Remember? It's 25% of the upper arm width.) But only half of that, or 1.75" worth, is going to go into this half of the armhole. Then, we know that we bound off 1" worth of stitches over the last ½" of rows. I'm not going to make you do the theorem to work this out here: The number comes out to be very close to 1⅛", or 1.125. (This number will be the same for *every* sleeve cap we make—as long as we decrease 1" worth of stitches over ½" worth of rows. So you can use this measurement of 1⅛" over and over again.) If we add these two together—1.75 + 1.125—we get 2.875 or 2.88". So the top of the sleeve and that final bind-off make up 2.88" of the curve of half the sleeve cap. If we subtract that number from the measurement of the armhole, we'll get what the rest of the sleeve cap should measure. So 9.66" (the armhole curve measurement) minus 2.88" equals 6.78". That's the remaining measurement in the sleeve cap. So how do we go about decreasing our stitches so that we get this exact measurement? We gotta calculate it. How? Well, I can tell you this: I've got a fever, and the only prescription is . . . more Pythagorean theorem!

Let's take a look. We know the diagonal needs to be 6.78". All we need is the length or the width to figure out the other side. Do we know the length? No, we have no freakin' clue. Do we know the width? No, but we can figure that one out. We know that the base of this sleeve cap is 12" (14" at the armhole, minus the 1" of bind-offs at *each* side). Let's just look at half of that number for now—6". From this, we will subtract half of the 3½" we remove at the top—which was 1.75": 6 − 1.75 = 4.25. And we subtract another inch from that, because that's how much we got rid of in the top ½" of rows. We are left with 3.25".

That's the base of our triangle! Now that we have two sides of the triangle—the diagonal and the width—we can figure out the length of this section of the sleeve cap. Length squared + 3.25 squared = 6.78 squared, which means that length squared + 10.56 = 45.97. Or 45.97 − 10.56 = 35.41 (length squared). Since the square root of 35.41 is 5.95, that's the height of this part of the sleeve cap. To make this

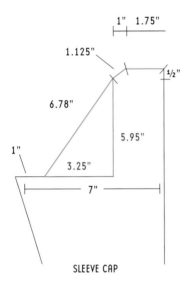

SLEEVE CAP

diagonal, we are going to need to decrease 3.25" worth of stitches over 5.95" worth of rows.

You know what? We can put our Pythagorean theorem away, because we're ready to put stitch counts into this sucker.

filling in the stitches

BACK AND FRONT

We'll start with the back. We begin with 102 stitches at the bottom, knit 2½" of ribbing, then we knit until the sweater is 13¼" long. Next, we bind off 5 stitches on each

side of the next two rows (that's 1" of stitches), and then we need to decrease 1 stitch each side every other row until we get to the width of the shoulders. We already figured out that this means 10 stitches on each side, but just as a reminder: We begin with 102 stitches, and after casting off those 5 stitches on each side we're left with 92 stitches. The width at the shoulders, 14.5", multiplied by our stitch gauge gives us 72.5, which we round down to 72. So we need to decrease from 92 to 72, which means we have to decrease 20 stitches altogether: 10 stitches on each side. We need to decrease 1 stitch each side every other row 10 times. Then we should knit straight until the armhole is 9" from the initial bind-off.

Okay, now we need to shape the shoulders. At this point, we have decreased the width of the body to the width of the shoulders, so we have 72 stitches on the needle. The neck was 7" wide, or 36 stitches. Subtracting the stitches for the neck from the stitches we have (72 − 36) leaves us with 36 stitches for the shoulders, 18 stitches on each side.

Now, we want to decrease these over 1" worth of rows. Our row count is 7.5 rows per inch, so we'll round it up to 8. We can bind off only at the beginning of our rows, so that really only gives us 4 rows over which we can bind off stitches. We have 18 stitches to bind off, and we want to divide those 18 stitches into 4 parts: 18 ÷ 4 = 4.5. We can't bind off only 4.5 stitches, so let's bind off 5 stitches twice, and 4 stitches twice. That will get rid of our 18 stitches over 1" of rows. After we've finished binding off the shoulders, we'll bind off the remaining neck stitches. And the back is done.

The front of the sweater is going to be the same as the back, except for the neck shaping. The neck starts 3" below the end of the sweater (remember, we're measuring from the end of the shoulder shaping here). This means we need to knit until the body measures 20¼". When the body is that length, we need to knit the shoulder stitches, then bind off the center 18 stitches, then bind off the remaining shoulder stitches. Subtracting 18 from the stitches I have at this point (72), I get 54, and dividing that in half I get 27. So I'll knit 27 stitches, bind off the next 18 stitches, and knit the remaining 27 stitches. Then I'll decrease 1 stitch at each neck edge every other row 9 times, and this knocks out the remaining 18 stitches. However, I also need to start worrying about the shoulder bind-offs at this point, so I have to remember that at the same time that I'm shaping the neck, I also have to start binding off the shoulders after the armhole is done, which will be when it is 9" long.

SLEEVES

For the lower part of the sleeve, we can borrow what we calculated for the raglan sweater in the previous chapter. We begin with 42 stitches at the wrist, knit in ribbing for 2½", then work in stockinette stitch. We want to get from those 42 stitches to the stitch count at the underarm, which is 14". Multiplying by our stitch gauge we get 70 stitches, and adding 2 stitches for the seams we get 72. This means we need to increase 30 stitches (72 − 42), and since we'll increase them two at a time, that gives us 15 increase rows. The length of this part of the sleeve is 18", and minus the 2½" of ribbing leaves us 15½". I want to get all my increases done at least an inch before I do the underarm bind-off, so I have only 14½" over which to increase my

stitches, or 108.75 rows, which I'll round down to 108. The Magic Formula says that means I need to increase each side every 8 rows 9 times, then every 6 rows 6 times. I need to continue knitting until the sleeve measures 18" from the cast-on edge. After that we bind off 5 stitches each side.

Okay, now we need to figure out the decreases for the diagonal. At this point, we've increased our sleeves to 72 stitches, then bound off 5 stitches each side, so we're left with 62 stitches. At the top of the sleeve we're going to bind off 3.5" (25% of the upper arm measurement), which will take up 18 stitches (3.5 × stitch gauge of 5 = 17.5, rounded to 18). We also plan to bind off an additional 1" on either side of that, which will take another 10 stitches altogether. So the top part of this sleeve—the last ½" of rows and the top—will use up 28 stitches; 62 − 28 = 34, and that's the number of stitches remaining to decrease. Doing them 2 at a time gives us 17 decrease rows, which we need to space over 5.95" worth of rows. (You remember that number, don't you? You gave a pound of your own flesh to calculate it on page 154.) So 5.95 multiplied by our row gauge of 7.5 gives us 44.62 rows, which we'll round down to 44. We need to space 17 decrease rows over 44 total rows. Magic Formula says that's every 2 rows 12 times, and every 4 rows 5 times.

In every instance so far, we've wanted our diagonals to be diagonals. However, here in Set-in Sleeveville, we kind

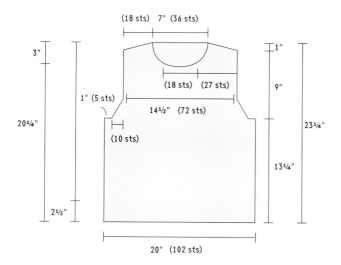

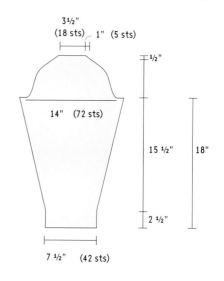

of prefer a curve over a diagonal. That means we want our decreases to start out fast at the beginning, get slower in the middle, then get fast again. But that is supereasy to do. We just split up our fast decreases—the ones that happen every 2 rows—and put half at the beginning and the other half at the end. Then we put our slower decreases—the ones that happen every 4 rows—in the middle. So here we'll decrease 1 stitch each side every 2 rows 6 times, then every 4 rows 5 times, then every 2 rows 6 times.

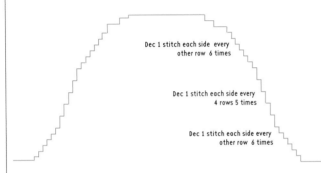

Dec 1 stitch each side every other row 6 times

Dec 1 stitch each side every 4 rows 5 times

Dec 1 stitch each side every other row 6 times

And now, we are really and truly done. You've accomplished what some might say is impossible: You've calculated a set-in sleeve cap! Do a little dance, make a little love, and get down tonight!

writing out the pattern

Whew boy! And now let's revel in the beauty of how this set-in sleeve pattern gets written out.

SIZE

Finished bust: 40"

Finished length: 23¼"

NEEDLES

US 8 (5mm) needles

US 6 (4mm) needles

US 6 (4 mm) 16" circular needle

GAUGE

20 sts and 30 rows = 4" in St st using size 8 (5mm) needles

BACK

With smaller needles, CO 102 sts.

ROW 1 (RS): K1, *k2, p2; rep from * to last st, k1.

ROW 2: P1, *k2, p2; rep from * to last st, p1.

Rep rows 1 and 2 until piece meas 2½" from beg, end with a WS row.

Change to larger needles. Work in St st until piece meas 13¼" from beg. BO 5 sts at beg of the next 2 rows —92 sts.

Dec 1 st at each side every other row 10 times —72 sts. Work even until piece meas 9" from armhole bind-offs.

BO 5 sts at beg of the next 4 rows, then BO 4 sts at beg of the foll 2 rows, then BO rem stitches.

FRONT

With smaller needles, CO 102 sts.

ROW 1 (RS): K1, *k2, p2; rep from * to last st, k1.

ROW 2: P1, *k2, p2; rep from * to last st, p1.

Rep rows 1 and 2 until piece meas 2½" from beg, end with a WS row.

Change to larger needles. Work in St st until piece meas 13¼" from beg. BO 5 sts at beg of the next 2 rows —92 sts.

Dec 1 st at each side every other row 10 times —72 sts.

Work even until piece meas 20¼" from beg, end with a WS row.

Work to center 18 sts, join a new ball of yarn, BO center 18 sts, work to end.

BO 5 sts at beg of the next 4 rows and 4 sts at beg of the foll 4 rows.

AT THE SAME TIME, when sweater measures 20¼" from beg, continue raglan decreases, work to center 18 sts, join a 2nd ball of yarn, BO center 18 sts, work to end. Working both sides at the same time, BO 1 st at each neck edge every other row 9 times. Work even at neck edge and cont shoulder decs until no sts remain.

SLEEVES

With smaller needles, CO 42 sts.

ROW 1 (RS): K1, *k2, p2; rep from * to last st, k1.

ROW 2: P1, *k2, p2; rep from * to last st, p1.

Rep rows 1 and 2 until piece meas 2½" from beg, end with a WS row.

Change to larger needles. Work in St st, inc 1 st each side every 8th row 9 times, then every 6th row 6 times —72 sts.

Work even in St st until piece meas 18" from beg, end with a WS row.

BO 5 sts at beg of the next 2 rows.

Dec 1 st each side every other row 6 times, then every 4th row 5 times, then every other row 6 times—28 sts.

BO 3 sts at beg of next 2 rows, then 2 sts at beg of foll 2 rows. BO rem sts.

FINISHING

Sew shoulder seams. Matching bind-off areas at armhole on sweater front and back to bind-offs at sleeves, ease sleeves into front and back of sweater body and sew.

With circular needle, pick up sts along neckline (see "One, Two, Pick up Stitch," page 162), and work in 2 × 2 rib for 1". BO loosely.

Sew side and sleeve seams.

details, details

n the three previous chapters, you learned a number of different ways to create a body and sleeves for a knit garment. However, there are a couple more details you need to work out before you have a truly completed sweater pattern. In this chapter, we'll deal with a few of those details, as well as how to calculate the amount of yarn you'll need in order to knit up the pattern you drafted.

ring Around the collar

NECKLINES AND FINISHES

In the examples above, we've made a 3" deep neckline and added 2" to the neckline width to allow for a crew neck finish. But this type of neckline does not have to be finished with a crew neck; it could have a turtleneck, roll neck, or split collar, to name just a few. Here are a number of necklines and finishes you can choose from when designing a sweater:

CROCHET/MOCK CROCHET EDGING: You don't need to add a collar to your project, but you shouldn't leave the neckline without any kind of finish at all. Not only is that unsightly—all those bind-offs and decreases have likely left a bumpy edge—but it's also too stretchy to hold its shape. One way to stabilize it and even out those bumps is to crochet around the entire neckline. The most common crochet edging is crab stitch, which is simply a single crochet worked from left to right instead of right to left. It's a great edging to use on a lace project or on a sweater with a deeper, wider neckline. Alternatively, if you're really opposed to crocheting, you can get a similar effect by picking up stitches around the neckline, knitting one row, and then binding off (loosely!) on the next row.

CLASSIC CREW NECK: For a classic crew, start with a neckline that is at least 3" deep. Pick up stitches around the neckline (see "One, Two, Pick up Stitch," page 162), and knit in a 1 × 1 or 2 × 2 rib for about ¾–1". Be sure to bind off *loosely,* or your head won't fit through.

TURTLENECK: A turtleneck is just a crew neck that keeps on going for 4 to 6". To make your turtleneck fold over nicely, start it on smaller needles, then change to larger needles when it is halfway done. Again, be sure to bind off loosely.

ROLL NECK: Start off as you do for a crew neck, but instead of knitting in ribbing or any other nonrolling stitch, knit in stockinette stitch for about 3–4". This collar will roll down on itself. A nice variation on this is to first knit a few rows of ribbing, then work in stockinette stitch for the rest of the roll neck. Or you could knit only 4 rows of stockinette stitch so that there is just enough fabric to roll over itself and cover up the neckline edging.

FUNNEL NECK: This is sort of like a turtleneck, in that it goes up the neck, but it doesn't fold over. It can be especially nice if you'd like to continue a stitch pattern (such as a cable) from the body of the sweater up to the neck. If you want to do that, it's easiest to put the back-neck stitches onto a stitch holder instead of binding them off, and do the same for the stitches at the bottom of the front neck. Pick up stitches from the sides of the front neck as usual, and knit till the neck is as long as you'd like.

SPLIT COLLAR: Pick up stitches around the neckline beginning at the front center of the neckline. Do not join into a round. Instead, knit back and forth in ribbing for as long as you want the collar to be—usually about 3". For a collar wider than this, start with a smaller needle and change to a larger size needle about halfway through so that the collar becomes wider around the outer perimeter and can lie flat.

V-NECK: A V-neck sweater requires a different neckline, obviously, than the crew neck we've been looking at up to now. While the back-neck width can remain the same, the front is split in the center, usually at the same point as the underarm shaping begins, and then decreases are worked so

crew neck   turtleneck   roll neck   split collar   boatneck   V-neck

that the V shape is exactly as wide at the top as the back neck. To do this, work out how many stitches need to be decreased over how many rows, and use the Magic Formula to calculate how these decreases should be made, ending your decrease at least 1" from the top of the sweater. If you have an odd number of stitches in your sweater body, resulting in an odd number of stitches for your back neck, place the center stitch on a stitch holder and work your decreases on the remaining stitches. If you have an even number of stitches, you'll need to create that center stitch later, when you pick up stitches for the edging (see "One, Two, Pick up Stitch," page 162).

In our sweater examples, our back neck was 36 stitches. This means that for a V-neck we have to decrease 36 stitches in the front as well, and we need to begin our shaping at the same point where the armhole begins—when the front measures 13¼". If our armhole depth is 10", in order to have our shaping done 1" before the top of the front, we have 9" of rows over which to work our decreases. Multiplying 9 by our row gauge of 7.5 gives us 67.5 rows over which to work these decreases, which we'll round down to 66. Since we'll be decreasing our 36 stitches 2 stitches at a time, that means we'll have to evenly distribute 18 decrease rows over those 66 rows. According to the Magic Formula, this means we'll need to decrease every 2 rows 3 times, and every 4 rows 15 times. Now, when we make our decreases or increases on sleeve bottoms or sleeve tops, it doesn't matter terribly much if you can see where the rate of increase or decrease changes, because this part of the sleeve is down under the arm or sewn into an armhole. But here on the V-neck, the decrease lines are smack dab front and center, and we want to make them look as even as possible. To do this, we'll alternate the "every 2 rows" and "every 4 rows" as long as we can. For this neckline, that means we would decrease 1 stitch each side every 2 rows, then every 4 rows, and repeat that 2 times more. Then we'd decrease 1 stitch every 4 rows 12 times.

For a V-neck edging, beginning at the lower left, pick up 3 stitches for every 4 rows along the diagonal, and 1 stitch for every stitch along the back. Place the center stitch, if you have one, on the needle, and if you don't, cre-

ate a stitch from the strand between the two center stitches with an invisible increase, like the make 1 (see page 104). Knit the edging as usual in a rib stitch, but make a double centered decrease with the center stitch and the stitch just before and after it (slip 2 together, knit 1, pass 2 slipped stitches over), and repeat that every 4 rounds. This edging, like the crew neck, should be ¾–1" wide.

BOATNECK: A boatneck is perhaps the easiest neckline of all to make, because it requires no neckline shaping and no neckline edging. The simplest form is to simply knit the front and back straight, with no shoulder shaping and no neck shaping, and knit the top ½" or more in ribbing or some other flat stitch. Stitch the shoulders together, leaving the center open. The boatneck itself should be about half the cross-back width, which means each shoulder will be 25% of this measurement (if you are working a boatneck on a drop-shoulder sweater, the shoulders will be wider than that).

Splitsville

DESIGNING A CARDIGAN

If you can draft a pullover sweater pattern, you can draft a cardigan, because it is basically the same as a pullover, except the front is split in half. What happens at the front edges—whether they are finished with some sort of band and then meet in the middle, or come together with a zipper, or overlap and connect with buttons and buttonholes—is the only additional factor you need to consider in working out a cardigan pattern.

The openings of cardigans are of two basic types: (1) they meet in the center; or (2) they overlap. A cardigan that zips closed is one that meets in the center, but so is one that has a fancy beaded edging. For this type of cardigan, the dimension of each front is simply half of a pullover front. However, these types of sweaters usually have a front band or edging knit or sewn on (see below for how to work cardigan bands), and you need to subtract the width of that band from the width of each front when working out your pattern. A cardigan that buttons closed needs to overlap in the center. For a buttoned cardigan, you need to widen each front exactly half the width of the front band (see below for basic band widths).

i'M witH tHe baNd

KNITTING FRONT BANDS FOR A CARDIGAN

A cardigan band goes from the bottom of the sweater up to the neckline; when the neck stitches are picked up later, they are picked up from both the sweater front and its front band. Cardigan bands are usually 1–2" wide, and if it is to be a button band, it should be twice as wide as the button itself (thus, a ¾" button would require a band that's 1½" wide). Bands are most often worked in a non-rolling stitch, such as ribbing, moss stitch, or garter stitch.

There are two ways to work the bands: One is to knit them along with the sweater front, and the other is to add them after the front has been completed. The challenge with knitting them at the same time is that because the band is worked in a different stitch than the rest of the sweater, it can also have a different row gauge. Garter stitch, for instance, takes many more rows to knit an inch of fabric than stockinette stitch does. So, if you want to knit the bands at the same time as the front, you must make a long swatch testing how the body and band stitches work together. You don't want the band stitch to make the fabric flare out or pull in at the edge.

One way to be certain that your edging is the same length as the sweater front is to pick up stitches from the front edge, and knit your band right onto it. Of course,

you have to be sure that you pick up exactly the right number of stitches for this to work, so you'll need to make a swatch with your edging stitch to gauge the number of stitches per inch. Then multiply the length of your sweater front (which you know from your schematic, or you can simply measure the completed front) by the band stitch gauge and pick up exactly that number of stitches, evenly, from the front band.

Another method is to knit the front band separately, then sew it on. The band usually goes from the bottom of the sweater up to the neckline. When the neck stitches are picked up later, they are picked up from both the sweater front and its front band.

When working button bands, work the side without buttonholes first. Then place pins where you'd like the buttons to be located; they should start at least ½" from the top of the band, and end at least ½" from the bottom. Space the remaining buttons evenly between these two points. Use the pins to help you place the buttonholes in the correct locations on the other band.

HoW MuCH YarN?

YOU DO THE MATH

It's not difficult to figure out how much yarn you need to knit up your pattern. Just grab your 5" × 5" swatch and weigh it (you may need a food or postal scale to get an accurate weight). This will tell you how many ounces of yarn it takes to knit an area of square inches of this size. To calculate the square inches, multiply one side of your swatch by the other side: in this case, 5" × 5" = 25 square inches.

Then go back to your schematic and, for the front and back, calculate its approximate area in square inches by multiplying its widest measurement (across the chest) by its longest measurement (the full length of the sweater front or back). For the sleeves, think of them as Tetris pieces. Imagine fitting them together side by side, with one right-side up and the other upside down. Then, to figure out the area of both sleeves, just take (width at the bottom of the sleeve + width at upper arm) × length of sleeve including the sleeve cap. Calculate the approximate area for the neck finishing (the height of the neck finish multiplied by the circumference of the neckline) and front bands if you're making a cardigan.

Add all areas together for the total area in square inches and divide by the square inches of your gauge swatch—in other words, you're trying to figure out how many gauge swatches it would take to make up this sweater area. Now multiply the result by the number of ounces or grams your gauge swatch weighed (see page 161). This is the number of ounces or grams of yarn you need to complete the project.

Finally, divide the number of ounces (or grams) of yarn you need by how many ounces (or grams) are in a single ball of the yarn you are using, and you'll get the total number of balls you'll need. Of course, if the yarn is in grams, you'll need to convert the weight from ounces to grams if you measured your swatch in ounces, and vice versa.

One, Two, Pick up Stitch
HOW MANY STITCHES TO PICK UP AROUND A NECKLINE

ou might think that the number of stitches to pick up around a neckline would be equal to the number of stitches bound off. In each of the preceding examples, we bound off 36 stitches for the back neck, and 36 stitches for the front, for a total of 72 stitches. So why wouldn't you just pick up 72 stitches? The reason is that the depth of the neckline also contributes to the total circumference of the neck. So a deeper neckline would require more stitches to be picked up, while a shallower neckline would require fewer. So use the following formula to calculate how many stitches need to be picked up around the neckline:

1. For every bound-off stitch on a horizontal edge (the back neck, and the bottom of the front neck), pick up 1 stitch.

2. For the straight, vertical rows along the sides, pick up 2 stitches for every 3 rows. That's because, in stockinette stitch, knit stitches are usually about two-thirds as tall as they are wide. How convenient!

3. For bound-off or decreased stitches along an angle (as on either side of the neck), pick up 3 stitches for every 4 rows. (We take up more stitches than in step 2 above because diagonals are sort of midway between vertical and horizontal lines—so we don't take as many as 100% of the stitches like we do on the horizontals, but we need more than the 66% we're taking on the verticals, so we make it 75%, or three-quarters.)

abbreviations

beg	begin(ning)(s)
BO	bind off
CC	contrasting color
ch	chain
cn	cable needle
CO	cast on
cont	continue(ing)
dec	decrease(ing)
dpn(s)	double-pointed needle(s)
est	establish(ed)
foll	follow(ed)(ing)(s)
inc	increase
k2tog	knit 2 sts together
k	knit
kfb	knit in front and back of st
kwise	knitwise
LH	left hand
m1	make 1: Pick up bar between sts and k tbl
MC	main color
meas	measure(s)
p	purl
p2tog	purl 2 sts together
patt(s)	pattern(s)
pfb	purl in front and back of st
PU	pick up
pm	place marker
pwise	purlwise
rem(s)	remain(s)(ing)
rep(s)	repeat(s)
rev St st	reverse Stockinette st: P on RS, k on WS
RH	right hand
rnd(s)	round(s)
RS	right side
s2kp	slip 2, knit, pass: slip 2 sts tog as if to k2tog, k1, pass the slipped sts over k1 st
sk2p	slip, knit 2, pass: slip 1 st kwise, k2tog, pass the slipped st over k2tog st
sc	single crochet
skp	slip 1 st kwise, k next st, pass the slipped st over k st
sl	slip
sl st	slip stitch
sm	slip marker
ssk	(slip 1 kwise) twice, insert LH needle into slipped sts and k2tog tbl
ssp	(slip 1 kwise) twice, slip sts back onto LH needle and p2tog tbl
sssk	(slip 1 kwise) 3 times, insert LH needle into slipped sts and k3tog
sssp	(slip 1 kwise) 3 times, slip sts back onto LH needle and p3tog tbl
St st	Stockinette st: K on RS, p on WS
st(s)	stitch(es)
tbl	through back loop
tog	together
WS	wrong side
wy	waste yarn
wyib	with yarn in back
wyif	with yarn in front
yo	yarn over

PART III
the patterns

LeiLa McMiLLan

DRESS TO IMPRESS

 dreamed up this Technicolor baby tunic as a smart way to use up some of the scrap yarn in my stash. I love using scraps because it lends itself to mixing patterns and colors easily. This dress is particularly fun to knit; while the colorwork looks like it was done with plenty of skillful, stranded knitting, in fact it was made with a variety of slip stitch patterns, so you only ever knit with a single color in any given row. The results are so impressive that once you get the hang of it, you'll wonder why you haven't been slip stitching forever.

STITCH PATTERN
LINEN STITCH (MULTIPLE OF 2 STS + 1)
ROW 1 (RS): K1, *sl 1 wyif, k1; rep from * to end.

ROW 2: Sl 1, p1, *sl 1 wyib, p1; rep from * to last st, k1.

Rep rows 1 and 2 for patt.

DIRECTIONS
Note: Always work first and last st of every row in St st using color indicated for row.

BACK
With larger needles and MC, CO 73 (83, 93) sts.

ROWS 1 AND 2: With MC, work in Linen st.

ROWS 3 AND 4: With D, work in Linen st.

ROWS 5, 6, 7 AND 8: With MC, work in Linen st.

SET-UP ROW 1 (RS): With A, k, inc 5 (7, 9) sts evenly across row—78 (90, 102) sts.

SIZE
S (M, L); 3–6 mos (9–12 mos, 18 mos)

Finished chest: 20½ (23½, 27)"

Finished length: 14¾ (16¼, 17¾)"

MATERIALS
Debbie Bliss *Baby Cashmerino* (55% wool, 33% microfiber, 12% cashmere; 50g/137 yd)

MC: 2 (3, 4) balls #008 Navy

A: 1 ball #026 Seafoam

B: 1 ball #029 Fuschia

C: 1 ball #608 Lt Lilac

D: 1 ball #032 Blue

E: 1 ball #023 Sienna

US 4 (3.5mm) needles

US 3 (3.25mm) circular needle

1 stitch holder

1 small button

Tapestry needle

GAUGE
23 sts and 32 rows = 4" in St st using larger needles

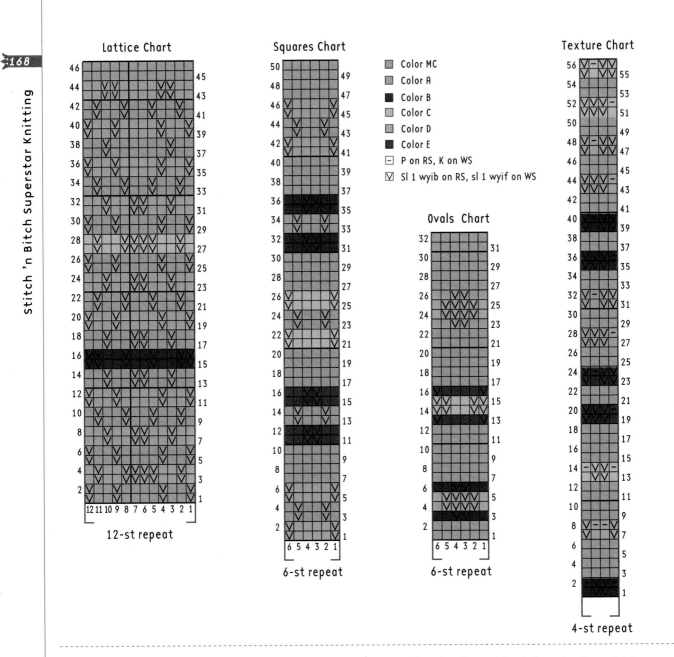

Lattice Chart

12-st repeat

Squares Chart

6-st repeat

Ovals Chart

6-st repeat

Texture Chart

4-st repeat

- ☐ Color MC
- ☐ Color A
- ■ Color B
- ☐ Color C
- ☐ Color D
- ■ Color E
- ⊟ P on RS, K on WS
- ☑ Sl 1 wyib on RS, sl 1 wyif on WS

SET-UP ROW 2: Purl.

Beg row 1 with stitch #10 and ending with stitch #3, work 46 rows of Lattice Chart, dec 1 st each side on row 13 and every foll 16th row—72 (84, 96) sts.

Cont with decs as est, beg row 1 with stitch #1 and ending with stitch #6, work 30 (40, 50) rows of Squares Chart—70 (80, 90) sts.

Working 2 (2, 1) more decs as est, beg row 1 with stitch

#5 (6, 1) and ending with stitch #2 (1, 6), work 32 rows of Ovals Chart—66 (76, 88) sts.

ARMHOLE SHAPING

With MC, BO 3 (4, 6) sts at beg of next 2 rows—60 (68, 76) sts.

Work 24 rows of Texture Chart while dec 1 st each side every RS row 3 times, then every 4th row 4 times—46 (54, 62) sts.

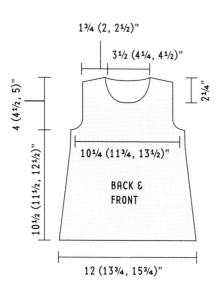

1¾ (2, 2½)"

3½ (4¼, 4½)"

4 (4½, 5)"

2¼"

10¼ (11¾, 13½)"

BACK & FRONT

10½ (11½, 12½)"

12 (13¾, 15¾)"

DIVIDE FOR BACK OPENING

NEXT ROW (RS): Cont with Texture Chart, with MC, k21 (25, 29) sts for right back. Place rem 25 (29, 33) sts onto a holder for left back.

RIGHT BACK

Turn and CO 4 sts for button band.

NEXT ROW (WS): With MC, k4, p to end.

Cont with row 27 of chart, complete a total of 45 (49, 53) rows of Texture Chart.

RIGHT NECK AND SHOULDER SHAPING

NEXT ROW (WS): With MC, BO 14 (16, 18) sts, p to end—11 (13, 15) sts.

NEXT ROW: With MC, BO 5 (6, 7) sts, k to end.

NEXT ROW: Purl.

BO rem 6 (7, 8) sts.

LEFT BACK

With MC and RS facing, rejoin yarn to rem 25 (29, 33) sts.

NEXT ROW (RS): With MC, k.

NEXT ROW: With MC, p to last 4 sts, k4.

Cont with row 27 of chart, complete a total of 46 (50, 54) rows of Texture Chart.

LEFT NECK AND SHOULDER SHAPING

NEXT ROW (RS): With MC, BO 14 (16, 18) sts, k to end—11 (13, 15) sts.

NEXT ROW: With MC, BO 5 (6, 7) sts, p to end.

NEXT ROW: Knit.

BO rem 6 (7, 8) sts.

FRONT

Work same as back until 16 (20, 24) rows of Texture Chart are complete.

LEFT NECK SHAPING

NEXT ROW (RS):

SIZES S AND M ONLY: *With MC, k1, ssk, k14 (15).*

SIZE L ONLY: *With MC, k19.*

Place rem sts onto a holder for all sizes.

NEXT ROW: With MC, BO 2 sts, p to end—14 (15, 17) sts.

Cont with Texture Chart, complete any rem armhole decs as for back and dec 1 st at neck edge on next 2 RS rows—11 (13, 15) sts. Work even until row 46 (50, 54) is complete.

LEFT SHOULDER SHAPING

NEXT ROW (RS): With MC, BO 5 (6, 7) sts, k to end.

NEXT ROW: Purl.

BO rem 6 (7, 8) sts.

RIGHT NECK SHAPING

Keep center 16 (20, 24) sts on holder. With RS facing, join MC to rem 17 (18, 19) sts.

NEXT ROW:

SIZES S AND M ONLY: *BO 2 sts, k to last 3 (3) sts, k2tog, k1—14 (15) sts.*

SIZE L ONLY: *BO 2 sts, k to end—17 sts.*

Cont with Texture Chart, complete any rem armhole decs as for back and dec 1 st at neck edge on next 2 RS rows. Work even until row 47 (51, 55) is complete—11 (13, 15) sts.

RIGHT SHOULDER SHAPING

NEXT ROW: With MC, BO 5 (6, 7) sts, p to end.

NEXT ROW: Knit.

BO rem 6 (7, 8) sts.

FINISHING

Block pieces to measurements. Sew shoulder seams.

NECKBAND

With RS facing and circular needle, using MC, PU and k14 (16, 18) sts across left back neck, 3 sts to shoulder, 20 sts down front side neck, 16 (20, 24) front neck sts on holder, 20 sts up front side neck, 3 sts from shoulder and 14 (16, 18) sts across right back neck—90 (98, 106) sts.

ROW 1: *K1, p1; rep from * to end.

ROW 2: Rib 3 sts, yo, k2tog, rib to end.

ROW 3: Rep row 1.

BO in rib.

ARMBANDS

With RS facing, and starting at underarm, using MC, PU and k66 (72, 80) sts evenly around armhole.

Work 3 rows in k1, p1 rib. BO in rib.

Sew side seams. Sew bottom edge of button band to inside. Sew small button opposite buttonhole.

ABOUT LEILA I make things, mend things, and am constantly fiddling with stuff. I was put off by knitting for a while, due to an unfortunate orange and green nylon tank top my grandmother made for me, but when I eventually took up knitting, I just couldn't stop. From the beginning, I always made up my own designs, as I don't follow orders very well. I live in St. Leonards-on-Sea, a seaside town on the south coast of England, with my husband and daughter. You can find me on Ravelry.com as LeilaBadblood.

DUTCH TOUCH

SIZE

S (M, L, XL)

Finished waist: 31 (35, 39, 43)"

Finished length: 25"

MATERIALS

Noro *Silk Garden* (45% silk, 45% mohair, 10% wool; 50g/122 yd), 11 (12, 13, 15) balls #8

US 7 (4.5mm) 40" circular needle

Spare circular needle for grafting

Waste yarn

8 stitch markers

Tapestry needle

1 (1, 1¼, 1½) yd 1" wide elastic for waistband

GAUGE

17 sts and 22 rows = 4" in St st

H olland is filled with the colors of dark blue water, bright blue skies, and lush green pastures. To my surprise, it's the exact color combination in the Japanese yarn Noro, and I used it to give this skirt a Dutch touch. I used short rows to create the pleats, which also divide the colors beautifully between each section. That shape and the vertical lines in the design have a slimming effect, and because the skirt is knit lengthwise, it hangs wonderfully. The wide elastic waistband makes it a dream to wear. Best of all, even after you've been sitting in it for a while, the skirt won't lose its shape.

SPECIAL ABBREVIATION

W&T (WRAP AND TURN): On RS, bring yarn between needles to front, sl next st onto RH needle, bring yarn between needles to back, return sl st to LH needle, turn.

On WS, bring yarn between needles to back, sl next st onto RH needle, bring yarn between needles to front, return sl st to LH needle, turn.

DIRECTIONS

Sizing Note: This skirt is knit a bit shorter than it will actually be once worn, because the weight of the skirt ensures that it will grow about 2 inches.

Pattern Notes: The last 7 sts in row 1 form the waistband facing. Slip all markers after row 1 as you come to them. Skirt length can be adjusted by working more or fewer sts between markers in this section. A longer skirt will require additional yarn.

Using provisional CO method and wy, CO 110 sts. Cont with working yarn.

ROW 1 (RS): K4, pm, (k15, pm) 5 times, k24, pm, k1, pm, k6.

ROW 2: P6, slip next st wyif, k to end.

SHORT ROW SECTION

ROW 3: K to 2nd marker, W&T.

ROWS 4, 6, 8, 10 AND 12: P to last marker, k4.

ROW 5: K to 3rd marker, W&T.

ROW 7: K to 4th marker, W&T.

ROW 9: K to 5th marker, W&T.

ROW 11: K to 6th marker, W&T.

ROW 13: K, picking up each wrap and k tog with wrapped st.

ROW 14: P6, slip next st wyif, k to end.

ROW 15: Knit.

ROW 16: P6, slip next st wyif, k to end.

Rep rows 3–16 (short-row section) 53 (60, 67, 74) times more, or to desired waist measurement. Work rows 3–13 once more, removing all markers on last row and leaving sts on needle.

FINISHING

Carefully remove wy and place sts onto a spare circular needle. Starting at the waistband end, graft first and last rows together using Kitchener st (see page 107) for St st or garter st as appropriate.

Fold waistband facing to WS and whipstitch in place, leaving a 1" opening. Cut elastic to length desired plus 1". Attach a safety pin to one end, insert through waistband casing, and sew ends together, leaving a ½" seam. Sew closed remaining 1" opening of facing. Weave in ends and block to measurements.

ABOUT CARLA I learned to knit in elementary school when I was seven years old but stopped during the '90s. I've been knitting again for the past six years or so, and more fanatically than ever. Stitch 'n Bitch and the Internet have had a large influence on what and how I knit, especially the community aspect of it. Every year my friend Hilly van der Sluis and I visit our knitting friends at the giant needlework convention in Paris (L'Aiguille en Fête) and the incredibly fun I Knit Day in London. But my roots remain in Holland, where Hilly and I have started our own business together, The Dutch Knitters (www.thedutchknitters.nl). We give workshops and promote knitting wherever and whenever we can, because everyone needs to learn that "knitting is chocolate for the mind." I live with five cats and my husband, Jan, in Utrecht, a city in the middle of the Netherlands. You can follow my adventures in the knitting world at my blog, Life 'n Knitting, www.lifenknitting.net.

JANA PIHOTA

BABY CORN

hile I wanted a comfortable easy-care dress to take along on a summer cruise, I couldn't find an existing knitting pattern for the baby-doll dress I envisioned. So indulging my fondness for natural fibers, textured stitches, and knitting in the round, I whipped up Baby Corn. Using gathers below the bustline, I created a figure-flattering skirt with an adjustable I-cord tie that could accommodate cruise-buffet indulgences. I played around with several complicated stitch patterns for the bodice before settling on the wrapped rib—I love its unusual texture. Finally, I chose 100% corn yarn to make Baby Corn cool, easy-care, and ecofriendly.

SPECIAL ABBREVIATION

W3 (WRAP 3): Wyif sl next 3 sts pwise, pass yarn to back, sl same 3 sts back to LH needle, pass yarn to front, sl sts back to RH needle.

SPECIAL STITCHES

WRAPPED RIB (MULTIPLE OF 6 STS)

RNDS 1–5: * P3, k3; rep from * to end.

RND 6: *P3, W3; rep from * to end.

Rep rnds 1–6 for patt.

ELONGATED ST ST (IN THE ROUND)

RND 1: *K1 wrapping yarn around needle 3 times; rep from * to end.

RND 2: *K1, dropping 2 extra loops off needle without working them; rep from * to end.

SIZE

S (M, L, XL)

Finished bust: 32½ (36, 39½, 43¼)"

Finished length: Approx 33 (33½, 34, 34½)" (from shoulder)

MATERIALS

SWTC *A-MAIZing* (100% corn fiber; 50g/143 yd), 10 (11, 12, 13) skeins #161 Ducky

US 7 (4.5mm) 24" circular needle

US 5 (3.75mm) double-pointed needles (2 only)

Stitch marker

Tapestry needle

GAUGE

20 sts and 30 rows = 4" in St st

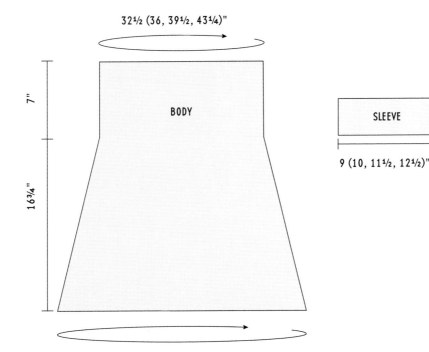

32½ (36, 39½, 43¼)"

7"

BODY

16¾"

48½ (54, 59½, 64¾)"

SLEEVE

3½"

9 (10, 11½, 12½)"

ELONGATED ST ST (WORKED FLAT)

ROW 1: *K1 wrapping yarn around needle 3 times; rep from * to end.

ROW 2: *P1, dropping 2 extra loops off needle without working them; rep from * to end.

DIRECTIONS

Note: This loose-fitting dress is knit in the round from the top down (you can adjust the length to your preference) with attached cap sleeves and I-cord tie. Note that the fabric will stretch some lengthwise when worn.

BODY

CO 162 (180, 198, 216) sts. Pm and join.

Work 5 rnds in St st.

NEXT RND: *K2tog, yo, k1; rep from * to end.

Work 5 rnds in St st.

Work 35 rnds in Wrapped Rib, ending with row 5.

Work 5 rnds in St st.

NEXT RND: *K2tog, yo, k1; rep from * to end.

NEXT RND: *K2, m1; rep from * to end—243 (270, 297, 324) sts.

Cont in St st, work approx 15" more, or 3" less than desired length.

NEXT RND: *K2tog, yo, k1; rep from * to end.

Work 3 rnds in St st.

Work 2 rnds Elongated St st.

Work 3 rnds in St st.

NEXT RND: *K2tog, yo, k1; rep from * to end.

Work 9 rnds in St st.

BO.

SLEEVES

CO 45 (51, 57, 63) sts, leaving a 24" tail for sewing.
Do not join.

Work 26 rows in St st.

NEXT ROW: *K2tog, yo, k1; rep from * to end.

Work 3 rows in St st.

Work 2 rows in Elongated St st.

Work 6 rows in St st.

BO, leaving 24" tail for sewing.

I-CORD TIE

With dpns, CO 3 sts.

Work in I-cord (page 110) for 63".

BO. Weave in ends.

FINISHING

Block sleeves and body. DO NOT STEAM OR IRON—
corn fiber yarn will melt at high temperatures.

Position side edges of each sleeve to top edge at inside of
dress bodice just above eyelets as desired. Using CO and
BO tails, sew in place.

Starting and ending at center front, thread I-cord tie
through upper row of bodice eyelets.

ABOUT JANA I have only been knitting the last
one-eighth of my life and deeply regret not starting earlier.
I always quilted, embroidered, cross-stitched, and hooked
rugs, but I seemed to have missed the knitting boat. Finally,
after opening Siren Song Stitchery in Cannon Beach,
Oregon, I taught myself to knit from the original *Stitch
'n Bitch* book. I've since moved on to financial industry
employment, but manage to knit three to four hours a day. I
live in fiber-friendly Portland, Oregon, with my obese yarn
stash and grand knitting aspirations. You can read about
my knitting adventures at hipknitizer.blogspot.com.

Laura Grutzeck

TULIP TOP

 once had a vintage blouse that I purchased at a flea market. I wore it so much that it was ragged after one summer. Looking sadly at my worn-out blouse, which had a cordlike trim that tied in a bow around the neck, I thought, "This trim looks like I-cord. I wonder if I could knit a top like this?" So I knit up some I-cord and a flat swatch, and it looked great—I knew the I-cord worked as a trim. The main challenge was that the original blouse was made of light, drapey rayon, so I knew I needed a yarn with drape. I decided on a worsted-weight cotton/wool blend, which would be cool and drapey, but still have some body. Once I knew what my knitted gauge was, I was able to translate a rough schematic into a knitting pattern. And voilà—I have a new version of my fave blouse that I hope becomes your favorite, too. It's perfect for spring, when the tulips come out, and it resembles them as well, with its sweet green stalk and bright pop of color at the neck.

SPECIAL ABBREVIATION

MK (MAKE KNOT): P3tog leaving sts on needle; working same 3 sts, k3tog leaving sts on needle, p3tog.

SPECIAL STITCH

KNOT PATTERN (MULTIPLE OF 10 STS)

RNDS 1–5: Knit.

RND 6: K1, *MK, k7; rep from * to last 9 sts, MK, k6.

RNDS 7–15: Knit.

RND 16: K6, *MK, k7; rep from * to last 4 sts, MK, k1.

SIZE

XS (S, M, L, XL)

Finished bust: 30 (34, 38, 42, 46)"

Finished length: 19½ (20½, 21½, 22½, 23½)"

MATERIALS

Brown Sheep *Cotton Fleece* (80% pima cotton, 20% wool; 100g/215 yd)

MC: 3 (3, 3, 4, 5) skeins #380 Dusty Sage

CC: 1 skein #310 Wild Orange

US 6 (4mm) 24" circular needle

US 5 (3.75mm) double-pointed needles

Stitch markers

Stitch holders

Tapestry needle

GAUGE

20 sts and 28 rows = 4" in St st using larger needles

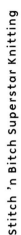

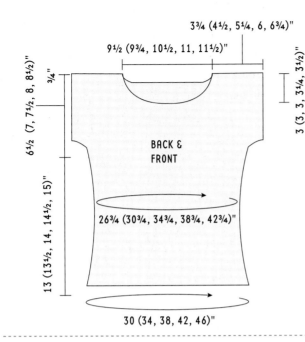

3¾ (4½, 5¼, 6, 6¾)"

9½ (9¾, 10½, 11, 11½)"

¾"

6½ (7, 7½, 8, 8½)"

3 (3, 3, 3¼, 3½)"

BACK & FRONT

13 (13½, 14, 14½, 15)"

26¾ (30¾, 34¾, 38¾, 42¾)"

30 (34, 38, 42, 46)"

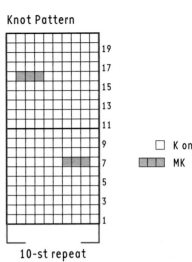

Knot Pattern

19
17
15
13
11
9
7
5
3
1

10-st repeat

☐ K on RS, P on WS

▨▨▨ MK

RNDS 17–20: Knit.

Rep rnds 1–20 for patt.

Note: When working back and forth, purl all odd-numbered rows.

DIRECTIONS

Note: This top is knitted in the round from the bottom up. After increasing for sleeves, work is separated for front and back. Front and back are knit separately, working flat rather than in the round.

Pattern note: As stitches are decreased and increased along the sides, the pattern will begin and end with a different number of sts; make sure the knots in rounds 6 and 16 of pattern remain centered between the knots worked on the last knot round.

BODY

With MC and circular needle, CO 75 (85, 95, 105, 115) sts, pm, CO 75 (85, 95, 105, 115) sts—150 (170, 190, 210, 230) sts. Pm and join.

Work in k1, p1 rib for 1".

Work in Knot patt until body meas 2½ (3, 3½, 4, 4½)" from beg.

WAIST SHAPING

DEC RND: *K2tog, work in patt as est to 2 sts before marker, ssk; rep from * once more.

Cont in patt as est, rep dec rnd every 8th rnd 3 times more—134 (154, 174, 194, 214) sts.

Work even in patt as est until body meas 7½ (8, 8½, 9, 9½)" from beg.

INC RND: *K1, m1, work in patt as est to 1 st before marker, m1, k1; rep from * once more.

Cont in patt as est, rep inc rnd every 8th rnd 3 times more—150 (170, 190, 210, 230) sts.

Work even in patt until body meas 13 (13½, 14, 14½, 15)" from beg.

SLEEVE SHAPING

Rep inc rnd EVERY rnd 5 times, end with an odd-numbered rnd (work an additional rnd if necessary)—170 (190, 210, 230, 250) sts.

DIVIDE FOR FRONT AND BACK

Work 85 (95, 105, 115, 125) sts in patt, remove marker. Place rem 85 (95, 105, 115, 125) sts onto holder for front.

BACK

Working back and forth, cont in patt as est on 85 (95, 105, 115, 125) sts until armhole meas 5½ (6, 6½, 7, 7½)", end with a WS row.

NECK AND SHOULDER SHAPING

NEXT ROW (RS): Work 21 (25, 28, 32, 36) sts in patt, join 2nd ball of yarn and BO 43 (45, 49, 51, 53) neck sts, work in patt to end—21 (25, 28, 32, 36) sts each side.

Working both sides at the same time, dec 1 st each neck edge every RS row twice—19 (23, 26, 30, 34) sts each side. Cont in patt as est until armhole meas 6½ (7, 7½, 8, 8½)".

Place both sets of shoulder sts onto holders.

FRONT

With RS facing, place front sts onto needle and attach yarn. Working back and forth, cont in patt as est until armhole meas 3½ (4, 4½, 4¾, 5)", end with a WS row.

NECK AND SHOULDER SHAPING

NEXT ROW (RS): Work 24 (28, 31, 35, 39) sts in patt, join 2nd ball of yarn and BO 37 (39, 43, 45, 47) sts, work in patt to end—24 (28, 31, 35, 39) sts each side.

Working both sides at the same time, dec 1 st each neck edge every RS row 5 times—19 (23, 26, 30, 34) sts each side. Cont in patt as est until armhole meas 6½ (7, 7½, 8, 8½)".

Place both sets of shoulder sts onto holders.

FINISHING

With RS tog, join front and back shoulders using 3-needle BO (page 103).

SLEEVE BANDS

With MC and dpns, PU and k60 (64, 70, 76, 80) sts evenly around sleeve opening. Pm and join. Work 4 rnds in k1, p1 rib. BO in rib.

NECK TRIM

With CC and dpns, CO 3 sts and work 9½" in I-cord (page 110). With RS facing and spare dpn, PU approx 20 neckline sts, picking up only the front loop of st and placing directly onto needle, starting 1" to left of beg of front neck BO. Cont to PU sts as you work around neckline.

NEXT ROW: On dpn with I-cord, *k2, ssk tog with neckline st, slide sts to other end of needle; rep from * until 1 neckline st rem.

Cont in I-cord on 3 sts for 9½". BO. Tie ends in a bow.

ABOUT LAURA I have been knitting ever since my mother taught me how in grade school. In addition to my day job as a librarian, I am a knitwear designer and freelance technical editor. I also work part-time at my LYS, Rosie's Yarn Cellar, because the great yarns and creative staff are an inspiration to me. I am the coauthor of *Knit So Fine: Designs with Skinny Yarn* (2008). I may be the only knitter out there without a blog, but you can always find me on Ravelry.com.

eLeNa rofenberg

ROCOCO SHAWL

As is the case with many of my designs, the Rococo Shawl came serendipitously from a client who wanted me to create a wrap in a rich orange with a textured body and ruffled edges. So I adapted a stitch I had previously used for some gloves and added ruffles to the border for a dash of drama. When you wear this shawl, you'll notice the way the right- and wrong-side textures layer when it folds on itself—I really love the look it creates. I have remade this shawl in tons of other colors, and it has become one of my very favorite pieces.

SIZE

Finished width: 14"

Finished length: 55"

MATERIALS

Elann *Peruvian Uros Aran* (50% highland wool, 50% llama; 50g/91 yd), 9 skeins #3052 Burnt Orange

US 9 (5.5mm) 36" circular needle

Tapestry needle

GAUGE

21 sts and 30 rows = 4" in Bas Relief st

STITCH PATTERN
BAS RELIEF (MULTIPLE OF 6 STS + 4)

ROW 1 (RS): K2, *p3, k3; rep from * to last 2 sts, k2.

ROW 2: K2, *p3, k3; rep from * to last 2 sts, k2.

ROW 3: K2, *p2, k4; rep from * to last 2 sts, k2.

ROW 4: K2, *p4, k2; rep from * to last 2 sts, k2.

ROW 5: K2, *p1, k5; rep from * to last 2 sts, k2.

ROW 6: K2, *p5, k1; rep from * to last 2 sts, k2.

ROW 7: K5, *p3, k3; rep from * to last 5 sts, p3, k2.

ROW 8: K5, *p3, k3; rep from * to last 5 sts, p3, k2.

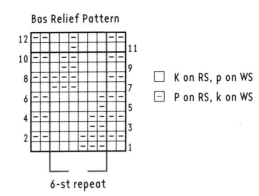

Bas Relief Pattern

6-st repeat

K on RS, p on WS

P on RS, k on WS

ROW 9: K5, *p2, k4; rep from * to last 5 sts, p2, k3.

ROW 10: K2, p1, k2, *p4, k2; rep from * to last 5 sts, p3, k2.

ROW 11: K5, *p1, k5; rep from * to last 5 sts, p1, k4.

ROW 12: K2, p2, *k1, p5; rep from * to last 6 sts, k1, p3, k2.

Rep rows 1–12 for patt.

DIRECTIONS

Pattern note: Shawl is knit lengthwise and end ruffles are picked up and knit upon completion of body.

BOTTOM RUFFLE

CO 432 sts.

ROWS 1 AND 2: Knit.

ROWS 3, 5, 7 AND 9 (RS): K2, p1, k5, *p1, k4; rep from * to last 9 sts, p1, k5, p1, k2.

ROWS 4, 6, 8 AND 10: K3, p5, *k1, p4; rep from * to last 9 sts, k1, p5, k3.

ROW 11: K2, p1, k2tog, k1, k2tog, *p1, [k2tog] twice; rep from * to last 9 sts; p1, k2tog, k1, k2tog, p1, k2—262 sts.

ROW 12: Knit.

BODY

Work 7 reps of Bas Relief patt, end with row 11—piece meas approx 12½" from beg.

NEXT ROW (WS): Knit.

TOP RUFFLE

ROW 1: K2, p1, kfb, k1, kfb, *p1, [kfb] twice; rep from * to last 7 sts, p1, kfb, k1, kfb, p1, k2—432 sts.

ROWS 2, 4, 6 AND 8: K3, p5, *k1, p4; rep from * to last 9 sts, k1, p5, k3.

ROWS 3, 5, 7 AND 9: K2, p1, k5, *p1, k4; rep from * to last 9 sts, p1, k5, p1, k2.

ROWS 10 AND 11: Knit.

BO.

END RUFFLE

With RS facing, PU and k 56 sts along short end of shawl, including edges of top and bottom ruffles.

ROW 1 (WS): K2, *kfb; rep from * to last 2 sts, k2—108 sts.

ROW 2: K2, p1, kfb, k1, kfb, p1, *k4, p1, k1, kfb, k1, p1; rep from * to last 11 sts, k4, p1, kfb, k, kfb, p1, k2—122 sts.

ROWS 3, 5 AND 7: K3, p5, *k1, p4; rep from * to last 9 sts, k1, p5, k3.

ROWS 4, 6 AND 8: K2, p1, k5, *p1, k4; rep from * to last 9 sts, p1, k5, p1, k2.

ROWS 9 AND 10: Knit.

BO. Rep on other end.

FINISHING

Block lightly.

ABOUT ELENA I am head-over-heels in love with knitting. When I am not knitting or designing, I am daydreaming about it. I have my wonderful mom to thank for teaching me to knit when I was a kid, and, probably, my grandmothers (one of whom was a seamstress and the other a weaver) for the gift of creating fiber goodness with my hands. Visit my shop on Etsy.com at TickledPinkKnits.etsy .com, and check out my second love, fine-art photography, at www.elenarosenberg.com.

MICHELLE CHO

TIPTOES

As a kid, I remember my mom having toe socks. Not just a pair or two, but a *lot* of them. To say I was fascinated with them would be an understatement. I would wear them at every opportunity. But once I was ten or eleven, my feet were already much bigger than my mom's, and so I left toe socks behind. Recently, my youngest sister, Janelle, developed a similar obsession with toe socks, so I set out to design a pair for her. Getting the toes just right was my biggest challenge. After much trial and error, I realized I needed to make the toes individually, then join them and start making the foot. Once I did that, the rest was a breeze. Now whenever I wear flip-flops and my feet get a bit chilly, I pull out my toe socks to warm my little piggies.

SPECIAL ABBREVIATION

W&T (WRAP AND TURN): On RS, bring yarn between needles to front, sl next st onto RH needle, bring yarn between needles to back, return sl st to LH needle, turn.

On WS, bring yarn between needles to back, sl next st onto RH needle, bring yarn between needles to front, return sl st to LH needle, turn.

DIRECTIONS

Note: These socks are worked from tips of toes to cuff using the Turkish CO (page 97). Each toe is individually made and then joined to form the sock.

SIZE

Women's M

Foot circumference: 7½"

Foot length: approx 9½"

MATERIALS

Koigu *KPM* (100% merino wool; 50g/175 yd)

A: 2 skeins #2231 Pink

B: 2 skeins #2163 Purple

US 1 (2.25mm) double-pointed needles (set of 5)

Waste yarn

GAUGE

36 sts and 50 rows = 4" in St st

TOES (MAKE 2 OF EACH, ONE EACH WITH A AND B)

TOE #1 (BIG TOE)

Using Turkish CO, CO 10 sts (5 sts on each needle).

RNDS 1 AND 2: Knit. Divide sts evenly over 4 dpns. Pm.

RND 3: [K1, m1, k3, m1, k1] twice—14 sts.

RNDS 4, 6 AND 8: Knit.

RND 5: [K1, m1, k5, m1, k1] twice—18 sts.

RND 7: [K1, m1, k7, m1, k1] twice—22 sts.

RND 9: [K1, m1, k9, m1, k1] twice—26 sts.

Cont even in St st until toe meas 2" or desired length. Break yarn leaving a 5" tail. Place sts on wy.

TOE #2

Using Turkish CO, CO 8 sts (4 sts on each needle).

RNDS 1 AND 2: Knit. Divide sts evenly over 4 dpns. Pm and join.

RND 3: [K1, m1, k2, m1, k1] twice—12 sts.

RND 4: Knit.

RND 5: [K1, m1, k4, m1, k1] twice—16 sts.

Cont even in St st until toe meas 2" or desired length. Break yarn leaving a 5" tail. Place sts on wy.

TOE #3

Work same as toe #2 until toe meas 1¾" or desired length. Break yarn leaving a 5" tail. Place sts on wy.

TOE #4

Work same as toe #2 until toe meas 1½" or desired length. Break yarn leaving a 5" tail. Place sts on wy.

TOE #5

Work same as toe #2 until toe meas 1¼" or desired length. Break yarn leaving a 5" tail. Place sts on wy.

RIGHT SOCK SET-UP

Using toe #1 in A, toe #2 in B, toe #3 in A, toe #4 in B, toe #5 in A, and one dpn (set-up Needle 1), PU 13 sts from toe #1, 8 sts each from toes 2 through 5—45 sts. With a second dpn (set-up Needle 2) and set-up Needle 1 to the back, PU the other half of the live sts that rem from each of the toes—90 sts total. Divide sts evenly over 4 dpns.

FOOT

Starting at toe #1, join B.

RND 1: K12, k2tog, [k6, k2tog] 3 times, k14, k2tog, [k6, k2tog] 3 times, k12—82 sts.

RND 2: K11, k3tog, [k4, k3tog] 3 times, k12, k3tog, [k4, k3tog] 3 times, k11—66 sts.

RNDS 3-14: Knit.

*Work 14 rnds in St st with A, work 14 rnds in St st with B; rep from * once more.

Change to A and work 7 rnds in St st.

HEEL

Work back and forth over first 33 sts.

ROW 1: K32, W&T.

ROW 2: P31, W&T.

ROW 3: K to one st before wrapped st, W&T.

ROW 4: P to one st before wrapped st, W&T.

Rep rows 3 and 4 until there are 10 wrapped sts on each side and 13 unwrapped center sts.

NEXT ROW (RS): K to first wrapped st, PU wrap and k tog with st, W&T.

NEXT ROW (WS): P to first unworked wrapped st, PU wrap and p tog tbl with st, W&T.

NEXT ROW: K to first double-wrapped st, PU both wraps and k tog with st, W&T.

NEXT ROW: P to first unworked double-wrapped st, PU both wraps, and p tog tbl with st, W&T.

Rep last 2 rows until all sts have been worked, end with a WS row.

LEG

Work 7 rnds in St st with A, work 14 rnds in St st with B.

*Work 14 rnds in St st with A, work 14 rnds in St st with B; rep from * once more.

Change to A and k 1 rnd.

Work 13 rnds in k3, p3 rib.

BO loosely in rib.

LEFT SOCK SET-UP

Set up toes in reverse order, and using one dpn (set-up Needle 1), PU 8 sts each from toes 5 through 2 and 13 sts from toe #1—45 sts. With a second dpn (set-up Needle 2) and set-up Needle 1 to the back, PU the other half of the live sts that rem from each of the toes—90 sts total. Divide sts evenly over 4 dpns.

FOOT

Starting at toe #5, join A.

RND 1: K7, k2tog, [k6, k2tog] 3 times, k24, k2tog, [k6, k2tog] 3 times, k7—82 sts.

RND 2: K6, k3tog, [k4, k3tog] 3 times, k22, k3tog, [k4, k3tog] 3 times, k6—66 sts.

Work remainder of left sock same as right sock, reversing stripe color sequence.

Weave in ends, using tails to close spaces between toes.

ABOUT MICHELLE In 2002, while I was pregnant with my second son, I taught myself to knit and have not put my needles down since. I was born, raised, and still live in Southern California with my husband and two sons, who keep me very busy. I am a self-proclaimed sports and fitness junkie who plays softball and soccer weekly, in addition to running and cycling. You can find out what I'm up to by visiting my blog at michellecanknit.blogspot.com.

elli stubenrauch

SQUIRRELLY MITTENS

nit in two colors of lovely Shetland wool, these too-cute mitts will keep your hands warm whether you're going for a late-fall bike ride or engaging in a winter snowball fight. I'd been a bit wary of colorwork, but it was time to get past my fear and attempt the "two-color tango," so I designed these mittens as a way to practice wrangling two colors at once. After I took the time to figure out the technique, I couldn't believe I'd waited so long to try it. I incorporated the squirrel chart into a simple Swedish-style mitten, and I've been addicted to stranded knitting ever since.

SPECIAL ABBREVIATIONS

M1L: Make 1 st by inserting LH needle from front to back under the CC strand between the 2 sts of the previous row, and k this loop tbl so it twists to the left.

M1R: Make 1 st by inserting LH needle from back to front under the CC strand between the 2 sts of the previous row, and k through the front of this loop so it twists to the right.

DIRECTIONS
CUFF

With CC, CO 64 sts. Distribute sts evenly over 4 needles. Pm and join, being careful not to twist.

RND 1: *K1 CC, p1 MC; rep from * around. Cont in corrugated rib for 13 rnds more.

Work 8 rnds of Chart 1.

SIZE
Woman's M

Finished circumference: 8¼"

Finished length: 9"

MATERIALS
Jamieson & Smith *2-ply Jumper Yarn* (100% wool; 25g/125 yd)

MC: 2 balls #48 Turquoise

CC: 2 balls #43 Dark Red

US 1 (2.25mm) double-pointed needles (set of 5)

Stitch marker

Waste yarn

Tapestry needle

GAUGE
36 sts and 42 rnds = 4" in St st over chart patt, after blocking

Chart 1

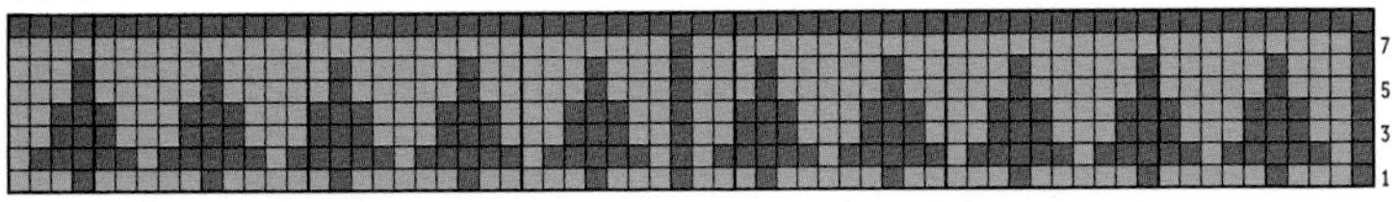

Chart 2

Chart 3

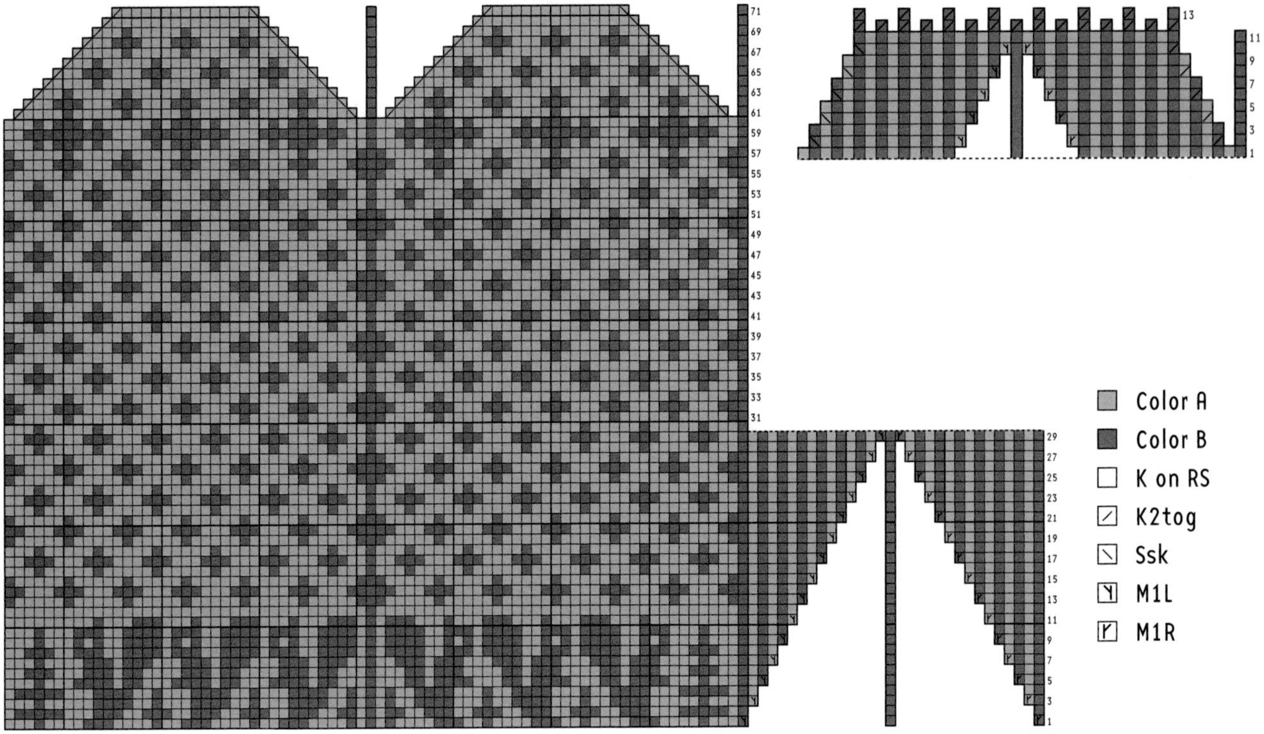

- Color A
- Color B
- K on RS
- K2tog
- Ssk
- M1L
- M1R

NEXT RND (INC): With CC, *[k4, kfb] twice, k5, kfb; rep from * 3 times more—76 sts.

HAND

Begin Chart 2, AND AT THE SAME TIME, beg inc for thumb as charted. ***Note:*** Incs are worked on either side of first st in rnd.

RND 30: Work to thumb; transfer 30 thumb sts to wy, work rem of rnd as charted.

Complete Chart 2, dec as indicated. With CC, graft rem sts together with Kitchener st.

THUMB

Distribute thumb sts evenly over 4 needles. Pm and join MC and CC between thumb and hand, leaving a 6" CC tail for sewing up. Work thumb in the rnd foll Chart 3.

When chart is completed, break yarn, leaving a 6" tail. Thread tail through rem sts, pull tight to close end and secure.

FINISHING

With CC tail, sew gap between thumb and hand closed. Weave in ends.

Make second mitten same as first mitten.

ABOUT ELLI **Descended from good Dutch-American folk who instilled hardworking and crafty values in me from an early age, I grew up to be a cartographer with a great fondness for designing colorwork mittens. I live in Bloomington, Indiana, where my current passions include genealogy, pirate LEGOs, praying mantises, and wearing foofy dresses. My husband facilitates domestic bliss by choosing not to comment on the yarn situation. The blog, Elliphantom Knits, can be found at www.elliphantom.com.**

HIP HOP BLANKET

SIZE

Finished width: approx 29"

Finished length: approx 29"

MATERIALS

Karabella *Aurora 8* (100% extrafine merino wool; 50g/98 yd)

A: 10 balls #18

B: 2 balls #1364

S. Charles Collezione *Micio* (60% nylon, 40% wool; 50g/110 yd)

C: 1 ball #01 White

US 10½ (6mm) 24" circular needle

Stitch markers

GAUGE

14 sts and 20 rows = 4" in St st using 2 strands held tog

 everal years ago there was a huge baby boom among my friends, and I needed a new baby pattern that would hold my interest and be fun to knit. The idea of bunnies hopped into my head, so I sketched the bunny shape, transferred it to graph paper, and plotted out the pattern. A lot of cutting and pasting went into positioning these rascally rabbits on the blanket until I was happy with the number of buns and the directions they faced. I love this design because the motif would be adorable on a sweater, a pillow, or whatever you can think of to satisfy your rabbit habit.

DIRECTIONS

Note: Entire blanket is worked with 2 strands held together. Bunnies may be knit using the intarsia method, or background yarn may be stranded behind bunny motif catching *every other* stitch for added strength and to avoid creating loops.

With A, CO 100 sts. Work 9 rows in garter st (k every row).

ROW 1 (WS): K7, p86, k7.

ROW 2: Knit.

Rep rows 1 and 2 until piece meas 3" from beg, end with a WS row.

NEXT ROW (RS): K9, pm, work Chart 1 over next 64 sts, pm, k to end.

Cont in patt as est, working rem 54 rows of chart between markers. Remove markers when chart is complete.

Rep rows 1 and 2 until piece meas 19" from beg, end with a WS row.

NEXT ROW (RS): K32, pm, work chart over next 61 sts, pm, k to end.

Cont in patt as est, working rem 34 rows of Chart 2 between markers. Remove markers when chart is complete.

Rep rows 1 and 2 until piece meas 26½" from beg, end with a RS row.

Work 9 rows in garter st.

BO.

ABOUT JENNIFER After six years as a jewelry designer in New York, the company I worked for closed, giving us the wonderful gift of a one-year compensation to find our dream job. Ever crafty, I found my dream job in the yarn world and began creating the GoKnit® Pouch, a drawstring pouch that allows knitters to carry their knitting projects around and knit while their yarn dangles from their wrist. My company, Knowknits®, has been around since 2005, offering accessories and designs to knitters all over the world. Please visit my website at www.knowknits.com and let me know what you think.

Chart 1

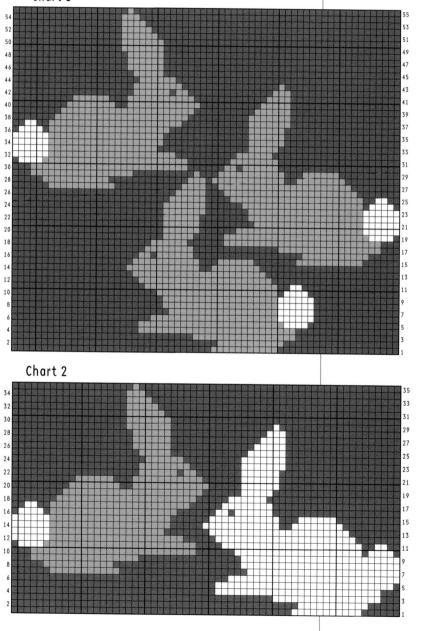

Chart 2

■ Color A
▨ Color B
☐ Color C

MANDY POWERS

STEEKS AND STONES

My son wanted a customized sweater, and he was very specific about it: zipper, skulls, and, of course, green snake eyes. I began the design with some ideas and a pencil, but when I knit a swatch using a scribbled chart, Jerry said it wasn't scary enough. Back to the drawing board. Then I came up with this creepy skull design that pleased both me and him. I decided to use steeks because they are terrific for colorwork. The steeks are placed where the openings will later be cut, and you always knit in the round, so no wrong-side colorwork rows have to be knit. The only downside to this method is that you can't try on the garment before cutting, and once you snip the steeks, there's no going back. This technique is not for the timid knitter, but I'll let you in on a little secret—steeking isn't as spooky as it seems.

SPECIAL ABBREVIATION

W&T (WRAP AND TURN): On RS, bring yarn between needles to front, sl next st onto RH needle, bring yarn between needles to back, return sl st to LH needle, turn.

On WS, bring yarn between needles to back, sl next st onto RH needle, bring yarn between needles to front, return sl st to LH needle, turn.

STITCH PATTERNS
GARTER STITCH IN ROWS

K every row.

Two rows make 1 "ridge." Count ridges from the RS.

SIZE

Child S (M, L) to fit child age 6 (8, 10)

Finished chest: 30 (32, 34)"

Finished length: 18¾ (20½, 21½)"

MATERIALS

Cascade Yarns *Cascade 220* (100% wool; 100g/220 yd)

MC: 3 (4, 4) skeins #4002 Charcoal

A: 2 (2, 3) skeins #8010 Cream

B: 1 (1, 1) skein #8894 Green

US 5 (3.75mm) 24" circular needle

US 3 (3.25mm) 24" circular needle

US 5 (3.75mm) 24" double-pointed needles (set of 5)

US 3 (3.25mm) 24" double-pointed needles (set of 5)

Crochet hook (C-2/2.75mm) for crocheted steeks

3 yd smooth cotton waste yarn

6 stitch markers

One 20" separating zipper in black

Sewing needle and matching thread

Tapestry needle

GAUGE

24 sts and 26 rows = 4" over chart patt using larger needles

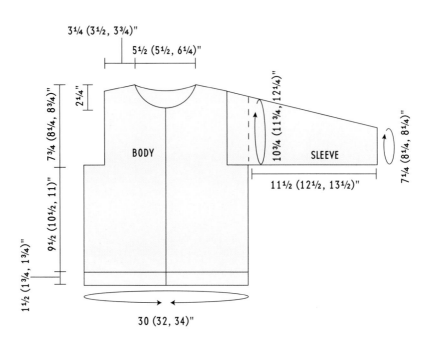

GARTER STITCH IN THE ROUND

RND 1: Purl.

RND 2: Knit.

Rep rnds 1–2 for patt.

Two rounds create 1 "ridge." Count ridges from the RS.

DIRECTIONS

Construction notes: This sweater is made in a tube from the bottom up. Steek stitches are used and later cut open at the center front, armholes, and neck. A 7-stitch steek is used for center front and neck steeks. To reduce bulk at the armhole steeks, a 5-stitch steek is used. Garter stitch sleeve caps are knit from the top then joined with the sleeves, which are knit from the cuff up, using Kitchener stitch. The collar, bottom hem, and front bands are knit last. Duplicate stitching is used to make random green skull eyes.

BODY

With MC and larger needle, CO 188 (198, 212) sts. Pm and join.

Join A and work 7 sts from Steek Chart 1, pm; starting with st indicated for size, work Skull Chart to end.

Work even in patt as est until piece meas 9½ (10½, 11)" from beg.

ARMHOLE STEEKS

Place underarm sts on hold and CO for armhole steek as foll:

Work 7 steek sts, work 35 (38, 41) sts of right front, place next 20 sts on wy, pm, using backward loop CO (page 88), CO 5 sts foll Steek Chart 2; work 71 (75, 83) sts of back, place next 20 sts on wy, pm, CO 5 sts foll Steek Chart 2. Work 35 (38, 41) sts of left front—158 (168, 182) sts.

Work even in patt as est until piece measures 15 (16½, 17½)" from beg.

Color MC
Color A
M M1

Skull Chart

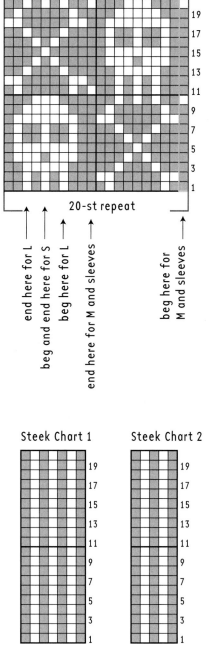

20-st repeat

end here for L
beg and end here for S
beg here for L
end here for M and sleeves
beg here for M and sleeves

Sleeve Chart

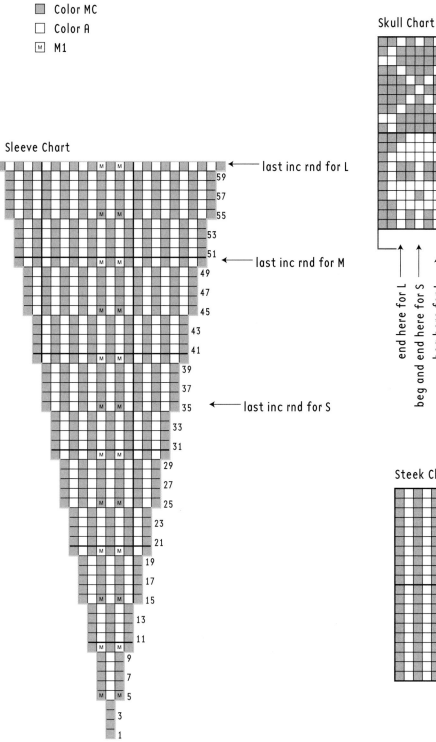

← last inc rnd for L

59
57
55
53
51 ← last inc rnd for M
49
47
45
43
41
39
37
35 ← last inc rnd for S
33
31
29
27
25
23
21
19
17
15
13
11
9
7
5
3
1

Steek Chart 1   **Steek Chart 2**

19   19
17   17
15   15
13   13
11   11
9   9
7   7
5   5
3   3
1   1

FRONT NECK SHAPING

BO 7 front steek sts. Work 9 (10, 11) sts in patt and place on wy. Work to end of rnd, break off yarns and place last 9 (10, 11) sts on wy. Pm for end of rnd, CO 7 sts foll Steek Chart 1, pm—140 (148, 160) sts.

RND 1: Work even in patt as est.

RND 2: Work 7 steek sts, with MC, (k1, ssk, k2), work in patt as est to last 5 sts, with MC, (k2, k2tog, k1).

Rep rnds 1 and 2 six times more—126 (134, 146) sts.

BACK NECK SHAPING

BO 7 front neck steek sts, 19 (21, 23) right front shoulder sts and 5 right armhole steek sts.

Work back and forth on back sts to raise back of neck as foll:

ROW 1 (RS): With MC, k to last back st, W&T.

ROW 2: With MC, k to last back st, W&T.

ROW 3: With MC, k to 6 sts before last wrapped st, W&T.

Rep last row 3 (5, 5) times more, end with a WS row.

NEXT ROW (RS): K to last back st, lifting wraps and k tog with wrapped sts, W&T.

NEXT ROW: Knit, lifting wraps and k tog with wrapped sts. Turn.

BO 19 (21, 23) sts for back right shoulder, k 33 (33, 37) back neck sts and place on wy, BO 19 (21, 23) sts for back left shoulder, 5 left armhole steek sts and 19 (21, 23) left front shoulder sts.

REINFORCE STEEKS

Using B and crochet hook, sl st crochet around both armholes, front neck, and front opening.

Cut neck steek ONLY in order for piece to lay flat. Wet, block, and lay flat to dry.

SLEEVES

Cut armhole steeks. With MC, sew shoulder seams.

With MC and smaller dpns, CO 44 (50, 50) sts. Pm and join. Beg with a p rnd, work 5 rnds in garter st. Change to B and work 4 rnds in garter st, then change to MC and work 6 (10, 10) rnds more in garter st—8 (10, 10) ridges.

SIZE S ONLY: *Inc 6 sts evenly across last rnd—50 sts.*

Change to larger dpns and attach A.

SET-UP RND: Substituting first st for Sleeve Chart, work rnd 1 of Sleeve Chart, pm, cont in Skull Chart patt as est to end of rnd.

NEXT RND: Work Sleeve Chart between markers at beg of rnd, work Skull Chart to end of rnd.

Rep last rnd, end increases for size as indicated—64 (70, 74) sts. Cont in patt as est until sleeve meas 11½ (12½, 13½)" from beg. Place sts on wy and set aside.

RIGHT SLEEVE CAP

Place 20 right underarm sts from body onto 2 dpns.

With MC, RS facing and larger needle, beg at lower back edge of armhole, PU and k64 (70, 74) sts evenly around (excluding 20 sts on dpns). Work back and forth as foll:

JOINING ROW: Sl 1, k to last st, ssk tog with next underarm st. Turn.

Rep joining row until 14 sts rem on dpns. Change to B and cont as est until 10 sts rem on dpns. Change to MC and cont as est until all sts on dpns have been worked, end with a RS row. Cut yarn and place sts on wy.

LEFT SLEEVE CAP

Work same as right sleeve cap, beg at lower front edge of armhole.

With MC, graft sleeves to sleeve caps beg at underarm. Use yarn ends to close any holes at underarm and reinforce.

FINISHING

Cut front steek.

BOTTOM BORDER

With MC, RS facing and smaller circular needle, PU and k181 (191, 205) sts across CO edge, excluding steek sts.

ROW 1 (WS): Knit.

ROW 2: K, dec 11 (11, 15) sts evenly across—170 (180, 190) sts.

With MC, k 3 (7, 7) more rows. Change to B and k 4 rows. Change to MC and k 4 rows—7 (9, 9) ridges. BO loosely.

COLLAR

Place neck sts onto smaller circular needle. With MC and RS facing, PU and k right front neck sts, PU and k10 (11, 12) sts along right neck shaping, k across back sts, PU and k10 (11, 12) sts along left neck shaping, k across left front sts—71 (75, 83) sts. With MC, k 3 (5, 7) rows; *change to B and k 4 rows; change to MC and k 4 (6, 6) rows; rep from * once more—10 (13, 14) ridges. BO loosely.

FRONT BANDS

With MC, RS facing and smaller circular needle, PU and k84 (93, 100) sts along front edge. K 3 rows— 2 ridges. BO loosely on the RS. Repeat for other side.

Weave in ends. Split the plies of a 1-yd length of MC in half and twist to strengthen. Use this thinner yarn and a sharp needle to whipstitch the facings in place, being careful not to let the thread show on the RS. With B, duplicate stitch green eyes on random skulls. Steam block front edges and sew in zipper.

ABOUT MANDY I learned to knit in '03 and can't seem to stop. I knit more hats than necessary, darn my holey handknit socks, and absolutely love colorwork. Recently I started passing on my love of knitting by teaching at my LYS. Most of this fiber fun is documented on my blog, zigzagstitch.wordpress .com. I live in North Carolina with my husband, who doesn't wear sweaters, and our two kids, who wear lots of them.

Serena Murphy

THE LIFE AQUATIC

ife Aquatic combines my love of color and classic, flattering shapes. I started with a traditional yoked sweater design, because it looks great on almost every body type, but gave it an updated, wider neck than the standard ski-style sweater. The yoke is done using the stranded knitting technique, which is fun, because you can use a lot of beautiful yarn colors instead of having to choose just one. As you can see, I took the ocean as my theme and as a cute way to combine colors, motifs, and shapes. A helpful tip on colorwork—remember to relax and keep a loose tension on the yarn. You'll thank me later.

SPECIAL ABBREVIATION

W&T (WRAP AND TURN): On RS, bring yarn between needles to front, sl next st onto RH needle, bring yarn between needles to back, return sl st to LH needle, turn.

On WS, bring yarn between needles to back, sl next st onto RH needle, bring yarn between needles to front, return sl st to LH needle, turn.

DIRECTIONS

This sweater is knit in the round from the bottom up, using one purl stitch for each side "seam." The body is separated at the armholes and worked separately, and the sleeves and body are then joined to work in the round at the yoke. Short rows are worked on the back to lengthen it.

SIZE

XS (S, M, L, XL)

Finished bust: 30¼ (34¼, 38¼, 42¼, 46¼)"

Finished length: 22¼ (22¾, 23½, 24¼, 25)"

MATERIALS

Brown Sheep *Nature Spun Sport* (100% wool; 50g/184 yd)

A: 6 (7, 8, 9, 10, 10) skeins #N78 Turquoise Wonder

B: 1 skein #109 Spring Break

C: 1 skein #116 Blue Boy

D: 1 skein #N64 Platte River Blue

E: 1 skein #N21 Mallard

F: 1 skein #145 Salmon

US 4 (3.5mm) 24" circular needle

US 5 (3.75mm) 24" circular needle

US 4 (3.5mm) double-pointed needles (set of 5)

US 5 (3.75mm) double-pointed needles (set of 5)

Stitch markers

Stitch holders

Waste yarn

GAUGE

24 sts and 26 rows = 4" in St st over chart patt using larger needles

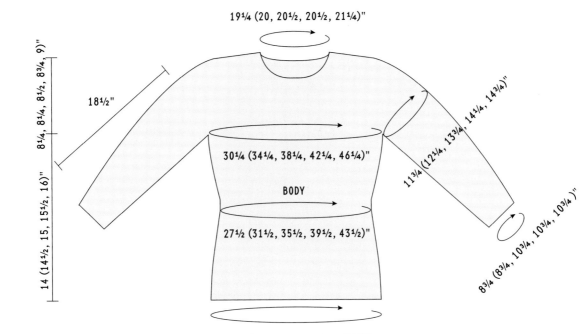

19¼ (20, 20½, 20½, 21¼)"

18½"

8¼, 8¼, 8½, 8¾, 9)"

14 (14½, 15, 15½, 16)"

30¼ (34¼, 38¼, 42¼, 46¼)"

BODY

27½ (31½, 35½, 39½, 43½)"

11¾ (12¼, 13¾, 14¼, 14¾)"

8¾ (8¾, 10¾, 10¾, 10¾)"

29½ (33½, 37½, 41½, 45½)"

BODY

With smaller circular needle and A, cast on 178 (202, 226, 250, 274) sts. Pm for beg of rnd and join.

SET-UP RND: *P1, pm, [k2, p2] 22 (25, 28, 31, 34) times, pm; rep from * once more.

Cont in rib as est for 4". Change to St st, k3 (3, 5, 7, 8) rnds, cont to p side seam sts as est.

WAIST SHAPING

DEC RND: *P1, sm, k2tog, k to 2 sts before next marker, ssk, sm; rep from *.

Rep dec rnd every 8 (8, 8, 9, 10) rnds twice more—166 (190, 214, 238, 262) sts.

K 3 rnds.

SHORT-ROW RND: P1, sm, k to 3 sts before next marker, W&T; p to 3 sts before marker, W&T.

K 1 rnd, working wrapped sts by lifting wrap onto needle and k tog with st. K 3 rnds.

INC RND: *P1, sm, kfb, k to 1 st before marker, kfb, sm; rep from *.

Rep inc rnd every 8 (8, 8, 9, 10) rnds 3 times more—182 (206, 230, 254, 278) sts.

K 8 rnds.

Work short-row rnd.

Cont in patt (working wrapped sts as before) until front of body meas 13¼ (13½, 14, 14½, 15)" from beg.

Work short-row rnd.

Cont in patt (working wrapped sts as before) until front of body meas 14 (14½, 15, 15½, 16)" from beg.

DIVIDE FOR FRONT AND BACK

NEXT RND: P1, sm, k to 5 (5, 5, 6, 6) sts before next marker; place next 10 (10, 10, 12, 12) sts on wy for underarm. Turn and p to 5 (5, 5, 6, 6) sts from beg of rnd; place next 10 (10, 10, 12, 12) sts on wy for other underarm—81 (93, 105, 115, 127) sts each on front and back. Turn.

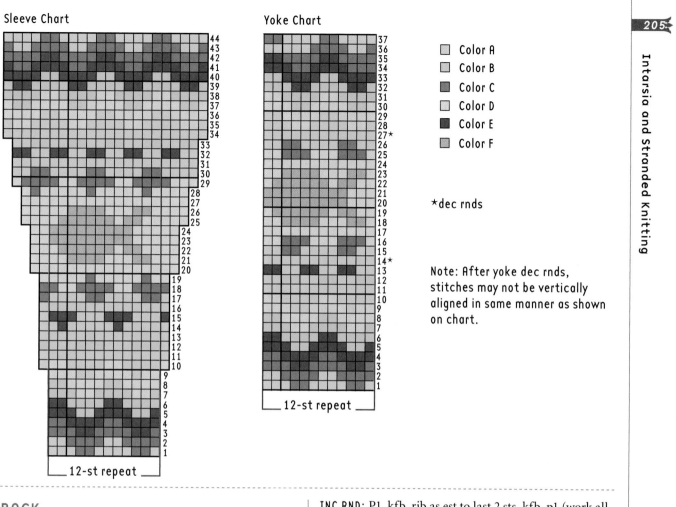

Sleeve Chart

Yoke Chart

☐ Color A
☐ Color B
☐ Color C
☐ Color D
☐ Color E
☐ Color F

*dec rnds

Note: After yoke dec rnds, stitches may not be vertically aligned in same manner as shown on chart.

12-st repeat

12-st repeat

BACK

NEXT ROW (RS): K2tog, k to last 2 sts, ssk.

NEXT ROW: Purl.

Rep last 2 rows twice more—75 (87, 99, 109, 121) sts. Place back sts onto holder.

FRONT

With RS facing, join yarn and work same as back.

SLEEVES

With smaller dpns and A, cast on 52 (52, 64, 64, 64) sts. Pm for beg of rnd and join; p1, [k2, p2] 12 (12, 15, 15, 15) times, k2, p1. Cont in rib as est for 1¾".

INC RND: P1, kfb, rib as est to last 2 sts, kfb, p1 (work all inc sts into rib patt).

Rep inc rnd every 6 rnds 3 times more—60 (60, 72, 72, 72) sts. Work even in rib until sleeve meas 5" from beg. K 3 rnds.

Change to larger dpns and work 44 rnds of Sleeve Chart, inc 1 st at beg and end of rnds 10, 20, 25, 29 and 34—70 (70, 82, 82, 82) sts.

Change to smaller dpns and cont in St st with A only, rep inc rnd every 8th rnd 0 (2, 0, 2, 3) times—70 (74, 82, 86, 88) sts. Work even until sleeve meas 18½" from beg.

NEXT RND: K to last 5 (5, 5, 6, 6) sts; place next 10 (10, 10, 12, 12) sts on wy for underarm—60 (64, 72, 74, 76) sts. Turn.

NEXT ROW (WS): Purl.

NEXT ROW: K2tog, k to last 2 sts, ssk.

Rep last 2 rows twice more, then p 1 row—54 (58, 66, 68, 70) sts.

YOKE

JOINING RND: With RS facing and smaller needle, k54 (58, 66, 68, 70) right sleeve sts, pm, k75 (87, 99, 109, 121) back sts, pm, k54 (58, 66, 68, 70) left sleeve sts, pm, and k75 (87, 99, 109, 121) front sts—258 (290, 330, 354, 382) sts. Pm for beg of rnd and join.

DEC RND: *Ssk, k to 2 sts before next marker, k2tog, sm; rep from * to end of rnd—250 (282, 322, 246, 374) sts.

SHORT-ROWS RND: K to 3 sts before back left marker, W&T, p to 3 sts before back right marker, W&T, k to end (working wrapped sts as before).

Rep dec rnd once more—242 (274, 314, 338, 366) sts.

K 1 (2, 3, 5, 7) rnds, dec 2 (4, 2, 2, 6) sts evenly around on last rnd—240 (270, 312, 336, 360) sts.

Work 37 rnds of Yoke Chart, making decs as folls:

RND 14: Dec 36 (42, 48, 48, 48) sts evenly around—204 (228, 264, 288, 312) sts.

RND 27: Dec 36 (42, 48, 48, 54) sts evenly around—168 (186, 216, 240, 258) sts.

RND 38: Change to smaller needles and cont in St st with A only, dec 44 (39, 57, 63, 67) sts evenly around—124 (147, 159, 177, 191) sts.

RND 39: Knit.

RND 40: Dec 0 (15, 19, 32, 32) sts evenly around—124 (132, 140, 145, 159) sts.

BACK NECK SHAPING

SHORT ROWS RND: K to 3 sts before back left marker, W&T, p to 3 sts before back right marker, W&T, k to 9 sts before back left marker, W&T, p to 9 sts before back right marker, W&T, k to end (working wrapped sts as before).

K 1 rnd.

NEXT RND: Dec 8 (12, 16, 21, 31) sts evenly around—116 (120, 124, 124, 128) sts.

Work in k2, p2 rib for ½". Bind off in patt.

FINISHING

Graft underarm sts using Kitchener st. Sew underarm seams. Weave in ends and block sweater to measurements.

ABOUT SERENA I live in the rainy forests of the Pacific Northwest. I started knitting one day on a whim after looking at a knitting book and realizing that there were some cool patterns and that I could actually make them myself. I quickly became knit addicted, and from there I began designing my own patterns. When I'm not knitting, I'm attending school, practicing yoga, reading, exploring the outdoors, and channeling my creativity into miscellaneous crafts and artistic pursuits. Check out my knitting blog at creativeoverload.wordpress.com.

SKULL ISLE SOCKS

SIZE

Woman's M

Foot circumference: 7"

Foot length: approx 9"

MATERIALS

Dale of Norway *Baby Ull* (100% merino wool; 50g/180 yd)

A: 1 ball #0090 Black

B: 1 ball #3718 Red

C: 1 ball #0010 White

US 1 (2.25mm) double-pointed needles (set of 5)

Stitch marker

GAUGE

36 sts and 48 rnds = 4" in St st over chart patt

SPECIAL ABBREVIATION

W&T (WRAP AND TURN): On RS, bring yarn between needles to front, sl next st onto RH needle, bring yarn between needles to back, return sl st to LH needle, turn.

On WS, bring yarn between needles to back, sl next st onto RH needle, bring yarn between needles to front, return sl st to LH needle, turn.

nitting socks with intricate colorwork is my favorite challenge. When I spotted this skull design on a silk-screened messenger bag, I had to figure out how to translate it to a sock. This project's name plays on Fair Isle knitting, which doesn't traditionally include skull motifs—though I think it should! The Fair Isle, or stranded, technique used here is superfun. If you make sure to carry your floats more loosely than you think you should, you'll avoid a too-snug leg. Though this pattern fits a 7–8" foot, it's totally versatile. Pick out a nice worsted-weight yarn and some size 3 needles if you want to make a cushiony house sock, or keep 'em light and easy in this comfy merino.

DIRECTIONS

Note: This sock is worked with a short-row heel so that the skull patt can continue, uninterrupted by gusset decreases, down the foot.

CUFF

With B, CO 64 sts. Divide sts evenly over 4 dpns. Pm and join. Break off B.

LEG

Join A and work in k1, p1 rib for 1".

Work 54 rnds of Skull Chart.

Skull Chart

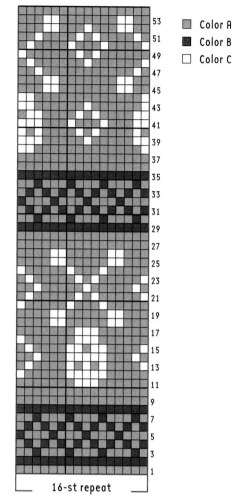

- ■ Color A
- ■ Color B
- □ Color C

53
51
49
47
45
43
41
39
37
35
33
31
29
27
25
23
21
19
17
15
13
11
9
7
5
3
1

⌞ 16-st repeat ⌟

HEEL

Work back and forth over first 32 sts with B.

ROW 1 (RS): K31 onto one needle, W&T.

ROW 2: P30, W&T.

ROW 3: K to 1 st before wrapped st, W&T.

ROW 4: P to 1 st before wrapped st, W&T.

ROWS 5–22: Rep rows 3 and 4. There should now be 11 wrapped heel sts on either side of 10 unwrapped center heel sts.

ROW 23: K to first wrapped st, PU wrap and k tog with st, turn.

ROW 24: Sl 1, p to first wrapped st, PU wrap and p tog with st, turn.

ROW 25: Sl 1, k to next wrapped st, PU wrap and k tog with st, turn.

ROW 26: Sl 1, p to next wrapped st, PU wrap and p tog with st, turn.

Rep rows 25–26 until all wraps have been worked.

FOOT

Divide sts evenly over 4 dpns, with beg of rnd at beg of heel. With RS facing, cont on all sts, work 54 rnds of chart. Break off A and C.

TOE

RND 1: Knit.

RND 2: *K1, ssk, k to end of dpn; k to last 3 sts of dpn, k2tog, k1; rep from * over rem 2 needles.

Rep rnds 1 and 2 until there are 32 sts.

Rep rnd 2 until there are 16 sts.

Break yarn, leaving a 12–14" tail.

Place sts on first 2 dpns onto a single dpn and sts from last 2 dpns onto a second dpn.

Graft toe using Kitchener st.

FINISHING

Weave in ends. Block to shape.

ABOUT CHRISSY I'm a former software architect who started designing knit patterns four years ago and am now surrounded by sketches on scrap paper, half-finished swatches, and bins full of yarn. I live in Portland, Oregon, with two kids, chickens, an extremely patient husband, and a very happy cat. In addition to having my own pattern line, I design for books and magazines. If you want to see more of my work, check out my website at www.gardineryarnworks.com.

rain o'brien

BUTTON IT!

hange the patch and you have a new sweater! This is what I came up with when I had two ideas for intarsia on a sweater I was making for a friend's baby, but time to knit only one. Button It! is one sweater with several supercute removable picture patches. When an idea hits, I usually start sketching on the nearest bit of paper, so I whipped up some animal pictures in my design journal, along with some calculations. Crunching numbers to work out the dimensions, I figured out the best way to center the intarsia on the patch and developed the basic shape of the sweater. I love how Button It! turned out—it's sweet, versatile, and practical. The patches are easier to manipulate than a whole sweater front and less work to undo if you make a boo-boo. What's best is that all of your intarsia work isn't wasted when the kid outgrows the sweater—simply knit a bigger one and button on the patch.

SIZE

6–12 months (2, 3, 4, 5 years)

Finished chest: 22 (24, 26, 28½, 30)"

Finished length: 10 (11, 12, 13, 14)"

MATERIALS

Debbie Bliss *Cashmerino DK* (55% merino wool, 33% microfiber, 12% cashmere; 50g/100 yd)

A: 4 (5, 6, 7, 8) balls #13 Cream

B: 1 ball #26 Pale Yellow

C: 1 ball #21 Brown

D: 1 ball #03 Tan

E: 1 ball #09 Blue

F: 1 ball #02 White

G: 1 ball #01 Black

H: 1 ball #11 Green

I: 1 ball #14 Orange

J: 1 ball #30 Caramel

K: 1 ball #10 Seafoam

US 3 (3.25mm) needles

US 6 (4mm) needles

Four 1" buttons

2 stitch holders or waste yarn

Tapestry needle

GAUGE

22 sts and 30 rows = 4" in St st using larger needles

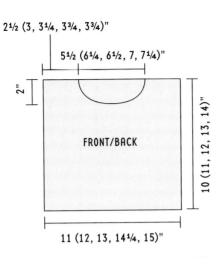

2½ (3, 3¼, 3¾, 3¾)"

5½ (6¼, 6½, 7, 7¼)"

2"

FRONT/BACK

10 (11, 12, 13, 14)"

11 (12, 13, 14¼, 15)"

11¼ (12, 12¾, 13½, 14¼)"

SLEEVE

8 (9, 10, 11, 12)"

7¼ (8, 8¾, 9½, 10¼)"

SPECIAL ABBREVIATIONS

M1L: Make 1 st by inserting LH needle from front to back under the horizontal strand between the 2 sts of the previous row, and k through the back of this loop so it twists to the left.

M1R: Make 1 st by inserting LH needle from back to front under the horizontal strand between the 2 sts of the previous row, and k through the front of this loop so it twists to the right.

STITCH PATTERN

LOOP ST (SEE CHART): K1 tbl leaving st on LH needle, bring yarn to front and wrap around thumb to make loop, bring yarn to back and k same st tbl, slip both sts off needle and pass 1st st over 2nd st.

DIRECTIONS

BACK

With smaller needles and A, CO 60 (66, 72, 78, 82) sts.

Work 8 rows in St st, end with a WS row.

EST RIB (RS): [K2, p2] to last 0 (2, 0, 2 , 2) sts, k0 (2, 0, 2, 2).

Cont in est k2, p2 rib for 5 rows more.

Change to larger needles and work in St st for 8½ (9½, 10½, 11½, 12½)" more, end with a WS row.

BO 14 (16, 18, 20, 21) sts, k next 32 (34, 36, 38, 40) sts and place on holder, BO rem 14 (16, 18, 20, 21) sts.

FRONT

Work same as back, until piece meas 6½ (7½, 8½, 9½, 10½)" above rib, end with a WS row.

NECK SHAPING

K16 (18, 20, 22, 23), k2tog, k24 (26, 28, 30, 32), ssk, k16 (18, 20, 22, 23).

RIGHT FRONT

P19 (21, 23, 25, 26); place rem sts onto holder.

DEC ROW (RS): K2, ssk, k to end.

Rep dec row every RS row 4 times more—14 (16, 18, 20, 21) sts.

Work even until front meas same as back, end with a WS row.

BO all sts.

LEFT FRONT

With WS facing, place first 20 (22, 24, 26, 28) sts onto holder for front neck. Join yarn to rem 19 (21, 23, 25, 26) sts and p to end.

DEC ROW (RS): K to last 4 sts, k2tog, k2.

Rep dec row every RS row 4 times more—14 (16, 18, 20,

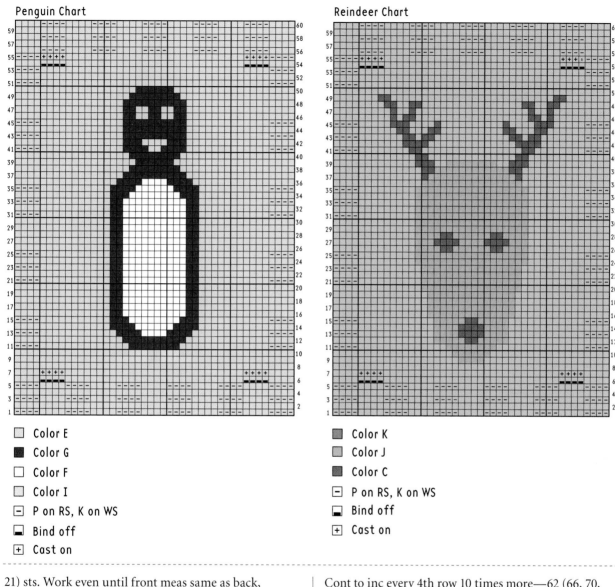

Penguin Chart

Reindeer Chart

□ Color E
■ Color G
□ Color F
□ Color I
⊟ P on RS, K on WS
▬ Bind off
⊞ Cast on

■ Color K
□ Color J
■ Color C
⊟ P on RS, K on WS
▬ Bind off
⊞ Cast on

21) sts. Work even until front meas same as back, end with a WS row. BO all sts.

SLEEVES (MAKE 2)

With smaller needles and A, CO 40 (44, 48, 52, 56) sts.

Work 8 rows in St st, end with a WS row.

Work 6 rows in k2, p2 rib.

Change to larger needles and St st.

INC ROW (RS): K2, m1, k to last 2 sts, m1, k2.

Cont to inc every 4th row 10 times more—62 (66, 70, 74, 78) sts. Work even until piece meas 6½ (7½, 8½, 9½, 10½)" from top of rib. BO all sts.

ANIMAL MOTIFS

With smaller needles and background color for motif, CO 44 sts. Start with a WS row at bottom left of chart; change to larger needles on row 6 and back to smaller needles on row 56.

When chart is complete, BO all sts.

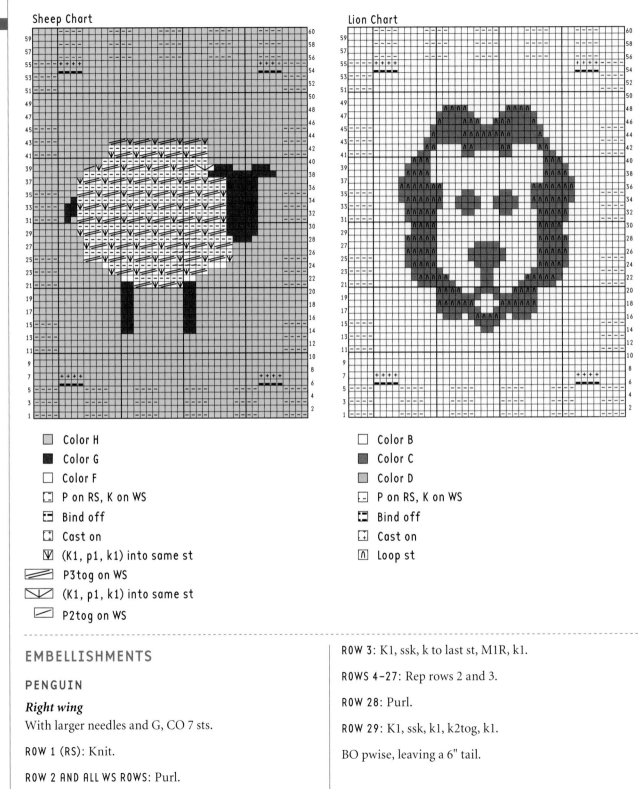

Sheep Chart

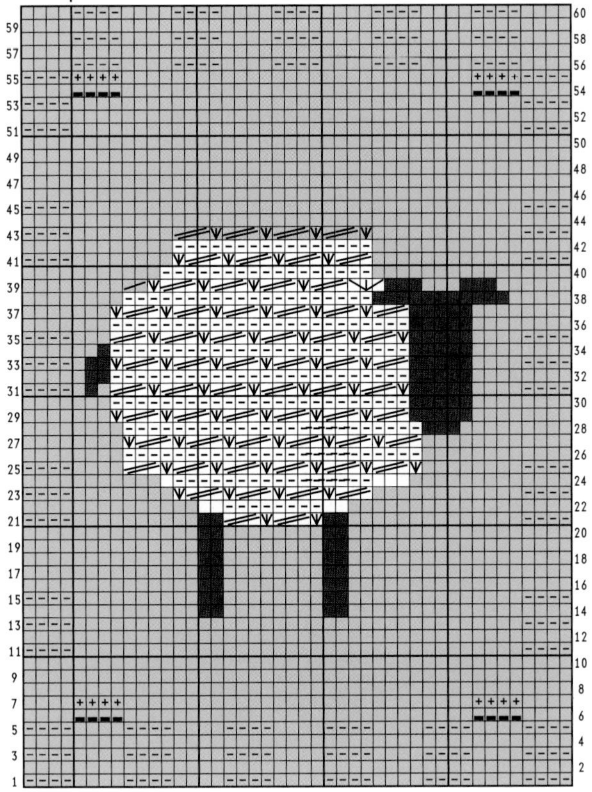

- Color H
- Color G
- Color F
- P on RS, K on WS
- Bind off
- Cast on
- (K1, p1, k1) into same st
- P3tog on WS
- (K1, p1, k1) into same st
- P2tog on WS

Lion Chart

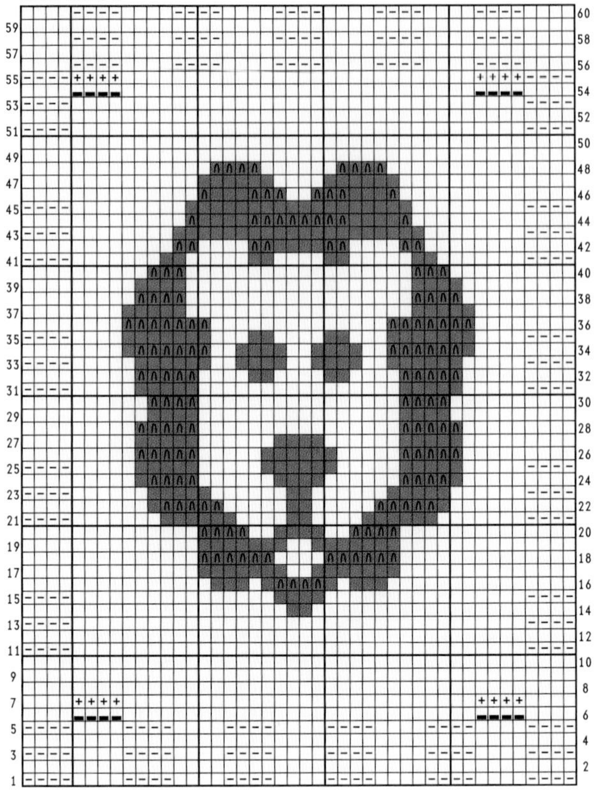

- Color B
- Color C
- Color D
- P on RS, K on WS
- Bind off
- Cast on
- Loop st

EMBELLISHMENTS

PENGUIN

Right wing

With larger needles and G, CO 7 sts.

ROW 1 (RS): Knit.

ROW 2 AND ALL WS ROWS: Purl.

ROW 3: K1, ssk, k to last st, M1R, k1.

ROWS 4–27: Rep rows 2 and 3.

ROW 28: Purl.

ROW 29: K1, ssk, k1, k2tog, k1.

BO pwise, leaving a 6" tail.

Left wing

With larger needles and G, CO 7 sts.

ROW 1 (RS): Knit.

ROW 2 AND ALL WS ROWS: Purl.

ROW 3: K1, M1L, k to last 3 sts, k2tog, k1.

ROWS 4–27: Rep rows 2 and 3.

ROW 28: Purl.

ROW 29: K1, ssk, k1, k2tog, k1.

BO pwise, leaving a 6" tail.

Sew wings to each shoulder at edge of belly.

REINDEER

Ears (make 2)

With larger needles and J, CO 8 sts.

ROW 1 (RS): Knit.

ROW 2: Purl.

ROW 3: K1, ssk, k2, k2tog, k1.

ROW 4: Purl.

ROW 5: K1, ssk, k2tog, k1.

ROW 6: P4tog.

Fasten off, leaving a 6" tail. Using tails, sew to side of head beneath antlers.

FINISHING

Sew right shoulder seam.

NECKBAND

With RS facing, smaller needles and A, starting at left shoulder, PU and k14 sts along left front neck, k20 (22, 24, 26, 28) front neck sts from holder, PU and k14 sts along right front neck and 32 (34, 36, 38, 40) back neck sts from holder—80 (84, 88, 92, 96) sts.

Work in k2, p2 rib for 6 rows.

Work in St st for 8 rows starting with a p row.

BO loosely.

Sew left shoulder seam, reversing seam on St st edge. Center sleeves over shoulder seams and sew in place. Sew side and sleeve seams, reversing seams on St st edges. Sew buttons to sweater front to correspond with buttonholes on motifs.

ABOUT RAIN I come from a long line of avid knitters—my grandmother even used to knit in the sidecar of my grandfather's motorcycle. My mum introduced me to the craft when I was nine years old, and it's been an obsession ever since. I love knitting for children, and, fortunately, my friends and relatives have kept up a steady supply. I now live in the French Alps and, recently, have traded in my needles for a pair of skis—though, I do often wonder if I could knit with the ski poles. You can read about my knitting exploits, or current lack thereof, at www.froginknots.blogspot.com.

jennifer tallapaneni

Lotus Bag

W hile in India for my wedding, I was inspired by all the beautiful floral and lotus prints—I knew I had to incorporate these motifs into a knit project. I also wanted to make a sturdy, nonfelted bag that could take a lot of abuse, as I tend to shove everything I possibly can into my purse. So I got to work making the Lotus Bag both stylish and strong. I chose double knit to reinforce the structure and combined it with intarsia to create seamless colorwork. Double knit also turned out to be a sneaky solution to making the handle strong and good-lookin', as it resembles stockinette stitch on both sides and it doesn't curl. If you're like me and want to put the "all" in "carryall," you'll be good to go with this sweet, perfectly sized tote.

DIRECTIONS

Construction notes: Front and back pieces are worked flat. The gusset/strap is worked as one piece in double knitting.

BACK

With MC and largest needles, CO 47 sts. Work 62 rows in St st, end with a RS row.

NEXT ROW (WS): Knit.

Work 7 more rows in St st beg with a k row.

BO all sts.

FRONT

With MC and largest needles, CO 47 sts. Work 11 rows in St st, end with a WS row.

SIZE

Finished width: 9½"

Finished length: 9"

MATERIALS

Knit Picks *Wool of the Andes* (100% Peruvian Highland wool; 50g/110 yd)

MC: 3 balls #23774 Chocolate

CC: 1 ball #23770 Tulip

US 6 (4mm) needles

US 4 (3.5mm) double-pointed needles

US 5 (3.75mm) double-pointed needles

¾" magnetic snap

Stitch markers (2)

1 sheet of plastic needlepoint mesh canvas

Tapestry needle

1 yd lining fabric

Sewing needle and matching thread

GAUGE

20 sts and 27 rows = 4" in St st on largest needles

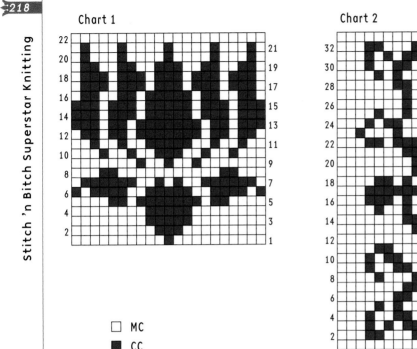

Chart 1

Chart 2

work rows 8–27
9 times

□ MC
■ CC

Note for Chart 2:
Each square represents two sts.
For RS rows, k the st on the
facing side in the color shown,
and p the corresponding st in
the opposite color. For WS
rows, k the st on the facing
side in the opposite color,
and p the corresponding st in
the color shown.

NEXT ROW (RS): K7, pm, work 21 sts of Chart 1, pm, k to end.

Cont in St st, working chart between markers. After chart is complete work 30 rows in St st, end with a RS row.

NEXT ROW (WS): Knit.

Work 7 more rows in St st beg with a k row.

BO all sts.

GUSSET/STRAP

With MC and smallest needles, CO 30 sts tightly.

ROWS 1–10: *K1, sl 1 wyif; rep from *.

Holding 2 of the larger dpns in your right hand and the work in your left, *slip 1 st onto the right front needle, then slip the next st onto the right back needle; rep from * to end.

Sts can now be distributed onto 3–4 dpns for working in the round. Work in St st until piece meas 14¾" from beg. Cut a piece of plastic mesh canvas 9½" × 2¼" and insert into the knitted tube down to the bottom.

Slip first 15 sts onto one needle and the last 15 sts onto another needle. Holding the needles parallel in your left hand, and one straight needle in your right hand, *slip 1 st from the left front needle, then slip the next st from the left back needle; rep from * to end. Cont with smaller dpns.

ROW 1: *With both colors held in back, k1 in MC, bring both strands to front, p1 in CC; rep from * to end.

ROW 2: *With both colors held in back, k1 in CC, bring both strands to front, p1 in MC; rep from * to end.

Rep rows 1–2 once.

Cont rep rows 1–2, working rows 1–14 of Chart 2. Work rows 8–27 (20-row rep) 9 times, then work final 12 rows.

Drop CC and complete gusset/strap with MC only.

NEXT ROW: *K1, sl 1 wyif, rep from * to end.

Rep last row 9 times more. Distribute sts on 3–4 larger dpns and work in the round until solid MC section meas 5¼".

BO ROW: K2tog, *k2tog, pass the 1st st over the 2nd st; rep from * to end.

FINISHING

Weave in all ends. Block all pieces. Cut two 1¾" × ¾" pieces of plastic mesh canvas.

With hem for the back piece folded over, insert the prongs of one half the magnetic snap through the hem layer and push a piece of canvas onto the back. Place the washer over the prongs in back and fold the prongs over. Rep for other half of snap on front piece. Sew down both hems over the plastic. With the plastic piece in the gusset on the bottom, sew front and back pieces to gusset.

LINING

Cut fabric into two 9½" wide × 8¾" long

pieces and one 27" × 3" strip. Press top ½" of each piece and both ends of strip to WS. With RS tog, sew the 3 raw edges of each piece to the strip using a ¼" seam. Place lining inside bag with WS tog. With sewing thread, carefully stitch in lining just inside folded hem of bag.

ABOUT JENNIFER A few years ago I stumbled across the first *Stitch 'n Bitch* book and knew right then I wanted to learn to knit. My combined love of art/design and mathematics/programming quickly led to me to discover their happy marriage in knitting design; I love the combination of creativity and technical details. I'm a multimedia developer by day and work on my designs by night. I live in Dallas, Texas, with my hubby and our endlessly amusing puppy, Aejaz. You can read more about me on my website www.pieKnits.com.

Laurie Undis

SHEEPY TIME

 y usual design for minisweaters is a basic chunky shape, because it's easier to work tiny garments without fussy shaping. I wanted to keep this baby cardi nice and simple. I also adore raglan sleeve construction for any size sweater, so I used it here. Since it was for my daughter, I asked her what it should look like. Naturally, she answered, "like little sheeps," and supplied me with a drawing. I translated her drawing into a cute silhouette and used a computer program to chart the shape of the sheep. I let her in on each step of the process, from designing the motif on the computer to holding the ball of yarn while I knit. She ended up loving the sweater because she helped, but I think any little kid will think it's great.

SIZE

3–6 months (1 yr, 2 yr, 4 yr)

Finished chest: 18 (20½, 22, 26)"

Finished length: 11 (12¾, 14½, 16)"

MATERIALS

MC: Karabella *Aurora 8* (100% merino wool; 50g/98 yd), 3 (4, 4, 6) balls #8167 Turquoise

A: 1 (1, 1, 1) ball #1250 White

B: 1 (1, 1, 1) ball #1148 Black

C: 1 (1, 1, 1) ball #851 Brown

US 7 (4.5mm) circular needle

US 7 (4.5mm) double-pointed needles

4 stitch holders

Stitch markers

Waste yarn

Three ½" buttons

GAUGE

20 sts and 28 rows = 4" in St st

DIRECTIONS

Pattern Note: Sweater is knit back and forth in one piece on a circular needle. Sheep are knit using intarsia method but stranding MC behind motifs.

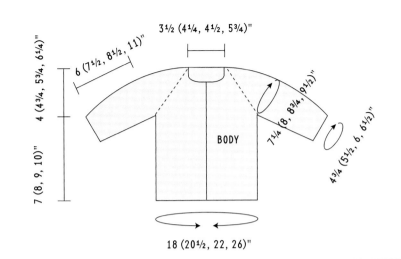

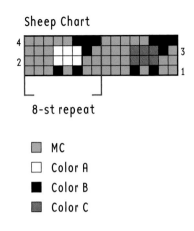

Sheep Chart

8-st repeat

☐ MC
☐ Color A
■ Color B
■ Color C

BODY

With MC, CO 89 (101, 109, 129) sts.

Work in garter st for 8 rows.

Work in St st for 3" more, end with a WS row.

NEXT ROW (RS): K6 (4, 4, 6), work Sheep Chart to last 3 (1, 1, 3) sts, knit to end.

Work rem 3 rows of Sheep Chart as est.

Cont with MC in St st until body measures 7 (8, 9, 10)" from beg, end with a WS row. Set aside.

SLEEVES

With MC and dpns, CO 24 (28, 30, 32) sts.

Work in garter st for 8 rows.

Pm and join to work in the round.

Work in St st, inc every 4th (6th, 6th, 6th) rnd 6 (6, 7, 8) times as foll:

K1, m1, k to last st, m1, k1—36 (40, 44, 48) sts after last inc.

Work even in St st until sleeve meas 6 (7½, 8½, 11)" from beg, ending 3 sts before end of rnd. Place next 6 sts onto holder and rem 30 (34, 38, 42) sleeve sts onto wy. Make second sleeve.

JOIN SLEEVES AND BODY

K19 (22, 24, 29) right front sts, pm, place next 6 sts onto holder, k30 (34, 38, 42) sleeve sts, pm, k39 (45, 49, 59) back sts, pm, place next 6 sts onto holder, k30 (34, 38, 42) sleeve sts, pm, k19 (22, 24, 29) left front sts—137 (157, 173, 201) sts.

RAGLAN SHAPING

Work 3 (5, 7, 7) rows in St st.

DEC ROW (RS): *K to 4 sts before marker, ssk, k4, k2tog; rep from * 3 times more, k to end of row.

Rep dec row every 4th row 2 (3, 4, 4) times more, then every other row 8 (8, 8, 10) times.

AT THE SAME TIME, when front edge meas 9½ (11¼, 12, 13¼)" from beg, shape neck as foll:

BO 3 (4, 5, 6) sts at beg of next 2 rows, then dec 1 st at each neck edge every RS row 3 times.

Bind off rem 37 (47, 53, 63) sts.

COLLAR

With RS facing and circular needle, PU and k49 (61, 69, 81) sts around neck opening.

Work in garter st for 1 (1¼, 1¼, 1½)". BO.

FINISHING

Graft underarm sts. Sew sleeve cuffs.

RIGHT FRONT BAND

With RS facing and circular needle, pick up and k47 (56, 60, 66) sts evenly along front edge. Work 6 rows in garter st. BO.

LEFT FRONT BAND

With RS facing, PU and k47 (56, 60, 66) sts evenly along front edge. Mark placement for buttonholes, the first ½" from top of neck, and the rem two buttonholes 1 (1, 1½, 1½)" apart. Work 3 rows in garter st. K next row, working a buttonhole at each marker by k2tog, yo. K 2 rows. BO.

Sew buttons opposite buttonholes.

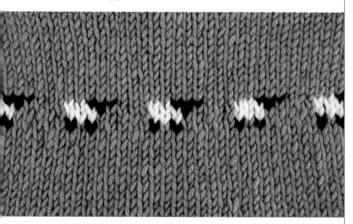

ABOUT LAURIE My grandmother taught me to knit doll blankets and dresses during the acrylic-covered '60s. Since then, I have knit endless amounts of yarn into more useful and lovely things. I live with my husband and children in Nashville, Tennessee, where I write patterns, teach others to knit, and hope I'll finally finish the afghan I started a year ago. See my patterns at knitloud.com and ninjaknits.com, and check out my haiku blog at haikuknitter.wordpress.com.

emily sessions

BOOKISH

This sweater was inspired by my love for vintage clothes, classic silhouettes, and librarian-chic styles. To draft the pattern, I took one of my own sweaters that fit well, laid it out on a flat surface, and measured across the hips, waist, and bust. Then I measured the length between hips and waist, waist and bust, and bust and shoulder seams. After sketching a sweater with these measurements, I knit a gauge swatch to see how many stitches per inch I'd get horizontally and vertically. Using my points of measurement and my gauge swatch along with some serious math (multiplying rows per inch by the distance between my points of measurement), I figured out which rows to decrease and increase. In my first try, I used size 3 needles with worsted-weight yarn, and my finished sweater was so stiff that it stood up on its own! So I started over with a new swatch on bigger needles. I learned a lesson here—your gauge swatch really does determine how sweet your sweater will be.

DIRECTIONS

BACK

Using cable CO method, CO 71 (81, 91, 101, 111, 121) sts.

ROW 1 (RS): K1, *k1, p1; rep from * to last 2 sts, k2.

ROW 2: P1, *p1, k1; rep from * to last 2 sts, p2.

Rep rows 1 and 2 four times more.

Work in St st for 8 rows.

SIZE

XS (S, M, L, XL, XXL)

Finished bust: 33½ (37, 41½, 45, 49½, 53)"

Finished length: 23 (23, 23½, 23¾, 24¼, 24½)"

MATERIALS

A: Cascade Yarns *Cascade 220* (100% wool; 100g/220 yd), 5 (5, 6, 6, 7, 7) skeins #8891 Turquoise

B: 1 skein #7816 Lt blue

C: 1 skein #8903 Lt green

D: 1 skein #8555 Black

Waste yarn

US 6 (4.25mm) 24" circular needle

2 stitch markers

2 stitch holders

Yarn bobbins

Tapestry needle

Ten ⅝" buttons

Sewing needle and matching thread

GAUGE

20 sts and 28 rows = 4" in St st

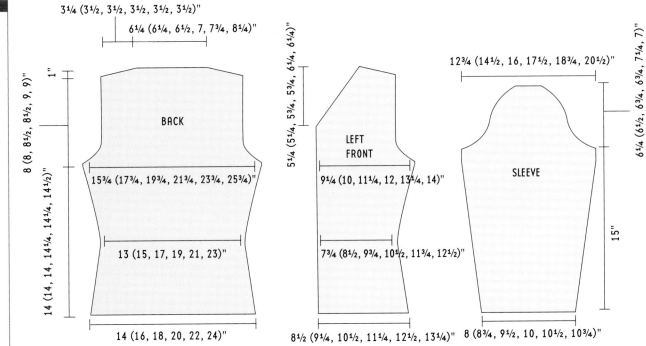

WAIST SHAPING

DEC ROW (RS): K2, k2tog, k to last 3 sts, ssk, k2.

Cont in St st, rep dec row every 8th row twice more—65 (75, 85, 95, 105, 115) sts.

Work even in St st for 7 (7, 7, 9, 9, 11) rows.

INC ROW (RS): K2, m1, k to last st, m1, k2.

Cont in St st, rep inc row every 8th row 6 times more—79 (89, 99, 109, 119, 129) sts.

Work even in St st until body meas 14 (14, 14, 14¼, 14¼, 14½)" from beg.

ARMHOLE SHAPING

BO 4 (6, 8, 10, 12, 14) sts at beg of next 2 rows.

DEC ROW (RS): K2, k2tog, k to last 4 sts, ssk, k2.

Cont in St st, rep dec row every RS row 3 (5, 6, 8, 10, 12) times more—63 (65, 67, 71, 73, 75) sts. Work even in St st until armhole measures 8 (8, 8½, 8½, 9, 9)".

SHOULDER SHAPING

BO 5 (5, 6, 6, 5, 5) sts at beg of next 2 rows, BO 5 (6, 6, 6, 6, 6) sts at beg of foll 2 rows, then BO 6 sts at beg of foll 2 rows. BO rem 31 (31, 33, 35, 39, 41) sts for back neck.

Note: Read all instructions before continuing. Patterning, armhole, and neck shaping take place at the same time.

LEFT FRONT

Using cable CO method, CO 42 (46, 52, 56, 62, 66) sts.

ROW 1 (RS): *K1, p1; rep from * to end. Pm at end of row to indicate front edge.

ROW 2: *K1, p1; rep from * to end.

Rep rows 1 and 2 four times more.

Work in St st for 8 rows, keeping 5 sts at front edge in rib for buttonband.

Argyle Chart

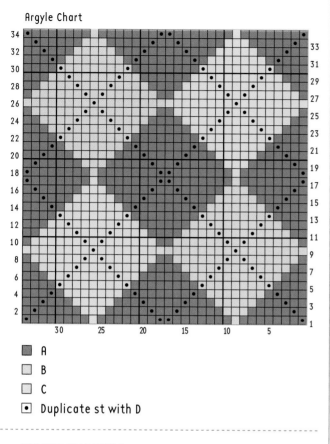

- ☐ A
- ☐ B
- ☐ C
- ☐ Duplicate st with D

WAIST SHAPING

DEC ROW (RS): K2, k2tog, k to last 5 sts, [p1, k1] twice, p1.

Cont in St st and rib as est, rep dec row every 8th row twice more—39 (43, 49, 53, 59, 63) sts.

Work even in St st and rib as est for 7 (7, 7, 9, 9, 11) rows.

INC ROW (RS): K2, m1, work in patt as est to end.

Cont in patt as est, rep inc row every 8th row 6 times more—46 (50, 56, 60, 66, 70) sts.

Work even until front meas 13 (13, 13, 13¼, 13¼, 13½)" from beg, end with a WS row.

Cont in patt as est, work Argyle Chart over St st section beg with stitch 11 (7, 1, 31, 25, 21) on row 1 until front meas 14 (14, 14, 14¼, 14¼, 14½)" from beg, end with a WS row. *Note:* End with stitch 17 at end of each RS row and beg with stitch 17 at beg of each WS row.

ARMHOLE AND NECK SHAPING

Adjusting RS row start points in Argyle Chart as necessary, BO 4 (6, 8, 10, 12, 14) sts at beg of next RS row.

DEC ROW (RS): K2, k2tog, k to last 5 sts, [p1, k1] twice, p1.

Rep dec row every RS row 3 (5, 6, 8, 10, 12) times more.

AT THE SAME TIME, when Argyle Chart is complete, dec 1 st at neck edge every RS row 17 (16, 18, 18, 21, 21) times as foll: K to last 7 sts, k2tog, [p1, k1] twice, p1.

SHOULDER SHAPING

AND AT THE SAME TIME, when armhole meas 8 (8, 8½, 8½, 9, 9)", BO 5 (5, 6, 6, 5, 5) sts at beg of next RS row. BO 5 (6, 6, 6, 6, 6) sts on foll RS row, and BO 6 sts on foll RS row. Place rem 5 rib sts onto holder.

BUTTON PLACEMENT

Sew 10 buttons in ribbed buttonband as foll: First button ½" below first neck dec and last button ½" above CO edge. Space remaining 8 buttons evenly between the two.

RIGHT FRONT

Using cable CO method, CO 42 (46, 52, 56, 62, 66) sts.

ROW 1 (RS): *P1, k1; rep from * to end. Pm at beg of row to indicate front edge.

ROW 2: *P1, k1; rep from * to end.

Rep rows 1 and 2 four times more.

AT THE SAME TIME, work buttonholes on RS rows opposite buttons on left front as foll: P1, k1, BO 2 sts, work to end of row. On next row, using backward loop CO method (page 88), CO 2 sts over BO sts.

Work in St st for 8 rows, keeping 5 sts at front edge in rib for buttonhole band.

WAIST SHAPING

DEC ROW (RS): P1, [k1, p1] twice, k to last 4 sts, k2tog, k2.

Cont in St st and rib as est, rep dec row every 8th row twice more—39 (43, 49, 53, 59, 63) sts.

Work even in St st and rib as est for 7 (7, 7, 9, 9, 11) rows.

INC ROW (RS): Work in patt as est to last 2 sts, m1, k2.

Cont in St st and rib as est, rep inc row every 8th row 6 times more—46 (50, 56, 60, 66, 70) sts.

Work even until front meas 13 (13, 13, 13¼, 13¼, 13½)" from beg, end with a WS row.

Cont in patt as est, work Argyle Chart over St st section beg with stitch 18 on row 1 until front meas 14 (14, 14, 14¼, 14¼, 14½)" from beg, end with a WS row. *Note:* End with stitch 24 (28, 34, 4, 10, 14) at end of each RS row and beg with stitch 24 (28, 34, 4, 10, 14) at beg of each WS row.

ARMHOLE AND NECK SHAPING

Adjusting WS row start points in Argyle Chart as necessary, BO 4 (6, 8, 10, 12, 14) sts at beg of next WS row.

DEC ROW (RS): P1, [k1, p1] twice, k to last 4 sts, ssk, k2.

Rep dec row every RS row 3 (5, 6, 8, 10, 12) times more.

AT THE SAME TIME, when Argyle Chart is complete, dec 1 st at neck edge every RS row 17 (16, 18, 18, 21, 21) times as foll: P1, [k1, p1] twice, ssk, k to end.

SHOULDER SHAPING

AND AT THE SAME TIME, when armhole meas 8 (8, 8½, 8½, 9, 9)", BO 5 (5, 6, 6, 5, 5) sts at beg of next WS row. BO 5 (6, 6, 6, 6, 6) sts of foll WS row, and BO 6 sts of foll WS row. Place rem 5 rib sts on holder.

SLEEVES

Using cable CO method, CO 40 (44, 48, 50, 52, 54) sts.

ROW 1 (RS): K2, *p1, k1; rep from * to end.

ROW 2: *P1, k1; rep from * to last 2 sts, p2.

Rep rows 1 and 2 four times more.

INC ROW (RS): K2, m1, k to last 2 sts, m1, k2.

Cont in St st, rep inc row every other row 0 (0, 0, 0, 0, 3) times more, every 4th row 0 (0, 3, 11, 17, 20) times, then every 6th row 11 (13, 12, 7, 3, 0) times—64 (72, 80, 88, 94, 102) sts.

Work even in St st until sleeve meas 15" from beg, end with a WS row.

CAP SHAPING

BO 4 (6, 8, 10, 12, 14) sts at beg of next 2 rows.

Using the foll dec rows as needed, dec every row 0 (0, 0, 2, 0, 4) times; every other row 8 (14, 17, 19, 22, 19) times; then every 3rd row 7 (3, 2, 0, 0, 0) times.

DEC ROW (RS): K2, k2tog, k to last 4 sts, ssk, k2.

DEC ROW (WS): P2, p2tog tbl, p to last 4 sts, p2tog, p2.

BO 3 sts at beg of next 4 rows. BO rem 14 (14, 14, 14, 14, 16) sts.

FINISHING

Sew shoulder seams. Set sleeves into armholes. Sew side and sleeve seams.

BACK NECK RIBBING

Place sts from 1 holder onto needle and cont in patt as est until rib fits across back neck, slightly stretched. Place sts from other holder onto a spare needle and join using 3-needle BO (page 103). Sew edge of ribbing to back neck edge.

DUPLICATE STITCH

With tapestry needle and D, finish Argyle Chart using duplicate stitch (page 81).

BUTTONHOLES

Using A and Buttonhole stitch (page 113), embroider around each buttonhole to reinforce.

ABOUT EMILY I've been knitting for about ten years, not counting some poorly conceived washcloths and doll capes I made as a kid. I love playing with new stitches and twists on basic patterns, and I'm always drawn to bright, saturated natural fibers. I also love sewing, photography, and embroidery. I sell my handmade iPod and iPhone cases at www.technocutie.com. I live in New York City with my wonderful husband and two cats.

SIZE

Finished height: 10"

Finished width: 14"

Finished depth: 4"

MATERIALS

Cascade Yarns *Cascade 220* (100% wool; 100g/220 yd)

MC: 2 hanks #8686 Chocolate

A: 1 hank #7825 Yellow-Orange

B: 1 hank #9444 Orange Heather

C: 1 hank #8886 Dk Purple

D: 1 hank #7808 Med Purple

E: 1 hank #8888 Lt Purple

F: 1 hank #8891 Turquoise Blue

G: 1 hank #9455 Heather Turquoise Blue

H: 1 hank #7803 Raspberry

I: 1 hank #7802 Fuchsia

J: 1 hank #9430 Leaf Green

K: 1 hank #9461 Heather Leaf Green

US 10 (6mm) needles

1 pair 25" leather handles in Grape (available from: www.muenchyarns .com/Pages/GraysonE.html)

Embroidery needle

FOR LINING

½ yd of lining fabric (48" wide)

½ yd iron-on interfacing (48" wide)

Sewing needle and matching thread

Plastic needlepoint mesh canvas, cut to fit bottom of bag

GAUGE

16 sts and 19½ rows = 4" in St st before felting

IN BLOOM

ketching flowers in my garden inspired the intarsia design on this cute bag. Within twenty-four hours, I went to my local yarn store, knit an intarsia swatch, felted it, and detailed the pattern. You could say I was superinspired to combine my love of felting, gardening, embroidery, and colorwork into one project. If you are a felting newbie, you'll be hooked after crafting this carryall. There's something magical about changing the knit portion you've worked so hard on into something completely different. I know you'll be excited to get to the embroidery, but take this felting advice: Let it dry. If you don't, the manhandling you'll do while embroidering will ruin your blocking job, big time, and we don't want that. Though this bag has several steps to completion, your patience will totally pay off when you have the cutest one on the block.

DIRECTIONS

With MC, CO 94 sts. Work 53 rows in St st, starting with a p row.

Work 140 rows of Intarsia Chart, BO on rows 35 and 36 and CO on rows 65 and 66 as indicated.

Work 15 rows in St st.

BO all sts.

FINISHING

With MC, sew each side seam using mattress st, matching patt where possible. Sew lower edges of sides and base together. Weave in ends.

To felt, place bag in a zippered pillow case and run through hot-wash cycle of washing machine with a few pairs of jeans and some tennis balls if you have them handy. Then using a small amount of detergent, wash bag on cold for a full cycle. Repeat as needed until you have achieved desired felting.

Block bag. I used 6 large (filled) tissue boxes stacked 3 per row. I like using tissue boxes because I can pin into them.

EMBROIDERY

Once completely dry, embellish with embroidery, following the chart.

With C, use French knots (page 85) to add texture to lupine flowers; with A, make French knots at centers of pink flowers.

With J, use satin stitch (page 85) for leaves of pink flowers and blue poppies.

With J, use chain stitch (page 83) for stems of pink flowers.

With J and K, use stem stitch (page 84) for stems of blue flowers.

With J and K, use fly stitch (page 86) for leaves.

Intarsia Chart

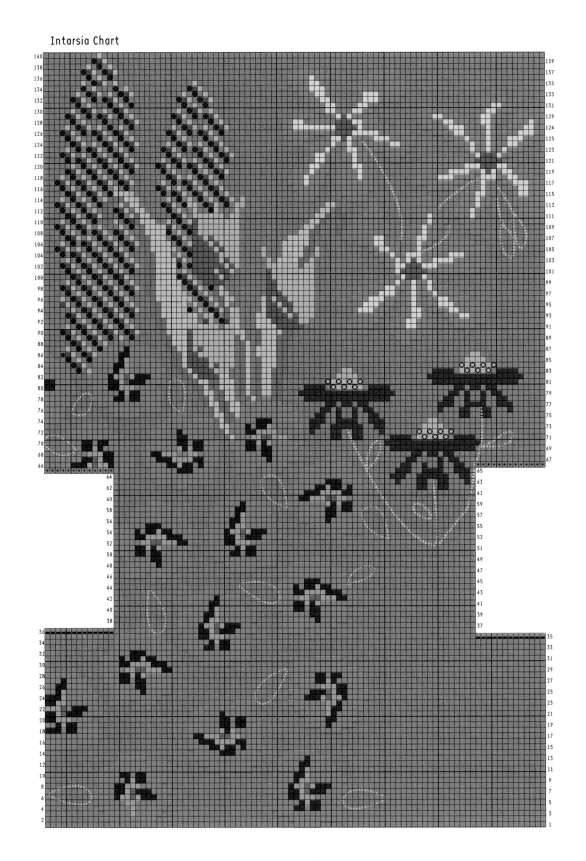

LINING

Measure the height, width, and depth (gusset) of your finished and blocked bag. Cut two pieces of lining that are (the width of the bag + 1¼") × (the bag height + ½ the bag depth + 1¼"). Cut two pieces of iron-on interfacing to these same dimensions.

Iron interfacing to WS of lining pieces.

ASSEMBLY

Align lining pieces with RS together and pin side edges. Sew side seams with ⅝" allowance. Press seams flat, then press open. Pin bottom edge 3" from each side. Sew bottom seam from sides toward center, leaving center open. Press seam as for sides.

To close bottom ends and form gusset, match side seams to bottom seams and flatten, then sew across with ⅝" allowance. Press seam as before.

Mark handle placement on knit bag. Cut four 2" × 2" pieces of iron-on interfacing. Turn knit bag inside out and iron interfacing to each spot and sew handles in place. Place bag into lining with RS together. Fold 2" knit hem over edge of lining and pin in place (ONLY through hem and lining). Sew lining in place. Tack plastic mesh into place at bottom of bag. Turn bag RS out through opening in bottom of lining and sew opening closed.

ABOUT KIMBERLI I'm so glad my mom took my pleas to learn to knit and crochet seriously. My day job as a milliner involves traveling between Asia and New York City, with occasional stops in Europe. My travels have allowed me to enjoy another hobby: learning cuisines, recipes, and cooking styles around the world. I love to knit, crochet, sew, entertain, write recipes, sing karaoke, garden, and enjoy all New York City has to offer. You'll often find me with a hat on my head, a smile on my face, and knitting in my bag. Read about my creations and travels at www.kimberlinewyork .blogspot.com.

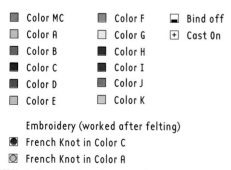

■ Color MC   ■ Color F   ▭ Bind off
□ Color A   □ Color G   ⊞ Cast On
■ Color B   ■ Color H
■ Color C   ■ Color I
■ Color D   ▨ Color J
□ Color E   □ Color K

Embroidery (worked after felting)
◉ French Knot in Color C
◎ French Knot in Color A
Embroidery in Colors J & K (see text)

NicoLe LaRocHe

SEA AND SURF SWEATER

ight and airy, this cotton sweater is perfect for spring days or cool summer nights. I always admired Knitty .com's Pomatomus sock pattern, designed by Cookie A, but since I rarely wear socks, I borrowed her brilliant stitch pattern to design this sassy shell. The stitch pattern itself is supergorgeous and reminds me of waves, so I made this sweater in a soothing blue and with a loose fit so that the stitches really shine. It's worked from the top down, so you can try on the sweater as you go and adjust the pattern for a stellar fit.

STITCH PATTERN
12-STITCH PATTERN

RND 1: *Yo, k2tog tbl, [p1, k1 tbl] 5 times; rep from * to end.

RND 2: *Yo, p1, k2tog tbl, [k1 tbl, p1] 4 times, k1 tbl; rep from * to end.

RND 3: *Yo, k1 tbl, p1, k2tog tbl, [p1, k1 tbl] 4 times; rep from * to end.

RND 4: *Yo, p1, k1 tbl, p1, k2tog tbl, [k1 tbl, p1] 3 times, k1 tbl; rep from * to end.

RND 5: *Yo, [k1 tbl, p1] twice, k2tog tbl, [p1, k1 tbl] 3 times; rep from * to end.

RND 6: *Yo, [p1, k1 tbl] twice, p1, k2tog tbl, [k1 tbl, p1] twice, k1 tbl; rep from * to end.

RND 7: *Yo, [k1 tbl, p1] 3 times, k2tog tbl, [p1, k1 tbl] twice; rep from * to end.

RND 8: *Yo, [p1, k1 tbl] 3 times, p1, k2tog tbl, k1 tbl, p1, k1 tbl; rep from * to end.

SIZE

S (M, L, XL)

Finished bust: 30¼ (35¼, 40½, 45½)"

Finished length: 19 (21½, 24, 26½)"

MATERIALS

Blue Sky Alpacas *Dyed Cotton* (100% cotton; 100g/150 yd), 4 (5, 6, 7) skeins #628 Azul

US 6 (4.25mm) 16" circular needle

US 6 (4.25mm) 24" circular needle

US 10½ (6.5mm) 16" circular needle

US 10½ (6.5mm) 24" circular needle

US 6 (4.25mm) double-pointed needles

US 10½ (6.5mm) double-pointed needles

2 stitch holders

4 stitch markers

Tapestry needle

GAUGE

14 sts and 18 rows = 4" in St st with larger needles

19 sts and 18 rnds = 4" in Patt st with larger needles

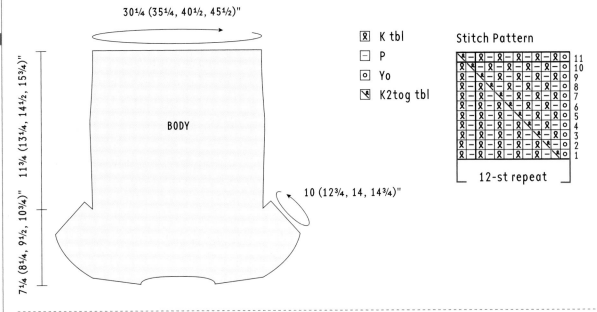

30¼ (35¼, 40½, 45½)"

11¾ (13¼, 14¼, 15¾)"

7¼ (8¼, 9½, 10¾)"

BODY

10 (12¾, 14, 14¾)"

⊻	K tbl
⊟	P
⊡	Yo
⊠	K2tog tbl

Stitch Pattern

12-st repeat

RND 9: *Yo, [k1 tbl, p1] 4 times, k2tog tbl, p1, k1 tbl; rep from * to end.

RND 10: *Yo, [p1, k1 tbl] 4 times, p1, k2tog tbl, k1 tbl; rep from * to end.

RND 11: *Yo, [k1 tbl, p1] 5 times, k2tog tbl; rep from * to end.

Rep rnds 1–11 for patt.

DIRECTIONS

Pattern note: Garment is knit in one piece from the top down. Begin with 16" circular needles and change to longer needles or dpns as necessary.

YOKE

With smaller 16" needles, CO 104 (124, 152, 172) sts. Pm and join. Work in k1, p1 rib for 5 rnds. Change to larger 16" needles. K38 (43, 50, 55) front sts, pm, k14 (19, 26, 31) left sleeve sts, pm, k38 (43, 50, 55) back sts, pm, k14 (19, 26, 31) right sleeve sts.

SIZES S AND L ONLY

Note: Each of the following rnds 1–10 adds 4 sts.

RND 1: *K1, work 12-st patt rep 3 (4) times, yo, k1 tbl, k1,

work 12-st patt rep 1 (2) times, yo, k1 tbl; rep from * once.

RND 2: *K1, work 12-st patt rep 3 (4) times, yo, p1, k1 tbl, k1, work 12-st patt rep 1 (2) times, yo, p1, k1 tbl; rep from * once.

RND 3: *K1, work 12-st patt rep 3 (4) times, yo, k1 tbl, p1, k1 tbl, k1, work 12-st patt rep 1 (2) times, yo, k1 tbl, p1, k1 tbl; rep from * once.

RND 4: *K1, work 12-st patt rep 3 (4) times, yo, [p1, k1 tbl] twice, k1, work 12-st patt rep 1 (2) times, yo, [p1, k1 tbl] twice; rep from * once.

RND 5: *K1, work 12-st patt rep 3 (4) times, yo, [k1 tbl, p1] twice, k1 tbl, k1, work 12-st patt rep 1 (2) times, yo, [k1 tbl, p1] twice, k1 tbl; rep from * once.

RND 6: *K1, work 12-st patt rep 3 (4) times, yo, [p1, k1 tbl] 3 times, k1, work 12-st patt rep 1 (2) times, yo, [p1, k1 tbl] 3 times; rep from * once.

RND 7: *K1, work 12-st patt rep 3 (4) times, yo, [k1 tbl, p1] 3 times, k1 tbl, k1, work 12-st patt rep 1 (2) times, yo, [k1 tbl, p1] 3 times, k1 tbl; rep from * once.

RND 8: *K1, work 12-st patt rep 3 (4) times, yo, [p1, k1 tbl] 4 times, k1, work 12-st patt rep 1 (2) times, yo, [p1, k1 tbl] 4 times; rep from * once.

RND 9: *K1, work 12-st patt rep 3 (4) times, yo, [k1 tbl, p1] 4 times, k1 tbl, k1, work 12-st patt rep 1 (2) times, yo, [k1 tbl, p1] 4 times; rep from * once.

RND 10: *K1, work 12-st patt rep 3 (4) times, yo, [p1, k1 tbl] 5 times, k1, work 12-st patt rep 1 (2) times, yo, [p1, k1 tbl] 5 times; rep from * once.

RND 11: *K1, work 12-st patt rep 3 (4) times, yo, [k1 tbl, p1] 5 times, kfb, k1, work 12-st patt rep 1 (2) times, yo, [k1 tbl, p1] 5 times, kfb; rep from * once—8 sts inc.

RNDS 12–22: Rep rnds 1–11, working the 12-st patt rep 4 (5) times and 2 (3) times between the inc sections.

SIZE S ONLY: *Rep rnds 1–10, bringing new 12-st reps into est patt—240 sts.*

SIZE L ONLY: *Rep rnds 1–21, bringing new 12-st reps into est patt—336 sts.*

SIZES M AND XL ONLY

RND 1: *K1, kfb, p1, k1 tbl, work 12-st patt rep 3 (4) times, yo, k2tog tbl, kfb, k1, kfb, p1, k1 tbl, work 12-st patt rep 1 (2) times, yo, k2tog tbl, kfb; rep from * once.

RND 2: *K1, p1, k1 tbl, p1, k1 tbl, work 12-st patt rep 3 (4) times, yo, p1, k2tog tbl, k1 tbl, k1, p1, k1 tbl, p1, k1 tbl, work 12-st patt rep 1 (2) times, yo, p1, k2tog tbl, k1 tbl; rep from * once.

RND 3: *K1, kfb, k1 tbl, p1, k1 tbl, work 12-st patt rep 3 (4) times, yo, k1 tbl, p1, k1 tbl, kfb, k1, kfb, k1 tbl, p1, k1 tbl, work 12-st patt rep 1 (2) times, yo, k1 tbl, p1, k1 tbl, kfb; rep from * once.

RND 4: *K1, k1 tbl, [p1, k1 tbl] twice, work 12-st patt rep 3 (4) times, yo, p1, k1 tbl, p1, k2tog tbl, k1 tbl, k1, k1 tbl, [p1, k1 tbl] twice, work 12-st patt rep 1 (2) times, yo, p1, k1 tbl, p1, k2tog tbl, k1 tbl; rep from * once.

RND 5: *K1, kfb, [p1, k1 tbl] twice, work 12-st patt rep 3 (4) times, yo, [k1 tbl, p1] twice, k1 tbl, kfb, k1, kfb, [p1, k1 tbl] twice, work 12-st patt rep 1 (2) times, yo, [k1 tbl, p1] twice, k1 tbl, kfb; rep from * once.

RND 6: *K1, [p1, k1 tbl] 3 times, work 12-st patt rep 3 (4) times, yo, [p1, k1 tbl] twice, p1, k2tog tbl, k1 tbl, k1, [p1, k1 tbl] 3 times, work 12-st patt rep 1 (2) times, yo, [p1,

k1 tbl] twice, p1, k2tog tbl, k1 tbl; rep from * once.

RND 7: *K1, kfb, k1 tbl, [p1, k1 tbl] twice, work 12-st patt rep 3 (4) times, yo, [k1 tbl, p1] 3 times, k1 tbl, kfb, k1, kfb, k1 tbl, [p1, k1 tbl] twice, work 12-st patt rep 1 (2) times, yo, [k1 tbl, p1] 3 times, k1 tbl, kfb; rep from * once.

RND 8: *K1, k1 tbl, p1, k2tog tbl, k1 tbl, p1, k1 tbl, work 12-st patt rep 3 (4) times, yo, p1, [k1 tbl, p1] 3 times, k2tog tbl, k1 tbl, k1, k1 tbl, p1, k2tog tbl, k1 tbl, p1, k1 tbl, work 12-st patt rep 1 (2) times, yo, p1, [k1 tbl, p1] 3 times, k2tog tbl, k1 tbl; rep from * once.

RND 9: *K1, kfb, p1, k2tog tbl, p1, k1 tbl, work 12-st patt rep 3 (4) times, yo, [k1 tbl, p1] 4 times, k1 tbl, kfb, k1, kfb, p1, k2tog tbl, p1, k1 tbl, work 12-st patt rep 1 (2) times, yo, [k1 tbl, p1] 4 times, k1 tbl, kfb; rep from * once.

RND 10: *K1, p1, k1 tbl, p1, k2tog tbl, k1 tbl, work 12-st patt rep 3 (4) times, yo, p1, [k1 tbl, p1] 4 times, k2tog tbl, k1 tbl, k1, p1, k1 tbl, p1, k2tog tbl, k1 tbl, work 12-st patt rep 1 (2) times, yo, p1, [k1 tbl, p1] 4 times, k2tog tbl, k1 tbl; rep from * once.

RND 11: *K1, kfb, k1 tbl, p1, k2tog tbl, work 12-st patt rep 3 (4) times, yo, [k1 tbl, p1] 5 times, k1 tbl, kfb, k1, kfb, k1 tbl, p1, k2tog tbl, work 12-st patt rep 1 (2) times, yo, [k1 tbl, p1] 5 times, k1 tbl, kfb; rep from * once.

RND 12: *K1, k1 tbl, [p1, k1 tbl] twice, work 12-st patt rep 4 (5) times, yo, [k1 tbl] twice, k1, k1 tbl, [p1, k1 tbl] twice, work 12-st patt rep 2 (3) times, yo, [k1 tbl] twice; rep from * once.

RND 13: *K1, kfb, k1 tbl, [p1, k2tog tbl] twice, work 12-st patt rep 3 (4) times, yo, p1, k1 tbl, kfb, k1, kfb, k1 tbl, [p1, k2tog tbl] twice, work 12-st patt rep 2 (3) times, yo, p1, k1 tbl, kfb; rep from * once.

RND 14: *K1, [p1, k1 tbl] 3 times, work 12-st patt rep 3 (4) times, yo, k1 tbl, p1, k2tog tbl, k1 tbl, k1, [p1, k1 tbl] 3 times, work 12-st patt rep 2 (3) times, yo, k1 tbl, p1, k2tog tbl, k1 tbl; rep from * once.

RND 15: *K1, kfb, k1 tbl, [p1, k1 tbl] twice, work 12-st patt rep 3 (4) times, yo, [p1, k1 tbl] twice, kfb, k1, kfb, k1 tbl, [p1, k1 tbl] twice, work 12-st patt rep 2 (3) times, yo, [p1, k1 tbl] twice, kfb; rep from * once.

RND 16: *K1, k1 tbl, [p1, k1 tbl] 3 times, work 12-st patt rep 4 (5) times, yo, [k1 tbl, p1] twice, k2tog tbl, k1 tbl, k1, k1 tbl, [p1, k1 tbl] 3 times, work 12-st patt rep 2 (3) times, yo, [k1 tbl, p1] twice, k2tog tbl, k1 tbl; rep from * once.

RND 17: *K1, kfb, [p1, k1 tbl] 3 times, work 12-st patt rep 4 (5) times, yo, [p1, k1 tbl] 3 times, kfb, k1, kfb, [p1, k1 tbl] 3 times, work 12-st patt rep 2 (3) times, yo, [p1, k1 tbl] 3 times, kfb; rep from * once.

RND 18: *K1, k1 tbl, p1, k2tog tbl, [p1, k1 tbl] twice, work 12-st patt rep 4 (5) times, yo, [k1 tbl, p1] 3 times, k2tog tbl, k1 tbl, k1, k1 tbl, p1, k2tog tbl, [p1, k1 tbl] twice, work 12-st patt rep 2 (3) times, yo, [k1 tbl, p1] 3 times, k2tog tbl, k1 tbl; rep from * once.

RND 19: *K1, k1 tbl, p1, k2tog tbl, k1 tbl, p1, k1 tbl, work 12-st patt rep 4 (5) times, yo, [p1, k1 tbl] 4 times, kfb, k1, k1 tbl, p1, k2tog tbl, k1 tbl, p1, k1 tbl, work 12-st patt rep 2 (3) times, yo, [p1, k1 tbl] 4 times, kfb; rep from * once.

RND 20: *K1, k1 tbl, p1, k2tog tbl, p1, k1 tbl, work 12-st patt rep 4 (5) times, yo, [k1 tbl, p1] 4 times, k2tog tbl, k1 tbl, k1, k1 tbl, p1, k2tog tbl, p1, k1 tbl, work 12-st patt rep 2 (3) times, yo, [k1 tbl, p1] 4 times, k2tog tbl, k1 tbl; rep from * once.

RND 21: *K1, k1 tbl, p1, k2tog tbl, k1 tbl, work 12-st patt rep 4 (5) times, yo, [p1, k1 tbl] 5 times, kfb, k1, k1 tbl, p1, k2tog tbl, k1 tbl, work 12-st patt rep 2 (3) times, yo, [p1, k1 tbl] 5 times, kfb; rep from * once.

RND 22: *K1, k1 tbl, p1, k2tog tbl, work 12-st patt rep 4 (5) times, yo, [k1 tbl, p1] 6 times, kfb, k1, k1 tbl, p1, k2tog tbl, work 12-st patt rep 2 (3) times, yo, [k1 tbl, p1] 6 times, kfb; rep from * once.

SIZE M ONLY: *Rep rnds 1–14, bringing new 12-st reps into est patt—288 sts.*

SIZE XL ONLY: *Rep rnds 1–22, then rows 1–4 once more, bringing new 12-st reps into est patt—384 sts.*

ALL SIZES: Place each set of 48 (60, 72, 84) sleeve sts onto stitch holders. Place rem 144 (168, 192, 216) sts onto needle, slipping first 1 (7, 1, 6) sts to RH needle and pm for beg of rnd.

BODY

Join yarn and complete 11-row patt as est beg with rnd 11 (5, 11, 5). Work until 7 (8, 9, 10) reps of Pattern st are complete, counting from beg of yoke. Change to smaller needles. Work 15 rows in p1, k1 tbl rib. BO in rib using larger needles.

SLEEVES

Place sts from holder onto dpns, slipping first 1 (7, 1, 6) sts to last needle and pm for beg of rnd.

SIZE S ONLY: *Work rnd 11 of Pattern st.*

SIZE M ONLY: *Work rnds 5–11 of Pattern st.*

SIZE L ONLY: *Work rnd 11 of Pattern st, then rnds 1–6 omitting YOs in last rnd—66 sts.*

SIZE XL ONLY: *Work rnds 5–11 of Pattern st omitting YOs in last rnd and end 2 sts from end of last rnd. K3tog tbl, *[p1, k1] 4 times, p1, k2tog tbl; rep from * 5 times more, [p1, k1] 4 times, p1—70 sts.*

ALL SIZES: Change to smaller needles. Work 6 rnds in rib as est. BO in rib using larger needles.

ABOUT NICOLE I'm a book designer living in New York City and have had a passion for fiber arts since high school. I learned the basics of knitting from my grandmother and taught myself multiple techniques, until I became obsessed with knitting sweaters—nothing else quite does it for me like finishing a handmade sweater. I've found many patterns unreliable, so I often create my own. I knit my boyfriend (now husband) a sweater every year, so I consider the boyfriend knitting curse broken. Check out pictures of my knits on my website, www .nicolelaroche.com.

COLORFUL CABLE HAT

SIZE

Finished circumference: 18¼"

MATERIALS

KnitPicks *Andean Silk* (55% superfine alpaca, 23% silk, 22% merino wool; 50g/96 yd)

MC: 1 skein Lettuce

CC: 1 skein Sangria

US 5 (3.75mm) double-pointed needles (set of 5)

Cable needle

Stitch marker

GAUGE

28 sts and 24 rows = 4" in chart patt

fter learning how to knit interlocked cables, but before the novelty of the technique wore off, I knew that I wanted to expand my options. With cables on the brain, I actually dreamed about knitting a hat that combined colorwork and cables. When I woke up, I set to work. While I knit, I found that the pairing of these two techniques was so intuitive that I was shocked to have never encountered it in patterns before. If you're a newbie like me to stranding for vertical stripes, take this advice: Keep a consistent yarn tension across the back by spreading your worked stitches evenly before beginning a new color. I'm guilty of skipping gauge swatches, but you may find it helpful to do a test run of this design.

SPECIAL ABBREVIATIONS

C4B: Sl 2 sts onto cn and hold in back, k2 MC, k2 MC from cn.

C4F: Sl 2 sts onto cn and hold in front, k2 MC, k2 MC from cn.

T2B: Sl 1 st onto cn and hold in back, k1 MC, p1 CC from cn.

T2F: Sl 1 st onto cn and hold in front, p1 CC, k1 MC from cn.

T3B: Sl 1 st onto cn and hold in back, k2 MC, p1 CC from cn.

T3F: Sl 2 sts onto cn and hold in front, p1 CC, k2 MC from cn.

STITCH PATTERN

CABLE PATTERN (MULTIPLE OF 16 STS)

RNDS 1 AND 11: *K2, p4, k2, p2, k4, p2; rep from * around.

RND 2: *T3F, p2, T3B, p2, C4F, p2; rep from * around.

Cable Chart

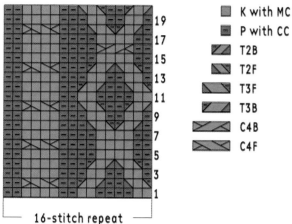

Legend:
- ▢ K with MC
- ▬ P with CC
- ⬚ T2B
- ⬚ T2F
- ⬚ T3F
- ⬚ T3B
- ⬚ C4B
- ⬚ C4F

Chart rows labeled: 1, 3, 5, 7, 9, 11, 13, 15, 17, 19

16-stitch repeat

RNDS 3, 9, 13 AND 19: *P1, k2, p2, k2, p3, k4, p2; rep from * around.

RND 4: *P1, T3F, T3B, p3, k4, p2; rep from * around.

RNDS 5, 7, 15 AND 17: *P2, k4, p4, k4, p2; rep from * around.

RND 6: *P2, C4B, p4, C4F, p2; rep from * around.

RND 8: *P1, T3B, T3F, p3, k4, p2; rep from * around.

RND 10: *T3B, p2, T3F, p2, C4F, p2; rep from * around.

RND 12: *T3F, p2, T3B, p2, k4, p2; rep from * around.

RND 14: *P1, T3F, T3B, p3, C4F, p2; rep from * around.

RND 16: *P2, C4B, p4, k4, p2; rep from * around.

RND 18: *P1, T3B, T3F, p3, C4F, p2; rep from * around.

RND 20: *T3B, p2, T3F, p2, k4, p2; rep from * around.

Rep rnds 1–20 for patt.

DIRECTIONS

Pattern notes: All k sts are worked in MC and p sts in CC throughout. Maintain a loose tension when stranding unused color in back of work, keeping in mind that cables naturally draw fabric in.

With MC, tightly CO 128 sts. Distribute evenly over 4 dpns, pm and join.

RND 1: With CC, k.

RNDS 2–5: *K2 MC, p4 CC, k2 MC, p2 CC, k4 MC, p2 CC; rep from * around.

Work 20 rnds of Cable Chart twice.

Remove marker, slip last st of last rnd onto LH needle. Pm for new end of rnd.

CROWN SHAPING

RND 1: *K2tog, k1, p4, k1, ssk, p1, ssk, k2tog, p1; rep from * around—96 sts.

RND 2: *K2, p4, k2, p1, T2F, p1; rep from * to end. Slip last 2 sts of rnd onto LH needle. Pm for new end of rnd.

RND 3: *K3tog, k1, p4, k1, sssk; rep from * around—64 sts. Slip last 2 sts of rnd onto LH needle. Pm for new end of rnd.

RND 4: *C4F, p4; rep from * around.

RND 5: *K2tog, ssk, p2tog, p2tog; rep from * around—32 sts. Slip last st of rnd onto LH needle and pm for new end of rnd.

RND 6: *T2B, T2F; rep from * to end. Slip last st of rnd onto LH needle and pm for new end of rnd.

RND 7: *K2tog, p2tog; rep from * around—16 sts.

FINISHING

Break yarn, leaving a 6" tail. Thread tail through rem sts, pull tightly to close top of hat and secure.

ABOUT SALLY In a Quaker meeting house, at age seven, I first wielded a pair of dowel rods I had run through a pencil sharpener and attacked a snarled mass of variegated acrylic yarn with vigor. I never finished my initial rectangle swatch, but that Christmas my sister did receive a lovingly crafted nose warmer. It wasn't until high school that I felt the desire to make a sweater. After that, I was hooked—when I wasn't knitting, I was sketching new projects in notebook margins, talking in exhaustive detail about the properties of yarns, or finding other ways to make a normally benign activity as obnoxious as possible. I'm currently a student at the University of Kentucky, studying anthropology.

Ysolda teague

GRETEL TAM

lipping through one of my many stitch dictionaries always gives me inspiration for a design. I found this basic lattice cable pattern while perusing the pages, and I liked it right away. But then I wondered what would happen if I used decreases that mimicked the cables to shape the hat, and I got really excited. That's when I started designing this tam. It took a lot of trial and error to get to the point where I had both the perfect flat circle and the shaping incorporated into the cables, but I think the effort was worth it. It's one of my fave designs, not just because the cables are superfun to knit, but because it's so easy to wear—Gretel really does seem to look good on everyone.

SPECIAL ABBREVIATIONS

C4B: Slip 2 sts onto cn and hold in back, k2, k2 from cn.

C4F: Slip 2 sts onto cn and hold in front, k2, k2 from cn.

T2B: Slip 1 st onto cn and hold in back, k1, p1 from cn.

T3B: Slip 1 st onto cn and hold in back, k2, p1 from cn.

T3F: Slip 2 sts onto cn and hold in front, p1, k2 from cn.

DIRECTIONS

Using tubular CO (page 95) and smaller circular needle, CO 96 sts. Do not join. Work the first 2 rows in k1, p1 rib, beg with p1. Convert to k2, p2 rib on next row as foll: P1, *k1, T2B, p1; rep from * to last 3 sts, k1, T2B. Pm and join.

RNDS 1-8: P1, *k2, p2; rep from * to last 3 sts, k2, p1.

RND 9: *P1, k2, m1, p1; rep from * to end—120 sts.

RND 10: *P1, k2, m1, k1, p1; rep from * to end—144 sts.

SIZE
Finished circumference: 18" (with negative ease, a fit measurement of 20–22")

MATERIALS
Classic Elite *Lush* (50% angora, 50% wool; 50g/123 yd), 2 skeins #4458 Lipstick

US 5 (3.75mm) 16" circular needle

US 7 (4.5mm) 16" circular needle, or size needed to obtain gauge

US 7 (4.5mm) double-pointed needles (set of 5)

Split-ring stitch marker or safety pin

Cable needle

Tapestry needle

GAUGE
16 sts and 24 rows = 4" in St st with larger needles

Change to larger circular needle.

RNDS 11-13: *P1, k4, p1; rep from * to end.

RND 14: *P1, C4B, p1; rep from * to end.

RND 15: *P1, k4, p1; rep from * to last 6 sts, p1, k2. Pm for new beg of rnd.

RND 16: *T3F, T3B; rep from * to end.

RND 17: *P1, k4, p1; rep from * to end.

RND 18: *Pfb, k4, pfb; rep from * to end—192 sts.

RND 19: *P2, k4, p2; rep from * to end.

RND 20: *P2, C4F, p2; rep from * to end.

RNDS 21-23: *P2, k4, p2; rep from * to end.

RND 24: *P2, C4F, p2; rep from * to end.

RND 25: *P2, k4, p2; rep from * to end. Remove marker and p2, k2. Pm for new beg of rnd.

RND 26: *T3F, p2, T3B; rep from * to end.

RND 27: *P1, k2, p2, k2, p1; rep from * to end.

RND 28: *P1, T3F, T3B, p1; rep from * to end.

RND 29: *P2, k4, p2; rep from * to end.

RND 30: *P2, C4B, p2; rep from * to end.

RNDS 31-33: *P2, k4, p2; rep from * to end.

RND 34: *P2, C4B, p2; rep from * to end.

RND 35: *P2, k4, p2; rep from * to last 8 sts, p2, k2. Pm for new beg of rnd.

CROWN SHAPING

RND 36: *T3F, p2, T3B; rep from * to end.

RND 37: *P1, k2, p1; rep from * to end.

RND 38: *P1, k1, ssk, k2tog, k1, p1; rep from * to end—144 sts.

RND 39: *P1, k4, p1; rep from * to end.

RND 40: *P1, C4F, p2, C4B, p1; rep from * to end.

RNDS 41-42: *P1, k4, p1; rep from * to end.

Change to dpns, dividing sts evenly over 3 needles.

RND 43: *P1, k1, ssk, k1, p2, k1, k2tog, k1, p1; rep from * to end—120 sts.

RND 44: *P1, k1, ssk, p2, k2tog, k1, p1; rep from * to end—96 sts.

RND 45: *P1, k2, p2, k2, p1; rep from * to end.

RND 46: *P1, k1, ssk, k2tog, k1, p1; rep from * to end—72 sts.

RND 47: *P1, k4, p1; rep from * to end.

RND 48: *P1, C4F, p2, C4B, p1; rep from * to end.

RNDS 49-50: *P1, k4, p1; rep from * to end.

RND 51: *P1, k1, ssk, k1, p2, k1, k2tog, k1, p1; rep from * to end—60 sts.

RND 52: *P1, k1, ssk, p2, k2tog, k1, p1; rep from * to end—48 sts.

RND 53: *P1, k2, p2, k2, p1; rep from * to end.

RND 54: *P1, k1, ssk, k2tog, k1, p1; rep from * to end—36 sts.

RND 55: *P1, k4, p1; rep from * to end.

RND 56: *P1, k1, ssk, k1, p2, k1, k2tog, k1, p1; rep from * to end—30 sts.

RND 57: *P1, k1, ssk, p2, k2tog, k1, p1; rep from * to end—24 sts.

RND 58: *P1, k1, ssk, k2tog, k1, p1; rep from * to end—18 sts.

FINISHING

Break yarn, leaving a 6" tail. Thread tail through rem sts, pull tight and weave in end. Sew ends of tubular cast-on together. For a crisper shape, block over an appropriately sized disc-shaped object such as a plate.

ABOUT YSOLDA Eternally creative, I was just getting into knitting when the first *Stitch 'n Bitch* book came out, and from it I learned the basics. Reading all of the designer bios was a huge inspiration, since it's always felt natural for me to make up my own designs. I was a student when I began designing knitting patterns, and now that I do it full-time, I can't imagine doing anything else. I sell original patterns on my website, www.ysolda.com, and I've completed two self-published books, *Whimsical Little Knits* 1 and 2, and am working on my third. I live by myself in Edinburgh, Scotland, which means I can leave knitting paraphernalia lying around everywhere without anyone complaining.

ANGeLA kreutzer

DOG-O-MATIC

One day I was hanging in the shade with my Chihuahua mix, Guppy, when I noticed he was shivering and needed to be wrapped up in the blanket we were sitting on. That's all I needed to get me going on the design for the Dog-O-Matic sweater to keep my pup cozy and cute. I started with the basic shape of a sock, then added leg holes and a neck hole. Obviously, when Guppy wore the sock it didn't fit all the curves and contours of his little bod, but the stretches and puckers served as a guide for where I'd decrease and increase stitches. Once I perfected the form-fitting structure in knit, I added the cables and a turtleneck, so Guppy would look oh-so-chic while strutting his stuff at the dog park. The sweater's shape is so straightforward that you can custom-fit it for any size dog just by plugging in some numbers.

SPECIAL ABBREVIATIONS

C6B: Sl 3 sts onto cn and hold in back, k3, k3 from cn.

C6F: Sl 3 sts onto cn and hold in front, k3, k3 from cn.

SIZE
Custom fit for any dog

MATERIALS
Cascade *Pastaza* (50% llama, 50% wool; 100g/132 yd), color 272, approx 100 yd per 7 pounds of doggy

US 8 (5mm) needles

US 6 (4mm) needles

Cable needle

Stitch markers

GAUGE
15 sts and 21 rows = 4" in St st

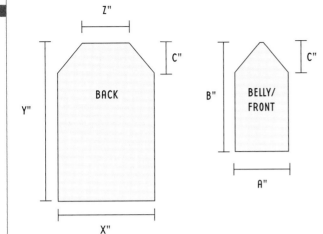

DIRECTIONS

TAKING MEASUREMENTS

Note: Round all measurements up to next whole number.

BACK

Armpit, across back, to other armpit = (X) inches
X = _____ inches wide

Length (from base of neck to tail)† = (Y) inches
Y = _____ inches long

   †or from base of neck to point desired

Neck measurement + 1 inch = (Z) inches
Z = _____ inches around

FRONT

Underside armpit to armpit = (A) inches
A = _____ inches wide

Bottom piece (from neck to belly) = (B) inches
B = _____ inches long

Length from base of neck to front of front legs = (C) inches
C = _____ inches long

Special note: X + A = total chest measurement

TOP OF SWEATER

Determine the number of sts to CO for the body by using measurement X and the stitch gauge (sts per inch = 3.75):

$(X \times 3.75)$ = _____ sts. Round to whole number divisible by 3 = _____ = number of CO sts for body.

With smaller needles, CO sts for body.

Work in k1, p1 rib for 1", ending after a WS row. Using st markers, divide sts evenly into 3 sections.

Change to larger needles.

ROW 1 (RS): K to 8 sts before marker, p2, k6, sm, p2, k to 2 sts before marker, p2, sm, k6, p2, k to end.

ROW 2: P to 8 sts before marker, k2, p6, sm, k2, p to 2 sts before marker, k2, sm, p6, k2, p to end.

ROWS 3 AND 4: Rep rows 1 and 2.

ROW 5: K to 8 sts before marker, p2, C6B, sm, p2, k to 2 sts before marker, p2, sm, C6F, p2, k to end.

ROW 6: P to 8 sts before marker, k2, p6, sm, k2, p to 2 sts before marker, k2, sm, p6, k2, p to end.

Rep rows 1–6 until body measures Y – C inches long, dec 1 st on last row if necessary to result in an even number.

SHOULDER SHAPING

Determine number of collar sts using measurement Z and sts-per-inch gauge:

$(Z \times 3.75)$ = _____ sts. Round up to an even number _____ = number of collar sts.

Determine the number of sts to be decreased:

(Number of sts on needle – number of collar sts) ÷ 2 = _____ rows of decreases. (2 sts dec—1 dec at the beginning of the row and 1 at the end—that's why you divide by 2.)

Determine the number of rows available for shaping using the row gauge:

$(C \times 5.25) =$ ____ rows for shoulder shaping.

Determine the rate at which to make the decreases (see "The Magic Formula," page 133).

For example, if you are going to do 5 rows of decreases, and you have 10 rows to do this, then you dec once for every 2 rows, or every other row.

Using RS and WS dec rows as foll to reach the desired number of collar sts:

RS DEC ROW: K1, ssk, k to last 3 sts, k2tog, k1.

WS DEC ROW: P1, p2tog, p to last 3 sts, p2tog tbl, p1.

If necessary, work even until back measures Y", increasing or decreasing on last row to a number divisible by 3.

TURTLENECK COLLAR

Change to smaller needles.

RS ROW: *K1, p2; rep from *.

Cont in rib as est for 4½" or desired length.

BO loosely in rib.

BELLY/FRONT

Determine number of sts to CO for front using measurement A and sts per inch:

$(A \times 3.75) =$ ____ sts. Round up to an even number ____ = number of CO sts for front.

Using smaller needles, CO sts for front.

Work in k1, p1 rib for 1". Change to larger needles.

Work in St st until piece meas B – C inches.

CHEST SHAPING

Determine number of decreases to be made on each side:

(Number of sts on needle – 2) ÷ 2 = ____ rows of decreases (1 st on each end) to be made.

Using the same number of dec rows that you used for the top of the sweater, determine the rate at which you dec (i.e., 5 dec, 10 rows = every other row):

Number of sts to dec (determined above) ÷ number of rows of dec = ____.

Using RS and WS dec rows as described above, dec 1 st each side at the required rate—2 sts rem. BO.

FINISHING

With *RS* of sweater top facing out, seam ribbed neckband section only. When you fold the turtleneck down, the WS shows and the seaming on the RS is hidden.

Seam the sweater top to the belly at the dec sections only.

Leaving a gap large enough for the front legs to fit through (best determined by trying it on), sew rem portion of sweater top to belly. Weave in ends.

ABOUT ANGELA By day I am the creator of Duet Yarns at A Swell Yarn Shop (www.aswellyarnshop .com) and by night I am a crusader against puppy mills and animal cruelty. I am also a crocheter, seamstress, soap maker, baker, gardener, farmer, and anything else that strikes my fancy. When I'm not crafting or crusading, you'll find me with my hubby traveling, playing Texas Hold 'Em, barbequing, camping, boating, clam digging, fishing, and whatever else we can come up with. I figure, life is short—why not do it all?

KAREN PAYZANT

LOVE ME OR LEAF ME BAG

What is more fresh or fun than a leaf motif? Anything I can create using a leaf design always tops my list; I just love their classic elegance. You can really put your own personal spin on this bag—add a stem or flower to the leaf cable or work it up in a luscious burnt orange or burgundy for a punchy autumnal feel. This bag is one of my favorite designs, mostly because of its great texture. Working with two strands of yarn throughout the body of this pattern can be a challenge, but it pays off—the durability and feel of your finished project will be wonderful.

SPECIAL ABBREVIATIONS

C5B: Slip 3 sts onto cn and hold in back, k2, k3 from cn.

C4B: Slip 2 sts onto cn and hold in back, k2, k2 from cn.

C4F: Slip 2 sts onto cn and hold in front, k2, k2 from cn.

SPECIAL STITCHES
LARGE LEAF PATTERN (OVER 9 STS)

ROW 1 (RS): P4, k1, p4.

ROW 2: K4, p1, k4.

ROW 3: P3, k3, p3.

ROW 4: K3, p3, k3.

ROW 5: P2, k5, p2.

ROWS 6 AND 8: K2, p5, k2.

ROW 7: P2, C5B, p2.

SIZE

Finished width: 17"

Finished height: 12", excluding handles

MATERIALS

Cascade Yarns *Cascade 220* (100% wool; 100g/220 yd), 3 skeins #7814

US 6 (4mm) needles

US 10½ (6.5mm) needles

Cable needle

Tapestry needle

1 pair 11½" bamboo handles

Optional: ⅔ yd each lining fabric and iron-on interfacing

GAUGE

16 sts and 20 rows = 4" in St st with larger needles and 2 strands of yarn held tog

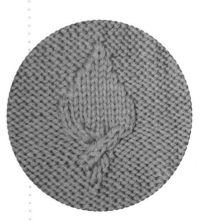

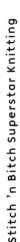

Large Leaf Chart

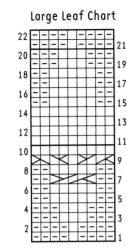

Small Leaf Chart

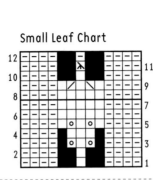

☐ K

⊟ P

⊙ Yo

☑ K2tog

◻ Ssk

◼ Sk2p

■ No stitch

▱ C4B

▱ C4F

▱ C5B

ROW 9: C4B, k1, C4F.

ROWS 10, 12 AND 14: Purl.

ROWS 11 AND 13: Knit.

ROWS 15 AND 17: Rep row 5.

ROWS 16 AND 18: Rep row 6.

ROW 19: Rep row 3.

ROW 20: Rep row 4.

ROW 21: Rep row 1.

ROW 22: Rep row 2.

SMALL LEAF PATTERN (OVER 9 STS)

ROW 1 (RS): P4, k1, p4.

ROW 2: K4, p1, k4.

ROW 3: P4, yo, k1, yo, p4.

ROW 4: K3, p3, k4.

ROW 5: P4, k1, (yo, k1) twice, p4.

ROWS 6 AND 8: K4, p5, k4.

ROW 7: P4, k5, p4.

ROW 9: P4, ssk, k1, k2tog, p4.

ROW 10: K4, p3, k4.

ROW 11: P4, sk2p, p4.

ROW 12: Knit.

DIRECTIONS

Pattern note: Body of tote bag is worked with a double strand of yarn.

FRONT

With larger needles and 2 strands of yarn held tog, CO 65 sts. Work 2 rows rev St st, begin with a RS (p) row.

ROW 1 (EST PATT): P1, *work row 1 of Large Leaf patt across next 9 sts, p9; rep from * twice, work row 1 of Large Leaf patt across next 9 sts, p1.

ROW 2: K1, *work row 2 of Large Leaf patt across next 9 sts, k9; rep from * twice, work row 2 of Large Leaf patt across next 9 sts, k1.

ROWS 3-22: Cont in est patt.

ROW 23: P10, *work row 1 of Large Leaf patt across next 9 sts, p9; rep from * twice, p1.

ROWS 24-44: Cont in est patt. When Large Leaf patt is complete, work even in rev St st for 3 rows, end with a RS row.

Change to smaller needles and break off 2nd strand of yarn, leaving a 6" tail for weaving in. Use single strand of yarn for remainder of front. Work 3 rows St st, beg with a WS (p) row.

ROW 1 (EST PATT): K4, *work row 1 of Small Leaf patt across next 9 sts, k3; rep from * to last st, k1.

ROW 2: P4, *work row 2 of Small Leaf patt across next 9 sts, p3; rep from * to last st, p1.

ROWS 3–12: Cont in est patt.

When Small Leaf patt is complete, work 4 rows even in St st.

DIVIDING ROW FOR HANDLE TABS (RS): K19, BO next 3 sts, k21, BO next 3 sts, k19.

Work first 19 sts in St st for 7 rows, beg with a p row. BO.

With WS facing, attach yarn to next 21 sts on needle and work the same as first 19 sts.

Rep for last 19 sts on needle.

BACK

With RS facing, using larger needles and 2 strands of yarn, PU and k 65 sts along bottom edge of front.

K 1 WS row.

Work same as for front.

FINISHING

Fold bag in half and sew side seams up to 6" from tab BO.

Fold tabs over bamboo handles and sew securely in place.

OPTIONAL: Line bag with coordinating cotton fabric reinforced with iron-on interfacing. Don't forget to add all sizes of pockets for your phone or gadgets!

ABOUT KAREN Born and bred in Nebraska, I began knitting at a very early age. After raising three children, and becoming a grandmother, I have found myself at a place where I have time again to create—and give in to my lifelong passion for yarn, texture, and design. Please visit my blog at through-karens-eyes.blogspot.com, where I write about my crafts, home, and lovely family. I do hope that you'll stop by and say hello.

LITTLE RED RIDING HOODIE

SIZE
S (M, L, XL)

Finished chest: 33 (37½, 41½, 46)"

Finished length: 22½ (22¾, 25¼, 26¾)"

MATERIALS
Rowan *Cashsoft DK* (57% extrafine merino wool, 33% microfiber, 10% cashmere; 50g/142 yd), 19 (21, 24, 27) skeins #512 Poppy

US 5 (3.75mm) needles

Cable needle

Stitch markers

Tapestry needle

19½ (20, 20½, 21)" medium-weight separating zipper

Sewing needle and matching thread

GAUGE
CO 37 sts. Row 1 (WS): K2, p12, k2, p9, k2, p8, k2. Row 2: P2, work 8-st cable, p2, work little leaf lace, p2, work 12-st plait cable, p2. Work in patt as est in row 2 for 4". Swatch should meas 4" wide.

his saucy little sweater combines elegant cable and lace patterns, while the hood adds a dash of attitude. Really versatile, it can be worn with a short skirt and tall boots on Saturday night or with comfy jeans for Sunday brunch. This was my first pattern design—and a learning experience, for sure. I began with a picture in my head of my ideal sweater and then sketched it out. I swatched a bunch before I found the perfect yarn. Completing the design was a very hands-on process—I just had to knit my way through it. When I reached the shoulders, I realized I needed a human form to get them right. A dress form was no help because it doesn't have arms! So I used my friend Linda and pinned the sweater right onto her T-shirt. I've worked out the kinks, so now you can whip up a sweater that will give you a great fit, too.

SPECIAL ABBREVIATIONS
C8B: Sl 4 sts onto cn and hold in back, k4, k4 from cn.

C8F: Sl 4 sts onto cn and hold in front, k4, k4 from cn.

STITCH PATTERNS
12-ST PLAIT CABLE
ROW 1 (RS): Knit.

ROW 2 AND ALL WS ROWS: Purl.

ROW 3: C8B, k4.

ROW 5: Knit.

ROW 7: K4, C8F.

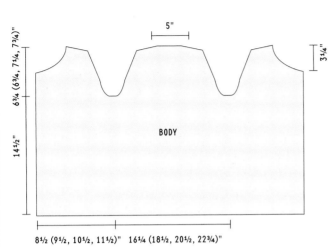

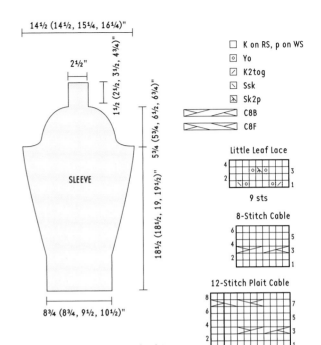

ROW 8: Purl.

Rep rows 1–8 for patt.

LITTLE LEAF LACE (OVER 9 STS)

ROW 1 (RS): K1, k2tog, yo, k3, yo, ssk, k1.

ROW 2: Purl.

ROW 3: K3, yo, sk2p, yo, k3.

Rep rows 1–4 for patt.

8-ST CABLE

ROWS 1 AND 5 (RS): Knit.

ROWS 2 AND 4: Purl.

ROW 3: C8B.

ROW 6: Purl.

Rep rows 1–6 for patt.

DIRECTIONS

Note: Be sure to swatch carefully with whatever yarn you choose. Consistent with traditional Aran techniques, this piece was knit with a smaller needle size to make the stitch patterns pop.

Pattern notes: Body is worked in one piece to underarm then divided for fronts and back. Sleeves are worked flat. Hood is picked up and worked after pieces are sewn together.

BACK

Using cable CO method (page 89), CO 298 (338, 374, 414) sts.

SET-UP ROW (WS)

SIZES S AND XL ONLY: P3, k2, p12, [k2, p2, k2, p9, k2, p2, k2, p8] 2 (-, -, 3) times, k1, pm, k1, [p2, k2] 2 times, p2, k2, [p8, k2, p2, k2, p9, k2, p2, k2] 2 (-, -, 3) times, p12, [k2, p2, k2, p9, k2, p2, k2, p8] 2 (-, -, 3) times, [k2, p2] 2 times, k1, pm, k1, [p8, k2, p2, k2, p9, k2, p2, k2] 2 (-, -, 3) times, p12, k2, p3.

SIZE M ONLY: P3, k2, p12, [k2, p2, k2, p9, k2, p2, k2, p8] 2 times, k2, [p2, k2] 2 times, p1, pm, p1, [k2, p2] 4 times, k2, [p8, k2, p2, k2, p9, k2, p2, k2] 2 times, p12, [k2, p2, k2, p9, k2, p2, k2, p8] 2 times, k2, [p2, k2] 4 times, p1, pm, p1, [k2, p2] 2 times, k2, [p8, k2, p2, k2, p9, k2, p2, k2] 2 times, p12, k2, p3.

SIZE L ONLY: P3, k2, p12, [k2, p2, k2, p9, k2, p2, k2, p8] 2 times, k2, p2, k2, p9, k2, p2, k1, pm, k1, [p2, k2] 3 times, p9, k2, p2, k2, [p8, k2, p2, k2, p9, k2, p2, k2] 2 times, p12, [k2, p2, k2, p9, k2, p2, k2, p8] 2 times, k2, p2, k2, p9, [k2, p2] 3 times, k1, pm, k1, p2, k2, p9, k2, p2, k2, [p8, k2, p2, k2, p9, k2, p2, k2] 2 times, p12, k2, p3.

ALL SIZES: 146 (166, 184, 204) back sts and 76 (86, 95, 105) sts each front.

ROW 1

SIZES S AND XL ONLY: K3, p2, 12-st Plait Cable, *[p2, k2, p2, Little Leaf Lace, p2, k2, p2, 8-st Cable] 2 (-, -, 3) times, p2, [k2, p2] 2 times, [8-st Cable, p2, k2, p2, Little Leaf Lace, p2, k2, p2] 2 (-, -, 3) times, 12-st Plait Cable; rep from * once, p2, k3.

SIZE M ONLY: K3, p2, 12-st Plait Cable, *[p2, k2, p2, Little Leaf Lace, p2, k2, p2, 8-st Cable] 2 times, p2, [k2, p2] 7 times, [8-st Cable, p2, k2, p2, Little Leaf Lace, p2, k2, p2] 2 times, 12-st Plait Cable; rep from * twice, p2, k3.

SIZE L ONLY: K3, p2, 12-st Plait Cable, *[p2, k2, p2, Little Leaf Lace, p2, k2, p2, 8-st Cable] 2 times, p2, k2, p2, Little Leaf Lace, p2, [k2, p2] 4 times, Little Leaf Lace, p2, k2, p2, [8-st Cable, p2, k2, p2, Little Leaf Lace, p2, k2, p2] 2 times, 12-st Plait Cable; rep from * twice, p2, k3.

Cont in patt as est until piece meas 14½" from beg, end with a WS row.

DIVIDE FOR FRONTS AND BACK

Work in patt to 6 sts before marker, join new ball of yarn and BO 13 sts; work in patt to 7 sts before marker; join new ball of yarn and BO 13 sts, work in patt to end—132 (152, 170, 190) back sts, 70 (80, 89, 99) sts each front.

ARMHOLE AND NECK SHAPING

Note: Read all instructions before continuing. Armhole and neck shaping take place at the same time.

Cont in patt as est, BO 6 sts at each armhole edge 3 times—96 (116, 134, 154) back sts, 52 (62, 71, 81) sts each front.

DEC ROW (RS): On right front, work in patt to last 4 sts, k2tog, k2; on back, k2, ssk, work in patt to last 4 sts, k2tog, k2; on left front, k2, ssk, work in patt to end.

DEC ROW (WS): On left front, work in patt to last 4 sts, ssp, p2; on back, p2, p2tog, work in patt to last 4 sts, ssp, p2; on right front, p2, p2tog, work in patt to end.

Rep last 2 rows 5 times more—72 (92, 110, 130) back sts and 40 (50, 59, 69) sts each front.

Work even until armhole meas 3¼ (3½, 4, 4½)".

NECK DEC ROW (RS): On right front, k2, sssk, cont in patt as est to last 4 sts of left front, k3tog, k2.

Rep neck dec every RS row 12 times more—72 (92, 110, 130) back sts, 14 (24, 33, 43) sts each front.

Cont even in patt as est on fronts and back until armhole meas 6¾ (6¾, 7¼, 7¾)", end with a WS row.

BO 7 (12, 17, 22) sts at beg of each armhole edge over the next 2 rows.

BO 7 (12, 16, 21) sts at beg of each armhole edge over next 2 rows. BO rem 44 back neck sts.

SLEEVE

Using cable CO method, CO 78 (78, 86, 94) sts.

SET-UP ROW (WS): [P2, k2] 1 (1, 0, 1) time, p0 (0, 6, 6), k0 (0, 2, 2), p8, k2, p2, k2, p9, k2, p2, k2, p12, k2, p2, k2, p9, k2, p2, k2, p8, p0 (0, 2, 2), k0 (0, 6, 6), [k2, p2] 1 (1, 0, 1) time.

ROW 1: [K2, p2] 1 (1, 0, 1) time, k0 (0, 6, 6), p0 (0, 2, 2), 8-st Cable, p2, k2, p2, Little Leaf Lace, p2, k2, p2, 12-st Plait Cable, p2, k2, p2, Little Leaf Lace, p2, k2, p2, 8-st Cable, p0 (0, 2, 2), k0 (0, 6, 6), [p2, k2] 1 (1, 0, 1) time.

Cont in patt as est until sleeve meas 6" from beg, end with a WS row.

INC ROW (RS): K2, m1, work in patt to last 2 sts, m1, k2.

Rep inc row every 4th row 7 times more, then every other row 18 times, working new sts in k6, p2 rib—130 (130, 138, 146) sts.

Work even in patt until sleeve meas 18½ (18½, 19, 19½)" from beg.

SHAPE CAP

Cont in patt as est, BO 6 sts at beg of next 6 rows—94 (94, 102, 110) sts.

DEC ROW 1 (RS): K2, ssk, work in patt to last 4 sts, k2tog, k2.

DEC ROW 2 (WS): P2, p2tog, work in patt to last 4 sts, ssp, p2.

Rep last 2 rows 3 times more—78 (78, 86, 94) sts.

Cont in patt as est, rep dec row 1 every RS row 15 (15, 18, 20) times—48 (48, 50, 54) sts.

Rep dec rows 1 and 2 three times—36 (36, 38, 42) sts.

BO 7 (7, 8, 10) sts at beg of next 2 rows—22 sts.

NEXT ROW (RS): K3, p2, 12-st Plait Cable, p2, k3.

Cont in patt as est for 1½ (2½, 3½, 4¾)" for saddle.

BO in patt.

HOOD

Sew front and back shoulders to saddles, leaving center 44 sts for back neck. Set sleeves into armholes. Sew sleeve seams.

With RS facing, start and end at beg of neck shaping, PU and k38 right front neck sts, 22 saddle sts, 44 back neck sts, 22 saddle sts, and 38 left front neck sts—164 sts.

SET-UP ROW (WS): P3, k2, p12, k2, p2, k2, p9, k1, p1, k1, p4, pm, k1, p1, k1, p12, k1, p1, k1, pm, p4, k1, p1, k1, p9, [k2, p2] 4 times, k2, p9, k1, p1, k1, p4, pm, k1, p1, k1, p12, k1, p1, k1, pm, p4, k1, p1, k1, p9, k2, p2, k2, p12, k2, p3.

INC ROW (RS): K3, p2, k12, p2, k2, p2, k9, p1, m1, k1, m1, p1, m1, [k1, m1] 4 times, sm, p1, m1, k1, m1, p1, m1, k12, p1, m1, k1, m1, p1, m1, sm, [k1, m1] 4 times, p1, m1, k1, m1, p1, m1, k9, p2, [k2, p2] 4 times, k9, p1, m1, k1, m1, p1, m1, [k1, m1] 4 times, sm, p1, m1, k1, m1, p1, m1, k12, p1, m1, k1, m1, p1, m1, sm, [k1, m1] 4 times, p1, m1, k1, m1, p1, m1, k9, p2, k2, p2, k12, p2, k3—204 sts.

NEXT ROW: P3, k2, 12-st Plait Cable, k2, p2, k2, Little Leaf Lace, k2, p2, k2, 8-st Cable, sm, k2, p2, k2, 12-st Plait Cable, k2, p2, k2, sm, 8-st Cable, k2, p2, k2, Little Leaf Lace, [k2, p2] 4 times, k2, Little Leaf Lace, k2, p2, k2, 8-st Cable, sm, k2, p2, k2, 12-st Plait Cable, k2, p2, k2, sm, 8-st Cable, k2, p2, k2, Little Leaf Lace, k2, p2, k2, 12-st Plait Cable, k2, p3.

Cont in patt as est until hood meas 13½". Using 3-needle BO (page 103), fold hood in half and close top of hood.

FINISHING

Beg at lower front corner, work 4-st attached I-cord (page 110) along right front edge, hood and left front edge. Using sewing needle and matching thread, sew in zipper.

ABOUT KATE

My mom may have taught me to knit when I was eight, but I did not become obsessed with wool until later in life. Now, when I'm not doing psychiatric evaluations in the local emergency room, hanging out with my kids, or working the school book fair, I'm hand-painting yarn and spinning fiber for my business, Dragonfly Fibers. A whole-hearted fiber fanatic, I spin, wash, and process raw fleeces, and, of course, knit. I can be found at fiber festivals up and down the East Coast and on DragonflyFibers.com.

LATTICE

Keyholes and wee little buttons are the two details that inspired the Lattice top. To these, I've added a cable pattern that is as fun to wear as it is to stitch—you can even work these cables without a cable needle, if you're feeling saucy. To put a flirty spin on the cabled sweater, I chose a slim silhouette, scoop neck, cap sleeve, and high ribbed body. I then set out to find the perfect stitch to match the looping keyhole detail. Many stitch dictionaries and swatches later, I met and fell in love with the interlocking lattice pattern. I knit gauge swatches, crunched numbers, and used my trusty TI-36 scientific calculator to graph the shaping of the sleeve caps, neck, and keyhole. I think all the effort paid off—the Lattice showcases your skills and is effortlessly adorable.

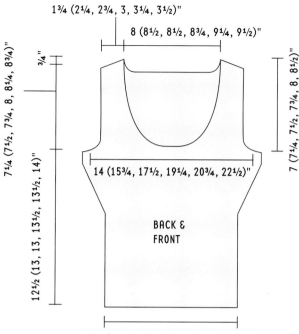

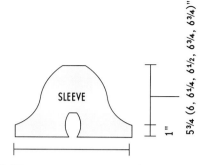

SPECIAL ABBREVIATIONS

C2F: Sl 1 st onto cn and hold in front, k1, k1 from cn.

C2B: Sl 1 st onto cn and hold in back, k1, k1 from cn.

M1P: Insert LH needle from back to front into the horizontal strand between last st and next st, p this strand through front loop.

T2F: Sl 1 st onto cn and hold in front, p1, k1 from cn.

T2B: Sl 1 st onto cn and hold in back, k1, p1 from cn.

SPECIAL STITCH

LATTICE CABLE PATTERN (MULTIPLE OF 6 STS)

ROW 1 (WS): *P1, k4, p1; rep from * to end.

ROW 2: *T2F, p2, T2B; rep from * to end.

ROW 3 AND ALL WS ROWS: Knit the k sts and purl the p sts.

ROW 4: *P1, T2F, T2B, p1; rep from * to end.

ROWS 6 AND 12: *P2, C2B, p2; rep from * to end.

ROW 8: *P1, T2B, T2F, p1; rep from * to end.

ROW 10: *P1, T2F, T2B, p1; rep from * to end.

ROW 14: *P1, T2B, T2F, p1; rep from * to end.

ROW 16: *T2B, p2, T2F; rep from * to end.

ROW 18: K1, p2, *p2, C2F, p2; rep from * to last 3 sts, p2, k1.

ROW 20: K1, p2, *p1, T2B, T2F, p1; rep from * to last 3 sts, p2, k1.

ROW 22: K1, p2, *p1, T2F, T2B, p1; rep from * to last 3 sts, p2, k1.

ROW 24: K1, p2, *p2, C2F, p2; rep from * to last 3 sts, p2, k1.

Rep rows 1–24 for patt.

DIRECTIONS

Pattern Notes: Garment is designed to have about ½"–2½" negative ease.

Lattice Cable Pattern

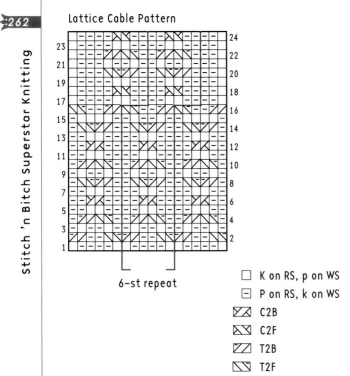

6-st repeat

☐ K on RS, p on WS
⊟ P on RS, k on WS
▨ C2B
▧ C2F
▤ T2B
▧ T2F

BACK

With smaller needles, CO 86 (98, 110, 122, 134, 146) sts.

ROW 1 (WS): P2, *k2, p2; rep from * to end.

ROW 2: K2, *p2, k2; rep from * to end.

Rep rows 1–2 for 8 (8½, 8½, 8½, 8½, 8½)", end with a WS row.

Change to larger needles.

SET-UP ROW (WS): P1, work row 1 of Lattice Cable patt to last st, p1.

INC ROW (RS): K1, M1P, work in patt to last st, M1P, k1.

Cont in patt, keeping first and last st in St st and increased sts in Rev St st, rep inc row every 6th row 5 (5, 5, 2, 2, 2) times more, then every 8th row 0 (0, 0, 3, 3, 3) times—98 (110, 122, 134, 146, 158) sts.

Work even in patt until back meas 12½ (13, 13, 13½, 13½, 14)" from beg, end with a WS row.

ARMHOLE SHAPING

Cont in patt as est, BO 6 (6, 7, 8, 10, 11) sts at beg of next 2 rows. Dec 1 st each side every row 3 (3, 5, 7, 8, 10) times—80 (92, 98, 104, 110, 116) sts.

Work even until armhole meas 7¼ (7½, 7¾, 8, 8¼, 8¾)", end with a WS row.

NECK AND SHOULDER SHAPING

BO 4 (5, 6, 7, 7, 8) sts at armhole edge, work in patt until there are 10 (13, 15, 16, 18, 19) sts on RH needle. Place rem unworked sts onto holder.

NEXT ROW (WS): K1, p2tog, work in patt to end.

NEXT ROW (RS): BO 4 (5, 6, 7, 7, 8) sts at armhole edge, work in patt to end.

NEXT ROW (WS): K1, p2tog, work in patt to end.

BO rem 4 (6, 7, 7, 9, 9) sts.

Leave center 52 (56, 56, 58, 60, 62) sts on holder for back neck and place rem sts onto needle. With RS facing, rejoin yarn and work in patt to end.

NEXT ROW (WS): BO 4 (5, 6, 7, 7, 8) sts at armhole edge, work in patt to end.

NEXT ROW (RS): K1, ssk, work in patt to end.

NEXT ROW (WS): BO 4 (5, 6, 7, 7, 8) sts at armhole edge, work in patt to end.

NEXT ROW (RS): K1, ssk, work in patt to end.

BO rem 4 (6, 7, 7, 9, 9) sts.

FRONT

Work same as back until front meas 13½ (14, 14, 14½, 14½, 15)" from beg, end with a WS row.

LEFT NECK SHAPING

Work in patt to center 14 sts. Place center 14 sts onto holder tog with rem sts for right neck and shoulder. BO 3 sts at the beg of the next 2 WS rows. Dec 1 st at neck edge every row 9 (11, 11, 11, 11, 13) times, every other row 4 (4, 3, 4, 6, 5) times, then every 4th row 2 (2, 3, 3, 2,

2) times—12 (16, 19, 21, 23, 25) sts.

Work even in patt until armhole meas 7¼ (7½, 7¾, 8, 8¼, 8¾)", end with a WS row.

LEFT SHOULDER SHAPING

BO 4 (5, 6, 7, 7, 8) sts at beg of next 2 RS rows. Work 1 row even. BO rem 4 (6, 7, 7, 9, 9) sts.

RIGHT NECK SHAPING

Keeping center 14 sts on holder, with RS facing, work across rem 33 (39, 42, 45, 48, 51) sts. Work 1 row even. BO 3 sts at the beg of next 2 RS rows. Dec 1 st at neck edge every row 9 (11, 11, 11, 11, 13) times, every other row 4 (4, 3, 4, 6, 5) times, then every 4th row 2 (2, 3, 3, 2, 2) times—12 (16, 19, 21, 23, 25) sts.

Work even in patt until armhole meas 7¼ (7½, 7¾, 8, 8¼, 8¾)", end with a RS row.

RIGHT SHOULDER SHAPING

BO 4 (5, 6, 7, 7, 8) sts at beg of next 2 WS rows. Work 1 row even. BO rem 4 (6, 7, 7, 9, 9) sts.

SLEEVES (MAKE 2)

Note: Keyhole and cap shaping are worked at the same time. Read through instructions before beginning.

With smaller needles, CO 35 (35, 41, 41, 47, 47) sts, with 2nd ball of yarn CO 35 (35, 41, 41, 47, 47) sts onto same needle. Work both sides at the same time.

ROW 1 (WS): P0 (0, 1, 1, 0, 0), k0 (0, 1, 1, 0, 0), *p2, k2; rep from * to last 3 sts, p1, k1, p1, drop yarn and work other side; p1, k1, p1, *k2, p2; rep from * to last 0 (0, 2, 2, 0, 0) sts, k0 (0, 1, 1, 0, 0), p0 (0, 1, 1, 0, 0).

ROW 2: K0 (0, 1, 1, 0, 0), p0 (0, 1, 1, 0, 0), *k2, p2; rep from * to last 3 sts, k1, p1, k1, drop yarn and work other side; k1, p1, k1, *p2, k2; rep from * to last 2 (2, 0, 0, 2, 2) sts, p0 (0, 1, 1, 0, 0), k0 (0, 1, 1, 0, 0).

Rep rows 1 and 2 twice more. Change to larger needles.

KEYHOLE

NEXT ROW (WS): P1, m1, k3, beg with row 13, work in Lattice Cable patt to last 7 sts, k2, k2tog, p1, k1, p1, drop yarn and work other side; p1, k1, p1, ssk, k2, work Lattice Cable patt to last 4 sts, k3, m1, p1.

Work 1 row even on both sides, keeping in patt as est.

DEC ROW (WS): Work in patt to last 5 sts, k2tog, p1, k1, p1, drop yarn and work other side; p1, k1, p1, ssk, work in patt to end.

Work 1 row even on both sides, keeping in patt as est.

DEC ROW (WS): Work in patt to last 5 sts, k2tog, p1, k1, p1, drop yarn and work other side; p1, k1, p1, ssk, work in patt to end.

Work even in patt for 8 rows.

INC ROW (RS): Work in patt to last 3 sts, M1P, k1, p1, k1, drop yarn and work other side; k1, p1, k1, M1P, work in patt to end.

Rep inc row every RS row twice more.

NEXT ROW: Work even in patt as est.

NEXT ROW: Work even in patt on first side, CO 4 sts using backward loop CO (page 88), cut 2nd ball of yarn leaving a 6" tail; cont to work other side and rem of sleeve with first ball.

SLEEVE CAP

AT THE SAME TIME, when sleeve meas 1" from beg, end with a WS row, BO 6 (6, 7, 8, 10, 11) sts at beg of next 2 rows.

Dec 1 st each side every row 2 (2, 4, 4, 4, 4) times, every 4th row 5 (5, 3, 6, 5, 7) times, then every other row 6 (8, 10, 6, 6, 2) times, then every row 8 (6, 9, 8, 13, 14) times. BO 3 sts at beg of next 2 rows. BO rem 16 (16, 16, 18, 18, 18) sts.

FINISHING

Block pieces to measurements. Sew shoulder seams.

NECKBAND

With RS facing and circular needle, starting at left shoulder seam, PU and k36 (36, 38, 41, 42, 43) sts along left front neck, k14 sts from front neck holder, 36 (36, 38, 41, 42, 43) sts along right front neck, 5 sts along right back neck, k52 (56, 56, 58, 60, 62) sts from back neck holder, and 5 sts along left back neck—148 (152, 156, 168, 172) sts. Pm and join.

RIB RND: K1, *p2, k2; rep from * to last 3 sts, p2, k1.

Rep last rnd 6 times more. BO in rib.

Set in sleeves. Sew side and sleeve seams. Weave in ends.

KEYHOLE CLOSURE

Sew buttons at edge of back section of sleeve in center of rib.

BUTTON LOOP: With crochet hook, leaving a 6" tail, ch 6 and fasten off. Using tails, attach ends of chain to edge of front section of sleeve to form button loop.

ABOUT MELISSA Although my grandmother taught me to knit when I was seven, I quickly lost interest in making Barbie tube dresses, but the allure of both fashion and knitting came back to me later in life. I studied at FIT and today am a full-time knitwear designer for a clothing company. I also have my own line of handknit patterns, Neoknits. In addition, I work part-time as the creative director for One Planet Yarn and Fiber. To follow my current projects, please stop by my knitting blog at neoknits.com.

SIZE

Finished width: approx 34"

Finished length: approx 29 (34)"

MATERIALS

Fleece Artist *Big Blue* (100% Bluefaced Leicester wool; 250g/288 yd), 3 (4) skeins Moss

US 10 (6mm) 40" circular needle

Tapestry needle

GAUGE

26 sts and 34 rows = 6" in patt st

pamela grossman

FERTILITY BLANKET

 was drawn to this bobble pattern, which I found in a book from my knitting library, because it looked . . . a bit obscene. I wondered if anyone else would share my dirty association. I whipped up a swatch and showed it to some girlfriends. "What does this look like to you?" A few unfazed responses offered "leaves" or "waves." "Really?" I asked, "Nothing familiar?" They finally exlaimed, "OMG! It looks like girly bits!" The Fertility Blanket was born from these suggestive bobbles, and it'll make a great gift for a gal pal—whether she's thinking of getting preggers or not. Not normally a bobble fan, I think they work adorably here, adding interest without kitsch, to make a sly celebration of ladyhood.

DIRECTIONS

Pattern notes: Wyib sl the 1st st of every RS row kwise. Wyif sl the 1st st of every WS row pwise.

Loosely CO 147 sts using the Old Norwegian CO (page 91).

SET-UP ROW 1 (WS): Sl 1, p to end.

SET-UP ROW 2 (RS): Sl 1, p1, *k1, [yo, k1] twice, p1, k3, s2kp, k3, p1; rep from * to last 5 sts, k1, [yo, k1] twice, p1, k1.

SET-UP ROW 3: Sl 1, k1, p5, *k1, p7, k1, p5; rep from * to last 2 sts, k1, p1.

ROW 1 (RS): Sl 1, p1, *k2, yo, k1, yo, k2, p1, k2, s2kp, k2, p1; rep from * to last 7 sts, k2, yo, k1, yo, k2, p1, k1.

Bobble Pattern

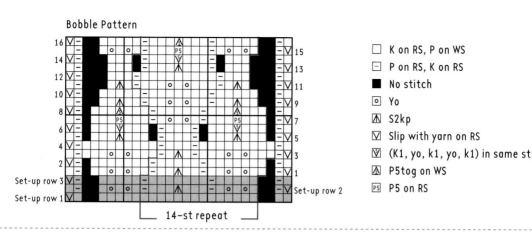

- □ K on RS, P on WS
- ⊟ P on RS, K on RS
- ■ No stitch
- ⊙ Yo
- ⅄ S2kp
- ⋎ Slip with yarn on RS
- ⋎ (K1, yo, k1, yo, k1) in same st
- ⋀ P5tog on WS
- P5 P5 on RS

14-st repeat

ROW 2: Sl 1, k1, p7, *k1, p5, k1, p7; rep from * to last 2 sts, k1, p1.

ROW 3: Sl 1, p1, *k3, yo, k1, yo, k3, p1, k1, s2kp, k1, p1; rep from * to last 9 sts, k3, yo, k1, yo, k3, p1, k1.

ROW 4: Sl 1, k1, p9, *k1, p3, k1, p9; rep from * to last 2 sts, k1, p1.

ROW 5: Sl 1, p1, *k3, s2kp, k3, p1, k3, p1; rep from * to last 11 sts, k3, s2kp, k3, p1, k1.

ROW 6 (BEG BOBBLE): Sl 1, k1, p3, (k1, yo, k1, yo, k1) in next st, p3, *[k1, p3] twice, (k1, yo, k1, yo, k1) in next st, p3; rep from * to last 2 sts, k1, p1.

ROW 7: Sl 1, p1, *k3, p5, k3, p1, k1, [yo, k1] twice, p1; rep from * to last 13 sts, k3, p5, k3, p1, k1.

ROW 8 (END BOBBLE): Sl 1, k1, p3, p5tog, p3, *k1, p5, k1, p3, p5tog, p3; rep from * to last 2 sts, k1, p1.

ROW 9: Sl 1, p1, *k2, s2kp, k2, p1, k2, yo, k1, yo, k2, p1; rep from * to last 9 sts, k2, s2kp, k2, p1, k1.

ROW 10: Sl 1, k1, p5, *k1, p7, k1, p5; rep from * to last 2 sts, k1, p1.

ROW 11: Sl 1, p1, *k1, s2kp, k1, p1, k3, yo, k1, yo, k3, p1; rep from * to last 7 sts, k1, s2kp, k1, p1, k1.

ROW 12: Sl 1, k1, p3, *k1, p9, k1, p3; rep from * to last 2 sts, k1, p1.

ROW 13: Sl 1, p1, *k3, p1, k3, s2kp, k3, p1; rep from * to last 5 sts, k3, p1, k1.

ROW 14 (BEG BOBBLE): Sl 1, k1, p3, *k1, p3, (k1, yo, k1, yo, k1) in next st, p3, k1, p3; rep from * to last 2 sts, k1, p1.

ROW 15: Sl 1, p1, *k1, [yo, k1] twice, p1, k3, p5, k3, p1; rep from * to last 5 sts, k1, [yo, k1] twice, p1, k1.

ROW 16 (END BOBBLE): Sl 1, k1, p5, *k1, p3, p5tog, p3, k1, p5; rep from * to last 2 sts, k1, p1.

Rep rows 1–16 eight (ten) times more, then rows 1–12 once more.

FINISHING

NEXT ROW (RS): Sl 1, k to end.

Cut yarn, leaving a 90" tail. Thread tapestry needle with tail and BO as foll:

BO ROW: *Working sts on needle from right to left, insert tapestry needle through the first 2 sts pwise, pull tail all the way through. Insert needle through the first st kwise. Pull tail through and snug, then slip first st off needle; rep from * to end.

Weave in ends. Block to shape.

ABOUT PAMELA By day I'm a mild-mannered schoolteacher. By night, I'm a compulsive knitwear designer. I wear a variety of hats and try to keep them jaunty. You can find me as Pamelamama on crafty social-networking sites, including Ravelry, Flickr, and Twitter. Stop by my blog at www.pamelamama.com, and say hello at my pattern shop and forum at www.woolywonder.com.

juLia fRank

SAXON THE CITY

able stockings were part of the ensemble I designed for my wedding, an occasion that included a parade, in the dead of winter, from the chapel to my flat in Budapest. I made the groom a "wedding sweater" for the big day and then realized that he'd be really warm while I'd freeze in my gown. Short on time and unable to snag good yarn in Budapest, I raided my stash for something that would work up quickly and still look wedding-worthy; I designed a pair of stockings with a gorgeous saxon braid pattern. As I started these thigh-highs, I realized what a quick knit they would be. The shaping became obvious as I established the center back stitch, even on the right leg, where you'll need to put on your knitter's thinking cap in order to reverse the shaping. It's helpful to keep in mind that the shaping happens *before* the cable pattern needle on the left leg, and *after* it on the right. Get a perfectly snug fit by knitting a size down from your own actual thigh measurement, and these thigh-highs will be begging for a parade.

SPECIAL ABBREVIATIONS

C2B: Sl 1 st onto cn and hold in back, k1, k1 from cn.

C2F: Sl 1 st onto cn and hold in front, k1, k1 from cn.

T2B: Sl 1 st onto cn and hold in back, k1, p1 from cn.

T2F: Sl 1 st onto cn and hold in front, p1, k1 from cn.

C3B: Sl 1 st onto cn and hold in back, k2, k1 from cn.

C3F: Sl 2 sts onto cn and hold in front, k1, k2 from cn.

C3L: Sl 1 st onto cn and hold in front, k2, k1 from cn.

SIZE

Thigh circumference: 11½ (12¾, 14)", unstretched

Ankle circumference: 7"

MATERIALS

Green Mountain Spinnery *Mountain Mohair* (30% mohair, 70% wool; 2oz/140 yd)

MC: 8 (9) skeins #6779 Raspberry

CC: 1 skein #6750 Raven

US 8 (5mm) double-pointed needles

Stitch marker

Cable needle

Tapestry needle

GAUGE

22 sts and 28 rows = 4" in St st

27 sts and 26 rows = 4" in k2, p1 rib, unstretched

Saxon Braid

47
45
43
41
39
37
35
33
31
29
27
25
23
21
19
17
15
13
11
9
7
5
3
1

16 rnd repeat
(work 9 times)

24-stitch panel

□	K
⊟	P
◪	K2tog
◩	Ssk
■	No stitch
◨	C2B
◪	C2F
◨	T2B
◩	T2F
◨	C3B
◩	C3F
◪	C3L
◨	C3R
◩	T3L
◨	T3R
◩	T3F
◨	T3B
◨	C4B
◪	C4F
◨	T4B
◩	T4F

C3R: Sl 2 sts onto cn and hold in back, k1, k2 from cn.

C4B: Sl 2 sts onto cn and hold in back, k2, k2 from cn.

C4F: Sl 2 sts onto cn and hold in front, k2, k2 from cn.

T3B: Sl 1 st onto cn and hold in back, k2, p1 from cn.

T3F: Sl 2 sts onto cn and hold in front, p1, k2 from cn.

T3L: Sl 1 st onto cn and hold in front, p2, k1 from cn.

T3R: Sl 2 sts onto cn and hold in back, k1, p2 from cn.

T4B: Sl 2 sts onto cn and hold in back, k2, p2 from cn.

T4F: Sl 2 sts onto cn and hold in front, p2, k2 from cn.

M1P: Insert LH needle from back to front into the horizontal strand between last st and next st, p this strand through front loop.

SPECIAL STITCH
SAXON BRAID PANEL (OVER 24 STS)

RND 1: [P2, k4, p2] 3 times.

RND 2: [P2, C4B, p2] 3 times.

RND 3: Rep rnd 1.

RND 4: P1, T3B, [T4F, T4B] 2 times, T3F, p1.

RND 5: P1, k2, p3, k4, p4, k4, p3, k2, p1.

RND 6: T3B, p3, C4F, p4, C4F, p3, T3F.

RND 7: [K2, p4, k2] 3 times.

RND 8: K2, p2, [T4B, T4F] twice, p2, k2.

RNDS 9 AND 11: K2, p2, k2, p4, k4, p4, k2, p2, k2.

RND 10: K2, p2, k2, p4, C4B, p4, k2, p2, k2.

RND 12: K2, p2, [T4F, T4B] twice, p2, k2.

RND 13: K2, [p4, k4] twice, p4, k2.

RND 14: T3F, p3, C4F, p4, C4F, p3, T3B.

RND 15: P1, k2, p3, k4, p4, k4, p3, k2, p1.

RND 16: P1, T3F, [T4B, T4F] twice, T3B, p1.

Rep rnds 1–16 for panel.

DIRECTIONS

Note: Read all instructions before continuing. Shaping and color changes take place at the same time.

LEFT STOCKING

With MC, CO 78 (86, 94) sts. Pm and join, distributing sts over 3 needles as foll: 24 sts on Needle 1; 28 (32, 36) sts on Needle 2; 26 (30, 34) sts on Needle 3.

SET-UP RND: Work Saxon Braid panel over 24 sts of Needle 1, k2, *p2, k2; rep from * to end.

Cont with MC in patt as est for 3 more rnds.

NEXT RND: Work in patt as est over Needles 1 and 2; for Needle 3, work to last 12 (16, 16) sts, p2tog (mark st for center back), work in patt to end—77 (85, 93) sts.

Work 4 rnds in patt.

Note: Rearrange sts on Needles 2 and 3 as necessary on the foll shaping rnds.

DEC RND: Work in patt to next set of p2 sts before center back, p2tog, work to next set of p2 sts after center back, p2tog, work in patt to end—75 (83, 91) sts.

Rep dec rnd every 5th rnd 1 (2, 3) times more —73 (79, 85) sts.

Work 4 rnds in patt.

DEC RND: Work in patt to next set of p2 sts before center back, p2tog, work in patt to end—72 (78, 84) sts.

Rep last dec rnd every 5th rnd 7 times more —65 (71, 77) sts.

AT THE SAME TIME, when stocking meas 3½", change to CC and work in patt and dec as est for 2½". Change to MC.

Cont even in patt as est until 5 16-rnd reps of Saxon Braid panel are complete or to desired length to knee.

KNEE DEC: Work in patt to 5 sts before center back st, ssk, work 7 sts, k2tog, work to end —63 (69, 75) sts.

Work 2 rnds in patt.

DEC RND (SIZES M AND L ONLY): *Work in patt to next set of k2 sts before last dec, ssk, work to next set of k2 sts after next dec, k2tog, work to end—(67, 73) sts.*

Complete 6th rep of Saxon Braid panel or work to base of knee.

CALF INC: Work in patt as est to center back st, M1P, p1, work in patt to end.

Work 1 rnd in patt.

INC RND: Work in patt to next p st before center back sts, M1P, p1, work to next p st after center back, p1, M1P, work in patt to end.

Rep inc rnd every other rnd once more—68 (72, 78) sts.

Complete 7th rep of Saxon Braid panel or work 10 rnds in patt as est.

CALF DEC RND 1: Work in patt as est to 4 sts before center back sts, [p2tog, k2] twice, p2tog, work to end—65 (69, 75) sts.

Work 2 rnds in patt.

DEC RND 2: Work in patt as est to 7 sts before center back st, p2tog, work 11 sts, p2tog, work to end —63 (67, 73) sts.

Work 2 (2, 3) rnds in patt.

DEC RND 3: Work in patt as est to 5 sts before center back st, ssk, work 7 sts, k2tog, work to end—61 (65, 71) sts.

Work 2 (2, 3) rnds in patt.

DEC RND 4: Work in patt as est to 4 sts before center back st, ssk, work 5 sts, k2tog, work to end—59 (63, 69) sts.

Work 2 (2, 3) rnds in patt.

DEC RND 5: Work in patt as est to 3 sts before center back st, ssk, work 3 sts, k2tog, work to end—57 (61, 67) sts.

Work 2 (2, 3) rnds in patt.

DEC RND 6: Work in patt as est to 5 sts before center back st, ssk, work 7 sts, k2tog, work to end—55 (59, 65) sts.

Work 2 (2, 3) rnds in patt.

DEC RND 7: Work in patt as est to 4 sts before center back st, ssk, work 5 sts, k2tog, work to end—53 (57, 63) sts.

Work 2 (2, 3) rnds in patt.

DEC RND 8: Work in patt as est to 3 sts before center back st, ssk, work 3 sts, k2tog, work to end—51 (55, 61) sts.

Cont even in patt as est, end with rnd 28 of Saxon Braid panel (rnd 12 of 16-rnd pattern, 10th rep or desired

number of reps). Work charted decs or as foll over Needle 1 and in patt as est over Needles 2 and 3:

RND 29: Ssk, [p4, k4] twice, p4, k2tog—22 sts on Needle 1.

RND 30: T2F, p3, C4F, p4, C4F, p3, T2B.

RND 31: P1, k1, p3, k4, p4, k4, p3, k1, p1.

RND 32: P1, T2F, [T4B, T4F] twice, T2B, p1.

RND 33: P2, k3, p4, k4, p4, k3, p2.

RND 34: P2, C3B, p4, C4B, p4, C3B, p2.

RND 35: P2, k2tog, k1, p4, k4, p4, k1, ssk, p2—20 sts on Needle 1.

RND 36: P1, T2B, T3L, T4B, T4F, T3R, T2F, p1.

RND 37: P1, k1, p3, k3, p4, k3, p3, k1, p1.

RND 38: T2B, p3, C3L, p4, C3R, p3, T2F.

RND 39: K1, [p4, k3] twice, p4, k1.

RND 40: K1, p2, T4B, T3L, T3R, T4F, p2, k1.

RND 41: K1, p2, ssk, p4, k2, p4, k2tog, p2, k1—18 sts on Needle 1.

RND 42: K1, p2, k1, p4, C2F, p4, k1, p2, k1.

RND 43: K1, p2, k1, p4, k2, p4, k1, p2, k1.

RND 44: K1, p2, [T3L, T3R] twice, p2, k1.

RND 45: K1, [p4, k2] twice, p4, k1.

RND 46: T2F, p3, C2B, p4, C2F, p3, T2B.

RND 47: K2, p3, k2, p4, k2, p3, k2.

RND 48: P1, T2F [T3R, T3L] twice, T2B, p1—18 sts on Needle 1.

HEEL FLAP

Using Needle 3, k7 (5, 6) from Needle 1. Redistribute sts as foll: 19 (21, 23) sts on Needle 3 for heel, 13 (14, 16) sts each on Needles 1 and 2 for instep. Drop MC and join CC. Turn to work WS row over heel sts.

ROW 1 (WS): Sl 1, p to end.

ROW 2 (RS): *Sl 1, k1; rep from * to end.

Rep these 2 rows 9 (10, 11) times more.

TURN HEEL

ROW 1 (WS): Sl 1, p9 (10, 11), p2tog, p1, turn.

ROW 2: Sl 1, k2, ssk, k1, turn.

ROW 3: Sl 1, p to 1 st before gap, p2tog, p1, turn.

ROW 4: Sl 1, k to 1 st before gap, ssk, k1, turn.

Rep last 2 rows (*omitting p1 and k1 at ends of last 2 rows for size M only*) until all sts have been worked—11 (11, 13) heel sts.

Drop CC and pick up MC. Pick up and k10 (11, 12) sts along side of heel flap; with new Needle 2, k across 26 (28, 30) instep sts; with new Needle 3, pick up and k10 (11, 12) sts along other side of heel flap and k2tog, k4 (4, 5) from first needle—56 (60, 66) sts. Pm for end of rnd.

GUSSET SHAPING

RND 1: For Needle 1, k to last 3 sts, k2tog, k1; for Needle 2, knit; for Needle 3, k1, ssk, k to end.

RND 2: Knit.

Rep last 2 rnds until 40 (44, 48) sts rem.

FOOT

Work even in St st until foot meas 2 (2¼, 2½)" less than desired finished length.

Redistribute sts as foll: 10 (11, 12) sts each onto Needles 1 and 3; 20 (22, 24) sts onto Needle 2. Change to CC.

TOE

RND 1: For Needle 1, k to last 4 sts, k2tog, k2; for Needle 2, k2, ssk, k to last 4 sts, k2tog, k2; for Needle 3, k2, ssk, k to end.

RND 2: Knit.

Rep last 2 rnds until 24 sts rem, then rep rnd 1 until 12 sts rem.

Slip first 3 sts of Needle 2 onto Needle 1; slip 3 sts of Needle 3 onto Needle 2—6 sts on each of 2 needles. Graft toe sts using Kitchener st (page 107).

RIGHT STOCKING

With MC, CO 78 (86, 94) sts. Pm and join, distributing sts over 3 needles as foll: 26 (30, 34) sts onto Needle 1; 28 (32, 36) sts onto Needle 2; 24 sts onto Needle 3.

SET-UP RND: K2, *p2, k2; rep from * to end of Needle 2, work Saxon Braid panel over 24 sts of Needle 3.

Cont with MC in patt as est for 3 more rnds.

NEXT RND: Work in patt as est over first 10 (14, 14) sts, p2tog (mark st for center back), work in patt to end—77 (85, 93) sts.

Work rem of stocking same as left side with patterning and leg shaping reversed.

. . . .

ABOUT JULIA Taught by my granny in the Hungarian tradition, I am a lifelong knitter. During the past thirty years I have followed my love of knitting across America, Europe, and, now, Iceland. I spent many years working and living on a sheep farm, and have taught knitting and spinning in yarn shops in New York, New Mexico, and California. For a while, I did all of this while keeping my day job as a structural steel welder and doing bronze sculpture restoration. In Iceland, along with making custom couture, exhibiting, and teaching, I collaborate with top designers and have a catalog of original designs that you can check out at www.julikaworks.com.

janice kang

LACED-UP SOCKS

For these pretty socks, I wanted a pattern that was visually intriguing—something with twisted stitches and lace. I turned to my knitting library for inspiration and found a stitch pattern that I modified to create a fancy stacked effect for the leg. I also separated the columns of motifs with a simple rib for a supercute fit. Sizing up the pattern was a toughie—just increasing the width of the rib between the columns threw off the balance of the whole pattern. After going back to the drawing board, I solved it with a bigger motif for the larger size. The details on these socks are so nice, it's a shame to cover 'em up with shoes!

SPECIAL ABBREVIATIONS

LT (LEFT TWIST): Insert RH needle tbl of 2nd st on LH needle and k, leaving st on LH needle; insert RH needle tbl of the first 2 sts on LH needle and k2tog; slip both sts off needle.

RT (RIGHT TWIST): Insert RH needle between 1st and 2nd st and k 2nd st tbl; k 1st st and slip both sts off the needle.

STITCH PATTERN
RIBBING
RND 1: *K1, p1, k1 (2), [p1, k2] 3 times, p1, k1 (2), p1, k1; rep from * around.

DIRECTIONS
CUFF
Using wy, CO 33 (37) sts. Do not join.

ROW 1 (RS): Using project yarn, *k1, yo; rep from * to last st, k1—65 (73) sts. Turn.

ROW 2 (WS): P1, k1, *sl 1 wyif, k1; rep from * to last st, p1. Turn.

SIZE
Women's M (L)

Foot circumference: 6½ (7½)"

Foot length: approx 9 (10)"

MATERIALS
Hand Jive *Nature's Palette Fingering Weight* (100% merino wool; 50g/185 yd), 2 (3) hanks #NP 103 Seafoam

US 1 (2.25mm) double-pointed needles

Stitch marker

Waste yarn

Tapestry needle

GAUGE
34 sts and 48 rnds = 4" in St st

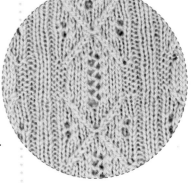

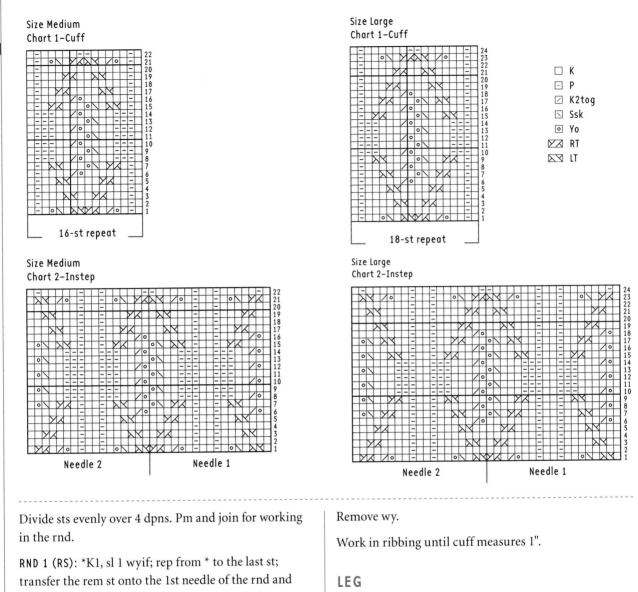

Size Medium
Chart 1-Cuff

16-st repeat

Size Large
Chart 1-Cuff

18-st repeat

☐ K
⊟ P
☑ K2tog
◻ Ssk
⊙ Yo
⊠ RT
⊠ LT

Size Medium
Chart 2-Instep

Needle 2   Needle 1

Size Large
Chart 2-Instep

Needle 2   Needle 1

Divide sts evenly over 4 dpns. Pm and join for working in the rnd.

RND 1 (RS): *K1, sl 1 wyif; rep from * to the last st; transfer the rem st onto the 1st needle of the rnd and pm for new beg of the rnd. Do not turn. 17 (19) sts on Needle 1; 16 (18) sts each on Needles 2, 3, and 4—65 (73) sts.

RND 2: K2tog, p1, *sl 1 wyib, p1; rep from * around—64 (72) sts; 16 (18) sts on each needle.

RND 3: *K1, sl 1 wyif; rep from * around.

RND 4: K1, p1, *sl 1 wyib, p1; rep from * around.

RND 5: *K1, p1; rep from * around.

RND 6 FOR SIZE L ONLY: *K1, p1, k1, m1, s2kp, m1; rep from * around.

Remove wy.

Work in ribbing until cuff measures 1".

LEG

Work 22 (24) rnds of Chart 1 twice, then work rnds 1–21 (1–23).

NEXT RND: Work 56 (63) sts of rnd 22 (24). Pm for new beg of the rnd.

Distribute sts over 3 dpns as folls: 16 (18) sts each onto Needles 1 and 2, 32 (36) heel sts onto Needle 3—64 (72) sts; turn.

HEEL FLAP

SET-UP ROW (WS): K3, p12 (14), pfb, p to end of row—33 (37) sts; turn.

ROW 1 (RS): P3, *k1, sl 1 kwise; rep from * to last 4 sts, k4; turn.

ROW 2 (WS): K3, p to end of row; turn.

ROW 3: P3, *sl 1 kwise, k1; rep from * to last 4 sts, sl 1 kwise, k3; turn.

ROW 4: Rep row 2.

Rep rows 1–4 six (seven) times more, then work rows 1–3 once more—32 (36) rows total including set-up row.

TURN HEEL

ROW 1 (WS): Sl 1, p17 (19), p2tog, p1; turn.

ROW 2 (RS): Sl 1, k4, ssk, k1; turn.

ROW 3: Sl 1, p to 1 st before gap, p2tog, p1; turn.

ROW 4: Sl 1, k to 1 st before gap, ssk, k1; turn.

Rep rows 3 and 4 until all heel sts have been worked, ending with a RS row—19 (21) sts.

GUSSET

SET-UP RND 1 (RS): With empty needle, PU and k15 (17) sts along side of heel flap; with empty needle, PU and k1 st along side of heel flap, 2 sts between heel and instep, then *work 16 (18) sts from next needle as foll: LT, k1, ssk, yo, k1 (2), p1, k2, p1, k1 (2), yo, k2tog, k1, RT; with empty needle, rep from *, PU and k2 sts between instep and heel, then 1 st along side of heel flap; with empty needle, PU and k15 (17) sts along side of heel flap, then k9 (10) from next needle, slip rem 10 (11) heel sts onto end of 1st needle; with empty needle, k8 (9), ssk, k15 (17)—86 (96) sts: 19 (21) sts each on 2 needles for instep and 24 (27) sts each on 2 needles for sole. Pm for beg of rnd.

SET-UP RND 2: For instep, (k2tog) 2 times, k5 (6), p1, k2, p1, k6 (7), k6 (7), p1, k2, p1, k5 (6), (ssk) 2 times—34 (38) sts; for sole, k48 (54)—82 (92) sts.

GUSSET SHAPING

RND 1: For instep, work rnd 3 of Chart 2; for sole, k1, ssk, k to last 3 sole sts, k2tog, k1—80 (90) sts.

RND 2: For instep, cont as est over Chart 2; for sole, knit.

RND 3: For instep, cont as est over Chart 2; for sole, k1, ssk, k to last 3 sole sts, k2tog, k1.

Rep rnds 2 and 3 until 64 (72) sts rem—17 (19) sts each on 2 needles for instep and 15 (17) sts each on 2 needles for sole.

FOOT

Cont working instep sts over Chart 2 and sole sts in St st until 3 reps of Chart 2 have been completed or foot meas approximately 1½ (2)" less than desired finished length.

TOE

SET-UP RND: With last sole needle, k1 from 1st instep needle and pm for new beg of rnd. Transfer last instep st onto 1st sole needle—16 (18) sts on each needle. For instep, *k6 (7), p1, k2, p1, k6 (7); rep from * once; for sole, knit.

RND 1: For instep, k1, ssk, work in patt as est to last 3 instep sts, k2tog, k1; for sole, k1, ssk, k to last 3 sole sts, k2tog, k1.

RND 2: Work even.

Rep rnds 1 and 2 until 20 (28) sts rem—5 (7) sts each needle.

FINISHING

On 1st needle of instep and 1st needle of sole: pass the 1st st over the 2nd st; on 2nd needle of instep and 2nd needle of sole: pass the last st over the 2nd to the last st—16 (24) sts—4 (6) sts each needle.

Graft toe sts using Kitchener st (page 107).

Weave in ends.

ABOUT JANICE Some of my earliest memories are of my mom knitting sweaters for the whole family; she was the one who taught me the basics. I really got into the craft when I discovered the San Jose Stitch 'n Bitch group a few years ago. Since then, I've met great friends and my fiber world has grown to include spinning and design. You can find me on my blog, knitflix.blogspot.com.

gryphon perkins

FRILLY FILLY SCARF

When I originally made this scarf, it was my first lace project and very early in my knitting career. The pattern is basic enough to knit as a near-beginner, but it creates an intricate finished product that packs a lot of punch. The horseshoe lace stitch pattern is easy to memorize, so it's a cinch to add repeats to make a wider scarf, or even a superluxe stole. Or you can knit two half-length scarves in different colors and sew them together for a striking two-toned look. With this lovely lace pattern, the options are endless.

SPECIAL STITCHES

HORSESHOE PATTERN
(MULTIPLE OF 10 STS PLUS 1)

ROW 1 AND ALL WS ROWS: Purl.

ROW 2: K1, *yo, k3, sk2p, k3, yo, k1; rep from * to end.

ROW 4: P1, *k1, yo, k2, sk2p, k2, yo, k1, p1; rep from * to end.

ROW 6: P1, *k2, yo, k1, sk2p, k1, yo, k2, p1; rep from * to end.

ROW 8: P1, *k3, yo, sk2p, yo, k3, p1; rep from * to end.

Rep rows 1–8 for patt.

DIRECTIONS

CO 31 sts loosely.

Work rows 1–8 of Horseshoe patt 38 times.

P 1 row.

SIZE

Finished width: 5"

Finished length: 53"

MATERIALS

Rowan *Kidsilk Night* (67% super kid mohair, 18% silk, 10% polyester, 5% nylon; 25g/227 yd), 1 ball # 608 Moonlight

US 8 (5mm) needles

Rustproof pins for blocking

GAUGE

25 sts and 23 rows = 4" in patt st, after blocking

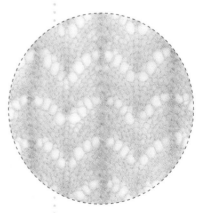

Horseshoe Pattern

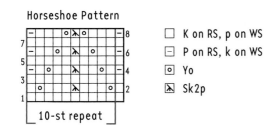

	K on RS, p on WS
	P on RS, k on WS
⊙	Yo
⋌	Sk2p

BO using Russian lace BO (page 102).

Weave in ends; do not cut excess until after blocking. Handwash and block to measurements using as many pins as necessary to keep side edges straight. Pin points at ends to emphasize scallops.

ABOUT GRYPHON After trying my hand at several other careers—philosopher, dancer, teacher, costumer, molecular biologist—I finally realized that all of it was just cutting into my knitting time. So I retreated to the country with my family, where I spend my days dyeing yarn, spinning wool, designing, knitting, and generally immersing myself in fiber. You can follow my adventures on my blog, www.sanguinegryphon.blogspot.com, and check out my handmade yarns at www.sanguinegryphon.com.

SIZE

Finished width: approx 12"

Finished height: approx 8", without handles

MATERIALS

Rowan *4-ply Cotton* (100% cotton; 50g/186 yds), 1 ball #138 Tutti Frutti

US 9 (5.5mm) needles

US 3 (3.25mm) double-pointed needles (set of 2)

Tapestry needle

GAUGE

Approx 13½ sts = 4" in patt

ELISA CONTOLINI AND THE PURL BEE

NO PLASTIC PLEASE MESH TOTE

For this snappy eco-tote, I was inspired by the Climbing Lace Trellis stitch pattern I found on Purl Bee, a knitting blog I adore. The stitch reminds me of those vintage, circular-handled net bags your granny might have had, but I updated it with pretty I-cord handles. In addition to being a quick knit and a great gift, the tote is an opportunity to reduce your use of wasteful plastic shopping bags. When the Purl Bee blog got wind of my pattern, they improved upon it by using the applied I-cord technique to knit the handle right onto the bag when done. Now you get to benefit from everyone's input. The lace stitch expands nicely to fit a day's worth of groceries, books, and flea-market finds. You can control the finished size of your bag with the thickness of whatever yarn you're using. I used a cotton, but

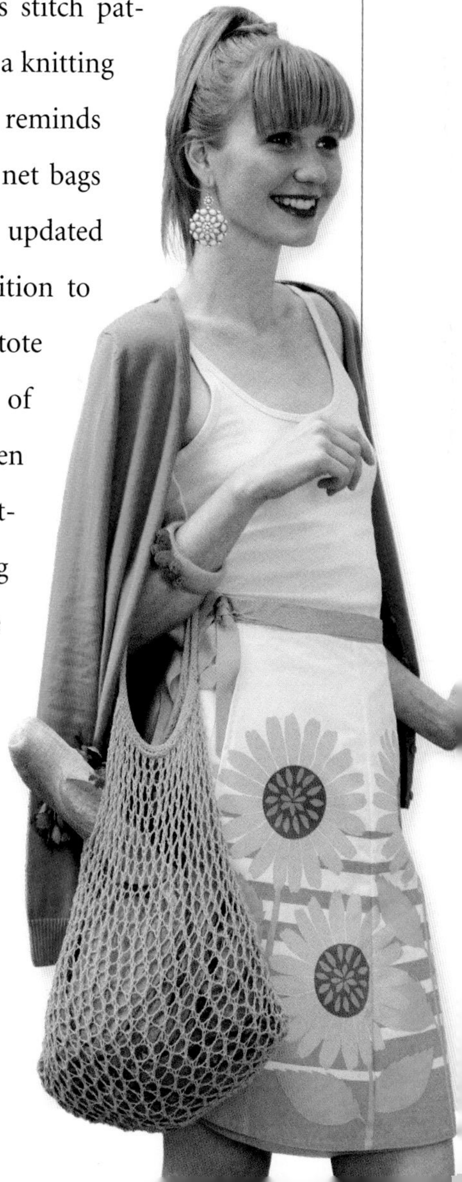

linen, hemp, and bamboo will also make a durable knit, and all are a perfect choice for the gal who wants to go green!

DIRECTIONS

With larger needles, CO 43 sts.

ROWS 1 AND 3 (WS): Sl 1, p to end.

ROW 2: Sl 1, k1, *yo, k2tog; rep from * to last st, k1.

ROW 4: Sl 1, k1, *ssk, yo; rep from * to last st, k1.

Rep rows 1–4 until piece meas approx 24" from beg (or twice desired height of bag).

BO loosely.

Fold piece in half lengthwise with RS tog so CO and BO edges form top of bag.

Starting 2" from top edge, sew or crochet side seams.

I-CORD BORDER/HANDLES

With dpns, CO 6 sts.

*K5, sl 1; with RS facing and starting at right top edge, PU 1 st and place on LH needle, k picked-up st and pass slipped st over it—6 sts. Slide sts to other end of needle. Rep from * across top edge of bag.

Cont to work unattached I-cord over 6 sts to desired length. Break yarn, leaving a 10" tail, and graft sts to CO sts. Rep on other side.

ABOUT ELISA AND THE PURL BEE

My mum taught me to knit when I was a child, but I rediscovered it twenty years later when I moved to Milan and needed a valid reason to postpone my daily chores. I still live in that same tiny, messy flat in Milan, where I love knitting during quiet, late nights when I'm the only one awake. The Purl Bee, the fabulous, project-driven blog launched by purlsoho.com's Joelle Hoverson, began in 2006 as a way for the craft artists at Purl Soho to show their latest work. My friendship with Joelle began shortly after, with the creation of this pattern.

ALYSSA CARLBERG

CRUSH

 rush is the name of this adorable shrug because it can be crushed into a tiny clutch for a night out in an itty-bitty dress, *and* because I guarantee you'll fall in love with it the first time you put it on. The fluffy mohair is surprisingly warm, doesn't wrinkle, and it's supersoft! Crush was inspired by a vintage pattern for a sweater from the '80s that incorporated the lovely lace design. Instead of a full sweater, I decided to wing it and craft a cute little shrug, so I used a dress form of my own measurements to guide the shaping. Once I had the twisted rib border for the back, I just imagined the shape of a sweaterlet as I stitched, and the pattern evolved. The collar and silhouette suggests the überfemme patterns of the '40s, and the branching lace on the back enhances the natural body shape. I hope you fall as hard as I did for this too-cute top.

SPECIAL ABBREVIATIONS

LT (LEFT TWIST): Insert RH needle tbl of 2nd st on LH needle and knit leaving st on LH needle; insert RH needle tbl of the first 2 sts on LH needle and k2tog; slip both sts off needle.

W&T (WRAP AND TURN): On RS, bring yarn between needles to front, sl next st onto RH needle, bring yarn between needles to back, and return sl st to LH needle, turn.

On WS, bring yarn between needles to back, sl next st onto RH needle, bring yarn between needles to front, return sl st to LH needle, turn.

SIZE

S (M, L, XL, XXL, XXXL)

To fit bust: 32–34 (36–38, 40–42, 44–46, 48–50, 52–54)"

Finished shoulder width: 16¾ (18¾, 20¾, 22¾, 24¾, 26¾)"

Finished waist width, unstretched: 13¼ (13¾, 14½, 15, 15½, 16)"

Finished back length not including collar: 11¾ (12¼, 13, 13½, 14, 14¼)"

MATERIALS

Rowan *Kidsilk Haze* (70% super kid mohair, 30% silk; 25g/229 yd), 2 (2, 3, 3, 3, 4) balls in #595

US 1 (2.5mm) 24–40" circular needle

US 4 (3.5mm) 24–40" circular needle

US 5 (3.75mm) 24–40" circular needle

3 stitch holders

8 stitch markers

Tapestry needle

GAUGE

24 sts and 28 rows = 4" in St st on largest needles

36 sts and 44 rows = 4" in twisted rib on smallest needles

Twisted Border

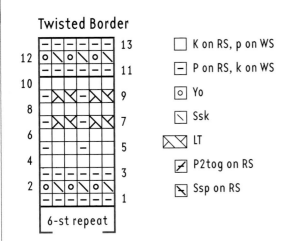

6-st repeat

☐	K on RS, p on WS
⊟	P on RS, k on WS
⊙	Yo
◺	Ssk
◿◺	LT
◿	P2tog on RS
◺	Ssp on RS

Branching Lace (BL)

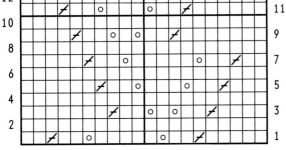

Branching Lace Mirrored (BLM)

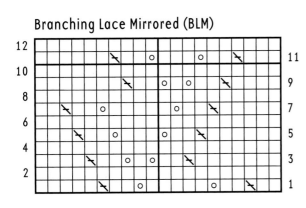

SPECIAL STITCHES

TWISTED RIB (MULTIPLE OF 2 STS)

ROW 1 (WS): *K1, p1; rep from * to end.

ROW 2: *K1 tbl, p1; rep from * to end.

Rep rows 1 and 2 for patt.

TWISTED BORDER (MULTIPLE OF 6 STS)

ROWS 1 AND 3 (RS): Purl.

ROW 2: *Yo, ssk; rep from * to end.

ROWS 4, 6, 8 AND 10: Purl.

ROW 5: *K2, p1; rep from * to end.

ROWS 7 AND 9: *LT, p1; rep from * to end.

ROW 11: Purl.

ROW 12: *Yo, ssk; rep from * to end.

ROW 13: Purl.

Rep rows 1–13 for patt.

BRANCHING LACE (BL) (OVER 20 STS)

ROW 1 (RS): K5, p2tog, k2, yo, k5, yo, k2, p2tog, k2.

ROWS 2, 4, 6, 8 AND 10: Purl.

ROW 3: K4, p2tog, k2, yo, k1, yo, k2, p2tog, k7.

ROW 5: K3, p2tog, k2, yo, k3, yo, k2, p2tog, k6.

ROW 7: K2, p2tog, k2, yo, k5, yo, k2, p2tog, k5.

ROW 9: K7, p2tog, k2, yo, k1, yo, k2, p2tog, k4.

ROW 11: K6, p2tog, k2, yo, k3, yo, k2, p2tog, k3.

ROW 12: Purl.

Rep rows 1–12 for patt.

BRANCHING LACE MIRRORED (BLM) (OVER 20 STS)

ROW 1 (RS): K2, ssp, k2, yo, k5, yo, k2, p2tog, k5.

ROWS 2, 4, 6, 8 AND 10: Purl.

ROW 3: K7, ssp, k2, yo, k1, yo, k2, ssp, k4.

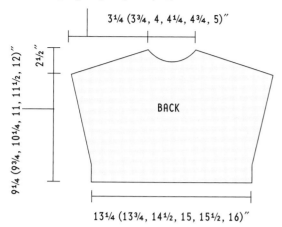

6¾ (7½, 8¼, 9¼, 10¾, 10)″

3¼ (3¾, 4, 4¼, 4¾, 5)″

2½″

9¼ (9¾, 10¼, 11, 11½, 12)″

BACK

13¼ (13¾, 14½, 15, 15½, 16)″

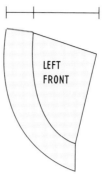

4″ 5½ (6¼, 7, 7¾, 8½, 9¼)″

LEFT
FRONT

ROW 5: K6, ssp, k2, yo, k3, yo, k2, ssp, k3.

ROW 7: K5, ssp, k2, yo, k5, yo, k2, ssp, k2.

ROW 9: K4, ssp, k2, yo, k1, yo, k2, ssp, k7.

ROW 11: K3, ssp, k2, yo, k3, yo, k2, ssp, k6.

ROW 12: Purl.

Rep rows 1–12 for patt.

DIRECTIONS
BACK

With smallest needle, CO 120 (124, 130, 136, 140, 144) sts.

Work in Twisted Rib for 2″, end with a RS row.
Change to medium-size needle.

Work dec row (WS) for your size:

SIZE S ONLY: *[P1, p2tog, p2, p2tog] 17 times, p1—86 sts.*

SIZE M ONLY: *P5, [p2, p2tog] 28 times, p7—96 sts.*

SIZE L ONLY: *P3, [p3, p2tog] 24 times, p7—106 sts.*

SIZE XL ONLY: *P3, [p5, p2tog, p4, p2tog] 10 times, p3—116 sts.*

SIZE XXL ONLY: *[P7, p2tog, p8, p2tog] 7 times, p7—126 sts.*

SIZE XXXL ONLY: *P8, p2tog [p16, p2tog] 7 times, p8—136 sts.*

Work 13 rows of Twisted Border as foll: Work 1 (3, 2, 1, 3, 2) sts in St st, work in Twisted Border patt to last 1 (3, 2, 1, 3, 2) sts, work in St st to end.

Change to largest needle.

BRANCHING LACE SECTION

SET-UP ROW (WS): K1, p19 (23, 27, 31, 35, 39), pm, p20, pm, k6 (8, 10, 12, 14, 16), pm, p20, pm, p19 (23, 27, 31, 35, 39), k1.

ROW 1: K to marker, sm, work BL, sm, k to next marker, sm, work BLM, sm, k to end.

ROW 2: K1, p to last st, k1.

ROWS 3–55 (59, 63, 67, 71, 75): Cont in patt as est and AT THE SAME TIME, work inc row as foll:

SIZE S ONLY: *Rows 8, 14, 22, 28, 36, 42, 50 (alternate between every 8th and 6th row, 7 times)—100 sts.*

SIZE M ONLY: *Rows 8, 14, 22, 28, 36, 42, 50, 56 (alternate between every 8th and 6th row, 8 times)—112 sts.*

SIZE L ONLY: *Rows 6, 12, 18, 24, 30, 36, 42, 48, 54 (every 6th row, 9 times)—124 sts.*

SIZE XL ONLY: *Rows 6, 12, 18, 24, 30, 36, 42, 48, 54, 60 (every 6th row, 10 times)—136 sts.*

SIZE XXL ONLY: *Rows 6, 12, 18, 24, 30, 36, 42, 48, 54, 60, 66 (every 6th row, 11 times)—148 sts.*

SIZE XXXL ONLY: *Rows 6, 12, 18, 24, 30, 36, 42, 48, 54, 60, 66, 72 (every 6th row, 12 times)—160 sts.*

INC ROW (RS): Work as row 1 to 2nd marker, sm, k2, yo, knit to 2 sts before next marker, yo, k2, sm, work as row 1 from 3rd marker to end.

SHOULDER AND NECK SHAPING

ROW 1 (WS): P to last 3 (3, 3, 4, 4, 4) sts, W&T.

ROW 2: Work in patt as est to last 3 (3, 3, 4, 4, 4) sts, W&T.

ROW 3: P to 3 (3, 4, 4, 5, 5) sts from last wrapped st, W&T.

ROW 4: Work in patt as est to 3 (3, 4, 4, 5, 5) sts from last wrapped st, W&T.

ROW 5: P to 3 (4, 4, 5, 5, 6) sts from last wrapped st, W&T.

ROW 6: Work in patt as est to 3 (4, 4, 5, 5, 6) sts from last wrapped st, W&T.

ROW 7: P to 3 (4, 5, 5, 6, 6) sts from last wrapped st, W&T.

ROW 8: Work 30 (34, 38, 42, 46, 51) sts in patt as est; join 2nd ball of yarn for right shoulder by k2 with both strands and drop new strand, work 12 sts in patt as est for back neck, cont in patt as est to 3 (4, 5, 5, 6, 6) sts from last wrapped st, W&T—32 (36, 40, 44, 48, 53) sts each shoulder.

LEFT SHOULDER AND NECK SHAPING

ROW 1 (WS): P32 (36, 40, 44, 48, 53), W&T.

ROW 2: Work in patt as est to 3 (4, 5, 5, 6, 8) sts from last wrapped st, W&T.

ROW 3: P to 1 (2, 2, 3, 3, 3) sts from last wrapped st, W&T.

ROW 4: Work in patt as est to 3 (4, 5, 6, 6, 6) sts from last wrapped st, W&T.

ROW 5: P to 1 (1, 2, 2, 2, 2) sts from last wrapped st, W&T.

ROW 6: Work in patt as est to 5 (5, 6, 6, 7, 7) sts from last wrapped st, W&T.

ROW 7: P to 1 (1, 1, 1, 2, 2) sts from last wrapped st, W&T.

ROW 8: K to 6 (6, 6, 6, 7, 7) sts from last wrapped st, W&T.

ROW 9: P to 1 st from last wrapped st, W&T.

ROW 10: K5 (6, 6, 7, 7, 9), W&T.

Break yarn and place 40 (45, 50, 55, 60, 65) left shoulder sts onto 1 stitch holder; place 15 (16, 17, 18, 19, 20) center neck sts onto 2nd holder, leaving 1 st on LH needle. With RS facing and 2nd ball of yarn, W&T around next st on the LH needle and move wrapped st to 2nd holder with neck sts.

RIGHT SHOULDER AND NECK SHAPING

With WS facing, work with yarn from 2nd ball of yarn.

ROW 1: P to 3 (4, 5, 5, 6, 8) sts from last wrapped st, W&T.

ROW 2: Work 28 (30, 33, 36, 39, 42) sts in patt as est, W&T.

ROW 3: P to 3 (4, 5, 6, 6, 6) sts from last wrapped st, W&T.

ROW 4: Work in patt as est to 1 (1, 2, 2, 2, 2) sts from last wrapped st, W&T.

ROW 5: P to 5 (5, 6, 6, 7, 7) sts from last wrapped st, W&T.

ROW 6: Work in patt as est to 1 (1, 1, 1, 2, 2) sts from last wrapped st, W&T.

ROW 7: P to 6 (6, 6, 6, 7, 7) sts from last wrapped st, W&T.

ROW 8: K to 1 st from last wrapped st, W&T.

ROW 9: P5 (6, 6, 7, 7, 9).

Break yarn.

FRONTS

With medium-size needles, CO 10 (10, 12, 12, 14, 14) sts for **Right Front (RF)**. With a 2nd ball of yarn, CO 10 (10, 12, 12, 14, 14) sts onto same needle for **Left Front (LF)**. Work both fronts at the same time, adding sts using backward loop CO method (page 88) where indicated.

ROW 1 (RS): LF/RF—Knit.

ROW 2: RF—K1, p to last st, sl 1, CO 4 (5, 5, 6, 6, 6) sts. LF—K1, p to last st, k1.

ROW 3: LF—K to last st, sl 1, CO 4 (5, 5, 6, 6, 6) sts. RF—Knit.

ROW 4: RF—K1, p to last st, sl 1, CO 2 (3, 4, 5, 5, 5) sts. LF—K1, p to last st, k1.

ROW 5: LF—K to last st, sl 1, CO 2 (3, 4, 5, 5, 5) sts. RF—Knit.

ROW 6: RF—K1, p to last st, sl 1, CO 2 (2, 3, 3, 4, 5) sts. LF—K1, p to last st, k1.

ROW 7: LF—K2, m1, k to last st, sl 1, CO 2 (2, 3, 3, 4, 5) sts. RF—K to last 2 sts, m1, k2.

ROW 8: RF—K1, p to last st, sl 1, CO 1 (2, 2, 2, 3, 4) sts. LF—K1, p to last 2 (2, 3, 4, 5, 6) sts, pm, p to last st, k1.

ROW 9: LF—K to marker, sm, k6, ssp, k2, yo, k to last st, sl 1, CO 1 (2, 2, 2, 3, 4) sts. RF—K8 (11, 14, 15, 18, 19), yo, k2, p2tog, k6, pm, k to end.

ROW 10: RF—K1, p to last st, sl 1, CO 1 (2, 2, 2, 2, 3) sts. LF—K1, p to last st, k1.

ROW 11: LF—K to marker, sm, m1, k5, ssp, k2, yo, k to last st, sl 1, CO 1 (2, 2, 2, 2, 3) sts. RF—K10 (14, 17, 18, 21, 23), yo, k2, p2tog, k5, m1, sm, k to end—22 (26, 30, 32, 36, 39) sts each side.

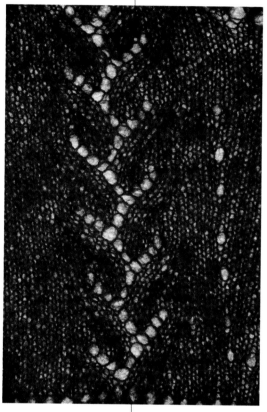

ROW 12: RF—K1, p to last st, sl 1, CO 1 (1, 1, 2, 2, 2) sts. LF—K1, p to last st, k1.

ROW 13: LF—K to marker, sm, k5, ssp, k2, yo, k to last st, sl 1, CO 1 (1, 1, 2, 2, 2) sts. RF—K12 (16, 19, 21, 24, 26), yo, k2, p2tog, k to end.

ROW 14: RF—K1, p to last st, sl 1, CO 1 (1, 1, 2, 2, 2) sts. LF—K1, p to last st, k1.

ROW 15: LF—K to marker, m1, sm, work BL (row 9), pm, k to last st, sl 1, CO 1 (1, 1, 2, 2, 2) sts. RF—K2 (6, 9, 12, 15, 17), pm, work BLM (row 9), sm, m1, k to end.

ROWS 16, 20, 24, 28, 30, 32, 36, 38, 42, 44, 48, 50 AND 52 (WORK EVEN ROWS): RF/LF—K1, p to last st, k1.

ROWS 17, 21, 31 AND 37: LF—K to marker, m1, sm, work BL, sm, k to end. RF—K to marker, sm, work BLM, sm, m1, k to end.

ROW 18: RF—K1, p to last st, sl 1, CO 1 (1, 1, 1, 1, 2) sts. LF—K1, p to last st, k1.

ROW 19: LF—K to marker, sm, work BL, sm, k to last st, sl 1, CO 1 (1, 1, 1, 1, 2) sts. RF—K to marker, sm, work BLM, sm, k to end.

ROWS 22, 26, 34, 40, 46 AND 54: RF—K1, p to last st, sl 1, CO 1 st. LF—K1, p to last st, k1.

ROWS 23, 35 AND 55: LF—K to marker, sm, work BL, sm, k to last st, sl 1, CO 1 st. RF—K to marker, sm, work BLM, sm, k to end.

ROWS 25, 29, 33, 39, 43, 45, 49 AND 53 (WORK EVEN ROWS): LF—K to marker, sm, work BL, sm, k to end. RF—K to marker, sm, work BLM, sm, k to end.

ROWS 27, 41 AND 47: LF—K to marker, m1, sm, work BL,

sm, k to last st, sl 1, CO 1 st. RF—K to marker, sm, work BLM, sm, m1, k to end.

ROW 51: LF—K to marker, m0 (1, 1, 1, 1, 1), sm, work BL, sm, k to end. RF—K to marker, sm, work BLM, sm, m0 (1, 1, 1, 1, 1), k to end.

ROW 56: RF/LF—K1, p to last st, k1—39 (44, 48, 52, 56, 60) sts each side.

CONTINUE FOR SIZES M (L, XL, XXL, XXXL) ONLY

ROW 57: LF—K to marker, m0 (1, 1, 1, 1), sm, work BL, sm, k to end. RF—K to marker, sm, work BLM, sm, m0 (1, 1, 1, 1), k to end.

ROW 58: RF/LF—K1, p to last st, k1.

ROW 59: LF—K to marker, sm, work BL, sm, k to end. RF—K to marker, sm, work BLM, sm, k to end.

ROW 60: RF/LF—K1, p to last st, k1—44 (49, 53, 57, 61) sts each side.

CONTINUE FOR SIZES L (XL, XXL, XXXL) ONLY

ROW 61: LF—K to marker, m0 (1, 1, 1), sm, work BL, sm, k to end. RF—K to marker, sm, work BLM, sm, m0 (1, 1, 1), k to end.

ROW 62: RF/LF—K1, p to last st, k1.

ROW 63: LF—K to marker, sm, work BL, sm, k to end. RF—K to marker, sm, work BLM, sm, k to end.

ROW 64: RF/LF—K1, p to last st, k1—49 (54, 58, 62) sts each side.

CONTINUE FOR SIZES XL (XXL, XXXL) ONLY

ROW 65: LF—K to marker, sm, work BL, sm, k to end. RF—K to marker, sm, work BLM, sm, k to end.

ROW 66: RF/LF—K1, p to last st, k1.

ROW 67: LF—K to marker, m0 (1, 1), sm, work BL, sm, k to end. RF—K to marker, sm, work BLM, sm, m0 (1, 1), k to end.

ROW 68: RF/LF—K1, p to last st, k1—54 (59, 63) sts each side.

CONTINUE FOR SIZES XXL (XXXL) ONLY

ROW 69: LF—K to marker, sm, work BL, sm, k to end. RF—K to marker, sm, work BLM, sm, k to end.

ROW 70: RF/LF—K1, p to last st, k1.

ROW 71: LF—K to marker, m0 (1), sm, work BL, sm, k to end. RF—K to marker, sm, work BLM, sm, m0 (1), k to end.

ROW 72: RF/LF—K1, p to last st, k1—59 (64) sts each side.

CONTINUE FOR XXXL ONLY

ROW 73: LF—K to marker, sm, work BL, sm, k to end. RF—K to marker, sm, work BLM, sm, k to end.

ROW 74: RF/LF—K1, p to last st, k1.

ROW 75: LF—K to marker, sm, work BL, sm, k to end. RF—K to marker, sm, work BLM, sm, k to end.

ROW 76: RF/LF—K1, p to last st, k1—64 sts each side.

SHOULDER SHAPING

ROW 1 (RS): LF—Work in patt as est. RF—Work in patt as est to last 3 (3, 3, 4, 4, 4) sts, W&T.

ROW 2: RF—P to last st, k1. LF—K1, p to last 3 (3, 3, 4, 4, 4) sts, W&T.

ROW 3: LF—Work in patt as est. RF—Work in patt as est to 3 (3, 4, 4, 5, 5) sts before last wrapped st, W&T.

ROW 4: RF—P to last st, k1. LF—K1, p to 3 (3, 4, 4, 5, 5) sts before last wrapped st, W&T.

ROW 5: LF—Work in patt as est. RF—Work in patt as est to 3 (4, 4, 5, 5, 6) sts before last wrapped st, W&T.

ROW 6: RF—P to last st, sl 1, CO 1 st. LF—K1, p to 3 (4, 4, 5, 5, 6) sts before last wrapped st, W&T.

ROW 7: LF—Work in patt as est to last st, sl 1, CO 1 st. RF—Work in patt as est to 3 (4, 5, 5, 6, 6) sts before last wrapped st, W&T.

ROW 8: RF—P to last st, k1. LF—K1, p to 3 (4, 5, 5, 6, 6) sts before last wrapped st, W&T.

ROW 9: LF—Work in patt as est. RF—Work in patt as est to 3 (4, 5, 5, 6, 7) sts before last wrapped st, W&T.

ROW 10: RF—P to last st, sl 1, CO 1 st. LF—K1, p to 3 (4, 5, 5, 6, 7) sts before last wrapped st, W&T.

ROW 11: LF—Work in patt as est to last st, sl 1, CO 1 st. RF—Work in patt as est to 3 (4, 5, 6, 6, 7) sts before last wrapped st, W&T.

ROW 12: RF—P to last st, k1. LF—Work in patt as est to 3 (4, 5, 6, 6, 7) sts before last wrapped st, W&T.

ROW 13: LF—Knit. RF—K to 5 (5, 5, 6, 7, 8) sts before last wrapped st, W&T.

ROW 14: RF—P to last st, sl 1, CO 1 st. LF—K1, p to 5 (5, 5, 6, 7, 8) sts before last wrapped st, W&T.

ROW 15: LF—K to last st, sl 1, CO 1 st. RF—K to 6 (6, 6, 7, 7, 8) sts before last wrapped st, W&T.

ROW 16: RF—P to last st, k1. LF—K1, p to 6 (6, 6, 7, 7, 8) sts before last wrapped st, W&T.

ROW 17: LF—Knit.

Do not break off yarn.

FINISHING

Join fronts to back at shoulder using 3-needle BO (page 103) starting at neck edge.

FRONT AND NECK EDGING

With RS facing and largest needle, starting at lower right front, PU and k89 (97, 108, 116, 124, 135) sts to neck, k20 (22, 24, 26, 28, 30) neck sts, then PU and k89 (97, 108, 116, 124, 135) sts along the left front edge—198 (216, 240, 258, 276, 300) sts.

K 1 WS row. Change to medium-size needle.

Work 13 rows of Twisted Border in reverse, beg with row 13 and end with row 1.

Change to smallest needle.

INC ROW (WS): K0 (3, 2, 0, 3, 2), m0 (1, 1, 0, 1, 1), *k2, m1, k3, m1; rep from * to last 3 sts, k2, m0 (1, 1, 0, 1, 1), k1—276 (302, 336, 360, 386, 420) sts.

Work in Twisted Rib for 2", beg with row 2 (RS).

BO loosely in k1, p1 rib.

Sew side seams along Twisted Rib and Twisted Border sections of fronts and back.

Weave in ends. Hand wash and lay flat to shape.

ABOUT ALYSSA My mother taught my two sisters and me to knit when we were kids. In 2005 my sister Kristen opened a yarn store, Modern Yarn, in Montclair, New Jersey, and I began knitting samples, custom projects, and original patterns for the store. Check out my work at www.theswatch.com, as well as on www.modernyarn.com. In the nonyarn world, I am getting my master's degree in public health at Johns Hopkins University and plan to return to medical school when I finish. I live in Baltimore with my fiancé and beautiful son (both of whom have worn many of my designs), as well as a dog and a cat (who have not donned my knits and never will).

THE EMPIRE STRIKES BACK DRESS

 s someone who is equal parts history buff, color addict, and fashion junkie, I came up with this design after thinking about how the French reinterpreted classical Greek and Roman costume in the early nineteenth century. I loved the long, loose silhouette and empire waist of those dresses, and I wanted to revamp that idea. So I chose feminine details that give a nod to the latter period, like short sleeves, a generous neckline, and a touch of lacy detail, but I gave the design a modern spin with a superbold color and a sizeable gauge. It's a pretty easy knit, and the silhouette is really flattering and versatile. For a punchy look, I wear mine with a tank or tunic dress in a contrasting color underneath.

STITCH PATTERN
LACE PANEL (OVER 17 STS)

ROW 1 AND ALL WS ROWS: K2, p to last 2 sts, k2.

ROW 2: P2, [k1, yo] twice, sk2p, k3, k3tog, [yo, k1] twice, p2.

ROW 4: P2, k1, yo, k3, yo, ssk, k1, k2tog, yo, k3, yo, k1, p2—19 sts.

ROW 6: P2, k1, yo, ssk, k1, k2tog, yo, sk2p, yo, ssk, k1, k2tog, yo, k1, p2—17 sts.

ROW 8: P2, k1, [yo, ssk, k1, k2tog, yo, k1] twice, p2.

ROW 10: Rep row 8.

Rep rows 1–10 for patt.

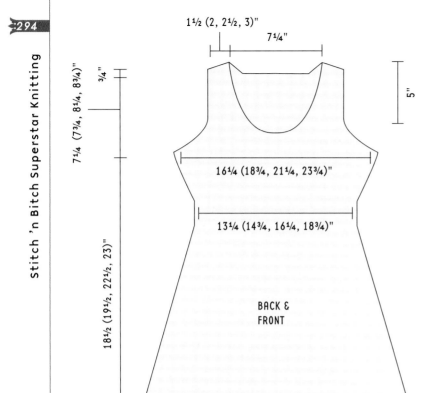

1½ (2, 2½, 3)"

7¼"

7¼ (7¾, 8¼, 8¾)"

¾"

5"

16¼ (18¾, 21¼, 23¾)"

13¼ (14¾, 16¼, 18¾)"

18½ (19½, 22½, 23)"

BACK &
FRONT

21¾ (24¼, 26¾, 29¼)"

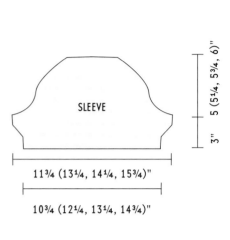

SLEEVE

5 (5¼, 5¾, 6)"

3"

11¾ (13¼, 14¼, 15¾)"

10¾ (12¼, 13¼, 14¾)"

DIRECTIONS

BACK

With larger needle, CO 87 (97, 107, 117) sts. Work 7 rows in k1, p1 rib. Work 3 rows in St st, beg with a p row.

DEC ROW (RS): K2, ssk, k to last 4 sts, k2tog, k2.

Cont in St st, rep dec row every 4th row 16 (18, 20, 20) times more—53 (59, 65, 75) sts.

Change to smaller needle, and work 7 rows in k1, p1 rib, beg with p1 on WS row.

Change to larger needle and work 3 rows in St st.

NEXT ROW (WS): P12 (14, 16, 20), pm, p1, pm, p27 (29, 31, 33), pm, p1, pm, p12 (14, 16, 20).

INC ROW (RS): K to first marker, yo, sm, k1, sm, yo, k to next marker, yo, sm, k1, sm, yo, k to end.

Rep inc row every 4th row 2 (3, 4, 4) times more—65 (75, 85, 95) sts.

Work 7 (5, 5, 7) rows in St st.

ARMHOLE SHAPING

BO 3 (4, 5, 6) sts at beg of next 2 rows; BO 3 sts at beg of foll 2 rows; BO 2 sts at beg of next 4 (6, 8, 10) rows; then BO 1 st at beg of foll 4 rows—41 (45, 49, 53) sts.

Cont even in St st until armhole meas 5 (5½, 6, 6½)", end with a WS row.

NECK AND SHOULDER SHAPING

K12 (14, 16, 18) and place these sts onto a holder, BO next 17 sts, k to end.

Lace Panel

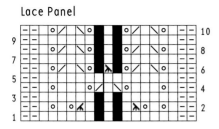

- ☐ K on RS, P on WS
- ⊟ P on RS, K on WS
- ⊘ K2tog
- ◩ Ssk
- ◉ Yo
- ◪ Sk2p
- ◪ K3tog
- ■ No stitch

LEFT SHOULDER

ROWS 1, 3, 5, 7 AND 9 (WS): Purl.

ROW 2: BO 2 sts, k to end.

ROWS 4, 6, 8 AND 10: K1, ssk, k to end.

ROW 11: BO 3 (4, 5, 6) sts, p to end.

ROW 12: Knit.

BO rem 3 (4, 5, 6) sts.

RIGHT SHOULDER

With RS facing, join yarn.

ROW 1 (RS): Knit.

ROW 2: BO 2 sts, p to end.

ROWS 3, 5, 7 AND 9: K to last 3 sts, k2tog, k1.

ROW 4 AND ALL WS ROWS: Purl.

ROW 11: BO 3 (4, 5, 6) sts, k to end.

ROW 12: Purl.

BO rem 3 (4, 5, 6) sts.

FRONT

With larger needle, CO 87 (97, 107, 117) sts. Work 7 rows in k1, p1 rib.

SET-UP ROW (WS): P35 (40, 45, 50), work row 1 of Lace panel over next 17 sts, p35 (40, 45, 50).

NEXT ROW: K35 (40, 45, 50), work row 2 of Lace panel, k35 (40, 45, 50).

NEXT ROW: P35 (40, 45, 50), work row 3 of Lace panel, k35 (40, 45, 50).

DEC ROW: K2, ssk, work in patt as est to last 4 sts, k2tog, k2.

Cont in patt as est, rep dec row every 4th row 16 (18, 20, 20) times more—53 (59, 65, 75) sts.

Change to smaller needle, and work 7 rows in k1, p1 rib beg with p1 on WS row.

Change to larger needle and work 3 rows in patt as est before rib.

NEXT ROW (WS): P12 (14, 16, 20), pm, p1, pm, work 27 (29, 31, 33) sts in patt as est, pm, p1, pm, p12 (14, 16, 20).

INC ROW (RS): K to first marker, yo, sm, k1, sm, yo, work in patt as est to next marker, yo, sm, k1, sm, yo, k to end.

Rep inc row every 4th row 2 (3, 4, 4) times more—65 (75, 85, 95) sts.

Work 7 (5, 5, 7) rows in patt as est.

ARMHOLE SHAPING

Cont in patt as est, work armholes same as for back until armhole meas 2¼ (2¾, 3¼, 3¾)", end with row 2, 6, 8 or 10 of Lace Panel—41 (45, 49, 53) sts.

NECK AND SHOULDER SHAPING

NEXT ROW (RS): K12 (14, 16, 18), p2, place these sts onto holder, BO next 13 sts, p2, k to end—14 (16, 18, 20) sts each side.

RIGHT SIDE

ROW 1 AND ALL WS ROWS: Purl.

ROW 2: BO 2 sts, k to end.

ROWS 4, 6, 8, 10, 12 AND 14: K1, k2tog, k to end.

ROWS 15–24: Work in St st.

ROW 25: BO 3 (4, 5, 6) sts, p to end.

ROW 26: Knit.

BO rem 3 (4, 5, 6) sts.

LEFT SIDE

With RS facing, join yarn.

ROW 1 (RS): Knit.

ROW 2: BO 2 sts, p to end.

ROWS 3, 5, 7, 9, 11 AND 13: K to last 3 sts, ssk, k1.

ROW 4 AND ALL WS ROWS: Purl.

ROWS 15–24: Work in St st.

ROW 25: BO 3 (4, 5, 6) sts, k to end.

ROW 26: Purl.

BO rem 3 (4, 5, 6) sts.

SLEEVES

With larger needle, CO 43 (49, 53, 59) sts. Work 5 rows in k1, p1 rib.

SET-UP ROW (RS): K21 (24, 26, 29), pm, k1, pm, k21 (24, 26, 29).

Work 2 rows in St st.

INC ROW (RS): K to first marker, yo, sm, k1, sm, yo, k to end.

Cont in St st, rep inc row every 4th row once more—47 (53, 57, 63) sts.

Work even in St st until sleeve meas 3" from beg.

CAP SHAPING

BO 3 (4, 5, 6) sts at beg of next 2 rows; BO 3 sts at beg of foll 2 rows; BO 2 sts at beg of next 2 rows —31 (35, 37, 41) sts.

DEC ROW (RS): K1, ssk, k to last 3 sts, k2tog, k1.

Rep dec row every RS row 8 (9, 10, 11) times more —13 (15, 15, 17) sts.

BO.

FINISHING

Block pieces. Sew shoulder seams. Set sleeves into armholes. Sew side and sleeve seams.

NECKBAND

Starting at center back neck with smaller circular needle, PU and k62 sts evenly around neck opening. Pm and join. Work 7 rnds in k1, p1 rib. BO in rib.

· ·

ABOUT TRICIA I am a thirty-five-year-old freelance fashion writer and designer who lives in Greenwich, Connecticut. I founded the popular online DIY street fashion community, Wardrobe_Remix, www.wardroberemix.com, and maintain a blog at www.bitsandbobbins.com. When I'm not obsessively knitting, crocheting, or sewing, I can be found cavorting with my tortie cat, Leela, my software architect husband, Peter, and our two-year-old daughter, Poppy.

· ·

Lien Ngo

NIP/TUCK

SIZE

XS (S, M, L)

Finished bust: 26¾ (32, 37¼, 42¾)"

Finished length: 22¾ (23¾, 25, 25¾)"

MATERIALS

Rowan *Bamboo Soft* (100% bamboo; 50g/112 yd), 6 (7, 8, 9) skeins black

US 3 (3mm) 24" circular needle

4 (4, 5, 5) ½" buttons

4 stitch holders

Stitch markers

Size C (3mm) crochet hook

2 cable needles

Tapestry needle

GAUGE

24 sts and 35 rows = 4" in Diamond Lace patt

In Diamond Lace patt: 2.9" width and 2.25" height = 1 patt repeat, blocked

n Hong Kong, I noticed lots of office ladies and businesswomen wearing snappy little sweaters with a cute bib detail. I started thinking about how I could make a knit bib. I use pin tucks here because they are a tailoring detail I've always loved—totally feminine but never fussy—but it took a while to translate pin tucks in knitting. I decided a very simple line of twisted knit stitches on a purl background was the way to go. Since this is essentially just a twisted rib, it shapes easily as an insert into the tee. Save yourself time with this pattern by knitting a large swatch and hanging it up before determining your gauge. The superflattering bamboo yarn tends to stretch a bit, so take that into consideration as you stitch.

SPECIAL ABBREVIATIONS

W&T (WRAP AND TURN): On RS, bring yarn between needles to front, sl next st onto RH needle, bring yarn between needles to back, return sl st to LH needle, turn.

On WS, bring yarn between needles to back, sl next st onto RH needle, bring yarn between needles to front, return sl st to LH needle, turn.

CT (CENTER TWIST): Sl 1 to RH needle, sl 1 onto cn and hold in front, sl 1 onto 2nd cn and hold in back, sl st on RH needle back to LH needle, k2tog, yo, k1 from cn in back, yo, sl st on cn in front back to LH needle, ssk.

SPECIAL STITCHES

TWISTED RIB (MULTIPLE OF 4 STS)

RND 1: *P3, k1 tbl; rep from * to end.

Rep rnd 1 for patt.

DIAMOND LACE (MULTIPLE OF 16 STS)

ROW 1 (RS): *K2, yo, ssk, k9, k2tog, yo, k1; rep from * to end.

ROW 2 AND ALL EVEN-NUMBERED ROWS: K on RS, p on WS.

ROW 3: *K3, yo, ssk, k7, k2tog, yo, k2; rep from * to end.

ROW 5: *K4, yo, ssk, k5, k2tog, yo, k3; rep from * to end.

ROW 7: *K5, yo, ssk, k3, k2tog, yo, k4; rep from * to end.

ROW 9: *K6, yo, ssk, k1, k2tog, yo, k5; rep from * to end.

ROW 11: *K6, CT (page 297), k5; rep from * to end.

ROW 13: *K5, k2tog, yo, k3, yo, ssk, k4; rep from * to end.

ROW 15: *K4, k2tog, yo, k5, yo, ssk, k3; rep from * to end.

ROW 17: *K3, k2tog, yo, k7, yo, ssk, k2; rep from * to end.

ROW 19: *K2, k2tog, yo, k9, yo, ssk, k1; rep from * to end.

ROW 20: K on RS, p on WS.

Rep rows 1–20 for patt.

DIRECTIONS

Construction Note: This tee is knit in one piece from the bottom up to the underarm and then worked back and forth. The bib is picked up and knit after the body is finished. The cap sleeves are picked up and knit down. Bib and cap sleeves are shaped by short rows.

BODY

CO 80 (96, 112, 128) sts, pm, CO 80 (96, 112, 128) sts—160 (192, 224, 256) sts. Pm and join.

Work 6 rnds in Twisted Rib.

Work in Diamond Lace patt until body meas 2½ (3, 3, 3½)" from beg.

DEC RND: *K1, k2tog, work to 2 sts before marker, ssk; rep from * once more.

Cont in patt as est, rep dec rnd every 6th rnd 6 times more—132 (164, 196, 228) sts.

Work even in patt as est for 2".

INC RND: *K1, m1, work to marker, m1; rep from * once more.

Cont in patt as est, rep inc rnd every 6th rnd 6 times more—160 (192, 224, 256) sts.

Work even in patt until body meas 16½ (17, 17, 17½)" from beg. Remove marker, k1, pm for beg of back—79 (95, 111, 127) back sts, 81 (97, 113, 129) front sts.

ARMHOLE SHAPING FOR BACK

ROW 1: Work in patt to 4 (4, 5, 6) sts from marker, W&T.

ROW 2 (WS): P to 4 (4, 5, 6) sts from marker, W&T.

ROW 3: Work in patt to 7 (7, 9, 9) sts from marker, W&T.

ROW 4: P to 7 (7, 9, 9) sts from marker, W&T.

ROW 5: Work in patt to 8 (9, 11, 12) sts from marker, W&T.

ROW 6: P to 8 (9, 11, 12) sts from marker, W&T.

Sizes M and L only
ROW 7: Work in patt to - (-, 12, 14) sts from marker, W&T.

ROW 8: P to - (-, 12, 14) sts from marker, W&T.

ROW 9: Work in patt to - (-, 13, 15) sts from marker, W&T.

ROW 10: P to - (-, 13, 15) sts from marker, W&T.

All sizes
ROW 7 (7, 11, 11): Work in patt to wrapped st, lift wrap and k tog with wrapped st, k to end, lifting wraps and k tog with wrapped sts.

ROW 8 (8, 12, 12): BO 8 (9, 13, 15) sts, p to end, lifting wraps and p tog with wrapped sts.

ROW 9 (9, 13, 13): BO 8 (9, 13, 15) sts, work in patt to end—63 (77, 85, 97) back sts.

Cont in patt as est on 63 (77, 85, 97) back sts until armhole meas 6¼ (6¾, 8, 8¼)", end with a WS row.

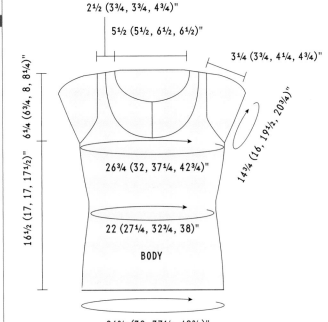

2½ (3¾, 3¾, 4¾)"

5½ (5½, 6½, 6½)"

3¼ (3¾, 4¼, 4¾)"

6¼ (6¾, 8, 8¼)"

14¾ (16, 19½, 20¾)"

16½ (17, 17, 17½)"

26¾ (32, 37¼, 42¾)"

22 (27¼, 32¾, 38)"

BODY

26¾ (32, 37¼, 42¾)"

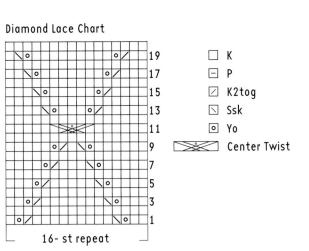

Diamond Lace Chart

19
17
15
13
11
9
7
5
3
1

16- st repeat

☐ K
⊟ P
☑ K2tog
◹ Ssk
⊡ Yo
▧ Center Twist

NEXT ROW (RS): Work 15 (22, 23, 29) sts in patt, BO center 33 (33, 39, 39) sts, work in patt to end—15 (22, 23, 29) sts each side. Place both sets of sts onto holders.

BIB OPENING AND ARMHOLE SHAPING FOR LEFT FRONT

Mark center st of front—40 (48, 56, 64) sts on either side of marked st. With RS facing, attach yarn to left front.

ROW 1: Work in patt to 8 sts before marked st, W&T.

ROW 2 (WS): P to last 4 (4, 5, 6) sts, W&T.

ROW 3: Work in patt to 13 sts before marked st, W&T.

ROW 4: P to last 7 (7, 9, 9) sts, W&T.

ROW 5: Work in patt to 17 sts before marked st, W&T.

ROW 6: P to last 8 (9, 11, 12) sts, W&T.

ROW 7: Work in patt to 19 (19, 21, 21) sts before marked st, W&T.

Sizes XS and S only (cont on sts of Left Front)
ROW 8: P to end, lifting wraps and p tog with wrapped sts.

ROW 9: BO 8 (9, -, -) sts, work in patt to last 21 sts, W&T.

ROWS 10, 12 AND 14: Purl.

ROW 11: Work in patt to last 22 sts, W&T.

ROW 13: Work in patt to last 23 sts, W&T.

ROW 15: Work in patt to first wrapped st, k to end (including marked st), lifting wraps and k tog with wrapped sts.

ROW 16: BO 25 sts, p to end—8 (15, -, -) sts.

Cont in patt until armhole meas 6¼ (6¾, -. -)".

Sizes M and L only (cont on sts of Left Front)
ROW 8: P to last - (-, 12, 14) sts, W&T.

ROW 9: Work in patt to last - (-, 25, 25) sts, W&T.

ROW 10: P to last - (-, 13, 15) sts, W&T.

ROW 11: Work in patt to last - (-, 29, 29) sts, W&T.

ROW 12: P to end, lifting wraps and p tog with wrapped sts.

ROW 13: BO - (-, 13, 15) sts, work in patt to last - (-, 30, 30) sts, W&T.

ROW 14: Purl.

ROW 15: Work in patt to last 31 sts, W&T.

ROW 16: Purl.

ROW 17: Work in patt to wrapped st, lift wrap and k tog with wrapped st, k to end (including marked st), lifting wraps and k tog with wrapped sts.

ROW 18: BO 32 sts, p to end.

Cont in patt on - (-, 12, 18) sts until armhole meas - (-, 8, 8¼)".

For all sizes
Place 8 (15, 12, 18) shoulder sts onto holder. Break yarn.

BIB OPENING AND ARMHOLE SHAPING FOR RIGHT FRONT

With RS facing, attach yarn to right front sts.

ROW 1 (RS): M1, work in patt to last 4 (4, 5, 6) sts, W&T.

ROW 2: P to last 9 sts, W&T.

ROW 3: Work in patt to last 7 (7, 9, 9) sts, W&T.

ROW 4: P to last 14 sts, W&T.

ROW 5: Work in patt to last 8 (9, 11, 12) sts, W&T.

ROW 6: P to last 18 sts, W&T.

Sizes XS and S only
ROW 7: Work in patt to wrapped st, lift wrap and k tog with wrapped st, k to end, lifting wraps and k tog with wrapped sts.

ROW 8: BO 8 (9, -, -) sts, p to last 20 sts, W&T.

ROWS 9, 11, 13 AND 15: Work in patt to end.

ROW 10: P to last 22 sts, W&T.

ROW 12: P to last 23 sts, W&T.

ROW 14: P to last 24 sts, W&T.

ROW 16: P to end, lifting wraps and p tog with wrapped sts.

ROW 17: BO 25 sts, work in patt to end.

Cont in patt on 8 (15, -, -) sts until armhole meas 6¼ (6¾, -,-)".

Sizes M and L only
ROW 7: Work in patt to last - (-, 12, 14) sts, W&T.

ROW 8: P to last - (-, 22, 22) sts, W&T.

ROW 9: Work in patt to last - (-, 13, 15) sts, W&T.

ROW 10: P to last - (-, 26, 26) sts, W&T.

ROW 11: Work in patt to wrapped st, lift wrap and k tog with wrapped st, k to end, lifting wraps and k tog with wrapped sts.

ROW 12: BO - (-, 13, 15) sts, p to last - (-, 30, 30) sts, W&T.

ROW 13: Work in patt to end.

ROW 14: P to last 31 sts, W&T.

ROWS 15 AND 17: Work in patt to end.

ROW 16: P to last 32 sts, W&T.

ROW 18: Purl to end, lifting wraps and p tog with wrapped sts.

ROW 19: BO 32 sts, work in patt to end. Cont in patt on - (-, 12, 18) sts until armhole meas - (-, 8, 8¼)".

For all sizes
Place 8 (15, 12, 18) shoulder sts onto holder. Break yarn.

LEFT FRONT BIB

With RS facing, start at left front shoulder, PU and k 1 st for every 2 rows along the vertical edge, and 27 (27, 35, 35) sts evenly across the front curve to the center for bib.

ROW 1 (WS): K3 (3, 4, 4), p1 tbl, k4, p1 tbl, k1 (1, 0, 0), turn.

ROW 2: P1 (1, 0, 0), k1 tbl, p4, k1 tbl, p3 (3, 4, 4), turn.

ROW 3: K3 (3, 4, 4), p1 tbl, [k4, p1 tbl] twice, k1 (1, 0, 0), turn.

ROW 4: P1 (1, 0, 0), [k1 tbl, p4] twice, k1 tbl, p3 (3, 4, 4), turn.

ROW 5: K3 (3, 4, 4), p1 tbl, [k4, p1 tbl] 3 times, k1 (1, 0, 0), turn.

ROW 6: P1 (1, 0, 0), [k1 tbl, p4] 3 times, k1 tbl, p3 (3, 4, 4), turn.

ROW 7: K3 (3, 4, 4), p1 tbl, [k4, p1 tbl] 3 (3, 4, 4) times, k4 (4, 0, 0), turn.

ROW 8: P4 (4, 0, 0), [k1 tbl, p4] 3 (3, 4, 4) times, k1 tbl, p3 (3, 4, 4), turn.

ROW 9: K3 (3, 4, 4), p1 tbl, [k4, p1 tbl] 4 times, k1 (1, 3, 3), turn.

ROW 10: P1 (1, 3, 3), [k1 tbl, p4] 4 times, k1 tbl, p3 (3, 4, 4), turn.

ROW 11: K3 (3, 4, 4), p1 tbl, [k4, p1 tbl] 4 (4, 5, 5) times, k3 (3, 1, 1), turn.

ROW 12: P3 (3, 1, 1), [k1 tbl, p4] 4 (4, 5, 5) times, k1 tbl, p3 (3, 4, 4), turn.

Sizes M and L only
ROW 13: [K4, p1 tbl] 6 times, k3, turn.

ROW 14: P3, [k1 tbl, p4] 6 times, turn.

ROW 15: [K4, p1 tbl] 6 times, k5, turn.

ROW 16: P5, [k1 tbl, p4] 6 times, turn.

All sizes
NEXT ROW (WS): Work in patt as est to last st of bib, ssk last st tog with next vertical st.

NEXT ROW: Work in patt as est to end.

Rep last 2 rows until 9 (9, 11, 12) vertical sts rem, end with a WS row.

LEFT NECK SHAPING

ROW 1 (RS): Work in patt to last 10 sts, W&T.

ROWS 2, 4, 6 AND 8: Work in patt as est to last bib st, ssk next st tog with next vertical st.

ROW 3: Work in patt to last 15 sts, W&T.

ROW 5: Work in patt to last 18 (18, 20, 20) sts, W&T.

ROW 7: Work in patt to last - (-, 22, 22) sts, W&T.

ROW 9: Work in patt to end, lifting wraps and work tog with wrapped sts.

ROW 10: BO 18 (18, 22, 22) sts, work in patt to last bib st, ssk next st tog with next vertical st—9 (9, 13, 13) bib sts and 4 (4, 6, 7) vertical sts.

ROWS 11 AND 13: Work in patt to last 3 sts, p2tog, p1— 7 (7, 11, 11) bib sts.

ROWS 12 AND 14: Work in patt as est to last bib st, ssk next st tog with next vertical st.

NEXT ROW: Work in patt as est to end.

Rep last 2 rows until all vertical edge sts have been worked—15 (22, 23, 29) sts. Place sts onto holder.

RIGHT FRONT BIB

With WS facing, start at left front shoulder, PU and p 1 st for every 2 rows along the vertical edge, and 27 (27, 35, 35) sts evenly across the front curve to the center for bib.

ROW 1 (RS): P3 (3, 4, 4), k1 tbl, p4, k1 tbl, p1 (1, 0, 0), turn.

ROW 2: K1 (1, 0, 0), p1 tbl, k4, p1 tbl, k3 (3, 4, 4), turn.

ROW 3: P3 (3, 4, 4), k1 tbl, [p4, k1 tbl] twice, p1 (1, 0, 0), turn.

ROW 4: K1 (1, 0, 0), [p1 tbl, k4] twice, p1 tbl, k3 (3, 4, 4), turn.

ROW 5: P3 (3, 4, 4), k1 tbl, [p4, p1 tbl] 3 times, k1 (1, 0, 0), turn.

ROW 6: K1 (1, 0, 0), [p1 tbl, k4] 3 times, p1 tbl, k3 (3, 4, 4), turn.

ROW 7: P3 (3, 4, 4), k1 tbl, [p4, k1 tbl] 3 (3, 4, 4) times, p4 (4, 0, 0), turn.

ROW 8: K4 (4, 0, 0), [p1 tbl, k4] 3 (3, 4, 4) times, p1 tbl, k3 (3, 4, 4), turn.

ROW 9: P3 (3, 4, 4), k1 tbl, [p4, k1 tbl] 4 times, p1 (1, 3, 3), turn.

ROW 10: K1 (1, 3, 3), [p1 tbl, k4] 4 times, p1 tbl, k3 (3, 4, 4), turn.

ROW 11: P3 (3, 4, 4), k1 tbl, [p4, k1 tbl] 4 (4, 5, 5) times, p3 (3, 1, 1), turn.

ROW 12: K3 (3, 1, 1), [p1 tbl, k4] 4 (4, 5, 5) times, p1 tbl, k3 (3, 4, 4), turn.

Sizes M and L only
ROW 13: [P4, k1 tbl] 6 times, p3, turn.

ROW 14: K3, [p1 tbl, k4] 6 times, turn.

ROW 15: [P4, k1 tbl] 6 times, p5, turn.

ROW 16: K5, [p1 tbl, k4] 6 times, turn.

All sizes

NEXT ROW (RS): Work in patt as est to last st of bib, p last st tog with next vertical st.

NEXT ROW: Work in patt as est to end.

Rep last 2 rows until 9 (9, 11, 12) vertical sts rem, end with a RS row.

RIGHT NECK SHAPING

ROW 1 (WS): Work in patt to last 10 sts, W&T.

ROWS 2, 4, 6 AND 8: Work in patt as est to last bib st, p next st tog with next vertical st.

ROW 3: Work in patt to last 15 sts, W&T.

ROW 5: Work in patt to last 18 (18, 20, 20) sts, W&T.

ROW 7: Work in patt to last - (-, 22, 22) sts, W&T.

ROW 9: Work in patt to end, lifting wraps and work tog with wrapped sts.

ROW 10: BO 18 (18, 22, 22) sts, work in patt to last bib st, p next st tog with next vertical st—9 (9, 13, 13) bib sts and 4 (4, 6, 7) vertical sts.

ROWS 11 AND 13: Work in patt to last 3 sts, k2tog, k1— 7 (7, 11, 11) bib sts.

ROWS 12 AND 14: Work in patt as est to last bib st, p next st tog with next vertical st.

NEXT ROW: Work in patt as est to end.

Rep last 2 rows until all vertical edge sts have been worked—15 (22, 23, 29) sts. Place sts onto holder.

SLEEVES

Join front and back shoulders using 3-needle BO (page 103).

With RS facing, starting at center of underarm, PU and k88 (96, 116, 124) sts evenly around armhole. Pm and join.

RND 1: K28 (32, 42, 46), pm, work next 32 sts in Diamond Lace patt, pm, k to end.

RND 2: K to marker, work next 32 sts in Diamond Lace patt, k to end.

ROW 3: Work in patt as est to 3 sts before end of rnd, W&T.

ROW 4: P to 3 sts before end of rnd, W&T.

ROW 5: Work in patt as est to 3 sts before last wrapped st, W&T.

ROW 6: P to 3 sts before last wrapped st, W&T.

Rep last 2 rows 7 (8, 10, 11) times more.

NEXT ROW: Knit, lifting wraps and k tog with wrapped sts.

NEXT RND: Knit, lifting wraps and k tog with wrapped sts.

Work 3 rnds in Twisted Rib. BO in patt.

FINISHING

Sew buttons to left front opening.

With crochet hook, work a row of sl sts along right front opening, making chain loops opposite buttons.

Wash and block to measurements.

ABOUT LIEN I learned to knit to get myself through grad school and started designing to keep myself sane during an imposed period of unemployment. Having first learned to knit at a Stitch 'n Bitch group, I have sought the company of knitting groups wherever I may be living. I've called three countries home since I started knitting and have found that knitters are a very diverse, international bunch—I'm never the only foreigner in any group. I'm an American expat living in Oxford with my English husband.

SUZI ANVIN

ENGLISH MESH LACE SKIRT

O n Fillmore Street in San Francisco, there's a fancy-schmancy boutique I always passed en route to work. One day, I saw a gorgeous lace skirt inside and I *had* to have it. Since it cost more than my wedding dress, I set out to knit one myself, but nary a pattern could be found. When some local yarn shop owners pointed out that a fitted skirt is really a tube, I boldly set out on my first design effort. I measured my waist and hips, swatched a ball's worth of yarn in different stitch patterns, and eventually settled on English Mesh Lace. An upside of lace knitting is that it requires less precise shaping than solid knitting techniques. Not only is it loads of fun making holes on purpose, but when you're done, you can wet and stretch the skirt for a magically perfect fit. I stuck some waist shaping into this pattern, but don't skip the blocking—you'll get a snug and sassy shape you'll love.

GAUGE SWATCH

CO 25 sts. Work 24 rows in English Mesh Lace (flat). P 1 row. BO loosely. Wet swatch and block to 4½" W × 4" H. When dry, fabric should still be able to stretch in all directions.

LACE EDGING

CO 4 sts.

ROW 1 (RS): Yo, k1, yo, k2tog, yo, k1—6 sts.

ROWS 2, 4 AND 6: P to last 2 sts, p2tog.

SIZE

XS (S, M, L, XL, XXL, XXXL)

To fit waist to 26 (29¼, 32½, 35¾, 39, 42¼, 45)"

To fit hips to 34½ (37¾, 41, 44¼, 47½, 50¾, 54)"

Finished length: 22"

MATERIALS

Dale *Baby Ull* (100% merino wool; 50g/180 yd), 3 (4, 4, 4, 5, 5, 6) balls #0007 charcoal

Size US 3 (3.25mm) 24" circular needle

Stitch markers (4 each in 2 different colors plus one additional to mark center)

Tapestry needle

1 yd fabric of contrasting color for lining (fabric width MUST be 1" wider than desired hip size)

Sewing needle and matching thread

One 6" invisible zipper

1½ yd ½" elastic for waistband

GAUGE

22¼ sts and 24 rows = 4" in English Mesh Lace, blocked

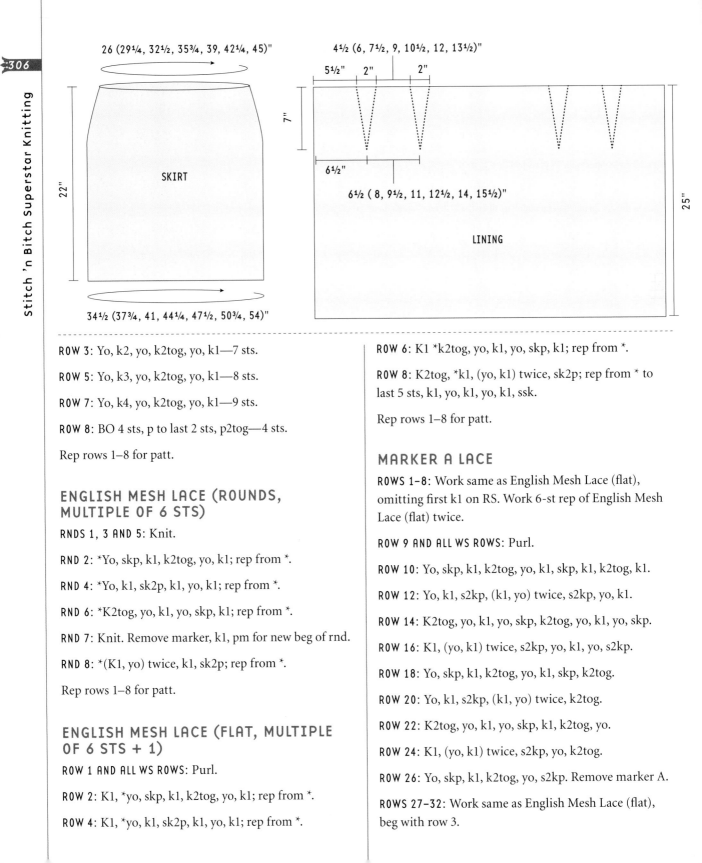

26 (29¼, 32½, 35¾, 39, 42¼, 45)"

SKIRT

22"

34½ (37¾, 41, 44¼, 47½, 50¾, 54)"

4½ (6, 7½, 9, 10½, 12, 13½)"

5½"   2"   2"

7"

6½"

6½ (8, 9½, 11, 12½, 14, 15½)"

LINING

25"

ROW 3: Yo, k2, yo, k2tog, yo, k1—7 sts.

ROW 5: Yo, k3, yo, k2tog, yo, k1—8 sts.

ROW 7: Yo, k4, yo, k2tog, yo, k1—9 sts.

ROW 8: BO 4 sts, p to last 2 sts, p2tog—4 sts.

Rep rows 1–8 for patt.

ENGLISH MESH LACE (ROUNDS, MULTIPLE OF 6 STS)

RNDS 1, 3 AND 5: Knit.

RND 2: *Yo, skp, k1, k2tog, yo, k1; rep from *.

RND 4: *Yo, k1, sk2p, k1, yo, k1; rep from *.

RND 6: *K2tog, yo, k1, yo, skp, k1; rep from *.

RND 7: Knit. Remove marker, k1, pm for new beg of rnd.

RND 8: *(K1, yo) twice, k1, sk2p; rep from *.

Rep rows 1–8 for patt.

ENGLISH MESH LACE (FLAT, MULTIPLE OF 6 STS + 1)

ROW 1 AND ALL WS ROWS: Purl.

ROW 2: K1, *yo, skp, k1, k2tog, yo, k1; rep from *.

ROW 4: K1, *yo, k1, sk2p, k1, yo, k1; rep from *.

ROW 6: K1 *k2tog, yo, k1, yo, skp, k1; rep from *.

ROW 8: K2tog, *k1, (yo, k1) twice, sk2p; rep from * to last 5 sts, k1, yo, k1, yo, k1, ssk.

Rep rows 1–8 for patt.

MARKER A LACE

ROWS 1–8: Work same as English Mesh Lace (flat), omitting first k1 on RS. Work 6-st rep of English Mesh Lace (flat) twice.

ROW 9 AND ALL WS ROWS: Purl.

ROW 10: Yo, skp, k1, k2tog, yo, k1, skp, k1, k2tog, k1.

ROW 12: Yo, k1, s2kp, (k1, yo) twice, s2kp, yo, k1.

ROW 14: K2tog, yo, k1, yo, skp, k2tog, yo, k1, yo, skp.

ROW 16: K1, (yo, k1) twice, s2kp, yo, k1, yo, s2kp.

ROW 18: Yo, skp, k1, k2tog, yo, k1, skp, k2tog.

ROW 20: Yo, k1, s2kp, (k1, yo) twice, k2tog.

ROW 22: K2tog, yo, k1, yo, skp, k1, k2tog, yo.

ROW 24: K1, (yo, k1) twice, s2kp, yo, k2tog.

ROW 26: Yo, skp, k1, k2tog, yo, s2kp. Remove marker A.

ROWS 27–32: Work same as English Mesh Lace (flat), beg with row 3.

Legend:
- ☐ K
- ⊟ P
- ☑ K2tog on RS, p2tog on WS
- ☐ Skp
- ⊙ Yo
- ☒ Sk2p
- ⊡ Bind off
- ■ No stitch

Lace Edging

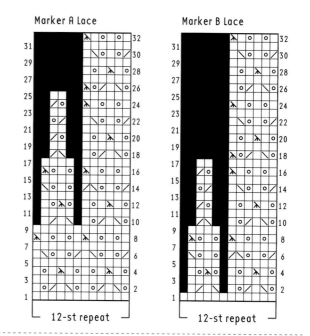

English Mesh Lace (rounds)

6-st repeat

*move marker 1 st to the left at end of R7

English Mesh Lace (flat)

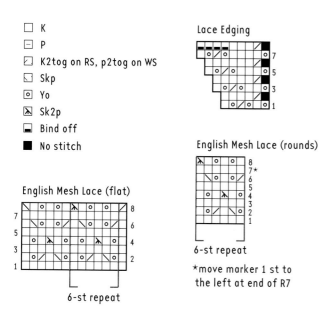

6-st repeat

Marker A Lace

Marker B Lace

12-st repeat

12-st repeat

MARKER B LACE

ROW 1 AND ALL WS ROWS: Purl.

ROW 2: Yo, skp, k1, k2tog, yo, k1, skp, k1, k2tog, k1.

ROW 4: Yo, k1, s2kp, (k1, yo) twice, yo, s2kp, yo, k1.

ROW 6: K2tog, yo, k1, yo, skp, k2tog, yo, k1, yo, skp.

ROW 8: K1, (yo, k1) twice, s2kp, yo, k1, yo, s2kp.

ROW 10: Yo, skp, k1, k2tog, yo, k1, skp, k2tog.

ROW 12: Yo, k1, s2kp, (k1, yo) twice, k2tog.

ROW 14: K2tog, yo, k1, yo, skp, k1, k2tog, yo.

ROW 16: K1, (yo, k1) twice, s2kp, yo, k2tog.

ROW 18: Yo, skp, k1, k2tog, yo, s2kp. Remove marker B.

ROWS 19–32: Work same as English Mesh Lace (flat), beg with row 3.

DIRECTIONS
EDGING

CO 4 sts. Work rows 1–8 of Lace Edging 32 (35, 38, 41, 44, 47, 50) times, end with row 7 of last rep. BO all sts in row 8 patt.

Note: Each repeat of the lace edging leaves 4 loops along the inner edge, formed by the yo at the beginning of each odd-numbered row. It may help to stretch these out as you go so they are easier to pick up later.

SKIRT

With RS facing, pick up each yo along straight edge of Edging—128 (140, 152, 164, 176, 188, 200) sts.

SET-UP ROW (RS): *K1, [k1, p1] in next yo; rep from * to end—192 (210, 228, 246, 264, 282, 300) sts.

Pm and join for working in the rnd. Work rnds 2–7 of English Mesh Lace, then rnds 1–8 thirteen† times more—112 rnds. CO 4 sts and turn.

†Add or subtract from this number to change length of skirt.

WAIST SHAPING

Note: Set-up row 1 establishes lace dec patterns and represents row 1 of Marker A and B Lace. Markers A and B indicate which chart to follow immediately after the marker.

SET-UP ROW 1 (WS): K4, pm, p18 (24, 24, 24, 24, 30),

pm A, p24 (24, 30, 30, 30, 36, 36), pm B, p24 (24, 24, 30, 36, 36, 36), pm B, p24 (24, 30, 30, 30, 36, 36), pm A, p30 (36, 30, 36, 42, 36, 42), pm A, p24 (24, 30, 30, 30, 36, 36), pm B, p24 (24, 24, 30, 36, 36, 36), pm B, p24 (24, 30, 30, 30, 36, 36), pm A, p0 (6, 6, 6, 6, 6, 12), CO 5 sts— 201 (219, 237, 255, 273, 291, 309) sts.

ROW 2: K4, beg with row 2 and k1, work 6-st rep of English Mesh Lace (flat) to next marker, *work Marker A or B Lace once, work 6-st rep of English Mesh Lace (flat) to next marker; rep from * to last 4 sts, k4.

ROWS 3–32: Cont patt as est—153 (171, 189, 207, 225, 243, 261) sts.

ROWS 33–40: Knit.

BO very loosely.

FINISHING

Sew edging seam. Handwash skirt and gently squeeze out excess water. Place skirt flat onto a pinnable surface and pin to desired measurements, stretching slightly to open up lace and using as many pins as necessary to create smooth edges. Stretch waistband to 1½". Fold zipper facings to either side and pin to ½" width; lace pattern should meet at opening. Pin each point of lace edging 2" below hemline. Leave pinned until thoroughly dry. Weave in ends.

SEWING INSTRUCTIONS FOR LINING

Cut a rectangle of fabric 1" wider than hip measurement of skirt and 25" in length (or 3" longer than desired skirt length). Using pins, mark for 2 darts along top edge of fabric 5½" and 7½" from either end. Mark for 2 more darts measuring from each inner marker as foll: XS—4½" and 6½"; S—6" and 8"; M—7½" and 9½"; L—9" and 11"; XL—10½" and 12½"; XXL—12" and 14"; XXXL—13½" and 15½". Mark base of darts 7" below the top edge of fabric 6½" from either end and then from each marker as foll: XS—6½", S—8", M—9½", L—11", XL—12½", XXL—14", XXXL—15½".

Fold fabric lengthwise, matching first 2 marks at top edge and creasing to base mark. Sew from top edge to base marker. Rep for other 3 pairs of markers.

With RS together and using a ½" seam allowance, sew back seam from lower edge to 7" below top edge. Press seam open. Fold 3" of lower edge to WS and press. Sew in place for hem.

Try on lining for fit. If too loose, take in more fabric with darts. If too tight, take out original darts and sew narrower darts.

Flip lace skirt inside out. With WS of skirt facing RS of lining, pin lace skirt and lining together, matching center front and zipper opening. Pin zipper facing of skirt to RS of lining. Pin zipper to zipper facing 1" below top edge and sew in place. Fold hem down over top edge of lining and sew in place working through both layers and creating a casing for the elastic. Insert elastic and secure at both ends.

ABOUT SUZI I am a child psychologist and started knitting when I discovered spinning at a Renaissance faire eight years ago. I'm admittedly picky about my knits, so I began designing my own patterns after learning the basics. I live in San Jose, California, with my husband, Peter, and a growing menagerie of pets, including one mouse, two bunnies, one cat, and one python—so far no one has eaten anyone else. I also run long distance, and completed my first marathon in August 2008. I am currently pursuing certification as a personal trainer with the hopes of working with obese children in my psychology practice. Check out my patterns at Suzi's Knits, www.suzisknits.com (and my private psychology practice at www.advancingminds.com).

LEAFY LACE CARDIGAN

SIZE

XS (S, M, L, XL)

Finished bust: 32 (36, 40, 44, 48)"

Finished length: 19¼ (21½, 23, 25½, 26½)"

MATERIALS

Cascade *Pima Tencel* (50% pima cotton, 50% tencel; 50g/109 yd), 8 (10, 12, 14, 15) balls #8374

US 7 (4.5mm) double-pointed needles

US 7 (4.5mm) 24" circular needle

Stitch markers in 2 colors (A and B)

Tapestry needle

GAUGE

20 sts and 28 rows = 4" in St st

This feminine cardigan is a testament to two things I adore—a lacy leaf motif and seamless construction. When I found this lace pattern in a Barbara Walker book, I dreamed up a cardi with cute cascading leaves to form a continuous border. Originally, the lace instructions were written out line by line, but I find charts are way easier to follow for lace, so I converted it to a chart and got stitchin'. To knit this cardigan in one piece, the front lace is knit as you create the body, and the bottom border is knit at a 90-degree angle to a live stitch edge so there's no sewing later. Your leafy lace will really pop if it's stitched in a natural material. And don't forget to block it! The result is a sweater that is fun to knit, nifty to finish, and can be worn with just about anything.

SPECIAL ABBREVIATIONS

M1L: Make 1 st by inserting LH needle from front to back under the bar between the 2 sts of the previous row, and k this loop tbl so it twists to the left.

M1R: Make 1 st by inserting LH needle from back to front under the bar between the 2 sts of the previous row, twist, and k through the front of this loop so it twists to the right.

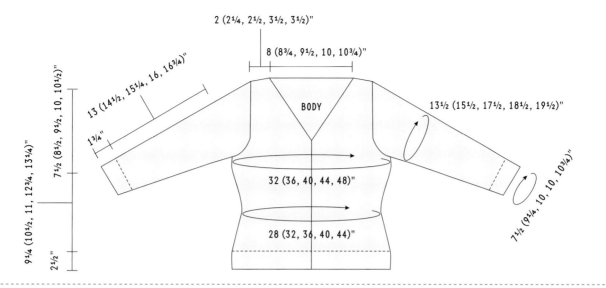

W&T (WRAP AND TURN): On RS, bring yarn between needles to front, sl next st onto RH needle, bring yarn between needles to back, return sl st to LH needle, turn.

On WS, bring yarn between needles to back, sl next st onto RH needle, bring yarn between needles to front, return sl st to LH needle, turn.

DIRECTIONS

Note: The sweater is knit in one piece to the underarms. The sleeves are knit in the round from the top down with short-row shaping in the shoulder cap.

BODY

Using a provisional cast-on and circular needles, CO 9 sts, pm A, CO 31 (36, 41, 46, 51) sts, pm B, CO 80 (90, 100, 110, 120) sts, pm B, CO 31 (36, 41, 46, 51) sts, pm A, CO 9 sts—160 (180, 200, 220, 240) sts.

ROW 1 (RS): Work Chart 1, sm, k to next marker A, sm, work Chart 2.

ROW 2: Work Chart 2, sm, p to next marker A, sm, work Chart 1.

Rep rows 1 and 2 until 10 rows are complete.

DEC ROW (RS): Work Chart 1, k to 3 sts before marker B, k2tog, k1, sm, k1, ssk, k to 3 sts before marker B, k2tog, k1, sm, k1, ssk, k to marker A, sm, work Chart 2.

Cont in patt as est, rep dec row every RS row 4 times more—140 (160, 180, 200, 220) sts.

Cont even in patt for 15 rows.

INC ROW (RS): Work Chart 1, k to 1 st before marker B, M1L, k1, sm, k1, M1R, k to 1 st before marker B, M1L, k1, sm, k1, M1R, k to marker A, sm, work Chart 2.

Cont in patt as est, rep inc row every other RS row 4 times more—160 (180, 200, 220, 240) sts.

Cont even in patt until back meas 9¼ (10½, 11, 12¾, 13¼)", end with a WS row.

DIVIDING ROW (RS): Work Chart 1, sm, k to marker B, sm, BO 4 (5, 5, 5, 6) sts, k to marker B. Turn.

BACK

Remove B markers. Work in St st, BO 4 (5, 5, 5, 6) sts at beg of next row, then BO 3 (3, 4, 4, 5) sts at beg of foll 2 rows—66 (74, 82, 92, 98) back sts.

DEC ROW (RS): K1, ssk, k to last 3 sts, k2tog, k1.

Rep dec row every RS row 2 (2, 3, 3, 4) times more—60 (68, 74, 84, 88) sts.

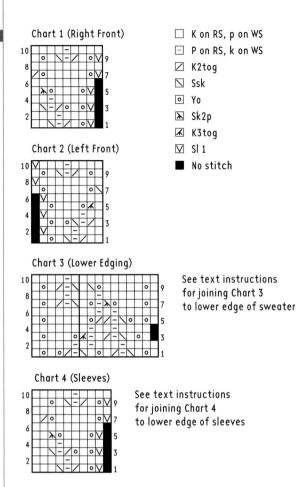

Chart 1 (Right Front)

Chart 2 (Left Front)

Chart 3 (Lower Edging)

See text instructions for joining Chart 3 to lower edge of sweater

Chart 4 (Sleeves)

See text instructions for joining Chart 4 to lower edge of sleeves

□ K on RS, p on WS

⊟ P on RS, k on WS

☑ K2tog

◩ Ssk

⊙ Yo

◩ Sk2p

◩ K3tog

◪ Sl 1

■ No stitch

Cont even in St st until armhole meas 7½ (8½, 9½, 10, 10½)", end with a WS row.

SIZES XS (S, M) ONLY: *BO 10 (12, 13) sts at beg of next 2 rows. Place rem 40 (44, 48) sts onto holder.*

SIZES L (XL) ONLY: *BO 9 sts at beg of next 2 rows, then BO 8 sts at beg of foll 2 rows. Place rem 50 (54) sts onto holder.*

RIGHT FRONT

With WS facing, attach yarn to armhole edge.

NEXT ROW (WS): BO 4 (5, 5, 5, 6) sts, p to marker A, sm, work Chart 1.

NEXT ROW: Work Chart 1, k to end.

NEXT ROW: BO 3 (3, 4, 4, 5) sts, p to marker A, sm, work Chart 1—33 (37, 41, 46, 49).

ARMHOLE DEC (RS): Work Chart 1, k to last 3 sts, k2tog, k1.

NEXT ROW: P to marker A, sm, work Chart 1.

Cont in patt as est, rep armhole dec every RS row 2 (2, 3, 3, 4) times more—30 (34, 37, 42, 44) sts. Work 1 row even.

NECK DEC (RS): Work Chart 1, sm, k1, ssk, k to end.

Cont in patt as est, rep neck dec every RS row 7 (9, 10, 11, 12) times more, then every other RS row 4 (4, 5, 5, 6) times—18 (20, 21, 25, 25) sts.

Cont even in patt as est until armhole meas 7½ (8½, 9½, 10, 10½)", end with a RS row.

SIZES XS (S, M) ONLY: *BO 9 (11, 12) sts, work Chart 1.*

SIZES L (XL) ONLY: *BO 8 sts, p to marker A, work Chart 1; work Chart 1, k to end; BO 8 sts, work Chart 1.*

Sew shoulder seam.

RIGHT NECKBAND

ROW 1 (RS): Work 9 sts of Chart 1, ssk last st together with first back neck st on holder. Turn.

ROW 2: Work next row of Chart 1.

Rep rows 1 and 2 until 20 (22, 24, 25, 27) back neck sts rem.

Place all sts onto holder.

LEFT FRONT

With RS facing, attach yarn to armhole edge.

NEXT ROW (RS): BO 4 (5, 5, 5, 6) sts, k to marker A, work Chart 2.

NEXT ROW: Work Chart 2, p to end.

NEXT ROW: BO 3 (3, 4, 4, 5) sts, k to marker A, sm, work Chart 2.

NEXT ROW: Work Chart 2, p to end.

ARMHOLE DEC (RS): K1, ssk, k to marker A, work Chart 2.

Cont in patt as est, work armhole dec every RS row 2 (2, 3, 3, 4) times more—30 (34, 37, 42, 44) sts. Work 1 row even.

NECK DEC (RS): K to 3 sts before marker A, k2tog, k1, sm, work Chart 2.

Cont in patt as est, rep neck dec every RS row 7 (9, 10, 11, 12) times more, then every other RS row 4 (4, 5, 5, 6) times—18 (20, 21, 25, 25) sts.

Cont even in patt as est until armhole meas 7½ (8½, 9½, 10, 10½)", end with a WS row.

SIZES XS (S, M) ONLY: *BO 9 (11, 12) sts, work Chart 2.*

SIZES L (XL) ONLY: *BO 8 sts, k to marker A, work Chart 2; work Chart 2, p to end; BO 8 sts, work Chart 2.*

Sew shoulder seam.

LEFT NECKBAND

ROW 1 (WS): Work 9 sts of Chart 2, p last st together with first back neck st on holder. Turn.

ROW 2: Work next row of Chart 2.

Rep rows 1 and 2 until no back neck sts rem.

Graft sts together with those from right neckband.

SLEEVES (MAKE 2)

Starting at center of underarm, with circular needle, pick up and k 1 st for each bound-off st—7 (8, 9, 9, 11) sts; PU and k27 (31, 35, 37, 38) sts to the shoulder seam, pm A; PU and k27 (31, 35, 37, 38) sts to the underarm sts; PU and k 1 st for each bound-off st—7 (8, 9, 9, 11). Pm B for beg of rnd—68 (78, 88, 92, 98) sts.

SET-UP ROW 1 (RS): K tbl 12 (14, 17, 18, 21) sts past marker A, W&T.

SET-UP ROW 2: Sl 1, p to 12 (14, 17, 18, 21) sts past marker A, W&T.

Remove marker A.

ROW 1: Sl 1, k to wrapped st, lift wrap onto needle and k st tog with wrap, W&T.

ROW 2: Sl 1, p to wrapped st, insert RH needle under wrap on RS, then into next st pwise, p these 2 sts tog, W&T.

Rep rows 1 and 2 until all except underarm sts have been worked. Cont in the rnd, k 9 (12, 12, 13, 16) rnds over all sts, picking up wraps on first rnd.

DEC RND: K1, k2tog, k to last 3 sts, ssk, k1.

Rep dec rnd every 6th rnd 8 (9, 6, 4, 3) times more, then every 4th rnd 6 (6, 12, 16, 18) times—38 (46, 50, 50, 54) sts.

Work even in St st until sleeve meas 13 (14½, 15¼, 16, 16¾)" from underarm. Place sts onto holder.

LOWER EDGING

Remove provisional cast-on and place sts onto circular needle. Position sweater with RS of left front facing.

CO 16 sts using cable CO (page 89).

JOINING ROW (RS): Work to last st of Chart 3, ssk last st together with the next st on body of sweater.

NEXT ROW: Work Chart 3.

Rep last 2 rows until all body sts have been worked. BO.

SLEEVE EDGING

CO 10 sts. Work rows 1 and 2 of Chart 4.

JOINING ROW (RS): With RS of sleeve edge facing, work to last st of Chart 4, ssk last st tog with the next st on edge of sleeve.

NEXT ROW: Work Chart 4.

Rep last 2 rows until all sleeve sts have been worked. BO.

Weave in ends.

ABOUT MOLLY In college I saw a friend knitting with huge fluffy yarn that felt amazing. I picked up the needles in 2002 and haven't put them down since (except, of course, to learn to spin). I've knit my way through a PhD program in materials science and engineering, marriage, having two amazing baby girls, and several moves across the country. Everywhere I go, I feel at home in the local fiber-arts scene.

SWEETHEART SWEATER

SIZE

S (M, L)

Finished bust: 33½ (39½, 45½)"

Finished length: 18½ (20½, 22½)"

MATERIALS

Red Heart *Bamboo Wool* (55% bamboo, 45% wool; 50g/87 yds), 10 (12, 15) balls #3920 Cayenne

US 7 (4.5mm) 24" circular needle

Tapestry needle

Straight pins

GAUGE

18 sts and 24 rows = 4" in St st

16 sts and 26½ rows = 4" in Sweetheart Lace patt

sing a vintage sweater pattern as my main inspiration for this Sweetheart pullover sweater, I added a smart ribbed yoke to pull the shoulder seam in and added an easy drape to the neckline. I'm in love with lace and the way it starts on paper as a crazy abbreviated knitting code and then magically turns into a pattern you can see growing on your needles. Don't let the lace grid overwhelm you; just concentrate on each row as you go, and, before you know it, you'll have a new sweater in your wardrobe! I guarantee you'll be pleased with the outcome: The ease of the yarn along with the open lace stitches gives this nifty sweater lots of stretch that flatters any figure.

SPECIAL ABBREVIATIONS

K4TOG: Knit 4 sts tog.

SSSSK: [Sl 1 kwise] 4 times, k4tog tbl.

SPECIAL STITCH

SWEETHEART LACE

ROW 1 (RS): K4, *yo, k2tog, k3, yo, k1, yo, k3, ssk, yo, k1; rep from *, end k3.

ROWS 2, 4, 6 AND 8: K2, p to last 2 sts, k2.

ROW 3: K4, *k1, yo, k4tog, yo, k3, yo, ssssk, yo, k2; rep from *, end k3.

ROW 5: K4, *k1, k2tog, yo, k5, yo, ssk, k2; rep from *, end k3.

ROW 7: K4, *k2tog, yo, k7, yo, ssk, k1; rep from *, end k3.

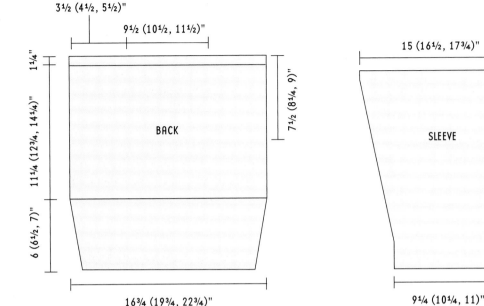
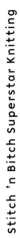

ROW 9: K3, k2tog, *yo, k9, yo, sk2p; rep from * to last 14 sts, yo, k9, yo, ssk, k3.

ROW 10: K2, p to last 2 sts, k2.

Rep rows 1–10 for patt.

DIRECTIONS

Notes: The first two and last two stitches of every RS and WS row of the body are knitted to create a selvage. These stitches are calculated into the instructions below.

The front and back pieces are knitted separately then sewn together at the shoulder and side seams before the stitches are picked up along the bottom to make the ribbed band.

This sweater is knit using circular needles, however the only time you knit in the round is when working on the bottom ribbed band. If you prefer, you can knit the front, back, and sleeves on straight needles.

BACK

CO 67 (79, 91) sts.

SET-UP ROW (WS): Knit.

Work rows 1–10 of Sweetheart Lace 7 (8, 9) times, then rows 1–4 once more.

RIBBED YOKE

NEXT ROW (RS): K2tog, k1, *p2, k2; rep from * to end— 66 (78, 90) sts.

Work in k2, p2 rib for 1¼", end with a RS row. BO kwise on WS. Pm 14 (18, 22) sts from each outside edge to indicate shoulder sts.

FRONT

Work same as back.

Sweetheart Lace

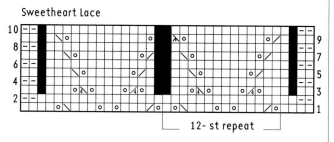

Work rows 1–10 7 (8, 9) times, then
work rows 1–4 once more

- ☐ K on RS, P on WS
- ⊟ P on RS, K on RS
- ⊙ Yo
- ☑ K2tog
- ◻ Ssk
- ⬙ Sk2p
- ◪ K4tog
- ◩ Ssssk
- ■ No stitch

ABOUT KARISSA

Gramma Rose taught me to knit when I was ten years old, and I feverishly made scarves for all of my Care Bears, then promptly forgot how to cast off. Ten years later, when I made myself a beautiful lavender cashmere scarf, I realized how much I love knitting. Since then, I've explored tough techniques, taught myself how to make my own patterns, and learned that special kind of patience that comes from casting on a sweater five times because you haven't allotted enough yarn. You can see my other knitting projects and various other adventures at my website, www.crackersandhoney.com.

SLEEVES

CO 42 (46, 50) sts. Work in k2, p2 rib for 2¾", end with a WS row.

INC ROW (RS): K1, m1, k to last st, m1, k1—44 (48, 52) sts.

Cont in St st, rep inc row every 6th row 12 (13, 14) times more—68 (74, 80) sts. Work even until sleeve meas 15 (16, 17)" from beg. BO.

FINISHING

Block pieces. Sew shoulder seams. Mark side edges of both front and back 7½ (8¼, 9)" down from shoulder seam. Position center of bound-off edge of sleeves on shoulder seams and sew in place between markers. Sew side and sleeve seams.

BOTTOM BAND

Starting at side seam, PU and k52 (64, 76) sts across cast-on edge of front, pm, PU and k52 (64, 76) sts across cast-on edge of back. Pm and join. Work in k2, p2 rib for 6 (6½, 7)". BO loosely pwise.

KaLani Craig

HAIKU

eceptively light with the steely strength of silk mohair, the Haiku is a sweater of opposites. The moment I first held a skein of supergorgeous Haiku, I wanted to take the contrasting elements of the yarn into the knitting itself, making a pattern that looked impressive but was still simple enough to stitch. I knew the paired yarn over/decrease sets of the Leaf Lace pattern in one of Barbara Walker's invaluable books of stitch patterns would make the shaping easy, even for a lace newbie. The shaping itself isn't too tricky, but I did design a fairly tough web-based shaping program to make the pattern-writing easier. Little did I know, this Haiku yarn would inspire one of my favorite sweaters as well as a cute series of customized patterns that I've crafted since.

SPECIAL STITCHES
LEAF LACE PATTERN (MULTIPLE OF 12 STS PLUS 1)

ROW 1 (RS): K1, *yo, ssk, k7, k2tog, yo, k1; rep from * to end.

ROW 2 AND ALL WS ROWS: Purl.

ROW 3: K1, *yo, k1, ssk, k5, k2tog, k1, yo, k1; rep from * to end.

ROW 5: K1, *yo, k2, ssk, k3, k2tog, k2, yo, k1; rep from * to end.

ROW 7: K1, *yo, k3, ssk, k1, k2tog, k3, yo, k1; rep from * to end.

ROW 9: K1, *yo, k4, sk2p, k4, yo, k1; rep from * to end.

ROW 11: K1, *k3, k2tog, yo, k1, yo, ssk, k4; rep from * to end.

ROW 13: K1, *k2, k2tog, k1, yo, k1, yo, k1, ssk, k3; rep from * to end.

ROW 15: K1, *k1, k2tog, k2, yo, k1, yo, k2, ssk, k2; rep from * to end.

ROW 17: K1, *k2tog, k3, yo, k1, yo, k3, ssk, k1; rep from * to end.

SIZE
S (M, L, XL, XXL, XXXL)

Finished bust: 34 (39, 43½, 48½, 53, 58)"

Finished length: 16½ (17, 19¼, 19½, 20¼, 20½)"

MATERIALS
Alchemy Yarns of Transformation *Haiku* (40% silk, 60% kid mohair; 25g/325 yd), 4 (4, 5, 5, 6, 7) hanks Koi Pond

US 5 (3.75mm) needles

US 4 (3.5mm) 24" circular needle

5 (6, 6, 7, 7, 8) ¼"–⅓" buttons of your choice

4 stitch holders

2 stitch markers

Waste yarn for provisional CO and lifeline

192 (216, 234, 264, 282, 306) size 6 or 8 seed beads (count includes 18 extra in case of breakage; be sure yarn fits through hole in bead)

Beading needle

Tapestry needle

Sewing needle and matching thread

GAUGE
20 sts and 28 rows = 4" in Leaf Lace patt using larger needles, after blocking

Each diamond motif measures 2¼"W x 3"L

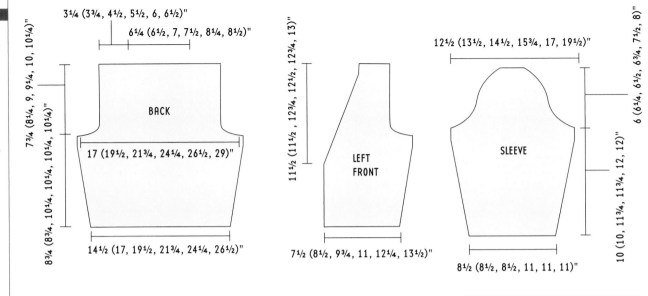

BACK

3¼ (3¾, 4½, 5½, 6, 6½)"

6¼ (6½, 7, 7½, 8¼, 8½)"

7¾ (8¼, 9, 9¼, 10, 10¼)"

8¾ (8¾, 10¼, 10¼, 10¼, 10¼)"

17 (19½, 21¾, 24¼, 26½, 29)"

14½ (17, 19½, 21¾, 24¼, 26½)"

LEFT FRONT

11½ (11½, 12¾, 12½, 12¾, 13)"

7½ (8½, 9¾, 11, 12¼, 13½)"

SLEEVE

12½ (13½, 14½, 15¾, 17, 19½)"

6 (6¼, 6½, 6¾, 7½, 8)"

10 (10, 11¾, 11¾, 12, 12)"

8½ (8½, 8½, 11, 11, 11)"

ROW 19: K2tog, *k4, yo, k1, yo, k4, sk2p; rep from * to last 12 sts, k4, yo, k1, yo, k4, ssk.

ROW 20: Purl.

Rep rows 1–20 for patt.

BEADED LACE (OVER 5 STS)

SB-YO-K2TOG (SLIP BEAD-YO-K2TOG): Slide bead to LH needle; with yarn in front, k2tog, passing working yarn over RH needle.

ROW 1 (RS): SB-yo-k2tog, m1, k1, k2tog with edge st—5 sts.

ROW 2: Sl first st on RH needle (edge st) to LH needle, p2tog, p4—5 sts.

ROW 3: SB-yo-k2tog, (yo) 3 times, ssk, k1—7 sts.

ROW 4: Sl first st on RH needle (edge st) to LH needle, p2tog, p1, (p1, k1, p1) into triple yo, p2—7 sts.

ROW 5: SB-yo-k2tog, sk2p, k1, k2tog with edge st—5 sts.

ROW 6: P5.

Rep rows 1–6 for patt.

BUTTONHOLE LACE (OVER 5 STS)

ROW 1 (RS): K1, k2tog, m1, k1, k2tog with edge st—5 sts.

ROW 2: Sl first st on RH needle (edge st) to LH needle; p2tog, p4—5 sts.

ROW 3: Yo, k2, yo, k2tog, k1—6 sts.

ROW 4: Sl first st on RH needle (edge st) to LH needle, p2tog, p5—6 sts.

ROW 5: K1, ssk, k2, k2tog with edge st—5 sts.

ROW 6: P5.

Rep rows 1–6 for patt.

PICOT EDGE (MULTIPLE OF 3 STS)

ROW 1 (WS): Purl.

ROW 2: *Sk2p, [yo] twice; rep from * to last 3 sts, sk2p.

ROW 3: P1, *(p1, k1) into double yo, p1; rep from * to end.

ROW 4: Knit.

ROW 5: Purl.

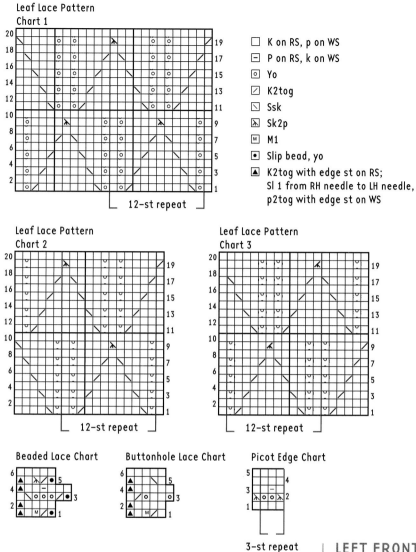

Leaf Lace Pattern
Chart 1

12-st repeat

□ K on RS, p on WS
⊟ P on RS, k on WS
○ Yo
☑ K2tog
◩ Ssk
⧄ Sk2p
Ⓜ M1
⊡ Slip bead, yo
▲ K2tog with edge st on RS;
   Sl 1 from RH needle to LH needle,
   p2tog with edge st on WS

Leaf Lace Pattern
Chart 2

12-st repeat

Leaf Lace Pattern
Chart 3

12-st repeat

Beaded Lace Chart

Buttonhole Lace Chart

Picot Edge Chart

3-st repeat

DIRECTIONS

Pattern note: As sts are increased, bring new sts into est patt. Because it is difficult to measure length before blocking piece, keep track of rows to ensure that front and back measure the same number of rows at body-shaping points.

BACK

Using provisional CO and larger needle, CO 73 (85, 97, 109, 121, 133) sts. P 1 WS row.

SIDE SHAPING

Work in Leaf Lace patt using Chart 1, inc 1 st each side every 8th (8th, 10th, 10th, 10th, 10th) row 6 times—85 (97, 109, 121, 133, 145) sts.

Work 12 (12, 10, 10, 10, 10) rows even in patt as est.

ARMHOLE SHAPING

Cont in Leaf Lace patt as est, BO 5 (5, 6, 6, 8, 8) sts at beg of next 2 rows— 75 (87, 97, 109, 117, 129) sts.

Dec 1 st each side every row 2 times, then dec 1 st each side every RS row 4 (6, 6, 7, 6, 8) times—63 (71, 81, 91, 101, 109) sts. Work 1 WS row.

Work 42 (42, 48, 46, 54, 52) rows even in patt as est.

NECK SHAPING

NEXT ROW: Work 16 (19, 23, 27, 30, 33) sts, BO center 31 (33, 35, 37, 41, 43) sts, work rem sts—16 (19, 23, 27, 30, 33) sts each shoulder.

Break yarn, leaving a 24" tail. Place shoulder sts onto stitch holders.

LEFT FRONT

Note: Read all shaping instructions before beginning. Side and neck shaping take place at the same time; neck and armhole shaping take place at the same time.

Using provisional CO and larger needle, CO 37 (43, 49, 55, 61, 67) sts. P 1 WS row. Pm to indicate side edge (RH edge with RS facing).

SIDE, NECK, AND ARMHOLE SHAPING

Work Leaf Lace patt using Chart 1 (2, 1, 2, 1, 2), inc 1 st at side edge every 8th (8th, 8th, 10th, 10th, 10th) row 6 times, then work even at side edge to beg of armhole shaping.

AT THE SAME TIME, when 36 (38, 46, 48, 52, 52) rows have been completed, beg neck shaping as follows: pm to indicate beg of shaping at neck edge (LH edge with RS facing). Dec 1 st at neck edge on next row and every foll 4th row 15 (13, 17, 16, 15, 15) times more, then every other row 0 (3, 0, 2, 5, 6) times.

AND AT THE SAME TIME, when piece is same length as back to beg of armhole shaping, end with a WS row and beg armhole shaping as foll:

BO 5 (5, 6, 6, 8, 8) sts at beg of next RS row.

Dec 1 st at armhole edge every row 2 times, then every RS row 4 (6, 6, 7, 6, 8) times.

Work even in patt as est until piece meas same as back.

Break yarn, leaving a 24" tail, and place rem 16 (19, 23, 27, 30, 33) sts on holder.

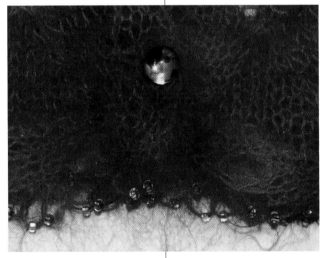

RIGHT FRONT

Using provisional CO and larger needle, CO 37 (43, 49, 55, 61, 67) sts. P 1 WS row. Pm to indicate side edge (LH edge with RS facing).

SIDE, NECK, AND ARMHOLE SHAPING

Work Leaf Lace patt using Chart 1 (3, 1, 3, 1, 3), inc 1 st at side edge every 8th (8th, 8th, 10th, 10th, 10th) row 6 times, then work even at side edge to beg of armhole shaping.

AT THE SAME TIME, when 36 (38, 46, 48, 52, 52) rows have been completed, pm to indicate beg of shaping at neck edge (RH edge with RS facing).

Dec 1 st at neck edge on next row and every foll 4th row 15 (13, 17, 16, 15, 15) times more, then every other row 0 (3, 0, 2, 5, 6) times.

AND AT THE SAME TIME, when piece is same length as back to beg of armhole shaping, end with a RS row and beg armhole shaping as foll:

BO 5 (5, 6, 6, 8, 8) sts at beg of next WS row.

Dec 1 st at armhole edge every row 2 times, then every RS row 4 (6, 6, 7, 6, 8) times.

Work even in patt as est until piece meas same as back.

Break yarn, leaving 24" tail, and place rem 16 (19, 23, 27, 30, 33) sts on holder.

LEFT SLEEVE

Using provisional CO and larger needle, CO 43 (43, 43, 55, 55, 55) sts. P 1 WS row.

Work Leaf Lace patt using Chart 2.

Inc 1 st each side every 6th (6th, 6th, 6th, 6th, 2nd) row 6 (10, 10, 8, 11, 1) times and every 8th (4th, 4th, 8th, 4th, 4th) row 4 (2, 5, 4, 4, 20) times—63 (67, 73, 79, 85, 97) sts.

CAP SHAPING

BO 5 (5, 6, 6, 8, 8) sts at beg of next 2 rows.

Dec 1 st each side on next row; every RS row 4 (3, 4, 3, 5, 5) times; then every 4th row 7 (8, 8, 9, 9, 10) times.

BO 5 (7, 7, 8, 8, 8) sts at beg of next 2 rows.

BO rem 19 (19, 21, 25, 23, 33) sts.

RIGHT SLEEVE

Work same as left sleeve using Chart 3.

FINISHING

Join shoulders using 3-needle BO (page 103). Set sleeves into armholes. Sew side seams.

Lace edgings are worked onto garment in sections.

BUTTONBAND

With RS facing and smaller needle, starting at neck shaping marker of left front, using a 32 (36, 36, 40, 40, 44)" tail to form sts, PU and k20 (24, 24, 28, 28, 32) sts along front edge to lower corner. Return to neck shaping marker and with RS facing and working yarn, Cable CO 5 sts.

Work 6-row rep of Buttonhole Lace 5 (6, 6, 7, 7, 8) times. Break yarn, leaving a 12" tail and leaving sts on needle.

BEADED LACE EDGING

Thread a new strand of working yarn onto beading needle and string 114 (132, 150, 168, 186, 204) beads.

Carefully remove wy from lower edge sts and place sts onto smaller needle—147 (171, 195, 219, 243, 267) sts.

Rejoin yarn to left front sts, cont with 5 sts on needle from buttonband to work 6-row rep of Beaded Lace patt 36 (42, 48, 54, 60, 66) times around lower edge of fronts and back AND AT THE SAME TIME, at each side seam, work 1 st from front and back together with edging; and on very last row of edging, work p2tog with edge st, p4.

BUTTONHOLE BAND

Using smaller needle, PU 20 (24, 24, 28, 28, 32) sts along right front edge to neck marker. Break yarn, leaving 12" tail, leaving sts on needle. Remove any unused beads. Slide sts to other end of needle in preparation to work a RS row.

Starting with 5 sts rem from Beaded Lace edging, work 6-row rep of Buttonband patt 5 (6, 6, 7, 7, 8) times.

BO.

SEW BUTTONS

Each yo in the Buttonhole Lace trim on right front serves as a buttonhole. Using needle and thread, sew 5 (6, 6, 7, 7, 8) buttons along buttonband seam of left front to correspond with buttonholes.

PICOT NECKLINE EDGING

With RS facing and smaller needle, PU and k3 sts from BO edge of Buttonhole Lace on right front, 57 (60, 63, 63, 66, 66) sts along front neck edge to shoulder seam, 34 (36, 38, 42, 42, 46) sts across back neck, 57 (60, 63, 63, 66, 66) sts down front neck edge and 3 sts across CO edge of Buttonhole Lace of left front—154 (162, 170, 174, 180, 184) sts.

Work 5 rows of Picot edging, then join last row to inside neck edge by *PU 1 st of neck edge on WS and k2tog with next st; rep from * to end.

Fasten off. Cut yarn, leaving 12" tail.

SLEEVE EDGING

Carefully remove wy from sleeve sts and place sts onto smaller needle, casting on 1 more st—44 (44, 44, 56, 56, 56) sts. Thread a new strand of working yarn onto beading needle and string 39 (39, 39, 48, 48, 48) beads. CO 5 sts and work 6-row rep of Beaded Lace patt 11 (11, 11, 14, 14, 14) times.

BLOCKING

Lace blocking isn't difficult, but it does require one unusual step: ends that are woven in and trimmed before blocking can work free during the blocking process. Weave in all ends, but do not trim. Wet block with untrimmed ends still intact, stretching lace pattern open to full dimensions in schematic. Pin yos from Beaded Lace patt open. Let dry completely and trim ends. Picot trim may require light steaming to lay flat.

ABOUT KALANI In college I found the meditative qualities of knitting were the perfect way to keep my fidgety instincts in check. I live with a whole lot of excess technology in Bloomington, Indiana, but not for long, because once I finish my PhD in medieval history, I'm hoping to return to Portland, Oregon, where I'm originally from. You can read more about my knitting life and see more of my patterns at www.hapagirl.com.

FLIRTY

SIZE

Women's L

Foot circumference: 8"

Calf circumference: 9½"

Foot length: approx 9¾"

MATERIALS

Brown Sheep *Cotton Fine* (80% pima cotton, 20% wool; 50g/222 yd), 3 balls #CW005 Cavern

US 1 (2.25mm) double-pointed needles (set of 5)

1 yd ¼" wide elastic

1⅔ yd ⅜" wide satin ribbon

Sewing needle and matching thread

GAUGE

30 sts and 40 rows = 4" in St st

nee-highs are my favorite socks because they are way more versatile than regular ankle socks. I wanted to knit a pair of lacy knee-highs but couldn't find a pattern that was just right, so I had to cook up this pattern on my own. These socks are knit toe-up because that makes it easy to determine when to start the increases for the calf shaping and the desired height. This technique is also great because, if you get tired of the project, you can bind off at any point after the ankle and still have a proper sock. Luckily, this pattern is way fun and it advances so swiftly you'll end up with lacy knee-highs in no time.

STITCH PATTERN

LACE PATTERN (MULTIPLE OF 10 STS)

RND 1: *K1 tbl, p2, yo, ssk, k1, k2tog, yo, p2; rep from * to end.

RNDS 2 AND 4: *K1 tbl, p2, k5, p2; rep from * to end.

RND 3: *K1 tbl, p2, k1, yo, sk2p, yo, k1, p2; rep from * to end.

Rep rnds 1–4 for patt.

DIRECTIONS

TOE

CO 12 sts. Knit 1 row. Rotate needle to cont across opposite side of CO. PU and k 12 sts across CO edge and place on 2nd dpn. Distribute sts evenly over 4 needles. Pm and join.

INC RND: *K to last 2 sts of needle, kfb, k1; for next needle, k1, kfb, k to end; rep from * to end.

Rep inc rnd every rnd until there are 48 sts. Cont in St st, rep inc rnd every other rnd until there are 60 sts. K 3 rnds.

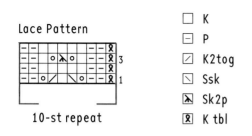

Lace Pattern

10-st repeat

	K
	P
	K2tog
	Ssk
	Sk2p
	K tbl

FOOT

Redistribute sts as foll: 15 sts each on Needles 1 and 2, 16 sts on Needle 3, and 14 sts on Needle 4. Beg of rnd is between Needle 4 and Needle 1 at center of sole.

RND 1: On Needle 1, k; on Needles 2 and 3, work Lace patt to last st of Needle 3, k1 tbl; on Needle 4, k.

Rep rnd 1 until foot meas 3" less than desired finished length, end with rnd 4 of Lace patt.

HEEL

With Needle 4, k15 from Needle 1, turn—29 heel sts.

ROW 1 (WS): Sl 1, p28, turn.

ROW 2 (RS): Sl 1 kwise, k28, turn.

Rep last 2 rows 14 times more—30 rows.

TURN HEEL

ROW 1 (WS): Sl 1, p18, p2tog, turn.

ROW 2: Sl 1 kwise, k9, ssk, turn.

ROW 3: Sl 1, p9, p2tog, turn.

Rep rows 2 and 3 until all sts have been worked, end with row 2—11 heel sts.

GUSSET

With Needle 1, PU and k16 sts along side of heel flap; work est patt across Needles 2 and 3; with Needle 4, PU and k16 sts along other side of heel flap, k6 heel sts; slip rem 5 heel sts onto Needle 1—74 sts. Pm for beg of rnd.

RND 1 (DEC): On Needle 1, k to last 3 sts, ssk, k1; on Needles 2 and 3, work in est patt; on Needle 4, k1, k2tog, k to end.

RND 2: On Needle 1, knit; on Needles 2 and 3, work in est patt; on Needle 4, knit.

Rep last 2 rnds until 60 sts rem. Rep rnd 2 as needed to end with rnd 4 of Lace patt.

LEG

SET-UP RND: On Needle 1, knit; on Needles 2 and 3, work in est patt; on Needle 4, cont in Lace patt.

Redistribute sts over 3 dpns if desired.

Cont even in Lace patt on all needles until leg meas 8" or desired length from set-up rnd, end with rnd 1 or 3 of Lace patt.

CALF SHAPING

INC RND 1: *K1 tbl, p1, pfb, k5, pfb, p1, k1 tbl, p2, k5, p2; rep from * to end—66 sts.

Cont even in Lace patt for 7 rnds, working additional p sts into patt as est.

INC RND 2: *K1 tbl, p3, k5, p3, k1 tbl, p1, pfb, k5, pfb, p1; rep from * to end—72 sts.

Cont even in Lace patt, working additional p sts into patt as est, until leg meas 12" from set-up rnd, end with rnd 4 of Lace patt.

Note: For shorter/wider calf, begin increasing sooner and rep both inc rnds with 7 rnds Lace patt between to calf width desired.

CUFF

EYELET RND: *K2, yo, p2tog; rep from * to end.

Work in k2, p2 rib for 1". BO loosely.

FINISHING

Block. Measure elastic so it fits snugly below knee plus 1". Thread elastic through eyelet rnd and sew ends tog. Thread ribbon through same path as elastic. Put on socks and tie a bow.

If you use a ribbon made out of satin or some other synthetic material, the ends should be "neatened" to avoid its unraveling. This can be done with the help of a candle: Cut the ribbon ends glancingly and move them slowly across the heat from the candle about 1" away from the flame! Do not place the ribbon straight into the flame! (About 1" is hot enough to melt the ribbon's ends without burning them.)

ABOUT VILMA When I was a little girl my mom kept her most valuable yarns and fabrics out of my reach to save them from my ambitious knitting experiments. Today I can relate to her hiding her stash, because my mini dachshund, Hertta, is even more interested in yarn than I am. Since Hertta moved in, I've had to be real careful about leaving my WIPs lying around, because in addition to nibbling yarn she also enjoys frogging my knitting projects. You can read about Hertta's yarn-demolishing exploits and other craft-related things on my blog, vilman.blogspot.com.

catherine shields

BEATRICE GLOVES

nitting with beads may seem intimidating at first, but once you get started, you'll see it's easy-peasy. I wanted to craft gloves because my hands were chilly on my morning bicycle commute, but I wanted them to be anything but ordinary. So I decided on this lovely lace pattern with a touch of beadwork. The most important tip for knitting with beads is to pick the right ones—you'll go nuts with beads that are too tiny to get onto your yarn, and bulkier beads will weigh your knits down. Save yourself a headache by choosing beads that are just barely big enough to string easily on. The Beatrice Gloves are a great project if you are a newbie to bead-knitting because they are small enough to get some good practice on, and you'll wind up with gloves that pack a really snazzy punch.

SPECIAL ABBREVIATION

KB (KNIT BEAD): Insert RH needle into st, slide bead to base of st, k1, pulling bead through to front.

DIRECTIONS

RIGHT GLOVE

String 102 beads onto yarn.

CO 48 sts. Divide evenly over 3 dpns. Pm and join.

Work in k1, p1 rib for 3".

K 1 rnd, inc 5 sts evenly around—53 sts. Divide over 3 dpns as foll: 24 sts on Needle 1, 15 sts on Needle 2, and 14 sts on Needle 3.

RND 1: K3, pm, work chart over next 21 sts, pm, k to end.

RNDS 2–32: K3, work chart between markers, k to end.

SIZE

One size (women's M)

Finished length: 11"

Finished circumference (at palm): 7½"

MATERIALS

Rowan *Scottish Tweed 4-ply* (100% wool; 25g/120 yd), 2 balls #016 Thistle

US 2 (2.25mm) double-pointed needles (set of 4)

Waste yarn for thumb gussets

204 size 6/0 seed beads

Stitch holder

2 stitch markers

Tapestry needle

GAUGE

28 sts and 40 rows = 4" in St st

Beaded Lace

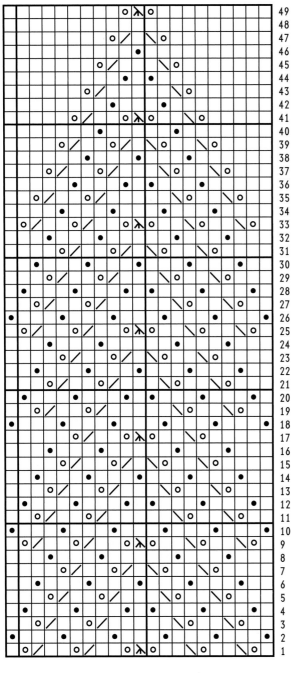

☐	K	
⊙	Yo	
⟋	K2tog	

⟍	Ssk	
⅄	Sk2p	
●	KB	

THUMB OPENING

RND 1: K3, work chart as est over next 21 sts, k3. Break off yarn, leaving an 8" tail. With wy, k7. Join main yarn and k to end.

RNDS 2–17: K3, work chart as est over next 21 sts, k to end.

Cont even in St st for 1¾" or to desired length to base of little finger.

FINGERS

Little finger

K7, place next 39 sts onto holder—14 little finger sts.

Divide sts onto 3 dpns. Pm and join.

Work in St st until finger meas 2¼" or to desired length.

DEC RND 1: *K2tog; rep from * to end—7 sts.

DEC RND 2: *K2tog; rep from * to last st, k1.

Break yarn. Thread tail through rem 4 sts, pull tight and fasten.

Upper hand

Place 39 sts from holder onto dpns. PU and k1 in base of little finger, k39, PU and k1 in base of little finger—41 sts. Pm and join.

K 2 rnds.

Ring finger

K7, place next 26 sts onto holder—15 ring finger sts.

Divide sts onto 3 dpns. Pm and join.

Work in St st until finger meas 2½" or to desired length.

DEC RND 1: *K2tog, rep from * to last st, k1—8 sts.

DEC RND 2: *K2tog; rep from * to end.

Break yarn. Thread tail through rem 4 sts, pull tight and fasten.

Middle finger

Place first 7 sts and last 6 sts from holder onto dpns. PU and k2 sts in base of ring finger, k13—15 middle finger sts. Pm and join.

Work in St st until finger meas 2¾" or to desired length.

Work decs and finish same as for ring finger.

Index finger
Place rem 13 sts from holder onto dpns. PU and k2 sts in base of middle finger, k13—15 index finger sts. Pm and join.

Work same as for ring finger.

Thumb
Remove wy and place 6 upper and 7 lower thumb sts onto 2 dpns. PU and k2 sts at right side of thumb opening, k7 from lower dpn, PU and k2 sts at left side of thumb opening, k6 from upper dpn—17 sts. Divide evenly over 3 dpns. Pm and join.

Work in St st for 2" or to desired length.

Work decs and finish same as for ring finger.

LEFT GLOVE

String 102 beads onto yarn.

CO 48 sts. Divide evenly over 3 dpns. Pm and join.

Work in k1, p1 rib for 3".

K 1 rnd, inc 5 sts evenly around—53 sts. Divide over 3 dpns as foll: 14 sts on Needle 1, 15 sts on Needle 2 and 24 sts on Needle 3.

RND 1: K29, pm, work chart over next 21 sts, pm, k to end.

RNDS 2-32: K29, work chart between markers, k to end.

THUMB OPENING

RND 1: K19. Break off yarn, leaving an 8" tail. With wy, k7. Join main yarn and k3, work chart as est over next 21 sts, k to end.

RNDS 2-17: K29, work chart as est over next 21 sts, k to end.

Cont even in St st for 1¾" or to desired length to base of little finger.

FINGERS

Work same as for right glove.

FINISHING

Weave in ends, closing any gaps between fingers.

ABOUT CATHERINE I have been knitting for about fifteen years—ever since my mother decided I needed to keep busy one family summer vacation. Originally from North Carolina, I now live in Santa Barbara, California, where I am working on a graduate degree in environmental science. When I'm not busy with school or knitting, I like to be outdoors or baking cupcakes. I hope to eventually move somewhere with colder winters and a longer sweater season. See my other knitting patterns and blog at www.studiomarlowe.com.

ruthie nussbaum

Coco

 got hooked on knitting with sequins when I saw master knitter and designer Lily Chin demonstrate bead-knitting at a New York City Knit-Out several years ago. I thought, "I could do this beading technique with sequins!" So I went straight home and began experimenting. I sketched this Chanel-style jacket because I wanted to take a classic look and jazz it up with some serious sparkle. It was hard to figure out the best way to get the sequins onto the yarn. The "helper thread" technique turned out to be the best solution to deal with yarn that is thicker than the sequin hole. With a little patience and precision, you'll see that your sequins will lie flat and provide maximum dazzle while creating a trim that is oh-so-chic.

SPECIAL ABBREVIATION

KS (KNIT SEQUIN): Insert RH needle into st tbl and wrap yarn around needle as if to k, slide sequin up to needle and complete st, pulling sequin through to front of work.

DIRECTIONS

BODY

String 402 (420, 462) sequins (page 76) onto yarn. Always string extra in case of breakage; these can always be removed later. Faceted sequins should be threaded with the cup side facing the ball of yarn.

CO 269 (281, 309) sts.

ROW 1 (WS): K1, *p1, k1; rep from * to end.

ROW 2: P1, *KS, p1; rep from * to end.

Rep rows 1 and 2 twice more, then rep row 1 once more.

SIZE

S (M, L)

To fit bust: 32–34 (36–38, 40–42)"

Finished bust: 36 (40, 44)"

Finished length: 18¾ (19¾, 21¼)"

MATERIALS

Debbie Bliss *Rialto* (100% merino wool; 50g/115 yd), 9 (11, 13) balls #14

2 packages (1,500 ct) 8mm faceted sequins in gold

US 6 (4.0mm) needles

US 6 (4mm) 40" circular needle

8 stitch markers

2 stitch holders

Tapestry needle

GAUGE

22 sts and 29 rows = 4" in St st

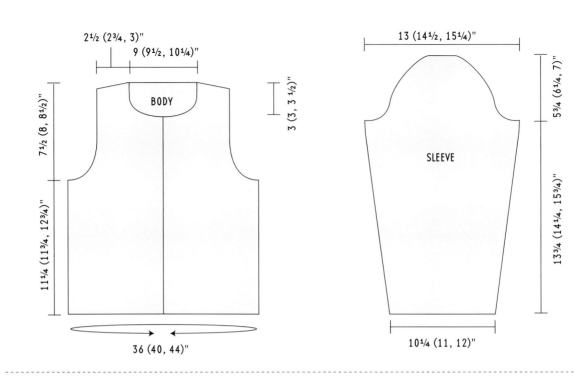

DEC ROW (RS): (P1, KS) 4 times and place these 8 sts onto a holder for right front band, [k2tog, k1 (3, 3), k2tog, k2] 15 (10, 8) times, [k2tog, k2] 9 (19, 35) times, [k2tog, k2, k1 (3, 3), k2tog] 16 (11, 9) times, place last 8 sts onto holder for left front band—182 (204, 224) body sts and 8 sts each front band.

Work body sts in St st until piece meas 11¼ (11¾, 12¾)" from beg, end with a WS row.

DIVIDE FOR FRONTS AND BACK

K35 (40, 44) and place these sts onto a holder for right front; BO 12 (14, 16) underarm sts; k88 (96, 104) sts and place these sts onto a holder for back; BO 12 (14, 16) underarm sts; k rem 35 (40, 44) sts for left front.

LEFT FRONT

NEXT ROW (WS): Purl.

ARMHOLE SHAPING

BO 2 sts at the beg of next 2 (3, 3) RS rows.

Dec 1 st at the beg of next 1 (1, 2) RS rows—30 (33, 36) sts remain.

Work even in St st until armhole meas 4½ (5, 5)", end with a RS row.

NECK SHAPING

BO 6 sts at beg of next WS row.

BO 2 sts at neck edge every WS row 5 (6, 7) times—14 (15, 16) sts.

Work even in St st until armhole meas 7½ (8, 8½)", end with a WS row.

SHOULDER SHAPING

NEXT ROW (RS): BO 7 (7, 8) sts, k to end.

Purl 1 row.

BO rem 7 (8, 8) sts.

RIGHT FRONT

Place 35 (40, 44) right front sts from holder onto needle and attach yarn to begin with a WS row.

Work same as left front, reversing all shaping.

BACK

Place 88 (96, 104) back sts from holder onto needle and attach yarn to beg with a WS row.

NEXT ROW (WS): Purl.

BO 2 sts at the beg of the next 4 (6, 6) rows.

Dec 1 st at each side of the next 1 (1, 2) RS rows—78 (82, 88) sts.

Work even in St st until armhole meas 7½ (8, 8½)", end with a WS row.

SHOULDER SHAPING

NEXT ROW (RS): K14 (15, 16), BO 50 (52, 56) back neck sts, k to end.

LEFT SHOULDER

BO 7 (7, 8) sts, p to end.

Knit 1 row.

BO rem 7 (8, 8) sts.

RIGHT SHOULDER

Attach yarn to beg with a RS row.

BO 7 (7, 8) sts, k to end.

Purl 1 row.

BO rem 7 (8, 8) sts.

SLEEVES

String 105 (111, 120) sequins onto yarn.

CO 71 (75, 81) sts.

ROW 1 (WS): K1, *p1, k1; rep from * to end.

ROW 2: P1, *KS, p1; rep from * to end.

Rep rows 1 and 2 twice more.

NEXT ROW: K1, *p1, k1; rep from * to last 2 sts, k2tog—70 (74, 80) sts.

DEC ROW (RS): K 0 (0, 2), [k3, k2tog] 7 times, k1 (4, 6), [k2tog, k3] 6 times, k2tog, k2 (3, 5)—56 (60, 66) sts.

Work 7 rows in St st.

INC ROW (RS): K1, m1, k to last st, m1, k1.

Rep inc row every 10th row 7 (3, 5) times more and every 0 (8th, 12th) row 0 (6, 3) times —72 (80, 84) sts.

Work even in St st until sleeve meas 13¾ (14¼, 15¾)" from beg, end with a WS row.

SLEEVE CAP SHAPING

BO 6 (7, 8) sts at beg of next 2 rows, then BO 2 sts at beg of foll 2 rows.

Dec 1 st each side every RS row 15 times, then every 4th row 1 (2, 3) times.

BO 3 (4, 4) sts at beg of next 4 rows.

BO rem 12 sts.

FINISHING

Block pieces to measurements.

Sew shoulder seams. Set in sleeves and sew sleeve and side seams.

RIGHT FRONT BAND

Place 8 right front band sts from holder onto needle. String 250 (260, 285) sequins and attach yarn to beg with a WS row.

ROW 1 (WS): Kfb, k1, *p1, k1; rep from * to end—9 sts.

ROW 2: P1, *KS, p1; rep from * to end.

ROW 3: K1, *p1, k1; rep from * to end.

Rep rows 2 and 3 until band meas same as body to neck edge, end with row 2.

Place sts onto holder. Sew front band to front edge.

LEFT FRONT BAND

Place 8 left front band sts from holder onto needle. String 250 (260, 285) sequins and attach yarn to beg with a RS row.

ROW 1 (RS): P1 in row below, *KS, p1; rep from * to end—9 sts.

ROW 2: K1, *p1, k1; rep from * to end.

ROW 3: P1, *KS, p1; rep from * to end.

Rep rows 2 and 3 until band meas same as body to neck edge, end with row 3.

Place sts onto holder. Sew front band to front edge.

NECKBAND

String approx 200 (210, 225) sequins. With RS facing, PU and k an odd number of neck sts as foll: 1 st for each BO or live st and 2 sts every 3 rows.

ROW 1 (WS): K1, *p1, k1; rep from * to end.

ROW 2: P1, *KS, p1; rep from * to end.

Rep rows 1 and 2, then rep row 1 once more.

BO in row 2 patt, placing sequins as est.

ABOUT RUTHIE I've been knitting since I was fifteen. For years, I kept my hobby under wraps for fear of being labeled a dork, as knitting was not the most popular activity among high school girls in the early '90s. I began designing knitwear as a teenager because I couldn't find any cute patterns to wear. Since then, I've had many of my designs published and have sold them online. After nine years in New York City, I now live in northern New Jersey, where I work as a school administrator. My current creative pursuits include weaving and glassblowing. See more of my work at www.ruthieknits.com.

SPARKLE SWEATER

SIZE

S (M, L, XL)

Finished bust: 34 (37½, 41, 44½)"

Finished length: 21½ (22, 23½, 23½)"

MATERIALS

Karabella *Aurora 8* (100% wool; 50g/98 yd), 10 (11, 13, 14) skeins #1148 Black

US 7 (4.5mm) 16" circular needle

US 7 (4.5mm) 29" circular needle

US 5 (3.75mm) 16" circular needle

US 5 (3.75mm) 29" circular needle

US 7 (4.5mm) double-pointed needles

US 5 (3.75mm) double-pointed needles

667 (726, 785, 866) size 6 clear glass beads (approx 120/10g), plus extra in case of rejects

Sewing needle with large eye, small enough to fit through beads

3 stitch markers

Tapestry needle

GAUGE

18 sts and 26 rnds = 4" in St st using larger needles

fter designing the Sparkle Hat for the original *Stitch 'n Bitch* book, I was hooked on making shiny, really fun pieces. Wearing a necklace of beads inspired me to whip up this sparkly, festive sweater, which features a glittery yoke with a shaped neckline. I tried to keep the design supersimple and stress-free, but getting the repeat right has made this a pattern for "thinking knitters," as you'll need to figure out how to decrease evenly around the yoke while maintaining the bead pattern. It's a toughie, but the dazzling outcome and new skills you'll gain will be worth it, I promise. I used Elizabeth Zimmermann's percentage system to get my sweater proportions, then tweaked the design to add waist shaping and more close-fitting sleeves. Finally, I added some more beading on the sleeves and hem because, well, it was a great excuse to add more sparkle!

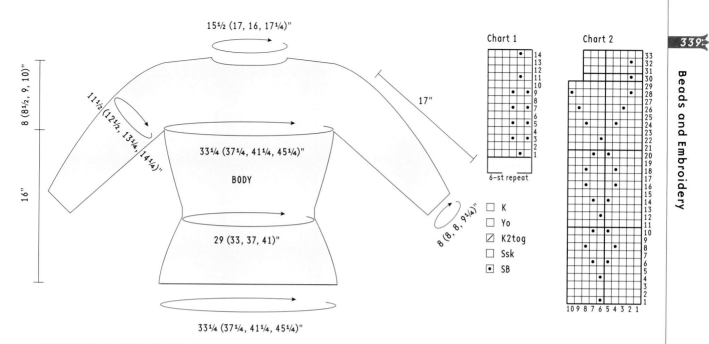

SPECIAL ABBREVIATIONS

SB (SLIP BEAD): Wyif, slide bead snugly up to needle, sl 1 st pwise, bring yarn to back.

W&T (WRAP & TURN): On RS, bring yarn between needles to front, sl next st onto RH needle, bring yarn between needles to back, return sl st to LH needle, turn.

On WS, bring yarn between needles to back, sl next st onto RH needle, bring yarn between needles to front, return sl st to LH needle, turn.

DIRECTIONS

BODY

With smaller 29" circular needle, CO 150 (168, 186, 204) sts. Pm and join.

Work in k1, p1 rib for 5 rnds.

Change to larger needle and k75 (84, 93, 102), pm, k to end.

Break yarn and string 275 (308, 341, 374) beads, pulling yarn out from ball and sliding beads down.

Rejoin yarn and work 14 rnds of Chart 1, adding beads by working SB where indicated.

WAIST SHAPING

DEC RND: *K2, k2tog, k to 3 sts before marker, ssk, k1; rep from * to end.

Rep dec rnd every 8th rnd 4 times more—130 (148, 166, 184) sts.

Work in St st for 6 rnds.

INC RND: *K1, m1, k to 1 st before marker, m1, k1; rep from * to end.

Rep inc rnd every 4th rnd 8 times more—150 (168, 186, 204) sts.

Work even in St st until body meas 16" from beg.

YOKE PREPARATION

K6 (7, 8, 9), place previous 11 (13, 15, 17) sts on wy for underarm, k to 6 (7, 8, 9) sts past next marker, place previous 11 (13, 15, 17) sts on wy for underarm, k to end—64 (71, 78, 85) sts rem each front and back. Put aside.

SLEEVES (MAKE 2)

String 66 (66, 66, 77) beads. With smaller dpns, CO 36 (36, 36, 42) sts. Pm and join.

Work in k1, p1 rib for 5 rnds.

Change to larger dpns and k 1 rnd. Work 14 rnds of Chart 1 AND AT THE SAME TIME, changing to larger 16" circular needle as needed, inc 2 sts every 12th (10th, 8th, 9th) rnd 8 (10, 12, 11) times as foll:

K2, m1, k to last st, m1, k1—52 (56, 60, 64) sts.

Work even in St st until sleeve meas 17" from beg.

K6 (7, 8, 9) and place previous 11 (13, 15, 17) sts on wy for underarm. Break yarn, leaving a 24" tail.

JOIN SLEEVES TO BODY

Using working yarn from body, *k41 (43, 45, 47) sleeve sts, k64 (71, 78, 85) body sts, k41 (43, 45, 47) sleeve sts, k32 (35, 39, 42) body sts, pm at center back for beg of rnd, k to end—210 (228, 246, 264) sts.

YOKE

Work even in St st for 3 (3½, 4, 5)".

DEC RND 1: Dec 0 (8, 6, 69) sts evenly around—210 (220, 240, 195) sts.

Work even in St st for 1 rnd.

Break yarn and string 260 (286, 312, 338) beads.

SET-UP RND: Beg with stitch #6 of Chart 2, work 5 sts of rnd 1 chart panel, *k11 (10, 10, 5) sts, work stitches 1–10 of Chart 2 once; rep from * to last 16 (15, 10, 10) sts, k11 (10, 10, 5), work stitches 1–5 of chart.

Cont working rnds 2–5 (2–7, 2–3, 2–15) of Chart 2 as est, inserting beads as indicated.

Note: Foll dec rnds are worked with beads. Adjust decs so beads will always be worked over a k st, not a dec. Change to shorter circular needle as needed.

DEC RND 2 [RND 6 (8, 4, 16) YOKE CHART]: Dec 50 (55, 60, 65) sts evenly around—160 (165, 180, 130) sts. Cont in est patt, work rnds 7–17 (9–21, 5–17, 17–29) of Yoke Chart.

DEC RND 3 [RND 18 (22, 18, 30) YOKE CHART]: Dec 50 (55, 60, 52) sts evenly around—110 (110, 120, 78) sts. Cont in est patt, work rnds 19–29 (23–29, 19–29, -) of Yoke Chart.

SIZE XL ONLY: *Skip to back neck shaping.*

DEC RND 4 [RND 30 (30, 30, -) OF YOKE CHART]: Dec 40 (33, 48, -) sts evenly around—70 (77, 72, 78) sts. Complete Yoke Chart.

BACK NECK SHAPING

Pm 20 (24, 28, 32) sts to each side of beg of rnd marker.

Knit to marker, W&T.

Purl to side marker, W&T.

Knit to 4 sts before side marker, W&T.

Purl to 4 sts before side marker, W&T.

K 1 rnd, picking up wraps and knitting them together with wrapped sts.

NECKBAND

Change to smaller 16" circular needle and work in k1, p1 rib for 5 rnds, dec 0 (1, 0, 0) st at beg of first rnd. BO loosely in rib.

FINISHING

Graft underarm seams using Kitchener st (page 107).

ABOUT SONYA I have been sewing, knitting, quilting, and making things for the past twenty years. I am happiest when surrounded by yarn, needles, buttons, sequins, fabric scraps, googly eyes, or anything sparkly. A New Englander at heart, I now live in Los Angeles with my husband and young sons, Elvin and Arthur. Currently, I am using crayons more than knitting needles.

kLara Norberg

MOONSHINE

SIZE

Finished wrist circumference: 5½"

Finished hand circumference: 7½"

Finished length: 6½"

MATERIALS

Blue Sky Alpacas *Alpaca Silk* (50% alpaca, 50% silk; 50g/146 yd), 1 skein #138 Garnet

US 6 (4mm) double-pointed needles

160 size 6 seed beads (#T6-319H Ruby Raspberry Lustre from Whimbeads)

Cable needle

Tapestry needle

GAUGE

22 sts and 31 rows = 4" in St st

ften my designs come from an idea of something I absolutely must have for myself. These beaded wrist warmers came to me when I was knitting a pair of socks. When I put the socks on my hands I realized that I really wanted to wear them on my wrists. This was my first foray into cable knitting, but since I wanted to adjust the pattern, I experimented a bit, and voilà—cabled socks became glammed-up, beaded wristlets, like sassy leg warmers for your daintier appendages. Their rock 'n' roll elegance makes them the perfect accessory to add some flair to your favorite jacket. Or you can always slip them on to warm your wrists while you knit!

Pearly Cable

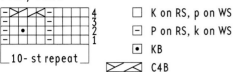

10- st repeat

☐ K on RS, p on WS

⊟ P on RS, k on WS

⊡ KB

◩ C4B

SPECIAL ABBREVIATIONS

C4B: Slip 2 sts onto cn and hold in back, k2, k2 from cn.

KB (KNIT BEAD): Insert RH needle into st, slide bead to base of st, k1, pulling bead through to front.

SPECIAL STITCH
PEARLY CABLE STITCH

RND 1: *K4, p1; rep from * to end.

RND 2: *K4, p1, k2, KB, k1, p1; rep from * to end.

RND 3: Rep rnd 1.

RND 4: *K4, p1, C4B, p1; rep from * to end.

Rep rnds 1–4 for patt.

DIRECTIONS (MAKE 2)
CUFF

String 80 beads onto yarn (see page 75).

CO 40 sts loosely.

Divide sts evenly over 4 needles. Pm and join.

Work 32 rnds in Pearly Cable st.

HAND

RND 1: *K4, p1; rep from * to end.

RND 2: *K4, p1, k2, KB, k1, p1; rep from * to end.

RNDS 3 AND 4: Rep rnd 1.

Rep rnds 1–3 once more.

NEXT RND: Knit.

PEARL EDGING

RND 1: *K1, KB; rep from * to end.

RNDS 2, 3 AND 4: Knit.

RND 5: *KB, k1; rep from * to end.

RNDS 6, 7 AND 8: Knit.

BO loosely. Weave in ends.

ABOUT KLARA I am a self-confessed chronic sockaholic. Socks make for speedy knitting projects; they're useful and portable enough to bring with you, which works for a mother of four with a hectic lifestyle. I live in Stockholm, Sweden, where I've always designed my own stuff. I had never written down my patterns until a few years ago—probably because I barely stick to a pattern myself and usually wind up knitting something completely different. A cardigan can end up a wrist warmer, a wrist warmer can end up a skirt. I love crafting and creating new things, as well as turning old things into new shapes. More information about me and some of my projects can be found at my blog, www.kristallklara.blogg.se.

TIGER LILY

always take a few extra steps for maximum cuteness when designing a stuffed animal. I look at photos of the animal I'm inspired by, pick out its defining characteristics, draw a sketch, work out the shape of each body part and, finally, I detail the face to give the toy loads of personality. Throughout the years, I've learned some tricks for making a toy look great, such as using mattress stitch for the seams to make them look tidier. Also, when stuffing the pieces, use filler that is one-third bigger than the body part, roll it in your hands until it's the same shape and size as the part, then carefully stuff the part. Follow these tips and you'll have a totally adorable tiger toy that would make an awesome baby or toddler gift. If you're making this for a young baby, you may want to replace the bead eyes with embroidery.

SIZE
Approx 9" tall

MATERIALS
Brown Sheep *Nature Spun Worsted* (100% wool; 100g/245 yd)

A: 1 ball (or approx 25g) #730 Natural

B: 1 ball (or approx 25g) #601 Pepper

C: 1 ball (or approx 25g) #N17 French Clay

D: 1 ball (or approx 25g) #307 Lullaby

E: 1 ball (or approx 10g) #522 Nervous Green

US 6 (4mm) needles

Size E/4 (3.5mm) crochet hook

Polyester fiber stuffing

1 pair safety eyes or ¼" buttons

Small amount of pink yarn for embroidering face

One or two ⅜" buttons for dress

Tapestry needle

GAUGE
22 sts and 32 rows = 4" in St st

DIRECTIONS
LEG (MAKE 2)
Beg at sole with A, CO 10 sts.

ROW 1 (WS): Purl.

ROW 2: K1, *m1, k1; rep from * to end—19 sts.

ROWS 3, 5 AND 7: Purl.

ROW 4: K4, *m1, k3; rep from * to end—24 sts.

ROW 6: Knit.

ROW 8: K8, [ssk] twice, [k2tog] twice, k8—20 sts.

ROW 9: P6, [p2tog] twice, [p2tog tbl] twice, p6—16 sts.

ROW 10: K7, k2tog, k7—15 sts.

Break off A and join C. For rem of leg, work stripes of 2 rows C and 2 rows B.

ROWS 11–13: Work in St st.

ROW 14: K2, m1, k11, m1, k2—17 sts.

ROWS 15–25: Work in St st.

ROW 26: K1, *k2tog; rep from * to end—9 sts.

Break off yarn. Thread end through rem sts and pull tight to gather. Sew back leg seam and sole, leaving an opening. Stuff and sew closed.

BODY

Beg at neck edge with B, CO 16 sts.

ROW 1 (WS): Purl.

ROW 2: K1, *m1, k1; rep from * to end—31 sts.

For rem of body, work stripes of 2 rows C and 2 rows B.

ROWS 3–5: Work in St st.

ROW 6: K8, m1, k15, m1, k8—33 sts.

ROWS 7–13: Work in St st.

ROW 14: K15, m1, k3, m1, k15—35 sts.

ROWS 15–17: Work in St st.

ROW 18: K3, m1, k1, m1, k27, m1, k1, m1, k3—39 sts.

ROW 19: Purl.

ROW 20: K16, ssk, k3, k2tog, k16—37 sts.

ROWS 21–23: Work in St st.

ROW 24: K15, ssk, k3, k2tog, k15—35 sts.

ROWS 25–27: Work in St st.

ROW 28: K1, *k2tog; rep from * to end—18 sts.

ROW 29: Purl.

ROW 30: *K2tog; rep from * to end—9 sts.

Break off yarn. Thread end through rem sts and pull tight to gather. Sew back seam to neck edge, leaving neck edge open. Stuff body.

RIGHT ARM

Beg at paw with A, CO 6 sts.

ROW 1 (WS): Purl.

ROW 2: K1, *m1, k1; rep from * to end—11 sts.

ROW 3: Purl.

ROW 4: [K2, m1] twice, k3, [m1, k2] twice—15 sts.

ROWS 5–7: Work in St st.

ROW 8: K1, [ssk] twice, [k2tog] twice, k6—11 sts.

Break off A and attach C. For rem of arm, work stripes of 2 rows C and 2 rows B.

ROWS 9–13: Work in St st.

ROW 14: K5, m1, k3, m1, k3—13 sts.

ROWS 15–23: Work in St st.

ROW 24: K1, *k2tog; rep from * to end—7 sts.

Break off yarn. Thread end through rem sts and pull tight to gather. Sew arm seam, leaving an opening. Stuff and sew closed.

LEFT ARM

Work same as right arm except work rows 8 and 14 as foll:

ROW 8: K6, [ssk] twice, [k2tog] twice, k1—11 sts.

ROW 14: K3, m1, k3, m1, k5—13 sts.

HEAD

Beg at back of head with C, CO 7 sts. Work in stripes of 2 rows C and 2 rows B.

ROW 1 (WS): Purl.

ROW 2: K1, *m1, k1; rep from * to end—13 sts.

ROW 3: Purl.

ROW 4: K1, *m1, k1; rep from * to end—25 sts.

ROWS 5-7: Work in St st.

ROW 8: [K2, m1] 4 times, k9, [m1, k2] 4 times—33 sts.

ROWS 9-18: Work in St st (last row should be C).

ROW 19: With C, purl.

ROW 20: With C, k8, [k2tog] twice, k9, [ssk] twice, k8—29 sts.

Break off C and work rem of nose with A.

ROW 21: Purl.

ROW 22: K1, [k2tog] 6 times, k3, [ssk] 6 times, k1—17 sts.

ROWS 23-25: Work in St st.

ROW 26: K1, *k2tog; rep from * to end—9 sts.

Break off yarn. Thread end through rem sts and pull tight to gather. Attach safety eyes or button eyes. Sew seam, leaving an opening. Stuff, adding extra to nose and cheeks to make them stick out, and sew closed.

EAR (MAKE 2)

With C, CO 9 sts.

ROW 1 (RS): Knit.

ROW 2: K1, ssk, k to end—8 sts.

ROWS 3-8: Rep rows 1 and 2—5 sts after row 8.

ROW 9: Knit.

ROW 10: [Ssk] twice, k1—3 sts.

Break off yarn. Thread end through rem sts, pull tight and secure end.

ASSEMBLY

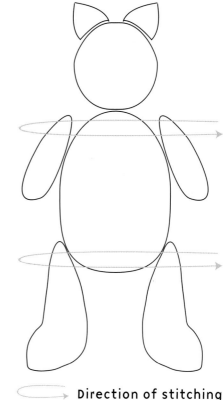

→ **Direction of stitching**

TAIL

With B, CO 9 sts.

Beg with a WS row, work 32 rows in St st stripes of 2 rows B and 2 rows C—16 stripes.

Break off C and attach A. Work 5 rows in St st.

Break off yarn. Thread end through sts and pull tight to gather. Sew seam.

FINISHING

With pink yarn, embroider nose and mouth.

OPTIONAL: Embellish stripes on head with duplicate st (see photo for placement).

Sew CO edge of ears to head. Sew head securely to open neck edge of body. Referring to diagram, thread approx

24" length of yarn through left arm approx ¼" from top, through body at shoulder, and through right arm; then again through arm, body, and left arm; pull tight. Repeat so yarn passes through each arm 3–4 times. Pull yarn tight so arms are secure, then fasten off yarn. Attach legs at lower edge of body in the same way as the arms. Sew tail to tiger's bum.

DRESS

FRONT

With D, CO 27 sts.

ROW 1 (WS): P3, *k1, p4; rep from * to last 4 sts, k1, p3.

ROW 2: Knit.

ROWS 3-20: Rep rows 1 and 2.

ROW 21: Rep row 1.

ROW 22: K1, *k2tog, k1, ssk; rep from * to last st, k1—17 sts.

Drop D and pick up E.

ROWS 23-24: With E, work in St st.

Drop E and pick up D.

ROWS 25-31: With D, work in St st.

BO.

BACK

Work same as Front through row 31.

ROW 32: Knit.

BO.

FINISHING

Sew side seams up to E stripe. With E, starting at side seam, work 1 rnd sc around front and back bodices, making a button loop on one or both back shoulders. Sew button(s) to front. Sew other shoulder seam if necessary.

ABOUT BARBARA I taught myself to knit while attending a university, when I got tired of buying ill-fitting acrylic hats and mittens. A toy rabbit was one of my first projects because it was small, quick, and taught me a bunch of useful techniques. Four years ago I was looking for something to do between jobs and thought people might buy my knitted animals. Fellow knitters quickly found them online and asked for patterns to make their own. Now I have a whole range of toy patterns available on my website (www.fuzzymitten.com), and though I'm busy with my family, fresh ideas just keep coming.

index

credits

Cover photograph by Michael Lavine

Cowgirl cover art by Enoch Bolles

Fashion photography by Gabrielle Revere

Wardrobe styling by Ellen Silverstein

Hair and makeup by Amy Schiappa

Project silos and detail photography by Eric Brown, Melissa Lucier, and Sophia Su

fashion

Page 171 Urban Outfitters: green belt and purple top; Lee Angel: bangles and ring. *Page 175* Family Jewels: shoes; Chan Luu: pearl bracelet; Lee Angel: rainbow bangles and floral gold bangles. *Page 183* Josette at Supplements NY: orange bangles. *Page 187* Chan Luu: black/silver tie bracelet; Lee Angel: jade/purple stones bracelet. *Page 217* Urban Outfitters: pink top and brown sandals; Lee Angel: bracelets. *Page 225* Urban Outfitters: jeans; Lee Angel: bangles. *Pages 229–230* Family Jewels: pink vintage dress; Chamak at Supplements NY: earrings. *Page 235* Lee Angel: pearl and silver pin, and studded bangle. *Page 239* Urban Outfitters: pleated scarf. *Page 243* Urban Outfitters: sweater and tank top. *Page 251* Family Jewels: vintage dress; Urban Outfitters: belt; Lee Angel: bangles. *Page 254* Urban Outfitters: shoes; Atomic Passion: sunglasses. *Page 259* Urban Outfitters: skirt. *Page 266* Lee Angel: tie bracelet. *Page 269* Urban Outfitters: plaid top; Chan Luu: bracelet. *Page 275* Urban Outfitters: dress; Chan Luu: bracelet. *Page 279* Chan Luu: bracelets. *Pages 281–282* Handmade By Hannah: skirt; Lee Angel: earrings; Josette at Supplements NY: bangles. *Page 285* Urban Outfitters: tank top; Screaming Mimi's: belt; Adia Kibur at Supplements NY: earrings. *Page 292* Urban Outfitters: earrings and turquoise underdress; Adia Kibur at Supplements NY: ring; Lee Angel: bangles; Chamak at Supplements NY: bracelet. *Page 298* Urban Outfitters: skirt; Lee Angel: bangles. *Page 305* Urban Outfitters: belt; Lee Angel: earrings and bangles. *Page 310* Lee Angel: necklace, bracelet, and bangles; Family Jewels: vintage bag. *Page 314* Lee Angel: bracelets and bangles; Urban Outfitters: chain braided bracelet. *Page 319* Urban Outfitters: jeans and necklace. *Page 324* Family Jewels: vintage skirt; Urban Outfitters: hat; Lee Angel: bracelet. *Page 329* Family Jewels: vintage suit. *Page 333* Screaming Mimi's: pink prom dress; Lily Posh at Supplements NY: gold pig bracelet and pink pearl bracelet; Chamak at Supplements NY: headband. *Page 337* Lee Angel: silver bangle. *Page 341* Lee Angel: necklace.